BIG DRAGON

The Future of China: What It Means for Business, the Economy, and the Global Order

DANIEL BURSTEIN
AND ARNE DE KEIJZER

A Touchstone Book
Published by Simon & Schuster

For Julie, who survived the dust storms of Yanan and whose
platinum-printed vision captured old Shanghai.

For David, born in the Year of the Dragon and connoisseur
of dragons everywhere.

—DANIEL BURSTEIN

For Helen, who climbed Huang Shan and reached
my heart, making it sing.

For Hannah, dancing into the future with grace, wisdom, and spirit.

—ARNE DE KEIJZER

And together, in mutual love and appreciation of our wonderful families.

 TOUCHSTONE
Rockefeller Center
1230 Avenue of the Americas
New York, NY 10020

First Touchstone Edition 1999

TOUCHSTONE and colophon are registered trademarks
of Simon & Schuster Inc.

Manufactured in the United States of America

10 9 8 7 6 5 4 3 2 1

The Library of Congress has cataloged the Simon & Schuster edition as follows:

Burstein, Daniel.
    Big dragon : China's future : what it means for business, the economy, and the global
order / Daniel Burstein and Arne J. de Keijzer.
        p.   cm.
    Includes bibliographical references and index.
    1. China—Economic conditions—1976– 2. China—Politics and government—1976–
3. Economic forecasting—China. 4. Entrepreneurship—China. 5. United States—
Foreign economic relations—China. 6. China—Foreign economic relations—United
States. 7. United States—Foreign relations—China. 8. China—Foreign relations—
United States. I. de Keijzer, Arne J. II. Title.
HC427.92.B84   1998
337.51—dc21   97-50092 CIP

ISBN 0-684-80316-X
ISBN 0-684-85366-3 (Pbk)

CONTENTS

INTRODUCTION

Present at the Creation

T HIS BOOK IS ABOUT the impact China will have on the global balance of wealth and power in the twenty-first century. We are particularly concerned with how the United States and China will interact not just in the next few years, but over the next several decades, and with the implications of those interactions for the economy, business, and the global order.

In our assessment, China remains positioned, if things go moderately well, to become the world's largest national economy sometime in the 2030s. Despite the setbacks associated with the current Asian financial crisis, the turmoil in world markets, and the slowing growth of economic output and foreign investment in China, we believe China will reemerge as a vibrant economy early in the next century and increasingly show itself as a super-power in every sense—economically, politically, militarily, culturally, tech-nologically.

China, however, will be different than any great power the world has ever seen. The political-economic system it will evolve—a unique hybrid of many influences, including elements of socialism as well as capitalism—will also be different than any system the world now knows.

The stakes for American business are of towering proportions. For a growth-hungry industrial world, the China market could represent what the New World meant for Europe several centuries ago: a huge new land of dynamic growth, possibility, and profit. It may also be the fulcrum of global competition, where companies compete for market share and control of the engines that drive cost curves down and consumer benefits up. To become the integrated, networked, and truly global corporation of the future, participation and even a measure of leadership in the China market may be a virtual requirement for all companies.

For nearly two decades it has been apparent that trade flows and capital flows, and the wealth and power that derives from them, are shifting from the old Atlantic-centric world to an increasingly Pacific-centric world. What has become evident more recently is that China lies at the heart of this Asian shift. The United States and the American business community are, of course, powerful and sometimes even dominant forces in the new Pacific-influenced order. China is in the process of dramatic changes, and Americans stand to benefit enormously from those changes *if* we understand and adapt to them properly.

Inevitably, different corporations will have different assessments of the opportunities and the risks, especially now that East Asia is trying to cope with a continuing and troubling economic shakeout that is the legacy of more than a decade of hypergrowth, overbuilding, overinvesting (often in the wrong sectors), as well as overleveraging.

China has obviously not been immune to the Asian flu. The thunderclaps of bad loans, collapsing currencies, failed banks, and plummeting equity prices that rolled through Thailand, Malaysia, Hong Kong, and South Korea, and that have been throttling the once mighty Japanese economy for years now, are bringing massive pressure to bear on China's emerging economic structure. Even now, the full impact cannot be calculated, either on China, which has, at this writing, not yet been thrown fully into the maelstrom of Asia's crisis, or on the other Asian countries, where enormous problems still fester. It is clear, however, that many American business and financial strategists are now spending more time thinking about protecting themselves from the downside dangers of Asian recessions, banking crises, and contagious effects on profits and equity values than they are about exploring new investment and opportunities in the region. And there are still plenty of reasons to worry: among them, the process of competitive devaluations of Asian currencies, which could lead to—choose your poison—global deflation and crisis, or "only" a record-shattering American trade deficit.

As the "Asia crisis" has spread to Russia, Latin America, and even Wall Street and Main Street, USA, China has worked indefatigably to stay on course with the growth and modernization of its economy. With Japan scarcely able to form a government (let alone pass meaningful legislation to address its banking crisis), with Suharto deposed in Indonesia and Mahatir on the ropes in Malaysia, with Bill Clinton mired in scandal, Boris Yeltsin unable to govern, and Helmut Kohl rejected by German voters, even the punditocracy of *The New York Times* concluded that China's leadership team, headed by President Jiang Zemin and Prime Minister Zhu Rongji, might be the world's most stable and consistent government.

And in Washington, where economists and Clinton administration officials huddled regularly in 1998 to worry about the crisis that was mushrooming into the worst threat to the world economy in half a century, China was almost universally seen as a critical player, if not *the* critical player. On the one hand, by continuing to grow its economy, even if more slowly than before, and by steadfastly refusing to join the Asian currency devaluation game, China was said to be keeping the Asian house of cards from falling down completely. On the other hand, the fear was rampant that if China were to fail, devalue its currency, and succumb to the Asia crisis, the worst-case scenarios would be unleashed upon the rest of the world economy, including the United States.

Thus, despite all the intense pretrip criticism of Clinton's July 1998 visit to China (criticism that centered on human rights, China's lack of internal democracy, its policies toward Tibet and Taiwan, and other moral and ideological considerations), most American leadership figures came to support the administration's efforts to warm up and improve Sino-U.S. ties. China's willingness to do the right thing in the face of the Asia crisis contrasted sharply with Japan's unwillingness and/or inability to do the right thing, making China appear to many as America's more logical partner in Asia, even though its total economy is still far smaller than Japan's.

China is not out of the woods yet. It is not clear that Beijing's leaders can live up to their oft-stated commitment not to devalue their currency, no matter how much "face" they have invested in taking the high road on this question and no matter how much pain they have already accepted (especially in Hong Kong, which is in a deep recession), in order to keep the Chinese renminbi and the Hong Kong dollar stable. Nor is it clear that Zhu Rongji's sound and well-intentioned course of domestic-led investment and State-Owned Enterprise reform can be implemented fast enough or thoroughly enough to continue to insulate China from the threats of Asian depression, an international credit crunch, asset price deflation, and other destabilizing external trends, let alone the magnifying internal economic challenges.

The Chinese trade surplus with the United States is rising to politically toxic levels, even if there is little real economic damage. And a new stream of protectionist edicts are coming out of Beijing that anger American businesses even as they defy Western logic: Why would they be making it more difficult for foreign companies to do business in China at precisely the moment they most need new foreign investment? Yet these measures have their own internal political peacekeeping in China. We can therefore expect this trend toward more difficult cross-border trade and investment to continue, becoming a potential new irritant in a U.S.-China relationship that is otherwise improving on an overall basis.

So there is much to worry about on the subject of China's short- and medium-term future. One way or another, however, we believe this extraordinary period of global crisis will pass. China, Asia, the United States, and the world economy will readjust over the next several years to new prices, new values, new realities, and a new global economic paradigm. The trade and capital shift toward Asia is likely to reestablish itself and even accelerate in the next decade. As it does so, the stage will be set for a new China rush.

Some of the more visionary global corporations see the current environment as a positive long-term opportunity for buying assets and investing at deflated prices in the region. Others see it as a reason to mute their enthusiasm, curtail their operations, and wait to see if and when Asian economies regain their growth trajectory. On this and other basic questions about China, some will get it right. More than a few will fail. Over the next quarter century, success or failure in China may be the margin of difference for some in the global competition. It may even be a leading indicator of the soundness of overall corporate growth strategies.

The stakes are equally high for government policymakers and the American public at large. The sheer size of tomorrow's Chinese superpower is enough to warrant reconsidering the future of just about every major global issue. But the challenge of understanding and dealing effectively with China is not about size and scale alone. The *different interests* that flow from China's history and different political-economic assumptions compound the challenge enormously. They require much more thoughtful analysis than they usually receive, either in the facile media discussions about investing in or doing business with China or in what passes for the process of political strategy formulation in Washington.

If we fast-forward several decades, we will find a world in which China and the United States are *the* two superpowers. Their power will have different sources, and they will have different ways of making their influence felt, different goals, and different strengths and weaknesses. In our judgment, the United States will still be the much more capable, in-depth, and efficient power, with far more advanced technology and more sophisticated mechanisms of projecting its influence globally, both in economic and military terms. Nevertheless, the aggregate size and the scope of China's economy, coupled with its centrality to Asia and its precedent-setting influence throughout the developing world, will make it a formidable and unique superpower in its own right. There will obviously be much to gain for both the United States and China through constructive partnership. But even more important, the dangers to both sides—and to the world—will be very great if the politics of confrontation dominate the relationship.

Unfortunately, what appeared in the early 1990s to be the beginning of a beautiful relationship soured in the frosty winds of a new cold war during the first four years of the Clinton administration. Despite the positive outcome of the administration's reassessment of its China policy in 1997, and President Clinton's successful trip in the summer of 1998, the improvement in relations is still too thin and weak to be certain of how long-lived such a trend will be. Dogged by his domestic scandal even as he traveled through China, Clinton has not been able to devote much attention to the kind of proactive and constructive relationship building needed to bridge the U.S.-China gap. It remains fashionable in some quarters in Washington, especially now that we have entered more economically uncertain times, to posit a "China Threat," a threat that Americans must prepare to confront and contain. Our view, however, is far more hopeful. China will challenge our society in profound ways and pose vexing problems. But on balance, we expect that the United States and China, as the two great nation-state superpowers of the twenty-first century, will find the way to compete, cooperate, and coexist peacefully.

The China we write about is one we have followed closely and experienced firsthand since we were in our twenties. Although we did not know each other at the time, we both made our first China journeys back in the early 1970s, when China was still caught up in the whirlwind of its Cultural Revolution. The dogmas and ideological passions of Maoism defined every outward aspect of what the visitor saw and experienced.

We were both—separately and to different degrees—captured by the romance of the Maoist rhetoric and the dream espoused by the Cultural Revolutionaries of creating a new utopian society in China. For both of us, coming to understand how the reality of China in the late 1960s and 1970s differed from Beijing's official party line about it (and just how severely *dystopian* the Maoist vision proved to be in practice for the Chinese people) ultimately involved powerful and emotionally wrenching life lessons. But among other salutary benefits, it taught us to look beneath the surface of Chinese society to understand the deep and complex forces that shape it. This is an important skill and a critical point of departure in looking at China today, even though its society has become more modern and open.

Traveling in China during that time period afforded us a chance to be present at the creation of modern Chinese "business" and the modern Chinese market economy. Despite the chaos and extremism of the Cultural Revolution, it was during the early 1970s that Deng Xiaoping's arguments about economy building were first beginning to be heard behind the walls of Zhongnanhai, the Beijing compound where the supreme leaders of the Chinese Communist Party dwell. After enormous political battles and the death of Mao, the resilient and tenacious Deng gained the upper hand politically. He began to bring the country's nightmare of fierce internecine struggle to an end. For the first time since the 1950s, China's political leadership began to define their tasks and the nation's future according to the needs of broad-based economic growth instead of political campaigns and ideological dogmas.

Thus, by the time of our travels in the late 1970s we were eating noodles at the first few private restaurants to open in China. We went down to the farms and met the various "rabbit ladies" and "chicken kings" who had made legally sanctioned private fortunes by raising their own animals and crops and selling them directly into the rudimentary market, instead of through the state system. We talked to managers of the first few enterprises that had discovered (usually with eurekalike brainstorms) the powers of advertising, marketing, and even mergers and acquisitions.

We witnessed the shift in the U.S.-China trade from "trading with the enemy" to the birth of what today is already a $100 billion a year relationship, on its way to becoming one of the central economic relationships in the world. We were asked by Chinese corporations for advice on everything from attracting foreign tourists to buying foreign steel fabrication plants. We advised major American and other foreign corporations as they tried to enter the market for the first time with products and services from rental cars to Western cosmetics. More recently we have been involved in significant corporate investments, venture capital start-ups, and LBOs of Chinese companies.

We vividly remember what it was like in the early 1970s to cross the little bridge at Lo Wu between Hong Kong's New Territories and the village on the Chinese side then known by its Cantonese name, Shimchun. It was as tense a border as any in the world, akin to crossing from West to East Berlin at Checkpoint Charlie during the height of the Cold War. On one side, American and British intelligence agencies kept their high-powered lens focused on who was coming and going. On the other side, ever vigilant "Red" Chinese border guards kept their weapons at the ready. In those days, almost everyone carried their own baggage across the bridge into China. Mao had made a point in his writings about the proletarian virtue of carrying one's own bags, so porters were in extremely short supply. And if you could find one, you wouldn't tip him. In the spirit of the prevalent slogan of the day, "Serve the People," tipping was disdained throughout China.

Walking across the bridge, you could almost hear the vacuum seal closing off the global economy behind. Ahead were big red signs with the sayings of Chairman Mao and the peasants of Shimchun tilling the green tropical rice fields as they had for centuries. Today, Shimchun is better known by its Mandarin name, Shenzhen. Business travelers coming from Hong Kong now arrive via superhighway in a speeding Mercedes or Lexus if they don't helicopter or fly in. Shenzhen has become a city of over a million people and the home to hundreds of foreign businesses. Most of the paddy fields have long since been devoured by the skyscrapers, department stores, and urban sprawl of this experimental "special economic zone."

The big red sayings of Chairman Mao are gone, replaced by equally prominent advertisements for Marlboro and other Western consumer goods. At the Shenzhen Shangri-La Hotel, there are plenty of porters eager to carry your bags, most of them too young to have read Mao's writings on the subject and all of them eager for tips. A single political billboard is visible on the hills above downtown Shenzhen. A visionary-looking Deng Xiaoping promises that China will not change its basic policy of economic reform and opening for one hundred years.

No one can possibly imagine what China will be like in one hundred years' time and have any hope of accuracy. The furthest we have gone in these pages is about three decades, which roughly balances the three past decades during which time we have been actively following developments in China. Knowing from firsthand experience how much China has changed in the last thirty years provides us with a certain personal framework for judging how much change is or is not possible in the next thirty.

From the vantage point of the middle of our lives, we have tried to think about what China will look like as we approach the later stages of our own lives. We have imagined what the interactions may be between China, the United States, and the rest of the world when our children, who today are not yet teenagers, arrive at the middle of *their* lives. We have sought, in short, to do what the Chinese have done for centuries: think long term—about decades instead of quarters; about the next era instead of the next year.

Significant new events affecting China, Asia, and U.S.-China relations have taken place since the hardcover edition of *Big Dragon* first appeared in March 1998. So far, nothing we have seen fundamentally changes the framework of analysis set forth within this book. Most new developments were forecast or alluded to in one way or another in the earlier volume. Nevertheless, our readers may wish to know our thoughts more specifically on at least some of these crucial developments:

The Crisis in the World Financial System

We touched on this issue briefly at the outset of this introduction. As this is a protean, constantly changing phenomenon defined by its volatility, it would be foolish to attempt too specific a forecast. However, it is worth making a few key observations:

• China has Asia crisis–like symptoms within its system, such as lack of transparency, too much government interference, insufficient market mechanisms, and crony capitalism writ large. Nevertheless, the problems of China's financial system do not necessarily arise from the same sources as the problems in other Asian countries, nor do they necessarily have the same solutions. China still has sufficient political control of certain issues to solve them politically. Currency value is a prime example: Since the RMB is not freely convertible and foreigners cannot play the Chinese currency market except in the most obscure ways, the currency cannot be devalued from external pressure as it was in Indonesia or Malaysia. Beijing might decide to devalue its currency in the future, but not for the reasons foreign experts usually suggest (i.e., to stay competitive on manufacturing cost with other Asian countries that have so greatly devalued their currencies). In our view, the incredibly low cost of Chinese labor (and the comparative efficiency of foreign manufacturing in China as compared to other Asian countries) keeps Chinese exports generally competitive—witness the rapidly rising trade surplus with the Untied States. China is therefore not compelled to devalue as some experts have suggested. If China devalues at all, our expectation is that it will be primarily to make foreign inward investment, which is currently falling precipitously, cheaper and therefore more attractive, so that foreign capital can again play the kind of invigorating role it did in the early '90s boom.

- Some interesting theories have also been spun to suggest that China deliberately held back on devaluation in 1997–98 in order to please Washington and therefore convince Americans that China was a more reliable partner and leader for Asia than Japan. To this interesting theory, we politely say, "bunk." While we note the highly responsible role that China has played in this difficult situation, and the degree to which that is appreciated in Washington, Chinese policy will continue to be driven by what is best for Chinese interests. Those Chinese thinkers who may be focused on the question of "who should lead Asia" tend to think about this in terms of decades and centuries. They are in no hurry to assume the costly burdens of leadership when they are still over their heads in the task of pulling China out of feudalism and into the modern age.

- Russia's economic implosion in the summer of 1998 has dealt a deathblow to anyone still dreaming about encouraging China to take the route of shock therapy, radical privatization, or quick electoral democratization. When Russia became a magnet for foreign investment in 1997 and the Russian stock market was briefly churning out billionaires and spectacular returns, there was a momentary renewal of the decade-old argument that China too should take this road. Russia's flameout has only served to validate the Chinese Communist Party leaders who have always argued that economic reform in China should be a slow, gradual, incremental process, with political reform on the back burner.

- America's own recent problems with speculative excess in our financial markets have diminished the credibility of Washington's argument that the solution to the Asia crisis lies in rushing more rapidly toward free and open financial markets. From precipitous stock market plunges to hedge fund blowups, what the Chinese have seen recently of U.S. financial markets is being used to reinforce the argument that the foreigners have no miracle potion and that China must find its own way.

- Even if China remains largely insulated from the full effects of the crisis felt by other Asian countries, there is no doubt that China is experiencing a major setback to its growth and modernization plans. The drying up of investor interest from other Asian countries, the collapse of demand for Chinese exports in other Asian countries, the severe recession in Hong Kong, and diminution of world financial markets' willingness to absorb public offerings of Chinese companies—all of these factors are bringing down the former double-digit trajectory of growth in China. Although we believe China will eventually resume a high growth track, those who invest and do business there will need to be even more patient than they have already been as the whole region digests what has happened to it and begins to rebuild.

President Clinton's Visit to China

In June 1998 Clinton's visit fulfilled *Big Dragon*'s number one policy recommendation (chapter 18) and demonstrated what a policy of "dynamic engagement" could accomplish. The "debate" about human rights Clinton held with Jiang Zemin on a live television broadcast, as well as the speech Clinton gave to students at Peking University (followed by a question-and-answer session with students), showed what a truly "normal" relationship and a policy of engagement could achieve. That is, the United States and China could cooperate closely, launch many constructive joint initiatives, and yet continue to disagree on some fundamental issues.

Clinton was right to go to Beijing. American ideas about democracy and human rights were heard because he was there, not because they were trumpeted by neo-isolationists in far-away Washington. Clinton's trip to Beijing achieved a truce in the cold war that had been brewing previously, a cold war we described in detail in this book. At least for a time, the "coming-conflict-with-China" school went into recess. The general discussion of China in the media, when not eclipsed altogether by economic concerns and domestic American political distractions, became less strident and inflammatory. (Of course, it has also helped that Clinton's political opponents, who had previously thought that China policy was an issue on which the president was vulnerable, now have better issues to indulge for their partisan purposes.)

Yet while the Washington-Beijing cold war has started to fade, the danger is that China policy remains a mile wide and an inch deep. While constructive dialogue is taking place and the overall atmosphere remains cordial and respectful, large, unresolved issues lurk just below the surface. A projected $60 billion annual trade deficit with China will certainly prove politically challenging in the 2000 election, particularly if there is a further downturn in the U.S. economy. U.S. exporters, meanwhile, are complaining that Beijing is beginning to close its doors by instituting import and investment curbs in key fields such as power generation, pharmaceuticals, machinery, and telecommunications. This may lead many of the affected companies—some of the largest and most politically influential in America—to rethink their hitherto strong enthusiasm for better U.S.-China ties. If another major "anti-human rights" or "anti-democracy" event occurs in China, or a new conflict arises over Taiwan, the cold war atmosphere could quickly—and disastrously—return.

Hong Kong

Nearly two years have elapsed since the transition of Hong Kong back to Chinese rule. Few of the major fears expressed by the pre-handover doomsayers about curtailment of rights and freedoms have come to pass. Hong Kong's life as a Special Administrative Region of China since July 1, 1997, has been marked with great success on the points that foreigners and critics were most concerned about. Ironically, while China has generally maintained the political status quo, Hong Kong has been hit with enormous unexpected challenges to its economic life posed not by greedy or power-hungry Chinese commissars, but by the impact of the capitalist-induced Asia crisis. Yet even faced with unprecedented economic challenges, China has been remarkably restrained and noninterventionist, at least to date. We feel that the positive general outlook expressed on Hong Kong when we wrote that section (see chapter 15) has been validated, although we are, of course, concerned about even the small political problems that have come to the fore.

It would be naive to think the challenge in Hong Kong is over or settled. Hong Kong must wrestle with a fascinating conundrum: It is universally acknowledged to be among the freest markets in the world, yet the value of its currency, under the U.S. dollar peg system, is set by political fiat. We suspect the Hong Kong dollar needs to be devalued significantly for the sake of the short-term interests of revitalizing the local economy. But many fear that any change in the U.S. dollar peg would be a sign that the status quo in Hong Kong has been abandoned. Squaring the circle—allowing the Hong Kong dollar to fall to a more rational market value and yet keeping stability and the status quo intact—will be a huge challenge in the period ahead.

The Acceleration of Internal Economic Reform

The selection of Zhu Rongji as prime minister in 1998 was a very positive portent. Senior American officials who have met with him, and most bankers and business leaders as well, come away with the impression that here is a Chinese political leader who has the courage, the vision, and the technical knowledge and skill to tackle China's economic challenges and move the country forward into the twenty-first century. His selection as prime minister tells us that the Chinese leadership knows it must forgo the "easy road" of ignoring the enormous fundamental problems of the economy. If anyone can prevent Asia crisis-type problems from boiling over in China, it would seem to be Zhu Rongji. However, as we often note in our discussions with American leaders and policymakers, it is important to remember that he is but one individual—an extremely important and capable person, to be sure—but one who must work in the framework of a collective leadership, the existing political and economic consensus, and the many limitations posed by China's stage of development. Even he, with his receptivity to new ideas and bold pronouncements about 8 percent annual growth and the overhaul of the State-Owned Enterprise system, cannot make these things happen without the kind of favorable circumstances that are suddenly in short supply.

At a more general level, we note that there has been a kind of a new "Beijing spring" developing recently in China. The range of ideas publicly discussed, the new spectrum of books and magazines being published, and the flourishing of the Internet and other new media are all positive, hopeful signs that an increasingly wide and sophisticated debate is taking place within China over many issues, including the most important matters about China's political and economic future. (We like to think that the publication of a Chinese edition of *Big Dragon,* which came about after a minor "bidding war" among leading publishers and was translated and published in record time to coincide with President Clinton's 1998 visit, is one small indicator of the expansion of ideas that can be officially published and discussed.) While there are many things that, unfortunately, still cannot be said in China and many viewpoints that cannot be freely heard, we are deeply impressed with how much opening has occurred in the last year or so.

A key mission of *Big Dragon* is to present China in its many dimensions, to avoid the quick sound bite and explore instead China's always complex, often ambiguous and contradictory realities. We have divided this book into five parts. Each provides a different, yet related, lens for looking at the China of today as well as tomorrow.

In Part I (Inside the New Cold War), we look at China through the window of the most troubling of all the issues on the table: the dangers of drifting into a destructive and unnecessary cold war between America and China. The Washington-Beijing relationship has undergone several shifts in the last decade. In the early 1990s, a bright, optimistic time prevailed. Then from 1993 to 1997, the environment was characterized by high profile ideological-political battles, virulent trade and economic disputes, the demonizing of China as a new "evil empire," China's provocative behavior on several fronts, and even military sparks over Taiwan. How and why the United States and China descended so quickly into this new cold war, what the stakes are for Americans, what could happen next, and how to avoid the worst-case scenarios are all subjects discussed in this first section.

In Part II (Benchmarking China), we illustrate some of the ways in which the heavy weight of China's past, its huge population, the feudal and then communist background of its political system, and other factors combine to constrain and shape the course of future change in directions other than that of a classic Western democratic market economy. Everyone knows China is "different" than the West. This section shows just how different.

In Part III (Jumping Into the Sea) we provide the "from-the-ground-up" view of these differences, profiling four entrepreneurs, including some of the richest and most successful private business people in China today. This section puts a human face on the complex questions associated with the concept of "ownership" and with creating a true "private" sector in China.

In Part IV (Geomancing the Dragon), we take what we know about China's past and present and project the trajectory of developments into the future between 2000 and 2024. We look at the future of the political system, at key issues such as Hong Kong and Taiwan, the emergence of new social and cultural values, and what exactly China's evolving new paradigm will mean for business, finance, and economics.

In the final section, Part V (Beyond the Cold War), we put forth some specific proposals for moving the U.S.-China relationship toward more of a partnership and away from the significant misunderstandings and mutual invective of the recent past. The partnership we suggest is one that recognizes differences—where "engagement" means dynamic interactivity, rather than serving as a euphemism for interference or incessant conflict.

To augment our analysis, we have placed some of our favorite facts, quotes, and comments about China in the margins. These are small, multifaceted pieces of glass, which together provide a kind of kaleidoscopic view. They are additive and interactive, but not necessarily directly related to the text. Readers should feel no compulsion to read each one. We don't always agree with those whom we have cited, but they provide ways of thinking about China we think valuable. Together, we believe these sidebars provide many rich details and insights relevant to any serious encounter with China's future.

Finally, a few housekeeping notes. We have converted the Chinese currency into U.S. dollars at the rate of approximately 8.4 (in other words, RMB 100 yuan works out to about $12). As to the use of the Chinese language, we have used the modern, pinyin system of romanization for names of people and places when they have relevance to post-1949 China (Mao Zedong, Beijing). But we have used the old Wade-Giles system of romanization (Lao Tse, Ching Dynasty) when the references are more familiarly associated with pre-1949 names, events, and places. This leads to certain minor inconsistencies, which we hope readers will appreciate as a meta-comment about Chinese ambiguities.

Weston, Connecticut
January 1999

PART I

INSIDE THE NEW COLD WAR

We have no fundamental conflicting interests. China will become a great power and have greater influence. We have to get used to this.

—HENRY KISSINGER

China's emergence as a superpower has been ominously likened to Germany's growing strength ten decades ago. That problem was "solved" by two hideous wars. It would be wise to find better ways to break China to the saddle and bridle of international dealings. How to do that may be the largest question of American life for a generation.

—GEORGE F. WILL

Our fashion is to have the enemy of the year. China is big, it's large on the map, it's yellow, so there is an under-the-surface racist element, and it fits very nicely an obsessive state of mind. I imagine it will last a couple of years, because China is big enough to sustain this obsession.

—ZBIGNIEW BRZEZINSKI

Strategy and Management

It is a hot, humid August night in Beijing in 1995. The U.S.-China relationship is in deep trouble, particularly as rhetoric escalates over the Taiwan issue, but on many other fronts as well. We have invited the editors of a new Chinese magazine called *Strategy and Management* to dinner. They have selected the place: the Peaceful Nation Hotel restaurant. This seems to be an in spot of sorts for China's growing cadre of neoconservatives, cultural nationalists, and others seeking to define a new, non-Western road for China's future. The hotel is shabby and run-down—a far cry from the glitzy new skyscrapers with atrium lobbies and sparkling shopping malls that now dot Beijing, courtesy in large part of foreign investors.

This is one of several dinners we will have at the Peaceful Nation this summer. The "home-style" cuisine apparently strikes a deep nostalgic chord in Chinese customers. We, however, find the virtues of this particular restaurant unfathomable. This divide is, no doubt, a sign of things to come.

Strategy and Management has been described to us as the Chinese equivalent of the *Harvard Business Review*, filled with "new ideas" and "key insights into the strategic trends" of the next century. A friend has mentioned that this publication seems to have high-level backing, particularly from some powerful people associated with the People's Liberation Army. We don't find this necessarily off-putting. After all, one of the most underreported stories of China's new economy is the role of the PLA's estimated 20,000 businesses. An economist we know who once wrote military biographies has recently written a manual on entrepreneurship for the PLA publishing house. It is at least plausible that the army could have a need to develop new management theory alongside new strategic doctrine.

The editors hand us copies of their magazine. An English version has now joined the bimonthly Chinese one. The cover has a glossy black finish and is far more elegantly printed than most documents in China. The masthead lists a number of extremely powerful Chinese advisors and honorary sponsors, including several senior military men.

Over drinks, we peruse the contents. It becomes clear that this is a magazine with a very distinct edge. The first photo-

"The swings of [China's] political life, the switches in its cultural moods, the lurches in its economy, the fact that its state hostility to foreign influences is so often accompanied by the flashes of a welcoming smile, all combine to keep us in a state of bewilderment as to China's real nature."

—JONATHAN SPENCE
THE SEARCH FOR MODERN CHINA

9

graph accompanying the first article is one of Vietnam War vintage: the famous image, rarely seen these days, of Phan Thi Kim Phuc, a nine-year-old girl running naked from a village after an American napalm bomb attack. This picture, worth much more than the proverbial thousand words in identifying the magazine's editorial stance, is accompanied by other oddities, the most incomprehensible of which is a twenty-three-page article by Lyndon LaRouche, the American political extremist (once of the "Left," now of the "Right"), who argues that China's present course of economic reform—and foreign investment in particular—will destroy the country. *This* we find truly surprising.

Over dinner, we ask: "You are said to be among the few groups doing work on cutting-edge issues concerning China and its future in the twenty-first century. What sorts of new concepts are you working with? What are some of your new ideas? Give us an example of one of the trends about the future you have identified."

The reply was instantaneous and sure: "That the United States will become the enemy of China."

Any other insights into China's future? Political system? Economic system? New institutions? How the State-Owned Enterprise problem will be solved? How the rule of law will be established? How to raise the living standards of 900 million peasants? The future of Chinese-Japanese relations? The role of American and foreign investment in continuing to fuel development and export growth?

Each of these questions is met with silence or beside-the-point comments. Everything comes back to one big, "new" line of reasoning: America has decided it cannot tolerate a strong, independent, economically successful China. Therefore, the United States is out to undermine China, stunt its growth, wreck its development, contain it militarily and strategically. The Soviet Union is gone, so America has decided to make China its enemy. Well, if America makes China its enemy, China must respond in kind. The twenty-first century will see the resulting clash.

That this would be *the* leading-edge "new idea" proffered in the 1990s by these Chinese intellectuals was more sad than shocking. After all, the modern U.S.-China relationship, a quarter-century in the making since Henry Kissinger's secret trip to Beijing in 1971, was visibly coming unraveled.

"America is the leader of the world, but not the god of the world. There is a big difference. Your power is limited. So don't go beyond it. Let others do their own job."

—CHEN XIAOLU
DIRECTOR, STANDARD
INTERNATIONAL CORP.

And the editors of *Strategy and Management* have their opposite numbers here at home. A growing and influential school of thought among American political strategists argues that it is *China* that has consciously decided to become *our* enemy, that it is China that has decided to threaten Asian stability and American global power, and that it is the United States that has no choice but to respond in kind, become adversarial with China, and prepare for a twenty-first century of conflict and clash.

CHAPTER 1

A New and Unnecessary Cold War Takes Shape

The End of History and the Burgers of Beijing

Things were not supposed to turn out this way.

It seems like ancient history now, but all through the 1980s, and even as recently as 1993–1994, the public discussion of China was dominated *not* by talk of conflict, clash, threats, and enmity, but by optimistic predictions of huge economic opportunity for American business. The Chinese drive toward modernity, markets, and democracy was seen as relentless and the pace as torrid. China's experience was seen as validating the new American vision of the post–Cold War world: since the Chinese, like everyone else, now aspired to American consumer goods and lifestyles, they would be prepared to do their part to fit into the American-influenced world order, which yielded such fruits to those who played by its rules.

There was no shortage of pundits to remind us constantly that the globalization of business and economics was the defining trend of the future. The rapidity with which China was becoming a major factor in international business was a prime case in point. Politics, ideology, nationalism, military muscle—all of these were widely thought to be powerful forces that had reached their zenith in the last half of the twentieth century and would now fade from the scene, yielding to the face of the twenty-first-century logic of consumerism, markets, technology, and the knowledge-based global economy.

This body of informed opinion saw economic competition as having replaced military conflict as the chief form of rivalry between great powers. "Hot" wars, along with cold ones, seemed utterly passé among major countries. The China problem, as it was perceived back then, was more likely to be economic than political and military. Would American manufacturing jobs eventually migrate entirely to China to take advantage of rock-bottom labor costs? How would the United States cope when China superseded it as the world's largest economy (as early as 2011, no less, according to some overenthusiastic forecasts made in 1994)?

Business and political leaders in the United States had absorbed almost by osmosis the thesis proffered by the social scientist Francis Fukuyama: the world had arrived at the "end of history." With the fall of the Berlin Wall and the end of the Cold War, humankind's long Darwinian search for an optimally efficient political-economic system was over. What everyone wants, what everyone needs, what everyone will thrive on the world over is a system of liberal democratic capitalism.

Yes, the Chinese still called themselves Communists and, yes, the Communist Party still ruled China with an iron grip. But how long could that last in the face of economic growth rates three to four times faster than America's, and one of the strongest surges of entrepreneurial energy the world had ever seen? One American manager of a China fund declared in 1994: "They may not wish to call it capitalism for their own political reasons, but by God, when I look at what's happening in China today I see not only capitalism at work, I see a very raw and energetic kind."

Political conflicts in Washington over China policy did not disappear entirely during this period of boomtown optimism. After all, the blood in Tiananmen Square was scarcely dry. On the 1992 campaign trail, Bill Clinton routinely criticized George Bush for "coddling dictators," signaling that, once elected, he was going to take a tough line with Beijing. When Clinton proved to be more pragmatic as president than his campaign rhetoric had suggested, congressional critics responded by turning the annual White House renewal of China's Most Favored Nation (MFN) trade status into a forum for venting their frustrations over continued Chinese abuses of human rights. But such conflicts were largely buried in an avalanche of exciting news about the expansion of American trade and investment, the adoption by the Chinese of more and more market-oriented mechanisms, and the ways supercharged growth rates were changing China's long closed and backward society.

The early nineties were a time of downsizing in much of corporate America, along with continuing recovery and readjustment to the multitude of new competitors in the world. The domestic American economy was mired in recession and slow growth at best, as were those of Europe and Japan. The Chinese market looked like manna from heaven to global corporations starved for growth at home. "If you want to be a growth company, you'd better be in growth markets," said the head of a New York investment bank, explaining the zeal for investing in China that seemed to appear almost overnight.

Jack Welch, the CEO of General Electric—America's largest company, measured by stock market capitalization—indicated that the Chinese market could be the center of gravity of his company's twenty-first-century growth strategy. Robert Allen, the CEO of AT&T, America's most widely held company, pointed out in an interview that over the next forty years more than half the global growth in the business of telephone lines and switches will be in China. "Next to China, all other opportunities around the world pale." William Warwick, who ran AT&T's operations on the ground in China, suggested that in the twenty-first century, global telephone companies, such as AT&T and its now independent Lucent equipment operation, could derive more revenue from China than from their "home" market. Motorola invested over $1 billion in China, where it immediately came to dominate the rapidly growing market for pagers and mobile phones. After just a few years, Motorola executives said their China operations were more profitable than those in Japan—where the company has been in business for more than thirty years.

At one of Beijing's busiest and most prestigious intersections, where Wangfujing Street meets Changan Boulevard, the American business visitor could sit at the world's biggest McDonald's, eat a passable cheeseburger, and dream the centuries-old foreign dream of selling one of everything to each Chinese. Watching a young couple on a date spend

The market to come:
"China is only 1 percent of our sales now, but it's one of the fastest-growing markets."

—BILL GATES
  CHAIRMAN, MICROSOFT

nearly a week's pay on Big Macs, Coca-Colas, and fries, it was possible to imagine that American values were indeed being universalized, even here, in what had so recently been one of the world's most zealously Communist societies. Even the McNotion that no two countries with McDonald's franchises had ever gone to war with each other seemed somehow profoundly true to some under the circumstances.

Not only fast-food outlets, but shopping malls, gleaming skyscrapers, superhighways, stock markets, and investment banks were all coming to China in a frenzy that frequently caused Western reporters to invoke the metaphor of the gold rush. Books appeared arguing that China would soon become the world's largest economy, that the American economy would get a powerful new growth kick from U.S. investments and trade with China, and that the West's encounter with a China-fueled Asia would be an enormous win-win situation for all concerned. The new global economic system—with its themes of private enterprise, venture capital, high technology, high growth, customer service, foreign investment, and free trade, and with its mantra "The market, the market, the market"—was taking hold among a quarter of humanity! No one captured the mood better than Morgan Stanley's chief strategist, Barton Biggs, who declared himself in 1993 to be "maximum bullish" on China.

Despite that optimistic atmosphere, our long experience with China told us that we should argue for a more cautious view. We were troubled by the fact that too many Americans in business and public policy failed to see just how different the Chinese experience was from our own, structurally, historically, and culturally. We wanted to argue that yes, American companies could make money and do well selling Big Macs and Coca-Cola to the Chinese, but in the world of political economy, you aren't necessarily what you eat. Taking in these long-forbidden fruits would not necessarily make the Chinese into a people insistent on establishing truly free markets or a truly free society.

Yes, the stakes were huge for American corporations, some of which might well thrive or founder, in the global competition of the twenty-first century, on the quality of their China strategy—or lack thereof. The sound strategies, we believed, would seek to localize and adapt American products, processes, and management techniques within the framework of the unique Chinese experience.

Then as now, we believed that China would create its own new political-economic paradigm, one that lies between traditional capitalism and traditional socialism and that combines elements of Asian and Western values. Those who expect the unleashing of rudimentary free-market forces to translate necessarily and quickly into a free society with free trade and fully democratic institutions will be enormously frustrated and ultimately disappointed.

Deng Xiaoping always believed that Mikhail Gorbachev's big mistake in the Soviet Union was to allow political freedom *before* he revamped the economy. Deng's view was economic modernization first, political reform much, much later—if ever. That China's gross domestic product has nearly trebled since 1985 (and China is now taken seriously as potentially the largest economy in the world), while the combined GDPs of the former Soviet republics have been halved (and Russia is considered a chaotic society and an economic basket case), lends at least circumstantial credibility to the wisdom of the Chinese road.

Because we envisioned China pursuing a very different political-economic model from the West, and because we were bullish enough on China to believe it would succeed in this course, we sensed that very significant conflicts would continue between China and the United States. The conflicts of the nineties, which ran the gamut from Taiwan, nuclear proliferation, and human rights to trade policy, intellectual property, and market access, would not be fully resolved any time soon. New, unforeseen conflicts would develop. Mindful of the stormy history of new superpowers arriving on the global scene, we foresaw some degree of systemic conflict as China emerged as a second all-around great power in a world where the United States, since the fall of the Berlin Wall, has been the sole superpower.

We planned this book as a critique of many kinds of wrongheaded American thinking about China. In particular, we thought it would serve as a warning against the excessive optimism and Pollyannaish school of thought that then pervaded American business. China is very different, and the Chinese will never be just like us, we wanted to say. But if we learn enough about China, understand just how different it is,

What a difference two decades makes: In 1974 Harvard economist Dwight Perkins wrote, "It would be sheer fantasy to imagine that China has the large market potential—let alone interest—to 'bail out' ailing American aerospace industries." Today, that picture looks very different indeed: "Without China, Boeing would be flat on its back," says Nicholas Heymann of NatWest Securities.

and develop creative ways to manage our differences, American business can still benefit from a huge new opportunity and the United States can still benefit strategically from partnership with China.

We saw China then—and still see it now in the light of all that has happened while we were at work on *Big Dragon*—as an extremely important opportunity for the United States in at least two different ways:

First, even if China does not develop in the way the Pollyannas had hoped, its economy will remain a vast potential market for American companies, a source of profits, and a generator of high-quality American jobs, almost 200,000 of which are already directly tied to the China trade (many more are tied indirectly). Low-cost labor and manufacturing in China, while possibly threatening some low-end American jobs, will continue to provide enormous cost savings for American consumers and industry, contributing to rises in American living standards and keeping global inflationary pressures at bay. Overall, China will be a massive new frontier of global growth where American entrepreneurs will build new empires and in which a great many American companies *must* participate to remain globally competitive.

Second, China's successful entry into the global economy and the global order will be of great value to American interests in spite of the very serious challenges that will have to be surmounted. A growing, prosperous, successful China will, on balance, contribute to the currently benign confluence of factors that has made the American system such a strong and dynamic leader in the world. On the other hand, a China that fails will make the world a much more dangerous place and end up commanding American attention for the negative and potentially costly purposes of defense rather than for the benefits of enhanced global economic competition and a bigger global pie.

In this book, we arm those thinking about China business strategies and policy concerns with what we believe is a balanced, nuanced, complex view of the events that may unfold. We forewarn readers that much of what we will see in China will be objectionable to our collective values as Americans. But we have to preserve American political capital and be careful about which battles we fight and when. Those we fight should be fought consistently, relentlessly, with clarity of purpose. Others should not be fought at all. And with respect to more than a few we might discover we are not as virtuous as we think. We urge more modesty on those engaged in the policy debate. Neither carrots nor sticks will be decisive in shaping China's future. What is decisive is the internal process, which outsiders can influence only at the margins.

The Great Leap Backward: From China Boom to China Threat

The pendulum of American thinking about China has swung wildly in the last few years—from optimism to pessimism, from hope to fear, from opportunity to threat, from the coming China boom to the coming conflict with China. Even though Clinton's successful visit to China in 1998 marked the triumph of a more rational "middle," anxiety, suspicion, anger, alarm, loathing, and even a renewed version of the old "yellow peril" continue to lie just beneath the surface in the public debate. The pendulum could easily swing again in favor of the dangerous rhetoric favored by the new cold warriors.

Just half a decade after Barton Biggs's statement, almost no one is still maximum bullish on China. Now the prevailing mood is more nearly the one reflected by *The Economist*'s rejoinder to Biggs: "Maximum Bullshit." As for Biggs himself, by the autumn of 1997 he had turned so bearish on the region that he was urging clients to empty their portfolios entirely of Hong Kong and Chinese stocks— a bit of advice that figured prominently among the multiple causes of the market crash that started in Hong Kong in late October, 1997, and spread like a prairie fire from there to every market in the world.

In the wake of the numerous economic and financial nightmares that engulfed Asia as 1998 began—plunging currencies and competitive devaluations, swooning stock markets, banks wobbling under mountains of bad debt, and the specter of deflation spreading across the region, many experts argued that it was only a matter of time before China would be engulfed by these same negative regional trends. Worries about recession in Asia and the unpredictable effects of financial volatility on new and not yet particularly stable Asian markets gave global business leaders pause for thought about new investments. American companies with significant business interests in Asia were suddenly punished

But for a lack of understanding . . . "If most Americans had even the foggiest idea of the change that has occurred in China they would be cheering [instead of looking for ways to punish China]."

—David M. Lampton
Former president,
National Committee
on United States–
China Relations

19

by the U.S. stock market, just as they had been rewarded for having capitalized on Asian growth in prior years.

Concern about the vitality and sustainability of Asian and Chinese growth patterns has led, quite legitimately, to caution on the part of many foreign businesses in 1998. But this new business realism was only one of two important pendulum swings in American attitudes toward China. Beginning in 1995–96 with China's increasingly muscular and shrill stance on Taiwan, and reaching a high point in 1997 with the coalescing of a powerful new anti-Beijing lobby made up of forces from both the Left and the Right, China emerged as a new kind of moral and political litmus test in American public policy. This pendulum swing may have already reached its extreme extension and may now be swinging back a bit, if one compares the mood and rhetoric in Washington circa 1998 to that of 1997. But powerful forces remain at work in the American political system trying to touch the nerve deep down in the American psyche where China can be portrayed as a new evil empire and a new national enemy.

Just as we oppose a Pollyannaish attitude, we reject this alarmism. We do not believe China poses a threat to the United States today, nor do we believe American policy should be designed to confront China in order to preempt a threat that may arise a decade or two from now. Of course, there are worrisome signs that China *might* become a strategic enemy of the United States in the future. But there are many years between now and then for American policy-makers to try to prevent such an eventuality, and plenty of time to prepare if the preventive course doesn't work.

Intelligent business and political strategy toward China must be rooted in accurate and realistic assessments of where China is coming from and where it is headed. The Pollyannas were wrong to assume that China would naturally evolve into a liberal, democratic, capitalist society. Today's Hawks are right to the degree they recognize how different our systems and values are. But they are wrong to believe that because the Chinese will not become liberal democrats on their own, America's interests will be served by trying to contain, constrain, and bludgeon China into accepting our way. Or that getting China to become more like us by these means is even a possibility.

Let's be clear: there would be no significant discussion of a

Is the West teaching China the wrong lessons? "China's ability to play Europeans and Japanese off against Americans when Washington criticizes Chinese policies is teaching it that belligerence, intolerance, corruption and other accouterments of totalitarianism will be tolerated by a great many countries so long as it waves commercial carrots."
The Wall Street Journal

"China threat" if Beijing's rhetoric and actions did not scare people. The "China threat" is not, as the editors of *Strategy and Management* would like to believe, a purely American invention made up out of whole cloth. Chinese behavior on many fronts—from Beijing's repression of dissidents, to its bullying of Taiwan, to allegations about gun-running corporations and contributions to Clinton campaign coffers—have demonstrated just how dangerously at odds the Chinese system is with our own values and our system's inner workings.

In America's view, the evidence shows that China has almost certainly sold nuclear equipment to Pakistan and missiles to Iran, and has occupied disputed islands in the South China Sea. Its factories wantonly crank out pirated American CD-ROMs and videos. Its corporations have procured dual-use technology from the United States under civilian guise, only to deliver it directly to the military establishment. Beijing promises to preserve the status quo in Hong Kong, then immediately moves to roll back civil liberties. Nationalism is on the rise in China, with a variety of prominent voices there declaring Washington the "enemy" and urging their fellow citizens to just say no to everything American.

Given this picture, it is entirely appropriate and realistic for Americans to be concerned. But certain American interest groups have found it expedient and useful for their own diverse agendas to turn what is legitimately a *challenge*—how to cope with the emerging Chinese superpower—into a sense of imminent *threat*. The question of how China may develop over the long term is being turned, by some influential voices, into a definitive answer—that China will be fascistic, expansionist, hegemonic, and inherently adversarial toward the United States.

"There is a big difference between acknowledging that the Chinese government behaves badly and believing that it represents a clear and present danger," observes Steven Erlanger of *The New York Times*.[1] But that difference has been increasingly blurred in a rash of recent articles, books, and news show talking heads arguing that China is already, or else is bound to become, a strategic foe of the United States. Our very civilizations are said to be motivated by such opposite impulses that they are destined to clash.

In the late 1980s, it might have been thought-provoking to predict a conflict between the United States and China. By the mid-1990s, it was tantamount to predicting the present.

"China is the only country still testing thermonuclear warheads with the goal of miniaturizing them to fit on ICBMs. Those missiles are aimed at us. I know it's not a popular thing to say, that China is a threat, but I think it is."

—GARY MILHOLIN
NUCLEAR-PROLIFERATION
EXPERT

The Washington-Beijing relationship had slid precipitously from amity toward enmity:

• Throughout much of the 1990s, leaders of the two countries could scarcely hold a successful ceremonial meeting. A brief encounter between Bill Clinton and Chinese President Jiang Zemin at an Asian leaders' summit meeting in Seattle turned into a famous moment of mutual anger and recrimination. The political atmosphere in Washington had veered into such an anti-China abyss in 1996 that Bill Clinton chose *not* to receive Jiang Zemin at the White House, even though Clinton would, in the months that followed, meet with two of Jiang's best-known critics, Martin Lee, the leader of Hong Kong's democracy movement, and the Dalai Lama, spiritual leader of Tibet. High-level summitry finally resumed in October 1997, when Clinton at last agreed to welcome Jiang to the White House. Although there was an effort on both sides to use this visit to warm up the relationship—and some substantive progress was, in fact, made—the agenda was a limited one. Powerful forces in the Congress and among special-interest lobbies sought to turn the visit into a platform for criticizing Chinese policies on Tibet and human rights and to oppose improved U.S. relations with China more generally. The protests outside the White House and the other venues where Jiang appeared drew as much media attention as the positive steps the two leaders agreed to take.

• Voices in Congress constantly argue for shutting down trade with China to punish it for its political sins. Denial of MFN—the normal trading privileges the United States extends to almost all countries—came perilously close to gaining a congressional majority in 1997. Extremist bills have swept through Congress seeking to cast China as America's national enemy and circumvent the president's constitutional authority to make foreign policy on matters concerning China. One such bill, for example, requires the president to apply for a special exemption from the Congress in order to allow a Chinese leader to visit the United States.

• American companies that have invested heavily in China, are highly regarded there, and are on the cusp of benefiting from the huge market forecast for so long are now witnessing the loss of prime business opportunities as Beijing vents its frustration with Washington on them.

• Our State Department routinely lists China among the world's worst violators of human rights.

• And our warships were dispatched to within 200 miles of the Chinese coast in 1996 to remind Beijing that the United States might intervene militarily if China tried to take Taiwan by force.

Even though the Clinton administration has moved toward a genuine improvement in relations with Beijing, and even as continued improvement remains the goal of many American business people despite recent economic uncertainties, the proponents of heightened confrontation with China have not lost their voice. Their arguments too often continue to set the terms for the debate. We are witnessing a new split in American leadership circles, with all-too-familiar echoes as "Hawks" and "Doves" debate various forms of "containment" versus "engagement." With the permafrost of the U.S.-Soviet conflict now gone, the Cold War has made a geological shift eastward, threatening, from time to time, to undermine better relations with China.

The 1998 vintage Bill Clinton appears to believe in working to narrow U.S.-China differences and expand the scope of the relationship, unlike the 1993–96 Bill Clinton, whose administration sought to confront Beijing over every imaginable issue. Recently, Clinton has spoken eloquently on the importance of a positive relationship with China and has even begun to use his bully pulpit (occasionally) to sell a confused and misinformed American public on the benefits of enhanced economic and cultural interaction between our two countries. Clinton's visit to Beijing in 1998 did much to improve the day-to-day dynamics. But, especially given his weakened political position, Clinton must avoid any initiative that would provide ammunition to the virulent lobby of anti-China Hawks.

In these dangerous times, those who still see the value in taking positive steps and building bridges and connections to China—following the basic concept behind the "constructive engagement" policy once articulated by the Clinton administration—are seen as softheaded and naive at best. At worst, they are derided as "appeasers," "sinopologists," and "dictator-coddlers" who are selling out the Chinese people as well as America's national interest.

Meanwhile, today's Hawks, who focus on proposing pen-

The great China debate (II): "There are Catholic priests and bishops that are in prison today. There are Protestant pastors that are in prison today. They've tortured and killed Buddhist monks and nuns. They have more gulags in China than they had in the Soviet Union. They've sold arms to Saddam Hussein that were used against American troops. There was foreign interference in our domestic elections, both trying to buy influence in Congress and in the administration. I really take issue with what the President said. I can't prove it, but I don't believe Ronald Reagan would extend MFN to China."

—Representative Frank Wolf (R-Va.)
May 17, 1997

alties and punishments for an errant Beijing that refuses to behave as Americans believe it should—along with those who hatch theories of how best to isolate and contain China, confront it, and overthrow its government—are the toast of Washington as they design the intellectual bait for today's political feeding frenzy.

The popular columnist George Will, for example, states baldly that "The strategic aim of U.S. policy is, and must be seen to be, the *subversion of the Chinese regime*" [emphasis added].[2] Current American policy toward China is nothing more than appeasement of aggression, adds the Naval War College's Arthur Waldron. What the United States should be doing is encircling China with military alliances and "[cutting] the ground out from under the Chinese hard-liners." The only long-term solution to the China threat, says Waldron, "is *a change in the regime,* in the direction of democracy" [emphasis added].[3]

In other words, the idea of building a U.S.-China strategic partnership, which has stood at the heart of public-policy discussions about China for the last two decades, is hopelessly out of fashion. For twenty-five years, since the Nixon-Kissinger days, American leaders have been working to come to grips with the reality of China, to recognize the legitimacy of its government, to learn to understand it on its own terms and seek common ground with it, and to appreciate its economic progress and success at delivering the goods to its people. But now the new vogue declares that what America should really be doing with China is *overthrowing its government.*

The Ironies of History

An old Chinese proverb warns, "Be careful what you wish for, because it may come true." The West now has in China what it has dreamed of for 200 years—a huge, thriving market, a vast emerging economy filled with opportunity, a new frontier in a world starved for dynamic growth. In one of history's great ironies, however, it appears that Washington was more comfortable with China in the 1970s, when it was still a dogmatic, extremist, Communist police state, than it is with the much more open, market-oriented, and modern country China has become.

Although China today is certainly not very democratic in the American sense of the word, it is arguably more democratic than it has been in 5,000 years of its own history. Its market for both trade and investment is more open than that of some other countries in the region. And yet, after an extraordinary twenty-year track record of Chinese successes at growing, changing, modernizing, and even stepping tentatively and partially into the Western light of democracy and markets, Washington treats China with more opprobrium today—and engages Beijing in less leadership-level dialogue—than it did when Beijing was a Maoist dictatorship in the 1970s.

The slide into confrontation and cold war is, incidentally, anything but costless to an American society already facing an age of limits on what government can do, and a Pentagon that has scaled down its "two-and-a-half-war" fighting capability to two-war capability and is currently headed down toward just one. Some have even begun to consider the economic and military costs. According to one such analysis:

> A real cold war with China could mean, at minimum, higher defense spending with more American troops abroad; a huge economic and trade disruption; a crisis with American allies in Asia; a much more disputatious United Nations Security Council, and probably more nuclear proliferation—in short, a much more dangerous and less predictable world.[4]

Toward Resolving the Cold War

No other country poses such significant business, economic, political, and strategic questions for the American agenda in the twenty-first century as China does. Especially in light of these high stakes, the widespread temptation in some circles to judgment about the nature of the China threat is particularly dangerous. U.S.-based corporations *could* be China's partner of choice in developing and modernizing its economy. The Chinese admire America's economic prowess and find Americans friendlier and much easier to deal with than the Japanese and far more decisive and leading-edge than Europeans. American business already stands a few steps inside the doorway of the Chinese market that foreigners

"Why is it that when China becomes a little stronger, a little more prosperous, you feel threatened? Why is the only China you want to deal with one that is poor and weak? We have always been the victim, never the aggressor. Look at history and you will see that when Columbus discovered the New World, he was brutal and turned people into slaves. When our great explorer Zheng He sailed throughout Asia to the coast of Africa he didn't colonize anywhere. He didn't take any slaves."

—SENIOR CHINESE GOVERNMENT POLICY ADVISOR

25

have sought to pry open for 200 years. But any reemergence of a cold war atmosphere will restrict the ability of American corporations to capitalize on the tantalizing opportunities just on the verge of coming to fruition.

The more it becomes conventional political wisdom that China is our adversary, the less possible it becomes to launch the fresh public and private-sector initiatives needed to put the relationship back on a positive course. Moreover, the more American policy and behavior come to look overtly like a strategic design to contain and control China, the more assertive and less cooperative China will assume it must become. Thus, to think of China as America's future enemy runs the risk of becoming a self-fulfilling prophecy.

Some American scholars and experts have argued that a cold war isn't even the worst-case scenario. At least four books have been published in the last two years by well-credentialed authors in which possible scenarios for a full-scale military war between the United States and China in the twenty-first century were detailed. To us, however, these scenarios represent some combination of undue alarmism about China's bellicosity, useful warnings to both sides to be more careful in their interactions, and marketing departments' belief that the best way to sell books about this complex relationship is to predict a U.S.-China war. No scenario should be ruled out in a book about great-power relationships, and we would not rule out a military showdown between the United States and China in the future. But although we have presented many futuristic scenarios in this book, we have not developed that one. The reason is very simple: we do not believe it will happen.

It is tragedy enough that conflict, confrontation, and cold war could result in enormous opportunities lost. In particular, the potential for compatibility and collaboration between Americans and Chinese—people who generally tend to like and admire each other personally, despite our cultural differences—could, in a different atmosphere, be harnessed to achieve many new ends.

Along the positive, constructive road of China's progress may lie the answer to the question of where the world's developed countries, which are now almost all slow-growth economies with rapidly aging populations, will get their energy and growth kicks in the first half of the next century. Today, fewer than one in four people lives in a "Have"

Questioning U.S. policy: "American policy toward China has assumed a cast that is more therapeutic than strategic. 'Constructive engagement' tries to punish China for its tantrums, then salve its feelings with assurances of regards. It is as if China were neurotic rather than vulnerable, and could be made to feel secure through expressions of esteem despite its circumference of actual and potential enemies and its relative military and economic weakness. American policy seems to do everything but talk consistently and clearly about where American and Chinese interests overlap and where they clash."

—ANDREW NATHAN
  COLUMBIA UNIVERSITY

economy—making the Haves of the world a very small minority surrounded by a sea of increasingly disenfranchised and embittered Have-Nots. Enrich China, integrate it into the world system, and the number of Haves automatically swells to half the world's population and the right example is set for other countries and peoples.

But in the space of a very few short years, the public-policy discussion about China has shifted from consideration of it as a potential partner and force for positive change in the world, to focus on how to isolate it and contain the dangers it presents. As Chas. W. Freeman, Jr., a former U.S. Foreign Service officer specializing in China and a former assistant secretary of defense, observed recently:

> In both Beijing and Washington, discussion of Sino-American relations is focused on the adverse consequences of estrangement and strategic hostility, rather than the advantages of friendship and entente. Almost no one seems to envision the possibility of broad cooperation in the coming decades. . . . The contrast with the . . . period from 1971 to 1989, when five successive American and Chinese administrations worked to advance a positive vision of Sino-American relations, could not be more stark.[5]

The urgent question, then, is not whether there will or won't be a Sino-American conflict in the future. Rather, it is how to permanently put behind us the conflict so much in evidence, even as the most recent events have been moving in a positive direction. How do we narrow the parameters of this conflict, instead of allowing it to widen, deepen, and escalate in the future? How do we resolve the cold war with China and set a positive course with mutual benefit for the twenty-first century? *That* is the crucial question of the moment.

CHAPTER 2

The Eagle and the Dragon (I): From Clipper Ships to Tiananmen Square

West Meets East

To think clearly and rationally about China and design an intelligent China business strategy, or to design a U.S. policy toward China, we must first know and understand something of China's historical experience, as well as the history of the West's interactions with it. Even a brief review of the epic saga of the interaction of East and West, and of U.S.-China relations in particular, is valuable to understanding the current context, as well as the potential future course of development.

Among the broad themes of this history is that the reality of China has often turned out to be other than what Americans either wished it or feared it to be. A second theme is the degree to which this relationship has been characterized by pendulum swings, mood shifts, cycles of excessive expectation followed by embittered disappointment and extreme reaction. Yet the relationship has endured just the same. And a third is just how deeply different the Chinese historical and cultural experience is from our own, and how carefully we need to think about what we can realistically change in China, what we can live with, and what we ourselves may have to adapt to in constructing a global economy and a peaceful relationship with the other superpower of the next century.

Asians, with their long historical memories, often think of Americans as comparative amnesiacs. And, to a very large degree, we are. The ability to put the past behind us and move on is a tremendously positive American cultural characteristic. But it also makes us more than a bit naïve about how other cultures and societies work.

In our collective amnesia, Americans sometimes find it hard to remember that there was a time when talking about trade balances with China, let alone investments there, would have been absurd and practically illegal. Or that several of the issues of concern today have been visited and revisited many times over the last two centuries. That we should learn some profound lessons from this storied history is clear. The question is, Will we?

In spite of the common notion that China is "inscrutable" and "exotic," Americans have managed to have a surprisingly close and even passionate relationship with it over the years. Our relationship with China actually predates the birth of the United States. When the Declaration of Independence was drafted, the clipper-ship era of the China trade was already in full swing. It was Chinese tea that American revolutionaries threw into Boston Harbor in 1773. Chinese silk, porcelain, and furnishings were almost as American as apple pie to George Washington's generation.

A Rip van Winkle who went to sleep in the 1790s would not be surprised to wake up today and discover the ubiquity of Chinese items on American shelves. Nor would he be surprised to learn that today's China trade was largely one-way. The Western battle to open China's door—along with the internal Chinese debate about how to be both "Chinese" and modern at the same time—is one of the enduring themes of world history in the second half of this millennium. Every businessperson trying to sell foreign goods to the Chinese and every politician trying to think through modern trade policy for dealing with China's soaring surplus should, at a minimum, understand just how long these matters have been debated.

Even as early as the 1760s, British colonial strategists and businessmen had begun to worry about their mounting trade deficit with China. The world's appetite for Chinese goods was immense, but Emperor Qianlong refused to

Better to let sleeping dragons lie? Sir Robert Hart, the famed British Inspector-General of Customs in China during the nineteenth century, was once told by a Chinese prime minister: "You are all too concerned with waking us up and setting us off on a new route; you will succeed in doing it, but you will regret it, because once we are awakened and set off, we will go faster and farther than you think, and a great deal more rapidly than you would like."

allow significant imports of foreign goods into China. Foreign traders chafed under restrictions that confined their activity to the single port city of Canton, where they had to follow strict procedures set down by the emperor for conducting their business through Chinese middlemen.

As foreign traders had to pay for their purchases in silver, and as they sold almost nothing back to the Chinese, a balance-of-payments problem arose that soon became a "source of alarm for the British government."[1] One attempted solution was to try to convince the emperor to open up China to free trade. Lord George Macartney was selected to travel to China on behalf of King George III to make this case in 1793.

Macartney was an able diplomat who had already succeeded in furthering London's goals in facing the challenges of foreign cultures: at the court of Catherine the Great in Russia, as governor of Grenada in the Caribbean, and as an administrator in Madras, India. He was among the first—but certainly not the last—to believe in applying a "universal" view of human and material interests to China.

To make Britain's demands more palatable, Macartney brought with him a vast array of state-of-the-art British manufactured goods as gifts. He also brought scientists, artists, and linguists. All this was to show Emperor Qianlong the wonders of the modern world, which could be his if China would only agree to a few essential proposals. (The proposals included British rights of diplomatic residence in Peking and the opening of new ports to international commerce.)

Emperor Qianlong was eighty years old and perhaps a bit senile. But he obviously recognized a deal with the devil when he saw one. Opening China up as Macartney proposed would have destroyed the Chinese imperial system. Instead of agreeing, Qianlong sent Macartney back to King George with a now-famous note in which he declared that China had everything it wanted and had not "the slightest need of your country's manufactures." Even if these articles were "ingenious," Qianlong said, he placed no value on them. They were "amusements for children" at best, and certainly no cause for China to turn its system inside out to accommodate British interests.

Macartney left China dismayed. But, like the Clinton administration envoys of today, he was sure it was only a matter of time before the Chinese caught on to the good sense of British ideas and values. He wrote in his diaries that it was "futile" for the Chinese to resist British goals, tantamount to trying to "arrest the progress of human knowledge." Impossible. China, he was convinced, would eventually see the light.[2]

The Macartney mission might have been the brainchild of today's Engagement school. But the next British tactic corresponds more to what the get-them-before-they-get-us containment school might have favored: opium. By introducing opium into China from their colonial lands in India, British traders solved their trade deficit. The opium trade exploded from less than 4,000 chests a year in 1790 to almost ten times that much by the 1830s. The flow of silver back to the British triggered an economic crisis in China. In the process, the opium trade dealt a body blow to the old Chinese imperial system, showing it to be ineffectual and corrupt and accelerating its already considerable decline.

In this increasingly polarized situation, the United States faced its first major crisis with China. A sailor named Terranova on an American ship, the *Emily,* accidentally killed a Chinese fruit seller in a small boat alongside when he dropped an earthenware pitcher into it. This caused the boat to capsize, drowning the woman. The Chinese authorities demanded that Terranova be turned over to their judicial system. The Americans refused and made a show of standing firm. But when the Chinese summarily shut down all trade with Americans in response, the captain of the *Emily* (which was presumably carrying a cargo of opium itself) ultimately agreed to offer up Terranova. The sailor was convicted in a quick trial and executed the next day.

As the British imports of opium rose ever higher, Emperor Daoguang decided to enforce a ban on the drug. A tense atmosphere ensued, thick with the inevitability of a clash. London debated whether Britain should go to war to protect the opium trade. Among the many contemporary echoes of this debate: the local traders dispatched William Jardine, a leading opium merchant (who would go on to found the venerable Hong Kong–based trading house Jardine, Matheson) with the equivalent of $20,000 to go back to London and lobby on their behalf. His mission was to convince

Manipulating your adversary: "Display profits to entice them. Create disorder in their forces and take them. If they are substantial, prepare for them; if they are strong, avoid them. If they are angry, perturb them; be deferential to foster their arrogance. If they are rested, force them to exert themselves. If they are united, cause them to be separated. Attack where they are unprepared. Go forth where they do not expect it. These are the ways military strategists are victorious."

—Sun Tzu
    The Art of War

Parliament and public opinion of the necessity of war over this issue—and to quash the influence of missionaries who were questioning the morality of the opium business.

The British ultimately responded by dispatching the fleet and mobilizing troops from India. What became known as the Opium War of 1839–1842 was on. Decimating the Chinese forces, the British blockaded ports, occupied Shanghai, and brought China's internal commerce to a standstill. The emperor had little choice but to accept a humiliating peace.

The Treaty of Nanking (1842), which formally concluded the hostilities, specified that China should make huge, treasury-draining reparations to Britain. It opened up five cities to British traders and ceded to them the virtually barren island of Hong Kong. Besides including many punishing provisions, the treaty ushered in China's century of deeply resented "unequal treaties," which gave foreigners (including Americans) trading privileges, special concessions, and special extraterritoriality rights that allowed them to set up their own fiefdoms inside Chinese cities but free from Chinese law. Indeed, it would be Chinese citizens who were subjugated inside these concessions, as in the case of the park for Europeans along the Bund in Shanghai with its notorious sign, still posted in the 1940s: "No Chinese or dogs allowed."

This history is learned by every schoolchild in China. Not just the Opium War, of course, but all that followed in the next century of Chinese humiliation at the hands of the West. From the late-nineteenth-century American campaign (sometimes altruistic but always also self-interested) to enforce an "open door" for foreign trade, to the anti-Western Boxer Rebellion and its suppression, to the brutal Japanese invasion and occupation of China in the 1930s and 1940s, the hundred years after the Opium War are seen by Chinese as a century of foreign oppression, weakness, and subjugation. Even members of the younger generation, far removed from the bitterness of old China, are getting their cultural education in how to nurse its wounds. "Opium War" is now the title of a CD-ROM game, with history told from a decidedly Chinese viewpoint amid slick graphics and video clips. It is also the title of an ambitious Chinese film, released to commemorate the return of Hong Kong a century and a half after it was lost as a result of the Opium War.

Among the class of people who shape Chinese political

"**It is worth remembering** that the elements of China's political and economic discourse we see today—concern over cultural contamination, fear of excessive foreign participation in the economy, the desire to protect domestic markets from foreign competition, and harsh rhetoric directed at perceived international malefactors—all form one dimension of a Chinese domestic dialogue that began in the 1850s."

—ROBERT A. KAPP
  PRESIDENT, U.S.-CHINA
  BUSINESS COUNCIL

philosophy and policy today, China is still seen as the victim of ruthless foreigners. Indeed, two centuries of foreign exploitation of China define the West in the Chinese mind far more than the last two decades of mutually beneficial trade and investment.

Missionaries and Demonizers

One concession the United States extracted from the Chinese in the 1844 Treaty of Wanghia was the right to establish churches and send missionaries, many of whom had already begun to arrive in China in the 1830s. After the treaty, a veritable flood of American missionaries poured into China, continuing well into the twentieth century. They fanned out all over China, convinced they could turn Chinese heathens into a nation of Christians. The missionaries were also influential in introducing Western medicine and science and contributing in various ways to what was already a rising indigenous strain of progressive, democratic thinking. They thought they were succeeding—until they were driven out of China completely by war and revolution. If they failed to "save" China spiritually or politically, the missionaries did succeed in making a lasting impression on *American* perceptions. "A great many Americans first heard of China when asked in Sunday school to contribute their pennies to missionary activities and thus came to feel they had a stake in the distant land."[3]

Many of those who interpreted China to Americans in the critical 1930s and 1940s were the sons (Henry Luce) and daughters (Pearl Buck) of such missionaries. Luce, the powerful founder and publisher of *Time* and *Life,* was perhaps the most influential of all those who envisioned the post–World War II world in America's image. He assured the American elite as well as the man on the street that China would someday be pro-American, democratic, Christian—and ruled by the supposed embodiment of all those values, Chiang Kai-shek. In addition, China was to be a capitalist bonanza for trade and investment in Luce's "American century."

American missionaries of another sort—thinkers and writers of the Left—also made their way to China in the 1930s and 1940s. Some made it as far as the hinterland

On America's temptation to force-feed its values to China: "Even the best food tastes sour if you stuff it into people's mouths by force."

—Vice foreign minister Li Zhaoxing

headquarters in Yanan of Mao Zedong and his Red Army. In the interviews with Mao and his revolutionary contemporaries conducted by Edgar Snow and Agnes Smedley, Americans heard a romantic and appealing version of the Chinese revolution, cast as an almost American story of good versus evil, poor versus rich, just versus unjust.

Missionaries of all types taught Americans to *care* about China's "backwardness," its immense poverty and suffering. But in doing so, they also infused the China policy debate with missionary zeal. They were not only convinced that Americans *could* change China, they believed it was a moral imperative to do so. That evangelical attitude lives on; many in business and among the architects of the Engagement policy are certain we can turn the Chinese into good capitalists and democrats (using technology and consumer goods instead of the Bibles of the missionaries). The Hawks, meanwhile, are certain that it is the West's responsibility to stand up to Beijing's tyranny and free the Chinese people.

History, of course, took a different path than the one envisioned by Henry Luce. The Communist vision triumphed; the capitalist-Christian one shattered. The subsequent dialogue over China in the 1950s became suffused with "sadness, anger, and dread. American efforts seemed to have been wasted, American ideals rejected."[4] Then came the McCarthy era, with its hunt for the witches who "lost China" and its alarm over the "yellow peril."

All through the 1950s and 1960s, Washington's official policy was to isolate China and overturn its Communist regime. The United States actively supported Chiang Kaishek, whose Nationalist forces had been routed by Mao Zedong's Communists in 1949. Chiang was driven off the mainland entirely, retreating to set up a rump regime on what was then the bucolic island province of Taiwan. From there, he vowed some day to reclaim the mainland— "Red China," in the parlance of the 1950s. In that ambition, Chiang was supported politically, militarily, and financially by American governments from Truman to Johnson. American policy of that era unstintingly endorsed the convoluted logic that tiny Taiwan was the "real" China, while the mainland, with its population seventy times greater, essentially didn't exist.

The United States not only refused to recognize the government in Peking (Beijing), it fought to keep China out of the United Nations. Washington used its then-awesome leverage to prevent most of America's allies from even establishing diplomatic relations with Mao's China.

If China didn't officially exist for the State Department of the 1950s and 1960s, it certainly existed for the Pentagon. China had, of course, been a major theater of World War II. The histories of both the Korean War of the early 1950s and, to a lesser extent, the Vietnam War of the 1960s, could be read as American wars with China. That hostility was also a constant component of the U.S.-Soviet Cold War all through the 1950s and 1960s; Washington saw China as Moscow's junior partner in aggressive pursuit of the triumph of global Communism.

From the compassionate concern for China of the 1930s and 1940s to the fear, hatred, and even paranoia of the 1950s, the pendulum had made a full swing. The 1960s began with John F. Kennedy and Richard Nixon debating who would stand up taller and tougher to the Chinese in the wake of the Quemoy and Matsu incident in the Taiwan Strait. The mood of the early 1960s was reflected in the popularity of the book, and later the film, *The Manchurian Candidate,* in which an aspiring American presidential candidate and scion of a leading family becomes wrapped up in an evil Chinese brainwashing plot to take over America.

The Cultural Revolution in China— and America

By the end of the turbulent 1960s, the pendulum of American thinking about China had started to swing again, this time toward better relations. It was pushed along by an unlikely alliance of two American camps of opinion. One camp was made up of liberals and radicals, inheritors of the leftist idealism of the 1930s. They tended to see something virtuous and admirable in the goals of China's revolution and its dramatic experiences. Or, at a minimum, they had come to believe that it was no longer sustainable for America to ignore China's existence, especially as the unpopular Vietnam War called into question American policy toward Asia more generally. The other camp was that of the Cold War strategists, who had come to realize that the idea of a monolithic Communist bloc was a myth, that the Sino-Soviet schism was very real, and that it was possible to play the

"I don't think we should be slapping China in the face. They are very concerned with 'face.' We keep slapping theirs. But no one else in the world is doing this. The Japanese don't. The Europeans don't. Germany's chancellor has visited China four times. We haven't had an American president or vice president go there in eight years. When their president came to the United Nations, our side didn't even want to have lunch with him."

—JIMMY ROGERS
INVESTMENT PUNDIT
(1996)

35

"China card" in America's global battle with the Soviet Union.

Both camps were very much affected by the tumult and changes of the Great Proletarian Cultural Revolution, launched in 1966 by Mao and his most radical colleagues. The Cultural Revolution threw China into turmoil, chaos, and near civil war for most of the next ten years, until Mao's death in 1976. It was an era of Maoist fanaticism run amok. Everything that smacked of China's ancient traditions, foreign influences, or real-world economics was to be destroyed. Cultural Revolution campaigns took aim at the icons of Chinese and Western culture from Confucius to Beethoven, seeking to eradicate the past completely in order to create the new Maoist Man. Anyone with any actual connections to the old landlord and capitalist classes, or to foreigners, or even to the loyal and dedicated Communist leaders whom Mao had singled out for attack was an immediate target. Many ended up jailed, tortured, killed, or sent to work for years at menial jobs and in remote countryside locations facing primitive and starvation conditions.

Those who would compare *today's* violations of human rights by the Chinese regime to Hitler, Saddam Hussein, and other "fascist" tyrants—a comparison often heard these days from the American media punditocracy—are missing entirely the context of how far China has come from those black days of the Cultural Revolution and how relaxed and comparatively free the life of today's average Chinese man and woman in the street has become.

Similarly, those who allege that Beijing's current irresponsible behavior seriously threatens world stability miss the context: how much more palpable the threat from China was in the days when millions of people waved Mao's Red Book and chanted slogans in support of armed struggle, people's war, and world revolution. In one telling incident early in the Cultural Revolution, for example, a British diplomatic outpost in China was briefly attacked. It was also a time when Beijing stepped up its clandestine support for Maoists the world over, providing arms for guerrilla wars against several Southeast Asian governments. Beijing even rattled its nuclear saber, stepping up testing programs and vociferously denouncing nuclear arms limitation talks as an imperialist conspiracy.

The spillover effects of the Cultural Revolution touched

much of Asia. Riots swept through Hong Kong. Even Japan was forced to close its universities for a year as Japanese student factions, inspired by events in China, engaged in pitched battles with the police and each other on campuses and in the streets of Tokyo.

Even though the Cultural Revolution was one of the darkest hours in Chinese history, many young Americans, too, were fascinated with the romance of it, rarely realizing the truth behind the Potemkin Village scenes of China shown to visiting foreigners. China presented the world with a utopian vision and a spirit of radical egalitarianism. The Mao-jacketed, Red Book–waving Chinese spouted all sorts of ideas that appealed to student radicals—about communes and collective living, about women holding up half the sky, about how it was inherently "right to rebel." The idea that Washington would not recognize the existence of "Red China," where a quarter of the world's population lived, seemed absurd to a generation to whom most of their elders' ideas and policies seemed absurd anyway.

As members of this generation and participants in the heady American enthusiasm that surrounded our discovery of China in the 1960s, we experienced firsthand disillusionment and disappointment when our vision of China turned out not to reflect the reality we saw upon our visits and through understanding, insights, and revelations that came as the years unfolded. Not unlike the nineteenth-century missionaries or the recent American evangelists of capitalism, we badly wanted China to be something other than what it turned out to be.

The self-destructive nature of the Cultural Revolution brought China to the brink of starvation and economic collapse. This background also needs to be understood when foreigners encounter what otherwise appears to be an unnecessary obsession with maintaining order and stability on the part of the current leadership. All this happened not long, long ago in ancient China, but a mere generation ago, and it is scarred deeply into the memory of every Chinese over forty.

Understanding China: "The world consists of contradictions. Without contradictions, the world would cease to exist. Our task is to handle these contradictions correctly. As to whether they can be resolved entirely to our satisfaction in practice, we must be prepared for either possibility; furthermore, in the course of resolving these contradictions we are bound to come up against new problems."

—MAO ZEDONG

Playing the China Card

Throughout his rule, Mao was concerned not only about his domestic enemies but also about those abroad, often to the point of xenophobia. Throughout the 1950s and 1960s—and especially during the early stages of the Cultural Revolution—Beijing directed shrill rhetoric at the "U.S. imperialists" (although Mao noted that America was really only a "paper tiger," easily defeatable on Asia's battle-fields). But his greatest anger came to be turned toward an enemy he perceived as even more dangerous: the "Soviet social-imperialists."

Mao had never been enthusiastic about Moscow, which had backed an opposing faction in the early days of China's revolutionary movement, had made known its displeasure with Mao's peasant-based ideology, and had lent only half-hearted support during China's civil war. The Soviets did support the rebuilding of China in the early 1950s, but the late 1950s and early 1960s saw the exchange of increasingly scorching polemics between Moscow and Beijing over Communist theory. In an effort to eradicate Soviet influence and assert China's total independence, Mao summarily dismissed thousands of Soviet advisors and engineers who were working in China on dams, power stations, bridges, roads, hospitals, and public buildings. By the late sixties the war of words had escalated into action: Soviet missiles were pointed at China, and huge armies were deployed against each other along their long common border. In 1969, Soviet and Chinese soldiers actually clashed in bitter border skirmishes in China's frozen north.

Mao had come to believe that the Soviet Union was encircling China militarily and aimed to destroy his revolution. His view may have been touched with paranoia, but it had a strong evidentiary basis. As Henry Kissinger recalls in his memoirs, "The number of Soviet divisions on the Chinese border had grown from 21 in 1969 to 33 in 1971, to 45 in 1973."[5] That background is critical to understanding the improbable realignment of strategic forces that began to bring the United States and China together again in the early 1970s. Mao made the first signal, suggesting in a highly studied yet apparently off-the-cuff remark to his old friend Edgar Snow that he would welcome a visit from Richard Nixon, whether as "a tourist or as President."

In a bold stroke of geopolitical genius, Secretary of State Henry Kissinger seized the moment. Going off the grid during a trip to Pakistan in 1971, he disappeared for a secret trip to Beijing. Kissinger had understood the depth of the Sino-Soviet antagonism and realized just how urgent Mao perceived the situation to be. In this crisis, he saw an opportunity for the United States to play the "China card" and stem the Soviets' rising tide of international aggression and expansion.

It was literally illegal for Americans to go to China in those days, although a trickle of travelers—most of them politically inclined toward Beijing's view of the world—risked prosecution and went anyway. (Even into the 1970s, the State Department still printed prominent warnings against travel to China right inside American passports.) But suddenly everything changed. The events played out quickly and dramatically. There was "Ping-Pong diplomacy": an American team of table tennis players touring Japan in 1971 received an impromptu invitation to visit Beijing, and the next year the Chinese team went to the United States, a trip that reached its climax at a warm and very public visit to the White House. Numerous other dramatic "firsts" made headlines out of events that would have been utterly mundane had they not involved breaking down the artificial wall of isolation that had stood between Americans and Chinese since 1949.

In 1972, President Richard Nixon made his unprecedented official visit to Beijing. The Kissinger and Nixon visits provided the first direct contacts ever between American leaders and their Chinese counterparts, Communist Party Chairman Mao Zedong and Premier Zhou Enlai. This flurry of diplomatic activity culminated in an undeclared peace treaty to end the long, undeclared U.S.-China war. The Shanghai Communiqué, perhaps the most deftly worded agreement between two great powers in modern diplomatic history, strongly implied that the United States endorsed the notion of one China. And the one China on which the United States would focus its diplomatic attentions was clearly the People's Republic of China, not Taiwan. Thus began the process of American recognition of China and normalization of relations.

Trading with the Enemy

In this very deep game, the Soviet threat—and all the attendant issues of nuclear missiles, troop deployments, and

Times have changed . . . and will change some more: At the time of President Nixon's first visit to china in 1972, Joseph Kraft, a respected journalist and Washington insider, wrote: "American security does not depend, in any clear and present way, on what happens on the mainland of Asia. Neither does American economic, cultural, or moral well-being."

proxy wars from Indochina to Afghanistan—was front and center. Economics, and the potential for U.S.-China business ties, always mattered. But they were a very secondary agenda item in the early stages of the rapprochement. Columnist Thomas Friedman, writing in retrospect, put it well:

> When Henry Kissinger and China's Zhou Enlai were first meeting in the 1970s to forge the strategic alignment between the two countries, Mr. Kissinger used to joke that he was constantly being badgered by U.S. businessmen who had dreams of selling "one billion pairs of underwear" to the Chinese. Ha, ha, ha, the two grand strategists would laugh in those big overstuffed chairs. What a joke! America selling things to Communist China, or, funnier yet, Communist China selling things to America. What a knee-slapper.[6]

Our own experiences in the early years of U.S.-China trade reflected some of the reasons for their amusement, but also showed the pent-up demand among Americans for doing business with China. A grand total of three American companies had been invited to visit the Canton Trade Fair in the fall of 1971. But after the Nixon visit, and as word spread that the United States might open trade relations with China, invitations became as eagerly and aggressively sought as the Holy Grail. By 1973 there were 106 American companies in attendance at the Canton Fair, including the likes of Westinghouse, Monsanto, Coca-Cola Asia, and the First National Bank of Chicago.

China was not ready for prime time as far as big business was concerned, however. The Canton Fair focused more on marginal ventures than on mainstream ones. Word had it that some people representing Barnum & Bailey had come, eager to buy a panda; the Chinese offered only goldfish. The biggest business was done in rugs, baskets, and textiles, and by small importers and middlemen, not multinational corporations. All faced restrictions similar to those Lord Macartney had encountered nearly two centuries earlier: business could be done only in Canton, and only through one of twelve government trade monopolies.

The irony that the businesspeople were pawns in a much larger political drama was not lost on those present. The vitriolic slogans of the Cultural Revolution were still visible underneath the single coat of varnish freshly applied to the

Beyond the billion pairs of underwear: Fifteen years ago only six in every 100 urban Chinese households had washing machines. Now, by one count, 86 do. In other consumer-product areas the market is just beginning to take off. The average Chinese drinks 15 colas a year; the average American drinks 800.

room doors at Canton's Tung Fang hotel. Thomas Friedman was right in his conclusion about the Kissinger–Zhou Enlai meetings: the relationship "was about one thing: the Soviet Union. It was about the United States and China forging a strategic partnership to counterbalance the Russian bear. It was not about one billion pairs of underwear."[7]

Today's young American investment bankers and other dealmakers have little time to reflect on the fact that everything they do today would have been doubly illegal in the China of a generation ago: the Chinese would have seen it as a case of foreign economic and political subversion and Washington would have classed it as prosecutable under the then current provisions of trade law prohibiting Americans from doing business with China.

Deng Xiaoping in a Stetson

For seventeen years, from the Shanghai Communiqué in 1972 to the unprecedented events of 1989, the compelling strategic logic of shared opposition to the Soviet Union barreled through any problems in the Sino-American relationship like a freight train. China was welcomed into the United Nations, and virtually every country of the world restored or established ties with Beijing. American relations with Taiwan were steadily downgraded and relations with Beijing upgraded until full normalization took place on New Year's Day, 1979. Numerous disagreements arose about America's continued arms sales and other involvements with Taiwan, but each of these was settled with new agreements and understandings, spurred on by the shared belief in the importance of a strong Sino-American relationship as a tool for checking Soviet expansion.

The deaths of Zhou Enlai in January 1976 and Mao Zedong in September of that same year triggered uncertainty and unprecedented domestic political convulsions. Jiang Qing, Mao's wife, and her three ultra-radical colleagues—known collectively as the Gang of Four—were all arrested and ousted from power, as were many of the leading ultra-Left figures of the Cultural Revolution. Deng Xiaoping, an early victim of Cultural Revolution purges, returned to power in 1978 and launched China on its course to reverse

"If the rate of growth of the productive forces in a socialist country lags behind that in capitalist countries over an extended historical period, how can we talk about the superiority of the socialist system?"

—Deng Xiaoping

41

the irrational policies of the past, introduce rational economics, and modernize China.

All this only enhanced the U.S.-China relationship at the time. Now China was not just a partner in the geostrategic alliance against the Soviet Union—siding with the United States in criticizing Moscow's invasion of Afghanistan, Soviet-Cuban adventures in Africa, and the Soviet-Vietnamese invasion of Cambodia—but was also beginning to de-Maoify, decommunize, and open up tantalizing business opportunities for foreign participation in its huge modernization drive. The American business community had been finding its way through the crack in the door Nixon had opened. With Deng's reforms unfolding, the door swung wide open and Americans could do some serious business.

As Deng Xiaoping emerged as China's paramount leader, Americans found him an appealing figure. That this tough, feisty, 4' 10" Sichuanese could have faced the brutally unforgiving Chinese system of political purges three times, stood up against the wrath of the Cultural Revolutionaries, and still survived was enough to make him a legend. But that he would ultimately come out on top and launch China on the road to a modern market economy was a tale of real American-style heroism. Unlike the remote and fearsome Mao, Deng also had a human side Americans could relate to. He had a passion for bridge and was considered an outstanding player. In his days as a student in France, he had acquired a lifelong taste for croissants. His droll humor was famous.

Deng's 1979 tour of America, which accompanied final formal normalization of U.S.-China relations, was a watershed in both countries. To the delight of the Chinese and American media alike, Deng immersed himself enthusiastically in his American experience. He wore a ten-gallon hat at a Texas rodeo and chowed down on barbecue. Everywhere he went, he deliberately encouraged the Chinese media accompanying him to beam pictures back home of how advanced American technology was and how big the houses were and how high American workers' living standards were.

Americans were flattered. Here was a Chinese Communist who appeared to understand the achievements of American capitalism and wished to emulate them. What Americans may not have grasped, however, was that Deng's enthusiasm for what he saw in America was conditioned by the struggle

"A great deal of verbal gymnastics goes on about whether reform and opening up are surnamed capitalism or socialism. . . . Some people say that with each dose of foreign capital we become more capitalist. . . . These people lack even the most basic common sense about developing capitalism. . . . China must watch out for the Right, but mainly against the Left."

—DENG XIAOPING
JANUARY 1992

he was leading in Beijing. He was not necessarily all that enamored of the American way, although he certainly understood its virtues. Rather, he saw an opportunity to use America's achievements to his advantage. He would jump-start Chinese economic reform by using the United States to offer his own people an image of what a modern country looked like. By showing them how far behind they were, he would help wake up the Chinese to the disaster they had experienced in the Cultural Revolution and how much time they had lost. He would inspire his own people to work harder to modernize—and he would get the added benefits of investment, technology transfer, and many other kinds of help from Americans increasingly interested in cultivating the China market. All the while, he would protect China from the still-menacing Soviet threat with an American umbrella that would come to include high-level military and strategic cooperation.

Deng's blunt pragmatism and his zeal for economic reform clearly marked him as someone with whom Americans could do business. As the first permanent correspondents from American news organizations arrived in Beijing, they found Deng always quotable, remarkably candid, and with a refreshing "American"-like spin on things. He graced the cover of *Time* magazine as "Man of the Year" twice—in 1978 and again in 1985. But Deng was obviously not without his faults in American eyes. Every China watcher knew that he slipped easily in and out of his support for "democracy." He used the intellectual ferment created at Beijing's Democracy Wall to expose his political opponents and consolidate his own position. But when he no longer needed this small island of free expression, he shut it down.

Then, too, the U.S. foreign-policy community had a hard time reconciling Deng the reformer with the incursion he launched into Vietnam in 1979, just after his U.S. visit. The Chinese attack on North Vietnamese border areas was meant to retaliate for Hanoi's aggressive expansion into Cambodia and its growing discrimination against ethnic Chinese in Vietnam. But even Americans generally predisposed to tacit support for China's role in opening up a second front against the Soviet-Vietnamese forces failed to grasp Deng's logic that China was invading Vietnam in "self-defense." (A cartoon at the time likened Deng to Lyndon Johnson. The message: First you wear the ten-gallon hat and eat barbecue;

Learning from capitalism: "Capitalism already has a history of several hundred years, and we have to learn from the peoples of the capitalist countries. We must make use of the science and technology they have developed and of those elements in their accumulated knowledge and experience which can be adapted to our use. While we will import advanced technology and other things useful to us from the capitalist countries—selectively and according to plan— we will never learn from or import the capitalist system itself, nor anything repellent or decadent."

—DENG XIAOPING

then something comes over you and you feel compelled to invade Vietnam.) The strategic consensus in support of a strong U.S.-Chinese relationship overwhelmed such concerns. Every American president from Nixon through Bush took the idea of fostering a warm relationship with Beijing—in order to have a China card to play against the Russians—as a key element of strategic policy.

Jimmy Carter was known for his strong "human rights" orientation, yet Carter, his cabinet, and his advisors were so committed in their support for normalization and a rapid upgrading of relations that Michel Oksenberg, a China specialist then serving on the National Security Council staff, recalls, "Everyone was for it." Similarly, although Ronald Reagan was known for his strong free-market bent and nativist suspicion of people who were, after all, still self-described Communists, he presided over a huge expansion in the relationship at every level from military cooperation to business to science. American public opinion also supported better relations with China with gusto. From Shirley MacLaine to Isaac Stern to Big Bird, American celebrities of every type had wonderful stories to tell about their experiences in China, as did most of the swelling numbers of ordinary American tourists.

By 1981, U.S.-China trade had reached a substantial volume—$5.6 billion a year. People like Washington State's Senator Henry Jackson (sometimes known as the "Senator from Boeing") personified the confluence of strategic and economic interest in the China relationship. Not only could Americans play the China card against Moscow, but companies like Boeing could sell a lot of airplanes as well. Senators from farm states were more than enthusiastic about the growing sales of American wheat and other agricultural commodities. As every high-level political and business leader who visited China in that era observed, "They need everything" to fulfill their modernization goals—and Americans wanted to sell it to them. The result was that the China trade boomed throughout the 1980s

1989: A Tale of Two Squares

Then came the fateful year 1989, when two spectacular events would fundamentally alter the thrust of the previous

Sound familiar? The effort by the U.S. corporate community to equate the national interest with its own when it comes to China isn't simply a phenomenon of the 1990s. Reflecting the arguments of business, Senator Henry Cabot Lodge said at the turn of the century: "All Europe is seizing on China, and if we do not establish ourselves in the East that vast trade, from which we must draw our future prosperity . . . will be practically closed to us forever."

seventeen years of U.S.-Chinese relations: the massacre in Beijing's Tiananmen Square and the fall of the Berlin Wall.

On June 4, 1989, the Chinese army was mobilized to oust student demonstrators and their supporters from Tiananmen Square. The decision to move violently against the students came after many weeks during which demonstrators, whose numbers swelled at times to a million people, had occupied the famous square, where several of China's most crucial battles over political power have been played out.

In the context of Chinese history, the incident should not have shocked Americans. But it did, of course, and on many levels. A bloody rout of protesters seemed so at odds with the picture of a modernizing, reforming, democratizing China to which Americans had grown accustomed. It was particularly shocking precisely because of how far China had come. The free flow of information was such that the Chinese students in the square were faxing regular communiqués around the world. CNN and other American news media were able to cover the events live and in-depth for weeks, until the plug was pulled on CNN in the final hours before the troops moved in.

Americans were not only comfortable with but enthusiastic about what was happening in China before Tiananmen. Deng Xiaoping's protégé Zhao Ziyang, who appeared to be presiding over much of the reform process, looked to foreigners like an extremely able technocrat with a big-picture vision of China as a modern, technologically advanced, liberal twenty-first-century society. The process seemed to fulfill American expectations about the virtuous circle of market economics and democratic politics: progress in economic reform creates a middle class and a large community of consumers and stakeholders in the economy; this leads to political reform and democratization, which in turn lead to more economic growth.

The violent repression in Tiananmen Square was a system shock to those who believed in this virtuous logic. That the army was called in to attack those who were seeking democratization and the rule of law, that Deng Xiaoping himself was the architect of the crackdown, that Zhao Ziyang ended up stripped of power and under house arrest for being too sympathetic to the demonstrators, that many of the evolving reforms stopped in Tiananmen's aftermath—all of this left

Beware the apocalypse: "Should China be reduced to a state like that of present-day Bosnia, no statesman in the world would be able to sleep."

—VICE PREMIER LI LANQING

Americans shocked, embittered, disappointed, and distrustful of the Chinese leadership. Washington responded with denunciations and lamentations—and by orchestrating investment and trade sanctions. Now it became Beijing's turn to become disappointed, embittered, and increasingly distrustful.

To Deng and other senior Chinese leaders, the decision to call the army into Tiananmen Square was all about preserving order and control. Certainly their own power and control were uppermost in their minds. But they were also concerned, as China's benevolent despots had always been, with the need to maintain their power in order to do good for the nation. In this case, they believed they needed stability to continue the economic reform. They were convinced that if they compromised or showed weakness, they would invite chaos and anarchy on a wide scale.

Totalitarians always wish to frame the mildest democratic opposition as a first step toward anarchy, but in the case of Tiananmen Square, Chinese authorities may have been more correct than democrats in the West will ever wish to acknowledge. On the seventh anniversary of the June 4 incident, one of the square's prominent young firebrands, Chai Ling, acknowledged in an interview that she and her faction were deliberately trying to provoke a military response and bloodshed in order to arouse the people to bring down the state.

Almost all the leaders of the Chinese Communist Party believed in 1989—and believe to this day—that had they not acted decisively to crush the rebellion, China would have been destabilized and ultimately would have gone the way of the then-unraveling Soviet Union. Did Americans want *that* outcome—just for the sake of free self-expression by muddled, immature students and rabble-rousers? The failure, as the Chinese saw it, of American public officials to acknowledge this and other larger historical points, combined with the post-Tiananmen pullback of American investment, reminded the Chinese of what they had always known: the West, and Americans in particular, could not be trusted.

June 4 would have been a turning point in the U.S.-China relationship in any event. But the events that took place just five months later in a square 10,000 miles away would have an even deeper and more lasting effect.

As the Berlin Wall came down in the Potsdamer Platz in

November 1989, it became clear to all that the Cold War between the United States and the Soviet Union was finally over. The China card was no longer perceived as valuable to Washington in dealing with chaotic and unstable Russia; certainly it was not as valuable as it had been in dealing with the stable, aggressive, nuclear-armed Soviet Union.

The corollary was true in China. Beijing and Moscow could now warm up their relations, free of the military and ideological obstacles that had embittered them since the Sino-Soviet split of the late 1950s. Just as Washington no longer needed a China card, Beijing no longer needed an American card against the Russians. So the 1990s began with Washington and Beijing deeply distrustful of each other in the wake of Tiananmen Square. The strategic glue of common anxiety about the Soviet threat, which had held the relationship firmly together for two decades, was rapidly melting away.

"To Get Rich Is Glorious!"

The West would not provide all the investment and technology China needed, Deng Xiaoping realized after Tiananmen: so be it. If Americans proved fickle, or surprisingly (for a nation of pragmatists) wedded to high-minded talk about human rights rather than to their own strategic and economic interests, China's modernization would not stop because of it.

On the one hand, there were issues of nationalism, pride, and face. Deng Xiaoping told Richard Nixon after the post-Tiananmen sanctions were imposed: "Don't ever expect China to beg the United States to lift the sanctions. If they lasted a hundred years, the Chinese would not do that."[8] But on the other hand, there were also alternatives. Deng and his colleagues realized they could open the door wider to the investors who would understand the nation's situation best: the "Overseas Chinese" from Hong Kong, Macau, Taiwan, and Southeast Asia.

Although these ethnic Chinese billionaires and millionaires were generally refugees (or the sons of refugees) from Mao's revolution, they, too, believed in the importance of stability and were largely unsympathetic to the student demonstrators of Tiananmen Square. Many were self-made

China's impact on the Asian economy:
"Eighty percent of China's external trade and 90 percent of foreign direct investment comes from cooperation with Asian countries. I think it's fair to say that China's economic growth is inseparable from economic cooperation with Asian countries."

—VICE PREMIER ZHU RONGJI

47

men with no education; they grew up poor and had spent their youth working eighteen-hour days. They had built autocratic business empires and had done so in countries or under political systems that had little democracy in their local cultures. These men's self-interest lay with China and the government in Beijing, whose modernization was putting their already successful companies at the center of growth in the global economy.

A Taiwanese investor's perspective: "China is the last gold mine of the twenty-first century."

—HSU BIN

For several very good reasons, the Overseas Chinese stepped up their investment in China after 1989. Their companies' excess liquidity was enormous because of the huge boom in the Hong Kong, Taiwan, and Southeast Asian economies. These vast cash flows could not be fully invested in their own economies, but had to be exported. For years the Overseas Chinese had been investing in America and the West as a hedge *against* China risk; now they saw the most advantageous investment opportunities as being *in* China.

Hong Kong investors faced a special difficulty. Their companies desperately needed China's cheap labor because the Hong Kong cost structure had become much too high. By moving their labor-intensive operations across the border into China, they could achieve the cost savings they needed to stay competitive. That move would also present them as helpful participants in building up the Chinese economy—surely a good political hedge against any dangers they might face after 1997, and probably a good business move toward integration within the emerging "Greater China" economy. During the late 1980s and early 1990s, almost all the remaining large-scale industrial manufacturing in Hong Kong was intentionally hollowed out. Manufacturing moved to China, while design, marketing, and trading functions remained in Hong Kong.

The already strong flow of Hong Kong and Overseas Chinese capital into China turned into a gusher. This was most true in Guangdong province and the Special Economic Zones (SEZs) such as Shenzhen, just across the border from Hong Kong, which had been set up on an experimental, less regulated and more open trading system and had been populated by young Chinese eager to learn and looking for opportunity. The combination of economic freedom in the south, the entrepreneurial instincts of the Cantonese, and the open spigot of Overseas Chinese capital combined to produce a spectacular boom.

In the early part of 1992, Deng Xiaoping moved to intensify that boom. Like Mao before him, and like Chinese emperors from the beginning of recorded history, he made a tour of the provinces. He was already nearly eighty-nine years old; this *nanxun* (literally, "southern journey") would be the starting point for the last major campaign of his life. For a man who openly admitted he knew little about modern economics, the campaign was particularly remarkable. It led to a spurt of economic growth and wealth creation unprecedented in Chinese history.

The place where growth was greatest—and where the strongest systemic shock to Chinese socialism was unfolding—was in the south. Guangdong province was enjoying an extraordinary wealth effect and boom. The process, however, was highly controversial. The northerners in Beijing were restless and increasingly critical of what they saw in the south. But Deng Xiaoping was not. On political matters, he took a hard line. The economy was a different matter; he was much more receptive to open policies and innovation, and he appreciated the usefulness of certain market forces. In Deng's view, authoritarian political controls were necessary, virtuous, and *best* maintained by high growth.

Through public appearances and pointed endorsements of the new methodologies he saw in action, Deng's inspection tour of the south lent unequivocal authority to the economic reform movement. "To get rich is glorious," he said, paraphrasing an old Chinese saying. If more Chinese became rich, they would enrich the nation on its path to modernization and prosperity. At every stop, as if he knew he was fighting his last battle, he called for greater opening to foreign trade and investment, for turning even faster toward the market, and for all of China to learn from the south.

Deng's tour kicked China's door wider open than it had ever been. From 1992 to 1994, as Deng himself grew increasingly frail and incapacitated, China enjoyed turbocharged growth and an economic boom topping all that had come before.

The Lure of the China Market

As China boomed, memories of Tiananmen began to take second place in the minds of American businesspeople and

"China's opening and reforms have changed the balance of world economic power in a few short years. Corporate chieftains from Paris to Tokyo have staked their own growth strategies on China's continued success. The U.S. nuclear industry, for instance, figures it alone could sell $60 billion worth of plants to China in the next 20 years."

—*BUSINESS WEEK*

policymakers. Although Beijing never retreated from its stance, the forces of time and opportunity eroded American objections to investing in China. Suddenly, China was the great global game, the hottest of the emerging markets, and the center of global growth. Americans could ill afford to stand aside. And so they did what Deng expected them to do: they rushed in.

The early 1990s saw nearly every American and Western company of significance race to capture a share of the market. Chinese companies were able to set up more than 100,000 joint ventures with foreign partners in the two years that followed Deng's southern tour. China investment funds proliferated on Wall Street and throughout Asia. A bidding war was on for Chinese talent. Foreign investment banks and brokerage houses were hiring young Chinese with English language skills and MBAs for $500,000 to $1 million a year.

In 1993 alone, foreign investors poured over $20 billion into China, several times the prior year's levels. And that figure would nearly double in 1994. By the end of 1996, twelve U.S. companies had demonstrated their confidence and excitement about China by investing more than $100 million each. The list, headed by Motorola, includes Arco, Coca-Cola, Amoco, Ford, United Technologies, PepsiCo, AT&T/Lucent, GE, General Motors, Hewlett-Packard, and IBM.

Going public on the New York Stock Exchange became the ultimate mark of prestige for Chinese companies wishing to be perceived as blue-chip. It was also a highly profitable business for their U.S. advisors and underwriters. One of eight such Chinese companies, Brilliance Automotive, became the most actively traded single company on the New York Stock Exchange one day in 1994.

The China boom of 1992–94 was, of course, unsustainable by definition, and produced its share of real estate bubbles and wild stock speculation, as well as several years of high inflation. Eventually, the Chinese authorities got back astride the tiger they had unleashed and slowed it down with tight money policies and austerity measures. By the time the spillover effect of the Asian financial crisis began to shrink China's growth rate, and Beijing had begun to adopt new measures to protect the domestic market, the Wild West gold rush atmosphere was definitely over. Foreigners, as well as Chinese, became more realistic about how much money could be made how fast.

Just three years after introducing its Head & Shoulders brand, Procter & Gamble saw it become China's best-selling shampoo—even though it cost 300 percent more than local brands.

But the China trade had become a large and growing force in the American and world economies. "Our container volume has gone up nearly fifty percent over the past two years, with half of that growth coming from China," said Don Wylie, director of trade and maritime services for the Port of Long Beach, California—just one prominent center among many that together have created a total of more than 400,000 China-related jobs in the United States.[9] Added Rick Younts, an executive with Motorola, the American company that from its headquarters in Schaumburg, Illinois, has invested more in China than any other firm: "Illinois jobs depend on trade, and trade with China is at the top of the list of future growth opportunities for a wide variety of industries."[10]

Groups such as the China Business Forum and the China Normalization Initiative brought together General Motors, Boeing, Motorola, and other major American exporters to help create better understanding of China in Washington and to lobby for closer U.S. political relations with Beijing in order to advance commercial, investment, and trade goals. Thus was born a basic dilemma in American policy toward China that will be with us for years to come. Even "schizophrenia" is not too strong a word for this phenomenon. Just as Washington began a period in which it would vow to get tougher with China, the business community was arguing for Washington to encourage a changing China in which American companies had a highly profitable ground-floor role to play.

CHAPTER 3

The Eagle and the Dragon (II): To the Brink

Is It Economics, Stupid? Or Stupid Economics?

George Bush, who was both an old China hand and an old Cold Warrior, tried to hang on to the semblance of a strategic Washington-Beijing relationship of the type Nixon and Reagan had favored. The aftermath of Tiananmen put severe constraints on the warmth of that relationship, but Bush continued to insist on the importance of a positive dialogue with the Chinese. The rapid rate at which business returned to China and the soaring trade and investment statistics seemed to buttress his case. In the 1992 election campaign, however, challenger Bill Clinton revived the moral issue. He argued that the Bush administration had sold out America's commitment to human rights in China by continuing to emphasize a positive business and diplomatic relationship even after Tiananmen, and that Bush was guilty of "coddling" the dictators in Beijing.

The Clinton election in 1992 set in motion the rapid decay of the Washington-Beijing political relationship. China was, of course, not the most prominent issue on which Bill Clinton would flip-flop, changing course several times. But it is a case study in the inconsistency endemic to an administration that believed in process over principle.

Arriving in office in 1993, the candidate who campaigned

under the famous rubric "It's the economy, stupid" chose to risk undercutting the renewed, post-Tiananmen economic relationship by putting Beijing in the dock not only over human rights but over almost every imaginable issue. The initial pressure for Clinton to follow this path of confrontation came mostly from the Democratic Party's Left, with its concerns about human rights and the potential for cheap Chinese labor to steal American jobs and put downward pressure on U.S. workers' wages.

But conservative Republicans were not far behind. While using every opportunity to urge Washington to get *out* of the lives of the American people, they wanted to get Washington *into* the lives of the Chinese people. The right-to-life movement wanted to use American aid and trade programs as levers to overturn China's family planning policies, for example. And the same politicians of the Right who liked the thought of putting "pampered" American prisoners to work on chain gangs wanted to deny access to the American market for goods made with Chinese prison labor.

With the early years of the Clinton administration focused almost exclusively on domestic policy and the White House as uninvolved in foreign affairs as it had been in modern memory, the shrewd political move was to lean into the winds of these pressures, adopt their causes, and let the China relationship fall where it might. As one observer summed up, "In the first term the White House was uninterested in spending political capital on China policy; in the second term it wishes to do so but risks running out of capital."[1]

The "Clinton I" years (the first Clinton administration, 1993–96) were dominated by more and more invective between Beijing and Washington, skirmishing and brinksmanship first over trade and later over Taiwan, threats of economic sanctions over intellectual property violations as well as nuclear weapons sales, and a constant upping of the political and even the military ante. The first post–Cold War American president had inadvertently brought back to U.S.-China relations the same emphasis on morality, ideology, and politics that had once characterized the U.S.-Soviet Cold War.

The Chinese were taken aback. "We don't do anything to harm U.S.-China relations," said Zhan Shiliang of the China Center for International Studies. "But now the U.S. puts so

How're we doin'? Not too good: "We grant China MFN status, and they arrest Harry Wu. We sign a trade agreement with them, and they pirate all our movies. No matter what we give, they consistently characterize American moves as 'hostile.' Quite simply, Beijing has more to gain by vilifying the U.S. than engaging it. As we continue to trade with China, we should at least end the utopian charade that we thereby democratize it."

—*THE NEW REPUBLIC*

much pressure on China—first human rights, then the economy. What for?"[2]

The Problem with the 800-Pound Gorilla

To be fair to the Clinton administration, it is undoubtedly worth noting that sometime in the early nineties geoeconomists and geostrategists began looking at what was happening in China from a whole different perspective. What had been the Amazing China Growth Story had segued into something new, different, and somewhat ominous: the Birth of a New Superpower.

Just as Clinton's best and most aware thinkers were settling into office in 1993, China was hitting the high point of the economic boom that followed Deng's southern tour of the previous year. Rapid growth had become the norm in the Chinese economy, but now it was zooming off the charts; the annual GDP growth rate was over 12 percent. When one thinks about China's massive base, and then compounds by annual growth of 10 percent or more, one could easily conclude that China will very quickly become the world's largest economy and eventually dwarf America's output. And that's just the conclusion the World Bank reached with a stunning report, which argued that China had already emerged as the world's third-largest economy after the United States and Japan, and was on its way to being number one by 2003.

The growth numbers used by the World Bank were flawed, as were aspects of the purchasing price parity methodology employed to calculate equivalencies between China's economy and those of the West. Nevertheless, the World Bank study made a powerful point: China was not just going to be another big emerging market. It was not just going to be another high-growth success story like the little Asian dragons that had come before—a good place to invest, manufacture, do business, and trade. No, China was the biggest dragon of them all. And it was on its way to becoming not just the world's biggest economy, but a global superpower.

The U.S.-China relationship was changed inalterably by this perception. After all, the rise of most great powers on the world scene over the last 500 years has triggered wars, revolutions, and epochal reordering of global wealth and power. The rise of China, in particular, as a new superpower is a totally unprecedented phenomenon. It raises questions about global interactions of economics and power relationships that the world has never before faced. To design a successful China policy is anything but a simple task. Although it is not clear that the Clinton team even now understands how great a power China might someday become, it has evidenced an inchoate sense of this destiny—and its policies have been a muddled attempt to keep the baby gorilla in the fold of the existing global order. Otherwise, the fear is, the baby will grow fast to its full 800 pounds and destabilize the world by writing its own rules and sitting wherever it wants.

"Sino-American Relations Are in Free Fall"

As hostilities increased, each side saw itself doing only what it had to do—reacting to the other's provocations and misbehavior, marshaling the appropriate show of economic, political, or military force to draw a line in the sand. The examples below—a far from comprehensive list—offer a picture of the downward spiral of the relationship in the first half of this decade:

• In keeping with campaign promises, the Clinton administration endeavored to "link" progress on human rights to renewals of China's MFN trading status. Although Clinton actually favored MFN, he needed to protect his flank by seeming to weigh considerations about human rights. This created an annual spectacle of China bashing in Congress and the media.

But using MFN as a club to bash China did not seem to work. After the first round or two of these debates, the Chinese dug in their heels and ceased making even cosmetic concessions to Washington on the release of dissidents, better treatment of political prisoners, and other human rights issues.

Clinton was now in an embarrassing quandary. The Chinese economy was booming. Big businesses wanted presidential assurances about continuing MFN as a way to keep trade growing. But Clinton had discovered that Beijing could not be bluffed or browbeaten into giving him even the shreds

"The premise of the China-threat lobby is this: What if China continues its explosive growth, does not crack up like the Soviet Union, waxes nationalistic, remains under the thumb of authoritarian leaders and strives for Asian military hegemony even as the United States grows weak and retreats from the Western Pacific? Won't we be sorry then that we kow-towed to Beijing back in the 1990s? But the odds of all these what-ifs coming to pass are exceedingly long."

—Walter A. McDougall
 Pulitzer Prize–winning
 historian

Explaining nationalism: "In China, people are dissatisfied—with the government, official corruption, authoritarianism, even the political system. But when people talk about the way the United States criticizes China, they don't separate themselves from the government. The attitude is: Whatever hurts the government hurts us all," said a leading next-generation government advisor, educated in the United States.

of evidence he needed to prove his case that linkage of MFN to human rights progress was working. As a result, he eventually moved to "de-link" MFN and human rights. In doing so he made the right move for maintaining the economic relationship, but set himself up for harsh criticism from the increasingly powerful domestic political forces he had originally set out to placate.

• Clinton dropped the presidential tradition of putting his ceremonial stamp of approval on the relationship: he refused to visit China personally during his first administration, not even sending Vice President Al Gore until the beginning of their second term in office. Few other senior representatives of the administration went to China either, and none went in much of a positive spirit except Commerce Secretary Ron Brown, whose China tours (on which he was accompanied by leading American CEOs) reflected his enthusiasm for using his department to promote American business opportunities abroad.

Secretary of State Warren Christopher visited Damascus twenty-nine times during the first four years of the Clinton administration, by one count. That was twenty-seven more times than he visited Beijing. When he went to Damascus, it was to gently encourage the dictator there to join the Mideast peace process, not to criticize his record on human rights—a record that would make the Chinese look comparatively warm and fuzzy.

• John Shattuck, a senior State Department official, detoured from his official China visit to meet with dissident Wei Jingsheng in 1994. Next, the administration signaled its support for the Dalai Lama—the exiled religious leader who is the embodiment of the Tibetan independence cause—by welcoming him in Washington for a meeting and photo op with President Clinton. While Americans were convinced of the high morality in these symbolic meetings, the Chinese took them as deliberate provocations—the rough equivalent of Chinese officials seeking meetings with the Unabomber or with the American militia leaders who don't recognize the sovereignty of the federal government.

• The case of Chinese dissident Harry Wu became a major issue in 1995, epitomizing the difference in the two countries' beliefs about human rights. Wu, who had documented abuses in the secretive prisons of the Chinese *laogai* (gulag) as an inmate, had managed to leave China and become an American citizen. In 1995, he tried to return to China, intending to further document prison labor abuses and publicize issues such as China's use of prisoners' bodies as sources of organs for transplant. Wu was arrested after he crossed one of China's most remote borders and was found traveling under a false name. The authorities charged him with spying, subversion, and treasonous offenses.

To the Clinton administration, the Wu case was one of an American citizen unfairly charged with crimes and being set up for a kangaroo court. To the Chinese, Wu was a troublemaker who had to be stopped. The war of nerves over Wu's fate dominated transpacific headlines for weeks. Eventually, after he agreed to a contrived confession, the authorities put him on a plane and sent him back to the United States. Wu then distanced himself from his confession, and the American side claimed victory. But by arresting, jailing, and sweating Harry Wu, the Chinese believed they had made their point to the audience they most wanted to hear it: Chinese dissidents at home and abroad.

• Washington threatened economic sanctions against China on several occasions and came quite close to implementing them twice during 1995–96 over Chinese piracy of American entertainment and computer software. Only eleventh-hour negotiations and China's reluctant agreement to curtail the most egregious violations (state-owned factories churning out thousands of pirated music CDs and computer CD-ROMs) prevented full-scale trade wars from erupting over intellectual property. Other trade conflicts flared up frequently over Chinese textiles flooding American markets. The United States filed sixty dumping cases against China between 1990 and 1996.

• Washington also threatened sanctions over Chinese arms sales, particularly sales of nuclear-related equipment to Pakistan. American intelligence authorities argued that China was behind a variety of sales to Iran and other countries considered enemies by the United States. On *these* issues, of greatest concern to American and global security, however, the Clinton administration chose to *avoid* pressing the Chinese, removing any remaining strand of logical consistency from America's China policy. An industry analyst raised the rhetorical question that said it all: The government

Be careful what you wish for . . . : "Hopes that China might now travel down the path of freedom seem to me undesirable, because it would be hell on earth if they were fulfilled. It is bad enough to have 250 million or so Americans all claiming the right to life, liberty, and the pursuit of happiness, each doing his own thing and letting it all hang out, each creating his own ethical code and religion, without also adding to that already dangerously large hodgepodge of individualism 1.2 billion more Chinese doing the same. One human-rights obsessed superpower determined to transform mankind in its image is quite enough."

—PEREGRINE WORSTHORNE
SPECTATOR (LONDON)

"won't punish the Chinese for nuclear proliferation, but for *Babe* and Arnold Schwarzenegger, they've got to pay?"[3]

• Learning early on from American threats of sanctions and other bluffs, the Chinese made it known that they would retaliate against the United States by closing their market to certain American goods if Washington imposed sanctions on China. Beijing also had its own version of "linkage." At two different flashpoints in the political relationship during this period (one involving Chrysler and Mercedes-Benz, the other involving Boeing and Airbus), the Chinese awarded much-sought-after deals to the European competitor, rather than the American company. Publicly, the Chinese indicated that the contracts were awarded for purely business and commercial reasons. Plausible explanations were provided to those who inquired. (Indeed, some say that Boeing is lucky not to have been stuck with the deal to help build a mid-sized passenger jet in China.) However, the timing of these major contract announcements left a silent message that could not have been clearer: Two can play at this game of global trade chicken.

As a senior Chinese diplomat confided to us:

> We can all argue that economics and politics are separate. To a degree, of course they are. And they are more separate today in China than they used to be. But politics and economics are linked, especially in a country like China. It will be impossible for American companies to succeed if the United States does not have a favorable policy toward China.

Feeding America's competitors: "The Chinese just bought 30 Airbus planes to reward Europe for not pushing human rights. The Europeans love the fight over MFN," says Ronald Woodward, president of the Boeing Commercial Airplane Group. Adds GM chairman John F. Smith, Jr., "What is the United States going to gain [by punishing China and depriving it of MFN status]? China can do business with any other country in the world."

• Acquiescing to critics who saw negative environmental and human rights implications, the United States refused to provide technical help to Beijing and withheld loan guarantees and insurance to American companies wanting to bid on China's Three Gorges Dam on the Yangzi River, the country's most important power project in a power-starved industrializing economy.

• The United States used its leverage to deny Beijing its most desired rite of passage into the modern world: the chance to host the Summer Olympics in 2000. Again, China's track record on human rights was the underlying issue.

• Eager to host other kinds of global events when it couldn't have the Olympics, Beijing agreed to host the United

Nations Women's Conference in 1995. But its clumsy, repressive handling of the event attracted extensive global criticism. Chinese authorities did everything possible to prevent the conference from serving as a meeting ground for demonstrators and nonofficial participants, refusing to cooperate with the thousands of women and organizations from around the world who, in past years, had made a tradition of meeting in parallel to the official session. Activists were searched and followed. It was thus understandable to Americans that when the first lady, Hillary Clinton, made up her mind to go to Beijing and address the conference, she would use her platform to criticize violations of human rights in China as well as the authorities' disrespect for the rights of the women from other countries who had gathered in Beijing. But China, which had had no presidential visit from Bill Clinton, considered the speech a deliberate affront.

• China was originally eager to join the first of the newly created multilateral institutions of the 1990s, the World Trade Organization (WTO). But the United States, with European support, moved to block entry until Beijing would acknowledge that, for WTO purposes, China is a "developed" country. In the complex bureaucratese of the WTO, a developed country loses certain economic preferences and must open more of its markets faster to foreign competition. Unwilling to give up the advantages associated with being a developing economy, the Chinese hammered away at Washington's absurd logic that would equate China's sub-$1,000-a-year per capita GDP with American and European averages more than twenty times higher. The United States now officially says it is working to get China into the WTO— after all, what kind of twenty-first-century world trade organization would *not* have China as a member? The results remain to be seen.

• Prominent private-sector American organizations railed against Chinese policies, appealing for boycotts of goods produced by Chinese prison labor, launching investigations into the horrors of China's orphanages, and pressing for Tibetan independence, among many other issues. Since the Chinese have little real understanding of American diversity of opinion and of how the private sector of a democratic society actually works, they frequently lump all these initiatives together as part and parcel of Washington's effort to

"Constructive engagement: a euphemism for doing business with thugs."

—Senator Daniel Patrick Moynihan (D-N.Y.)

undermine the relationship and attack China. What's more, most of these private efforts have had the support of enough members of Congress to lend credence to the Chinese theory that they reflect official American government policies.

• As China flexed its military muscles in the mid-1990s with minor ventures at Mischief Reef and other contested coastal islands and waterways, American pundits and foreign-policy experts began to see China becoming a dangerous combination of economic and military superpower. The need to contain this increasingly powerful China became the media flavor of the month in early 1995. Essayist Charles Krauthammer, for example, argued in *Time* that China was a country whose expansiveness knew no bounds and whose ruthless leaders were capable of just about anything. "Containment of such a bully must begin early in its career."[4]

• The very mention of "containment"—a word loaded with the Cold War history of American policy toward the Soviet Union—infuriated Beijing. Chinese media editorials fired salvos back at *Time, The Economist,* and others arguing for containment. The Chinese responses were no more consistent than American policy. Some argued that no one needed to contain China, because China threatens no one. Others argued that no one could contain China or stop China from achieving its destiny.

In Beijing, everything the United States did smelled of a conspiracy to harm China's interests. "Senior members of China's military and political establishment have come to believe the United States is actively conspiring to undermine China politically, economically, and militarily," began a typical report in China's daily press. And as Henry Kissinger summed up the situation in testimony before Congress in July 1995, "Sino-American relations are in free fall."

All the above-mentioned events and issues wounded the relationship and intensified the sense of danger in both capitals. But what drove the situation into crisis was an extremely large chunk of salt rubbed in those wounds—the issue of Taiwan.

Brinksmanship in the Straits of Taiwan

As it had been at several turning points in the past, Taiwan policy was at the crux of U.S.-China antagonisms in 1995–

96. In the spring of 1995, Washington cut Beijing to the quick by allowing Lee Teng-hui, Taiwan's president, to make a private visit to the United States. Ostensibly, Lee's purpose was to give a talk at Cornell University, which he had once attended. Yet behind this seemingly innocuous "private" visit by Lee to his "alma mater"—where he did a brief graduate stint—lay vast geopolitical machinations, profound policy issues, and political brinksmanship that would involve Washington, Beijing, Taipei, Hong Kong, and Tokyo.

As every China watcher knows, Taiwan has always been an extremely sensitive issue in Beijing. It is a litmus test of nationalism, patriotism, and military virility. In the post–Deng Xiaoping transition, it has assumed a special place on the Chinese agenda. The military has largely stayed away from the internal debate on matters of economic and political reform. But Taiwan is another story. On this issue, the septuagenarian and octogenarian military leaders insist on being heard. And their position is clear. Taiwan is the equivalent of an American "motherhood" issue. The elderly military leaders will tolerate no watering down of China's commitment to reunify Taiwan with the motherland someday.

Ever since Washington severed relations with Taiwan and established relations with China in the late 1970s, refusal to grant visas to Taiwan's leaders had always seemed a politically inexpensive way to show loyalty to the principle of "one China." American business could have a massive trade and investment relationship with Taiwan, and U.S. arms sales to Taiwan would be tolerated by China—within certain strict limits. But the quid pro quo for China's indulgence on these very substantive American involvements with the Taipei government was an insistence that Washington adhere in matters of protocol (such as issuing visas) to strict nonrecognition of Taiwan.

To those in the know, Washington's refusal to allow Taiwanese leaders to visit the United States could be read as implicit American support of China's view of the matter: Taiwan is merely a province of China; its officials have no political legitimacy and certainly no right to seek its acceptance as an independent entity or country; all matters concerning Taiwan's political status, its future, and its ultimate reunification with the motherland are to be decided by Chinese without outside interference.

For sixteen years, American governments were able to

One Chinese businessman's opinion on why the United States and China are arguing over Taiwan: "The United States is like a man who divorced his first wife [Taiwan], took a second wife [China], and then the first wife comes back for a visit and tries to move back in. Now the second wife is very mad!"

—ZHANG WEI
  CHAIRMAN, EAST CHINA
  HOLDINGS

keep this dance going, even as Taiwan emerged as one of the world's significant economies in its own right, liberalized its political structure, and developed a pro-independence constituency. In Washington before the age of Bill Clinton and Newt Gingrich, good relations with Beijing were always seen as more important than inflaming Chinese opinion over the symbolism of allowing a Taiwanese leader to visit the United States.

Taiwanese politicians, in concert with a significant community of American supporters (concentrated among right-wing Republicans), had been trying for years to wangle an official invitation for a senior leader, or even just a "private" visit—anything that could be used as a wedge in the argument over the legitimacy of Taiwan's status or be used as a precedent to force the United States to reconsider its bent toward Beijing in favor of even a small tilt back in the direction of Taipei.

Inside Taiwan's own complex political world, Lee Teng-hui was trying to consolidate his grip on power as he prepared to compete in the island's first democratic presidential election. To succeed, he needed to distinguish himself from two trends. One was the old Kuomintang (KMT)—the disciples of Chiang Kai-shek and the descendants of those who had fled from the mainland to Taiwan. (Lee Teng-hui is Taiwan's first native-born Taiwanese leader.) The other was a small but growing movement among intellectuals and the emerging middle class in favor of outright independence for Taiwan. Lee saw, in the daring idea of forcing America to allow him a visit, the opportunity to outflank the open supporters of independence and demonstrate his efficacy as a leader and a spokesperson for Taiwan's future.

The stunning Republican congressional victory of November 1994 put Bill Clinton momentarily on the ropes and vaulted Newt Gingrich, long a Taiwan supporter, to the pinnacle of congressional power as speaker of the House. As a result of the election, more than seventy freshmen Republicans joined the Congress, some of them specifically pro-Taiwan, many of them not particularly knowledgeable about the question. But they were generally certain they opposed Bill Clinton's policies, including MFN status for China.

These populist Republicans didn't much care that in its first two years the Clinton administration had generally been much tougher on Beijing than Republicans George Bush and

Ronald Reagan. Gingrich's Republicans were breaking with many old Republican traditions, backing off from their historic role as the apostles of big business to become the champion of white suburban middle-class males and the Christian Coalition. Giving "bad" China a poke in the eye was not only easy, it was good politics.

The business community was urging Republicans to tread lightly on the Taiwan issue for the sake of American trade and investment interests in China. But Newt and Company had other ideas. Gingrich was cavalier and led a highly provocative challenge to Beijing on the Taiwan issue. Although he purported to be a great student of history, he seemed to know little about Chinese history. In a famous interview, he declared that China should "just get over it" and accept the reality of Taiwanese independence. This was so impolitic that Henry Kissinger, whom Gingrich had asked to serve as his foreign-policy mentor, had to chastise his student.

In 1995, with a movement to welcome Lee Teng-hui gaining momentum in Congress, Secretary of State Warren Christopher assured Chinese officials that the White House would block the pro-Taiwan lobby's efforts to grant Lee a visa. But Christopher had misread the zeal of the just-elected 104th Congress. Only weeks later, the new Congress passed a resolution supporting Lee's right to make a private visit. The vote was 397 to 1. The administration thus found itself too isolated to risk blocking the visit. It had too many other battles going on with Congress to allow China policy to become a major issue.

The Clinton administration later told the Chinese that the Lee visit was a necessary accommodation to Republican pressure. "We tried to explain to them," confided a senior State Department official, "that in a democracy, the president does not control every issue. We never told them we would *prevent* Lee from visiting; we only said we would 'resist' a visit. They chose to believe that meant we would block it, but that was not the meaning of what we told them. They are going to have to learn that American democracy is a messy process."

Beijing found this truthful explanation unconvincing. The leadership suspected that everything happening in Washington was part of a devious anti-China plot. As *The Wall Street Journal* reported, "For many Chinese leaders, it seems unlikely that a powerful and sophisticated nation like the

The eagle and the dragon: Five leading Republican conservatives got together to write an OpEd piece for *The Wall Street Journal* which said, in part: "We should not demonize China. There is no new Cold War, and China is not a new Cold War enemy."

United States should have no strategy toward China"—or that it would allow that strategy to be disrupted by the opposition.[5]

The first reaction from Beijing was somewhat muted. But then the tough-minded military men made clear to Jiang that this was the kind of issue on which he had to demonstrate his mettle if he was to retain their favor as the preeminent successor to Deng Xiaoping. A line in the sand was drawn in Beijing, as much as between Beijing and Washington. Jiang had to prove to his domestic constituencies that he could stand up to the United States.

Soon Beijing was positioning the Lee visa as a heinous American crime. Torrential verbal denunciations ensued. China recalled its ambassador and canceled bilateral negotiations and cooperation on several fronts, then set about responding to the perceived American treachery with the mechanism Washington found most reprehensible: carrying out military "tests" off the coast of Taiwan that included firing live artillery rounds near Taiwanese towns and ports.

Traveling in Beijing during that period, we could not avoid being lectured about the Taiwan issue everywhere. We went for an interview with a senior official of the Ministry of Foreign Affairs. The discussion was supposed to have focused on China's long-term interactions with Japan, Russia, and other parts of the world. Instead, it turned into a ninety-minute harangue on American perfidy over the Taiwan matter.

We pointed out that China was not being singled out. The Clinton administration had granted a visa to Sinn Fein leader Gerry Adams (suspected by some of involvement with terrorist IRA actions) over Britain's opposition. Yet every effort we made to explain the logic of the American position was met with outright rejection. Ominously, we were told that just as the American president might have to placate our Congress, so the Chinese leaders might have to respond to theirs, which wanted an even more forceful response to the United States.

At lunch at a think tank connected to the People's Liberation Army, we were told by a retired general, in words that recalled the rhetoric of the Cultural Revolution:

> America has always tried to undermine and subvert China, but it has failed every time. First, you backed

Future shock: In the spring of 1994, eight admirals, about forty captains, and a handful of policy analysts gathered at the Naval War College in Newport, Rhode Island, to play out a war game scenario with China, set in the Taiwan Strait for the year 2010. Five times the game was played and each time the Chinese won, using technologically advanced missiles to knock out U.S. carriers before they could put their defenses up.

Chiang Kai-shek, but he fled from China. Then you propped up the Taiwan regime for years. Then you attacked China in Korea. Now, you are doing it again. But you will fail again.

The same Chinese intellectuals and publications that had recently been willing to discuss the merits of Taiwan's economic policy and how it might be applied to China were now claiming shrilly that if Taiwan had ever had any success it was because the United States had used it as a "base to attack China," and because "the CIA had conspired with Chiang Kai-shek to steal China's gold." Now, it was alleged, the "foreign imperialists" were still on the colonialist path and were, among other sins, trying to prevent China from doing what it would never allow itself to be kept from: liberating Taiwan.

The reality was that the actual China-Taiwan relationship was quite good at that moment in 1995, at least in most respects, and it remains good today. An unprecedented senior-level dialogue between Chinese and Taiwanese leaders was in the works, and cross-strait economic ties were booming. In the good dialectical-materialist approach Mao's philosophy has taught them, today's Chinese leaders have chosen to "aim the main blow" on the Taiwan question at Washington, rather than Taipei, so as not to cut themselves off from the benefits of the growing cross-strait economic relationship.

The war of words with the United States over Taiwan continued in crisis mode for more than a year. As two different election campaigns unfolded on Taiwan, China upped the ante, carrying out military tests that served as scarcely concealed messages to the independence forces on Taiwan about who was the ultimate master of Taiwan's fate.

The China That Says No

By 1996, the cold-war atmosphere was driving intellectuals in both societies to extreme pronouncements. In a book entitled *China Can Say No* (modeled on the notorious Japanese book *The Japan That Can Say No*), three journalists and a professor rang up the domestic Chinese cash registers with an alarmist but best-selling view of U.S.-China relations.[6] One of the authors, Song Qiang, a thirty-one-year-old jour-

It's not a matter of what kind of government is in place in Beijing: "Whoever is in power in China, Beijing will often seem to us to be prickly, mulish and fiercely independent—France cubed."

—NICHOLAS KRISTOF
FORMER BEIJING BUREAU CHIEF
THE NEW YORK TIMES

nalist, said it was a well-known fact that "The U.S. wants to destroy China's dream of becoming an economic superpower." The points made by Song and his coauthors ranged from the thought-provoking to the ridiculous: The CIA has launched a campaign to undermine China's social stability. These efforts include distributing pamphlets encouraging Chinese youths to have sex. Even TV specials by Chinese-American anchorwoman Connie Chung are part of this conspiracy. . . . China's foreign policy is too weak. China should get much tougher with the West. Indeed, Chinese youth should be even more nationalistic than their comparatively restrained leaders; they should prepare to seize Taiwan by force. . . . The United States has set up an "anti-China club" and is recruiting others, including Japan and Vietnam, to oppose China's claims to Taiwan and the Spratly Islands. . . . Motorola and other U.S. companies have sent third-rate technology to China, while Hollywood has launched a cultural invasion with movies that promote violence and individualism. . . . The United States has no right to preach to China about human rights. American abuses of human rights are much worse—from the beating of Rodney King to the violence against illegal Hispanic immigrants in California.

Chinese officials are embarrassed by the crude arguments in this book and in the various sequels and successors it has spawned (*China Still Says No; China Will Always Say No;* and a whole bookshelf full of such titles) and insist they don't agree with its arguments. Veteran China watchers know *China Can Say No* is an extreme and sensationalized version of only one current of thought, articulated primarily by young and inexperienced academics and journalists. Other books with much more positive views of the United States have also been published, such as the popular *Studying in America,* by Qian Ning, the son of China's foreign minister.

Yet most books published in China these days have considerable nationalist bite on the subject of how the United States has been treating China. In *Megatrends China,* an authoritative book compiling essays by leading Chinese political scientists and military scholars, the U.S. military is portrayed as actively seeking war with China in order to split and destroy it. And a poll by the semiofficial China Youth Research Center reports that the *China Can Say No* authors are not unrepresentative of their generation's opinions.

Yankee go home?
In a survey published by *China Youth News* in May, 1996, 90 percent felt that United States behaves "hegemonistically," with expansionist aims toward China. Ninety-one percent said US has been "unfriendly" in handling the issue of Taiwan. "Several years ago, we naively thought the United States wanted to help China instead of subvert it," says Anthony Chen, a 27-year-old banker who had taken part in the 1989 democracy movement and admired the United States. "Nowadays, we're all convinced that the U.S. government wants to destroy China."

Some 90 percent of young people believe the United States seeks to dominate China, and 86 percent believe the American human rights argument is based on "malice" toward China. These numbers may be overstated; nevertheless, they are not far out of line with the skew of opinion we have found in interviews.

If some opinions in Beijing have increasingly sounded fierce and alarmist, the same is true in America. A. M. Rosenthal, the former editor of *The New York Times* and now a columnist for that newspaper, compares China with Nazi Germany, Imperial Japan, and Saddam Hussein's Iraq. Beijing's government, he says, "is the most dangerous kind—a paranoid political dictatorship trying to balance itself atop a huge, nationalistic and virtually independent military machine."[7]

The xenophobes and ultranationalists on both sides are curiously linked, not only by their criticisms of each other but by their views on the politics of trade. "I Won't Get On a Boeing" is one of the designed-to-provoke chapter titles of *China Can Say No*. The authors call for a boycott of American products that have proliferated in China, from Boeing airplanes to Coca-Cola. They seek to rid their country of the cultural influences and political ties that develop when China does business with Americans. Acknowledging they were once "attracted to the ways of the West," two of the authors now say they believe the Chinese—and, for that matter, all Asians—must "say no" to American things in order to express their "sense of loss and resentment at this overwhelming Western influence."[8]

The *Times*'s Abe Rosenthal takes much the same approach from the other side of the spectrum. He, too, believes in just saying no to export products—Chinese products coming into the American market. Shoppers at holiday time should reject the shelves full of Chinese-made toys in American stores and tell merchants they aren't buying. Rosenthal invokes Harry Wu's argument that it is particularly shameless for Chinese companies to benefit from exporting Christmas merchandise to the American market while the Chinese government cracks down on Christians and other seekers of religious freedom at home.

As the leaders of the two countries jawboned over the terms of trade—each side flirting with sanctions and other trade-war tools, trying to benefit and profit more than the

Prodding on the new cold war: "The Chinese Communist government is an immoral, genocidal regime that doesn't deserve to be traded with on the same basis as democratic countries."

—REPRESENTATIVE DANA ROHRABACHER (R-CALIF.)

other—some extremists in both countries sought a much more sweeping trade confrontation: one that would lead to no trade at all. And when China lobbed artillery rounds in Taiwan's direction and the American president dispatched aircraft carriers to the region—to the accompaniment of loose talk about how Chinese missiles were capable of hitting Los Angeles and about how Washington should be trying to contain China—it seemed clear the relationship had hit bottom. The new cold war had been joined.

Even the possibility of a hot war could no longer be ruled out entirely. "China: Friend or Foe?" blared the *Newsweek* cover that week, complete with an ominous photo of a battle-ready Chinese soldier staring at Americans through his binoculars.[9]

The Left and the Right

The anti-China vogue of the mid-1990s was bipartisan. Forces on both the Left and the Right found it convenient to make China policy a matter of political passion and zeal, almost as if American politics could not function without the organizing principle provided by a common enemy and the need to wage a crusade against it.

Consider the special issues devoted to China of both *The New Republic* on the intellectual Left and *The Weekly Standard* on the intellectual Right, published almost simultaneously around the time of the death of Deng Xiaoping in February 1997. Most of the American media took Deng's passing from the scene as an occasion to look back on the phenomenal achievements of the Chinese economic reform he had led since 1978, although virtually all commentators balanced this miracle-growth story by recalling Deng's tarnished legacy of having presided over the bloodbath in Tiananmen Square. But both *The New Republic* and *The Weekly Standard* thought the time was right to issue clarion calls to arms against China and its American conciliators and appeasers.

"The policies of the Chinese regime are *the* leading threat to . . . peaceful order," editorialized *The Weekly Standard*.[10] A dozen get-tough-with-China articles were featured, with contributors ranging from Senate Foreign Relations Committee chairman Jesse Helms to Richard Bernstein and Ross H. Munro, coauthors of *The Coming Conflict with China,* which has become the bible of the China Threat school. In one of these articles, Michael Ledeen of the American Enterprise Institute argued in passionate terms that the crusade against Chinese tyranny was the "litmus test for American foreign policy." Summoning up the language of the twentieth century's great wars, Ledeen declared that taking a stand against China was the ultimate moral test of "the will and wisdom of the West." China, he said, "is the last of the great dictatorships of this century of wicked dictators, and if we fail in this final challenge it will call into question our previous triumphs."[11]

The New Republic's special issue on China included a lead editorial entitled "Destructive Engagement," a play on words criticizing constructive engagement. Dismissing the Deng Xiaoping era as the "modernization of tyranny" and as the continuation of Communist politics as usual merged with "the economics of fascism," the editors announced, as if it were indisputably true, that "The most important fact about China is that it has embarked on a program of massive militarization. . . . It is only a matter of decades before China becomes the other military superpower on earth." The conclusion? If China is to be engaged at all, "the United States, in the name of its values and its interests, must engage China *adversarially*" [emphasis added].[12]

Or consider Republican House Speaker Newt Gingrich and Democratic Minority Leader Richard Gephardt. They are similarly critical of Clinton-era policy toward China—and similarly interested in using Clinton's alleged softness in the face of the Chinese threat as a campaign issue in the congressional elections of 1998 and the presidential campaign of 2000.

Looking back nostalgically to the 1980s, Republican Hawks recall the great success of Ronald Reagan's unswerving rhetorical devotion to freedom and the popularity of his crusade against the "evil empire" of the Soviet Union. Where in the 1990s can one find an issue of freedom on a similar scale? Where can one find a new and frightening evil empire? China is the obvious answer.

The Left, too, looks back nostalgically on its themes of the 1980s. When Dick Gephardt gave a 1997 speech on China

> **"Any rational policy toward a rising, threatening China** would have exactly these two components: 1) containing China as it tries relentlessly to expand its reach, and 2) undermining its pseudo-Marxist but still ruthless dictatorship."
>
> —CHARLES KRAUTHAMMER
> *TIME*

policy to the Economic Club of Detroit, he made the extreme and almost absurd claim that Chinese "slave labor" was producing most of the trade deficit. He declared that MFN was both immoral on human rights grounds and a threat to American labor. In these lines of reasoning he was repeating protectionist themes he had used against the Japanese in campaigning for the presidency in 1988.

Consider further the politics-makes-strange-bedfellows strategy of influential cultural conservatives such as former Reagan administration official Gary Bauer. He hopes "to form a common bond with human rights advocates and trade protectionists on the left," people whom the ideologues of the Right normally cannot countenance, notes columnist Albert Hunt of *The Wall Street Journal*.[13] Bauer runs the Family Research Council, a right-wing Christian think tank absorbed with such issues as abortion. He is particularly zealous in attacking China's heavy-handed family planning policies, including the incentives and penalties meant to limit families to one child, and the millions of abortions performed annually in China.

Individual Americans have many different views on the religious or moral implications of China's family planning policies. But restraining the growth of the world's most populous nation is almost indisputably virtuous if one seeks to promote economic development in China, improve its prospects of democratization, and make it likelier to play a stable and moderate role in the world (not to mention promote more rational use of the earth's resources). Chinese policies in this regard serve Chinese interests, America's interests, and the world's. Yet in the present atmosphere, the moral and ideological extremism of a Gary Bauer is bringing to life the old saw about how politics makes for strange bedfellows. His Protestant-based movement is now joined at the anti-China hip with the Catholic Church, as well as the AFL-CIO and members of Congress from New York's Bill Paxon to Texas's Dick Armey, to oppose MFN and expansion of trade with China.

In the face of rising criticism from both the Left and the Right, Clinton had to abandon his plan to seek permanent MFN status for China in 1997—a solution that would have removed much of the annual political theatrics from this issue. "We've never seen anything quite like this," said a White House official, referring to the combination Clinton-

An American expatriate's view of the U.S. political debate on China:
"When you are over here you feel a little bit like Kafka's cockroach. You are able to look at life in America and politics there and say, Is this the country from which I come? Why am I hearing all these bizarre things? The China I see doesn't look like the China they are talking about. Yeah, they have their warts; but we have our warts, too."

and-China bashing by this odd emerging coalition of right-wing Republicans and left-wing Democrats. "This is driving a real wedge that leaves us with only the moderate Democrats and the moderate Republicans." [14]

Fear of China and criticism of the Clinton administration's "soft" stance are becoming a theme of nascent presidential campaigns, not only that of Dick Gephardt but also those of Pat Buchanan and Ross Perot, the perennial populists always in search of a foreign enemy. China bashing now brings Jesse Helms together with Ted Kennedy; some of Hollywood's most flamboyant directors and stars with the Christian Coalition; the editorialists of the far-right *Human Events* with well-known liberal columnists such as Anthony Lewis and Mary McGrory.

With more than a hint of whipping up the old "yellow peril" fear, right-wing publications have begun referring to Beijing's leaders as the Chinese Communists again, while the chairman of the Senate Foreign Relations Committee says he will go back to calling the nation Red China. The left-wing media prefer to discuss China's treatment of Tibet and dissidents by invoking images of the Chinese leaders as new fascists, in the mold of the Nazis.

Such voices are commanding attention in large part because there is no strong leadership to remind Americans of the benefits and opportunities offered by the China relationship, or of the progress that has been made in China on many major issues of concern. The Clinton administration, which spent its first few years primarily making the same arguments as its current critics, switched gears only recently, with the president beginning to speak in favor of a more positive relationship with China. In connection with his 1998 visit to China, Clinton spoke eloquently about China, articulating a positive, constructive definition of American interests in better relations. But he is so stained with his own personal scandal, as well as the continuing shadow of the Chinese connection in the campaign scandal of 1996, that his credibility on this issue is constantly in question.

Coffee or Tea?

The interplay between our two complex and interlinked societies is never all black or all white. We now know, for example, that even as our relationship with China was

Who has more prisoners? The ratio of the number of prisoners per 100,000 people in China to the number per 100,000 in the United States is 2:5.

—*HARPER'S INDEX*

headed toward rock bottom, the Clinton-Gore election machine was raising funds for its 1996 campaign from Chinese, Taiwanese, and other Asians and Asian-Americans who were concerned about improving U.S.-China relations. Even as the official media in Beijing were excoriating Clinton in the harshest terms, a local Chinese brewery found it advantageous to pay for its executives to have the chance to meet the Clintons and to use the resulting group portrait for advertising and publicity.

The Chinese government has, as of this writing, denied any official involvement in Clinton campaign contributions. And the Clinton administration has denied being influenced in its China policy by the many contributions we now know the Democratic National Committee solicited and received from individuals and companies with significant China-related business interests. Both sides may have narrow, technical ways of making plausible denials of what everyone can see is the plain truth. Nevertheless, the now infamous White House coffees and other fund-raising techniques constitute a new and fascinating chapter in the history of U.S.-China relations.

Let us stipulate at the outset that we don't approve of breaking campaign finance laws. Although we find the entire American system of campaign finance corrupt and dangerous to the real national interest, we believe that if the law says foreign campaign contributions should not be accepted, then it is wrong for top government officials to flout it. Having said that, however, we would like to offer several relevant ways to look at the "Donorgate" scandal and go beyond the pious punditry on this subject.

First, Americans professing to be shocked—shocked!—that the Chinese might somehow try to influence our political process should wake up to the reality that our China policy is plenty interventionist too. Americans champion Chinese dissidents, provide asylum to political critics of the Beijing regime, and finance opposition forces on a wide variety of causes. American funds are granted or withheld to influence Chinese policies on birth control, the environment, and other issues. The annual debate over MFN and the whole line of reasoning that runs, in effect, "If you accept our agenda on changing your political system, we will give you access to our market for trade," is a very significant intervention in the Chinese domestic political process.

All these efforts may be called constructive engagement,

if that euphemism appeals. At bottom, however, they are interventions in the Chinese political process, meant to reward those who are friendly to American ideas and punish those who are not. Since China does not have a multiparty system with periodic election campaigns for national office, Americans cannot intervene in that particular form of politics—yet. However, various arms of the U.S. government have done exactly that for years, in election campaigns from Latin America to Europe to Japan.

With no Chinese electoral system to try to manipulate, Washington does the next best thing. Through money, market access, and other means, Americans try to shape Chinese politics in a direction favorable to what those doing the shaping believe our national interests to be. The federally funded National Endowment for Democracy reportedly spent $2 million in 1996 on efforts to democratize China. The journalist David Mastio studied this issue and concluded that Americans routinely do the same kinds of things the Chinese are accused of doing, with only one major difference: "The fact is the Chinese are pikers when it comes to sticking their noses in other people's business." By Mastio's estimate, four federally funded programs alone, including the Voice of America, spent $16 million in 1996 on trying to influence politics in China, while the Chinese stand accused of trying to donate a comparatively puny $3 million or $4 million to the Democrats.[15]

What is new about Donorgate is that now two are playing this game—although the Chinese are still clumsy at it. But with the high moral dudgeon characteristic of post–Cold War American triumphalism, the pundits assume that Americans may rightly intervene in China's affairs: we, after all, are working for democracy and the good of the Chinese people. If we intervene in their affairs it is for virtuous and moral reasons. But when *they* intervene in our affairs, it is for sleazy and evil reasons, to corrupt our system and manipulate our leaders into appeasing their aggression.

Whatever one thinks of Donorgate, reality suggests we had better get used to it. As futurists Alvin and Heidi Toffler have observed:

> The concept that foreign-linked funding is necessarily inappropriate is based on obsolete conceptions of both sovereignty and nationhood. It is based on the idea that states

Department of unexpected stereotypes: In designing the "American Dream Park" in Shanghai, its American owners chose the Art Deco façades of Miami as inspiration for its main street. Said the company's president: "This is what most people in China think of the U.S.A. You know, *Miami Vice* and all that."

have absolute sovereignty and that nations are closed systems. All of that is coming apart as we move into the global economy. . . . It is time to recognize that politics, like economics and information, is going transnational.[16]

For years, American evangelists of democracy have urged the Chinese to get more involved in politics Washington-style. Trade lawyers, lobbyists, and PR specialists have told Chinese officials on countless occasions that the art of democratic politics includes and indeed necessitates lobbying as well as campaign donations. After the Lee Teng-hui visit, the Chinese asked these American experts and consultants why the United States had allowed it to occur. They may not have wished to hear the full explanation (including the fact that many in America found Taiwan more democratic than China), but one piece of the answer the Chinese heard over and over again (and *did* find credible) was *money politics*. The Chinese were told that just one of Taipei's contracts with U.S. lobbyists was worth $4.5 million and that pro-Taiwan forces spent at least $2 million and perhaps as much as $20 million on the Lee visit—from an endowment contribution to Cornell, to PR specialists, to lobbying on Capitol Hill, to congressional campaign contributions.[17] They were told that Taiwan had mastered this art long ago—and that they had better master it, too, if they wanted to compete.

The Senate held campaign finance hearings to look into this issue, with Tennessee's senator Fred Thompson declaring at the outset that he would produce evidence of Chinese government attempts to influence the 1996 presidential election. But after weeks of hearings, even Republican staffers acknowledged that no hard evidence had turned up. According to one press account, the key figures in the fund-raising scandal—John Huang and Charlie Trie—seemed "just as interested in hitting up allies of China's archenemy, Taiwan," as in raising money from pro-Beijing sources.[18]

Evidence of a Beijing connection may well eventually surface. But it is also highly plausible that Asian businesspeople such as Mochtar and James Riady of the Indonesia-based Lippo Group (whose close ties to Bill Clinton date back to his days as Arkansas governor) would have wanted to buy a seat at the head table of American political debate for their own business interests, quite apart from any inspiration or pressure from Beijing.

Those on the fairly long list of families and business empires from Thailand to Taiwan that have been identified as Clinton campaign donors—a group epitomized by the Riadys—are, by and large, the success stories of capitalism in Asia. They represent at least one significant chunk of the forces for which the United States wishes to make and keep Asia safe. So it is interesting to see what they think about China and why they may have been interested in trying to influence White House policy in the first place.

In 1995, a year before the Donorgate scandal broke, and before very many people in the United States had heard of the Lippo Group, we sat down with its chief Hong Kong representative, J. P. Lee, to discuss the situation in China. The Lippo Group was then at work on a variety of real estate and power plant projects in China, including building a small city from scratch, complete with residential and industrial facilities. The site was in Fujian, a brief boat trip away from Taiwan.

Though Washington-Beijing tensions were at a crisis point over Taiwan, Lee seemed quite relaxed about the issue. "In the end, there will be more and more contacts between Taiwan and China. Economically, there is no turning back for China." Lee then offered this overall assessment:

> China is a risk for us, but it is an acceptable risk—a medium-term risk for long-term gain. We anticipate rates of return of 25 to 35 percent a year on our China investments. We are not naïve. We know the Chinese could close the door and shut down these projects. But we don't think they will.
>
> They really do wish to have the rule of law, but this takes time. If foreign businesses and governments contribute positively to China's development, they will help China change in a positive direction. If they antagonize China and confirm Beijing's fear that all foreigners want is to try to dominate China, it will cause a negative reaction.

The message from Lee, as well as from many other highly successful capitalists in Hong Kong, Taiwan, and throughout Southeast Asia, is that they are more worried about Asia's future if the United States antagonizes China than they are about any "China threat" to their countries and their interests.

Donorgate in the context of the new Chinese reality: The Yongquan temple has become the first Buddhist monastery in China to buy television advertising time. It paid $24,000 to get on the 8 A.M. *Good Morning, Fujian* program and promote tourism to the mountain retreat. "We will buy additional television time to improve our communications with the outside world," said Master Pufa, the temple abbot.

Newt Gingrich got a similar message from *his* allies. He had positioned himself as a defender of Hong Kong's freedoms in 1997 by urging that Congress extend China's MFN status only for six months instead of a full year. His argument was that if China were kept on a shorter MFN leash, it would have to be more circumspect about how it handled the Hong Kong transition. No thanks, came the answer from Hong Kong's leading democrat, Martin Lee, as well as from Chris Patten, the last British colonial governor and a well-known critic of Beijing. Despite the concerns that both Lee and Patten have about Chinese behavior, they explained to Gingrich that Hong Kong's livelihood depends on MFN, that people of almost all political factions in Hong Kong and throughout the region favor MFN for China, that the best prospects for Hong Kong's benign treatment under Chinese rule lie with a Beijing that is economically successful, and that the best prospects for democracy in China lie in the space for liberalized politics created by prosperity, not the bunker mentality of a foreign-induced recession.

"It's a little much for us to say we're more in favor of Hong Kong than the people of Hong Kong," Gingrich admitted in a moment of candor.[19] Noting the zeal of Gingrich and other members of Congress in 1997 to use MFN as a club to bash China for its policy on Hong Kong, one critic likened such behavior to the old Vietnam War tactic of "burning down the village in order to save it."

It is possible, of course, that American politicians, who enjoy the benefits of distance and perspective, could be more right about the future of China and the region than the people who live there. After all, many big capitalists in wartime China mistakenly thought their support for Mao's united front against the Japanese would protect them and even afford them a privileged position in the post-1949 revolutionary order. More than a few Americans warned them not to fall for that trap.

However, if those who live on the scene and are most aware of its challenges and opportunities believe the United States should be playing a more cooperative role, Washington should at least listen to their voices. Not uncritically, of course. But the White House should be sure it is hearing from this global constituency. For better or worse, these are at least some of our "allies" in Asia.

Rethinking and Rethinking Again

At some point in late 1995 or early 1996, concurrent with the attempts to target special campaign fund-raising efforts at Asians and Asian-Americans, the Clinton administration clearly began to be concerned that it was drifting too far into the vortex of a counterproductive and destructive relationship with China. The weekend before the 1996 presidential election, *The New York Times* attempted to summarize the Clinton record on China. Noting that four years earlier he had pledged to stop Chinese "dictators" from engaging in missile sales, nuclear proliferation, and human rights abuses—all while opening Chinese markets to American goods—the article pointed out that Clinton found himself still dealing with all the same issues: "Today, the same 'dictators' rule, only they seem stronger because they have spent four years standing up to what they call 'American power politics' and 'pressure tactics' and 'interference.'" Chinese leaders had long since abandoned the approach of the 1970s, when they eagerly sought American approval in the interests of a strong relationship. The lesson the Chinese had learned? "Intransigence is rewarded when it comes to dealing with Washington."[20]

Another biting commentary was that of *The New Republic*, which also summed up the situation as a failure on all counts: "The Clinton administration has abandoned human rights without opening the Chinese market. A case could be made for jettisoning human rights in favor of national security or for economic gain. But the Clinton administration has ended up with the worst of all possible worlds. It has traded them away for nothing."[21]

On reading these and similar summaries, Clinton's advisors might well have thought they would have little to lose by trying a fresh approach. Certainly, with his 1996 campaign victory behind him, the president began to consider his historical legacy. Perhaps he did not want the U.S.-China relationship destroyed on his watch. Or perhaps American business leaders convinced him that their interests, and those of America as a whole, were being hurt by the negative atmosphere between Washington and Beijing.

Clinton's China advisors may also have begun to understand that a mood shift had taken place in China. Jiang Zemin had stood up to the United States over Taiwan and

Needed perspective: At the height of the MFN-renewal debate in 1997, leading Republican luminaries Jeane Kirkpatrick, Jack Kemp, Lamar Alexander, Steve Forbes, and Donald Rumsfeld said this: "Those whose concerns about China's human rights practices have led them to advocate nonrenewal of MFN status may wish to consider the following. In the life of the ordinary Chinese citizen, there is more freedom in the economic realm than any other. Trade can help maintain that freedom, and help expand that freedom to other realms of China's culture and society."

pursued a brazen and bellicose course to its end. In doing so, he had proven to his military and other domestic constituencies how tough he could be. Having done it once, he did not have to continue doing it. And, with Deng Xiaoping's death imminent, Jiang needed as much support and as few crises as possible.

Talk, Talk, Fight, Fight

Whatever the explanation, by early 1997 Clinton sounded more positive and upbeat about China than at any time in the prior four years. His State of the Union message reflected this new view as well. For the first time, the president was talking seriously about going to China himself. In the spring of 1997, Vice President Al Gore made a visit to Beijing (albeit a stilted and chilly one). President Jiang Zemin visited the United States in the fall.

Suddenly, all the emotional "ghosts and monsters" (to use Mao Zedong's phrase) that popped out over the Taiwan issue in 1995–96 seemed to have gone back in their box. Chinese officials no longer found it necessary to browbeat every American they met with the official party line on Taiwan.

Perhaps Beijing was only recycling a leaf from Mao's old playbook: "First go back and then get a better run for a bigger leap forward." But the issue faded so much that Chinese leaders were even able to smile through a 1997 visit by Newt Gingrich during which he warned that the United States would retaliate militarily if China used force to reunify with Taiwan. Of course they might have been smiling because they didn't believe him (most American experts do not believe the United States would actively intervene militarily in such a crisis). But a year earlier Gingrich's remarks would almost certainly have set off a fusillade of rhetorical denunciations. Now, they were taken in stride.

In a 1997 interview, Jiang Zemin pointed out that Taiwan remains "the most important and sensitive issue in Sino-U.S. relations," and urged the United States to "handle the Taiwan question cautiously."[22] Calm as these words were compared to the prior invective, they nevertheless underscored the continuing problem, as did Jiang's oft-repeated reminder, "I am fully confident that eventually Taiwan will be reunified with the motherland."

That Taiwan will remain both a tripwire and a touchstone of U.S.-China relations for years to come was made evident

"**America cannot remain silent** about the basic lack of freedom—speech, religion, assembly, the press—in China. Were we to do so, we would not only betray our own tradition, we would also fail to fulfill our obligations as a friend of China."

—NEWT GINGRICH
SPEECH AT PEKING
UNIVERSITY, APRIL 1997

by the American president's own visit to Beijing in March, 1998. In the United States, Clinton made headlines for his "spontaneous" debate on human rights at a televised, live postsummit press conference with President Jiang Zemin. In China, however, Clinton made far greater news when, several days later, he acceded to his hosts' insistent request that he personally and publicly endorse Beijing's so-called Three Noes policy toward Taiwan: no independence for Taiwan; no "one China, one Taiwan"; and no support for Taiwan's entry into world bodies.

American willingness to mouth the rhetoric China wants to hear on the Taiwan issue does not mean this issue is behind us. Memories are short and the next visa issue to Lee Teng-hui, or the next U.S. arms sale to Taiwan, or the next round of Capitol Hill enthusiasm for seating Taiwan at the United Nations could trigger a repeat of the whole crisis.

Although China appears now to be prepared to act more circumspectly toward Taiwan, rumors still circulate that Beijing might unilaterally set a date for Taiwan's reunification. The date would be far off—2010, say—just as the 1997 date was once far off for Hong Kong. But any such move on Beijing's part would provoke a firestorm of negative American reactions and a new crisis in and around Taiwan.

Another possibility is an "accidental crisis" in which Lee Teng-hui's long-dominant KMT party loses power as a result of corruption and crime scandals. The "cleaner" Democratic Progressive Party (DPP), whose leaders lean much more toward outright independence for Taiwan, would step into the breach. If the DPP came to power, Beijing might feel compelled to act to prevent the political momentum from turning toward a declaration of independence.

Moreover, Taiwan is not the only issue that could trigger the next Washington-Beijing crisis. Until new policies are put in place, and a new effort to reforge a long-term strategic partnership is designed, the relationship could be thrown into another frenzy of anger and recrimination at almost any point—by something that happens in Hong Kong or Tibet, by a dissident's case in China, or by a revelation about Chinese arms sales or campaign contributions. What has improved in the last year are the cosmetics and theatrics of the relationship. That is preferable to escalating conflict and confrontation, but it should not be confused with substantive progress toward minimizing the long-term dangers of this relationship.

American policy toward China explained: "Here's the deal," says an American official explaining U.S. efforts to assure the independence of Hong Kong after the transition. "After July 1 we pretend that Hong Kong isn't part of China, even though it is. And we still insist that Taiwan is part of China, even though it isn't."

Both sides are following Mao's old dictum on how to handle negotiations: "Talk, talk, fight, fight." For the time being, Washington and Beijing seem to be back in the talking phase. But the fighting phase may return after both sides have exhausted the benefits of talking about a very limited agenda that includes no long-term solutions to the underlying problems. It will return all the faster if the Hawk arguments continue to be ascendant in Washington. As some of China's more strident neonationalists warn: "There should be no illusion that relations will be qualitatively improved by visits from high-level American officials. . . . Barring revolutionary change in American foreign policy, the confrontation between China and America will be a protracted one."[23]

We should also guard against illusions about Jiang Zemin's fine words when he says he favors an improved relationship with the United States. In what strikes us as an apocryphal story that yet contains a kernel of truth, a German magazine reported that on Jiang's return from a European tour he told senior military leaders back home, "Anyone who criticizes me for clinking glasses with Western leaders should know that this is only for tactical reasons. . . . I am aware of the fact that the West remains our chief enemy."[24]

One of China's most sophisticated academic experts on the United States argues that even if the relationship improves, perceived hostility toward China has inflicted long-term damage to America's credibility and that of younger Chinese intellectuals attracted to American ideals. Often called upon by the leadership to explain Washington's actions, he believes he has to put a different spin on his own expert opinion in order even to continue to be heard:

> You cannot say to our leaders that a country like the United States does not seek maximum power. You waste your time trying to explain that their policies are not intended to dominate China, but arise from their own domestic political contradictions. You can argue that the United States has become too weak or powerless to successfully dominate China—that, they will listen to. But you cannot say that Americans do not have the intention to dominate China. . . .
>
> Clinton cheated the Chinese people by allowing Lee Teng-hui to visit the United States. Whenever there is a problem of this type, the leftist view gets heard more and the volume on it goes up. The realistic, pragmatic view suffers.

A young veteran of the democracy movement in Tiananmen Square who turned to financial services after 1989 describes the situation in even starker terms: "Several years ago, we naively thought the United States wanted to help China instead of subvert it. Nowadays, we're all convinced the U.S. government wants to destroy China."[25]

Indeed, as Beijing-Washington relations thawed in 1998, this kind of hyperbole was less often heard. But in times of tension these kinds of views will return—and not just among the leaders, but among many of the educated youth, intellectuals, technocrats, and entrepreneurs on whom so much of China's future depends. The mirror image of this phenomenon is also taking place among Americans, especially the young people who attend rock concerts benefiting free-Tibet campaigns and fill the theaters for the new wave of Hollywood films critical of China.

The Context Is Crucial, and That Context Is Progress

Lost from view in the current American swing from China boom to China threat are the very real, remarkable, and sustained accomplishments of the Chinese over the last two decades. We are not told very often anymore how successful the Chinese have been (to mention just a few accomplishments) at:

- lifting nearly a quarter of the world's people out of poverty and backwardness and doubling total economic output faster than any other major economy in history;
- creating, almost overnight, a sizable middle class whose total membership is as large as America's entire population and whose real incomes have risen ten times faster than American real incomes in the 1990s;
- decommunizing one of the world's most rigid centrally planned economies and shifting a significant portion of economic activity toward market mechanisms, while welcoming foreign enterprises into the heart of the Chinese economy;
- keeping the inefficient and essentially bankrupt State-Owned Enterprises running long enough to prevent the social dislocation of "shock therapy" and begin to shift the locus of economic activity gradually toward the private and quasi-private sectors, which now account for roughly half of Chinese economic output;

"China will be the world's largest economy within a few decades. Along the way, it has almost certainly raised more people from poverty to near prosperity in a shorter time than any society has ever done."

—*NEWSWEEK*

- creating enough macroeconomic policy coordination tools to have tamed rampant inflation (which many foreign experts thought was untamable); established a working central banking system, nascent financial and commodities markets, and a real estate market; and brought the currency (the renminbi) to the verge of full international convertibility;

- developing an extensive system of contested free elections for thousands of local posts that is now moving from the village level up to towns, expanding the legislative power and the quality of the debate in the once rubber-stamp National People's Congress, and passing laws to govern dozens of major commercial and civil issues previously covered by no written law;

- allowing a vast expansion of the media and more freedom of expression and access to information (on thousands of topics, if not the still-sensitive political ones) than modern China has ever seen; increasing consumer choice and labor mobility; and allowing some significant new religious, personal, and lifestyle freedoms;

- surviving (thus far) the post–Deng Xiaoping transition without purges and violence, making this the first smooth change of leadership in China's twentieth-century history.

Those most vociferous about the China threat don't seem very aware of or interested in the enormous positive changes that have shaken Chinese society in the last two decades. But it is only in the context of how much has been achieved that one can understand the negative and dangerous indicators for what they are: worrisome, important, but only a small part of the total mosaic of late 1990s Chinese reality—and not yet by any means the definitive part.

For along with the anti-Americanism, the xenophobia, the populist nationalism, and the ham-handed arrogance toward Taiwan, there has also been steady progress toward the development of checks and balances, the rule of law, real debate within the leadership, and the growth of competing interest groups. In our view, these *indigenous* factors will matter far more in the long run to restraining the irresponsible use of Chinese power than any Machiavellian webs of interests the Engagement camp might spin, or any confrontational pressures the Hawks might bring to bear.

CHAPTER 4

Competing and
Cooperating with the
World's New Economic
Superpower

As if the political dilemma were not significant enough, the economic challenge presented by China's rise is perhaps of even greater consequence to America's future. If and when Washington and Beijing overcome the present negative phase of their political relationship, they will do so in a world that feels the economic impact of China more strongly, for that impact grows by the week and month.

China's emergence as a twenty-first-century superpower has transcendent, wide-ranging implications for global business and finance, for technology, and for the social and cultural environment in which they operate. From the performance of stock markets to the quality of the air we breathe, to job growth and wages in American industries, the "China difference" will be felt in our daily lives. Indeed, it is already very much in evidence. For example, if the Chinese ever became wealthy enough to own and drive automobiles the way Americans do, their gasoline consumption would quickly drain most known oil reserves, while choking the world in pollution. And if the Chinese could afford to eat as much beef per capita as Americans do, there would probably not be enough grazing land on the planet to supply the demand. If every Chinese ate as much fish as every Japanese, China would consume the equivalent of the entire annual global fishing catch. One could go on and on with many more illustrations of the unprecedented ways China could affect the rest of us.

However, we do not join those who see China as *so* big, and its future *so* world-shaking that the whole success or failure of economic globalization hangs on its evolution. There are those who argue that China is *the* issue of our times and that everything depends on whether America gets it right or wrong. That is not our view. Other issues—from the digital electronics revolution to the aging society, to name but a few—will also be of critical importance. But even a realistic, unromanticized forecast of the size and scope of the China opportunity suggests that it will be *one* of the most important markets and a key theater of global competition for many American corporations. Moreover, China's growth over time into the world's largest single nation-state economy will profoundly affect the rest of the world, shaping some key contours of the twenty-first-century global economy.

Put aside the tempestuous ideological arguments over human rights, military budgets, and missiles, and look instead at where we think China will have its greatest impact on the United States: economic challenges and opportunities. Or, let us say, "political-economic"—for in dealing with China economics can never be severed from political issues. Following are nine commentaries on various pieces of the Chinese political-economic puzzle—the challenges as well as the opportunities.

1. China Ascendant: From Main Street to Wall Street, from the Boardroom to the Beltway

Even though its total economic output today is still quite modest—closing on England's and about twice the size of 1996 Korea's—China is already starting to show superpower-sized influence on global markets. In 1996, it outstripped Japan to become the world's largest crude-steel producer. This pattern will probably be repeated with one industrial product after another in the coming years.[1]

China, the last great growth market: AT&T and its spinoff company, Lucent, believe their equipment sales in China may eclipse their U.S. business after the turn of the century. They are no doubt encouraged by estimates that the number of phone lines per 100 people is expected to quintuple (from 4.5 to 21) by the year 2000.

"At no time in history has there been such a cataclysmic change where the economic power of a major part of the world was suddenly dumped on the world economy," observes Paul H. O'Neill, chairman and CEO of Alcoa.[2] In particular, the impact of China's rise on the American economy and American life generally is immediate, direct, and startling. Consider just a few indicators:

• The U.S. trade deficit with China has already emerged as a very large economic and political question. Analysts had predicted that the U.S. monthly trade deficit with China might exceed the U.S. deficit with Japan near the end of the decade. Instead, that watershed event occurred for the first time in July 1996. Ever since, China has been increasingly perceived as America's leading trade problem.

"The issue now is *China's* economy, stupid," observed a *Washington Post* analysis of the tasks before the Clinton administration leading up to the year 2000. The stakes in dealing with China may not yet be as dramatic as they are in a showdown with the Japanese over autos, but, says the *Post,* they are more important: "Trade experts fear that the world's free-trade regime will come under increasingly severe pressure if one of its biggest participants continues to play by such totally different rules."[3]

• Significant chunks of labor-intensive industry have already moved almost entirely to China: toys, textiles, plastics, consumer electronics, hand tools, and other low-priced manufactured items. As every Christmas shopper knows, more toys are made in China than anywhere else. Indeed, there may be five-year-olds who think Santa Claus lives in China, since everything he brings seems to come from there.

• Nor is China's growing manufacturing muscle confined to cheap wares and low-tech industries. Owing to a combination of cultural characteristics and the design of the educational system, China is able to produce world-class scientists and engineers in physics, electronics, computer science, biotechnology, and many other leading-edge fields. The research firm International Data Group reports that more than half of PCs sold in China are now domestic brands.

Andy Grove, CEO of Intel, the world's most successful microprocessor company, observed in 1995 that he thought in ten years his biggest competition in the microprocessor business would come not from other American companies,

"China," said the older man to The **Graduate:** "It is no secret that the days of substantial growth in the U.S. automotive market are over—this is a mature market, so the growth must come from outside North America, notably Asia . . . [and] China is the ideal cornerstone for growth in Asia."

—JOHN F. SMITH
CHAIRMAN, GENERAL MOTORS

not from Japan, and not from Korea or India, but from China. Asked just one year later if he stood by that forecast, Grove replied, "Yes—but probably in eight years."[4]

China has at least 350,000 information technology engineers, earning an average $105 per month. An American engineer earns about *twenty-nine times* more, providing foreign companies with a compelling reason for doing even complex and highly skilled manufacturing jobs in China.

Why Deere & Co. and other agricultural-equipment manufacturers are salivating over the China market: In China today, a single tractor is shared by nearly 600 farmers, and there are more than 9,000 farmers for every harvester. Just imagine the sales to be made as Chinese agriculture modernizes. In the United States, for example, the average farmer not only has his own tractor, he is likely to have two . . . and there is one harvester for every four farmers.

• Growth dynamics are so strong in China that quite a few American companies are already experiencing direct positive impact on their bottom line from their China operations. GE is closing in on its goal of a $1-billion-a-year China business by 2000. The insurance company AIG has more than 5,000 salesmen in Shanghai selling life insurance—a product post-1949 China hadn't seen before—door-to-door.

Motorola's sales in China now account for 12 percent of the company's worldwide revenue. China has become the world's largest market for pagers, surpassing the installed base of the United States over the last two years. And Motorola is the best-selling pager in China.

Avon opened for business in China in 1990 with a six-month supply of goods—which lasted three weeks. By 1996, there were more Avon ladies in China than anywhere else in the world. Even when, in 1998, Avon, along with Amway and other competitors, got hit with a damaging ban on direct selling, allegedly to prevent fraud and abuses of consumers, the company quickly found a way around the ban by starting retail outlets and converting independent "ladies" into teams of sales representatives who bring the customers in the door, and continues to do business full force.

The recent recessionary pressures in Asia and slowing growth curves in China may put a damper on some of these bright numbers. But the foreign companies that have led the way into China generally see slower growth as a new complexity in their business plans, not a reason to abandon the market.

• China has amassed over $100 billion in foreign currency reserves, making it one of the world's two or three largest foreign-reserve holders. Even markets for U.S. Treasury debt—through which Washington finances its deficits—have begun to take on a bit of Chinese flavor. Until the early nineties, the Chinese were essentially nonplayers. But after

1995, their interest began to snowball. Japan remains the leading foreign purchaser of American government debt, but China is coming up fast. In the first half of 1996, for example, the Chinese bought $11.8 billion worth of U.S. Treasury debt, making them Uncle Sam's third best foreign customer. "They definitely have the capacity to move the market," says one New York–based Treasury bond trader.[5]

Putting the Chinese purchase of Washington's debt in a macroeconomic context, Dwight Perkins, a Harvard economics professor, notes, "The U.S. doesn't save enough. China is doing the U.S.'s saving for it," helping America maintain its investment levels, just as Japan and other nations have done for the last fifteen years.[6] (Of course, with Japanese influence in the Treasury market came major political questions—an issue that could well be reprised with China in the future.)

Incredible as it may seem today, one solution to the problem of underfunded pension and retirement plans throughout the developed world may involve the recycling of capital surpluses from China and other emerging markets. The Chinese could, in effect, end up bailing out Social Security and Medicare in the United States twenty-five years from now, when these programs would otherwise be running $1-trillion-a-year deficits.

• Events in China have often driven the U.S. commodities markets up or down. American farm exports were aided by a sudden reversal in China's trade patterns in 1995, for example, when the Chinese imported corn for the first time in five years, boosted wheat imports by 250 percent, and quadrupled their cotton imports—mostly from the United States.[7] Not only these commodities but also gold, oil, and sugar have been dramatically affected by production in China and its trade patterns.

Developments in China can also have a profound impact on the share price of American stocks. Wal-Mart stock dropped $1.75 a share in a rising market on the day a news report linked the retailing giant with a Chinese company that allegedly mislabeled clothing to avoid U.S. import quotas. In an otherwise up day during the historic bull market of 1997, the stock price of Motorola dropped 11 percent when the company announced pager sales in China were "experiencing a larger-than-normal seasonal downturn."[8]

The Dragon drives the Bulls on Wall Street: In November 1996, shares of Federal Express rallied nearly 3 points on news that the company would expand its delivery area in China by 20 cities a year over the next five years. "China is a very big market and there is no one there except for Federal Express," said one analyst who covers the company.

The link between Hong Kong stocks and the fortunes of U.S. investors is a mixed tale. The runup to record highs at the time of the Chinese takeover of Hong Kong in the summer of 1997 fattened the portfolios of many U.S. mutual funds investors. Then, the crash of the Hong Kong market obliterated a major chunk of those profits just a few months later. For a few days in the fall of 1997, the roller-coaster volatility of Hong Kong—swinging up and down in increments of ten percent and more on a daily basis and having a domino effect on other global markets in the process—glued American investors to Internet investing sites on their computers and CNBC on cable television, and gave millions of people a real-life lesson in the complex interconnections between the Asian and American economies.

• American computer companies are thriving in China's booming market for personal computers, with IBM, Compaq, and Apple among the market leaders. Although Microsoft continues to be concerned about illegal duplication of its software, Bill Gates reached agreements at the highest levels with Chinese officials (including President Jiang Zemin) on this subject; ever since, China has said it will standardize around Microsoft's Windows 95 operating system for its PCs. "We're looking at one hundred percent growth as far as we can see," said Bryan Nelson, head of Microsoft's Greater China division.[9]

• China has a deep impact on the local economy in many parts of the United States. In Kansas, 120 companies have banded together into an alliance designed to remind Washington of the state's vital interests in exports to China. In California, a similar alliance has 350 members. Nationally, more than a thousand businesses support the Business Coalition for U.S.-China Trade. United Technologies, an important Connecticut employer that already enjoys revenues of $750 million from its China business, lobbies the Connecticut congressional delegation to support MFN; General Motors, with fifteen ventures in China and more in the pipeline, takes responsibility for convincing the Michigan delegation of the importance of keeping trade ties with China.

• Even some of the most traditional slices of Americana are affected by the China trade. The New Orleans gourmet restaurant business has become the scene of a pitched battle between local crawfish and Chinese imports. With Chinese crawfish selling at $3.50 a pound and the local catch at $8.00,

Louisiana fishermen have asked the U.S. Commerce Department for protective tariffs to safeguard their business and their way of life. The American importing companies, which pay their Chinese workers the equivalent of 15 cents an hour, argue that American consumers are getting the best of this deal, which they undoubtedly are. However, with Chinese crawfish reaching sales three times greater than the American catch, the U.S. International Trade Commission decided to intervene in 1997 with measures to limit the import of the Chinese product.

Thus, from Main Street to Wall Street, and from the boardrooms of corporate America to the Beltway and even to the bayou, American businesspeople, decision makers, and ordinary citizens alike are aware that something historic and significant is happening on the other side of the world—and that it is increasingly affecting our pocketbooks and bottom lines.

2. Are the Chinese Stealing American Jobs?

MIT's sage of modern capitalism, Lester Thurow, predicted in the early nineties that China would have a very substantial impact on the wages, living standards, and lifestyles of a significant percentage of American workers, particularly those without college educations and specialized skills:

> Think about it: Several hundred million Chinese workers are joining the global labor force. They are willing to work for less than $100 a month. They are educated as well [as] or better than the average American manufacturing worker. They are more disciplined, more motivated, and willing to work longer hours under much more difficult circumstances.
>
> With that for competition, how does anyone in the United States manufacture anything cost-effectively and profitably? The answer is, they don't. We will either lose these jobs to China and other emerging markets, or American wages will be forced down.

Some aspects of Thurow's gloomy forecast are already coming true. The hope that China would be a huge market for American exports is being tempered by mercantilist real-

The giant sucking sound: "China regularly extorts know-how and high-skill jobs from American companies like Boeing. As a condition of sales, it forces businesses to manufacture parts of their products within its borders and to transfer technology to Chinese partners. Beijing's aim is to set up its own industrial giants and supplant our suppliers in sectors like aerospace, semiconductors and automobiles."

—ALAN TONELSON
THE NEW YORK TIMES

ity. The Chinese are more willing to import what they need than either the Japanese or the Koreans were at a similar stage of development. But Beijing's economic policy still has a strong anti-import bias. Like the Japanese in the 1960s and 1970s, the Chinese strongly prefer local production by foreign companies. Local production creates jobs, transfers technology, and teaches skills. Since the government still controls access to the market, it can steer foreign companies into transferring some of their most advanced technology. Most managers of foreign companies operating in China today believe they *must* manufacture locally for maximum success.

Boeing, for example, eager to capitalize on China as the world's fastest-growing market for aircraft, agreed to build half the fuselage for its new generation of 737 jets at a military plant in Xian. American labor leaders worry that Boeing will give the Chinese access to the company aircraft design and then shift skilled production jobs to Chinese workers—losing not only American jobs but possibly the American competitive edge as well. "Now there is Boeing in China and Boeing here. . . . One hand of Boeing is competing with the other," observes AFL-CIO secretary-treasurer Richard L. Trumka.[10]

Some American companies worry that the technology transfer bar may be raised too high. Reflecting on a "lost" opportunity to construct a $1 billion joint-venture minivan plant, which Chrysler had pursued aggressively for a number of years, company chairman Robert Eaton speculated about what would have happened had Chrysler "won": "They wanted us to set them up as a world-class competitor to Chrysler, and pay for it, too."[11]

Despite the competitive threat China poses as a low-wage manufacturing center, almost all economists recognize important benefits in the U.S.-China trade relationship. Not all manufacturing is going to move to China, despite the attraction of low wages. American manufacturing has experienced a renaissance in recent years as companies have finally gotten it right on quality and developed all sorts of ways to use information systems to add efficiency and value to the manufacturing process. China's low wages do not threaten most of American industry, as long as the American side keeps moving up the ladder of skill, productivity, and knowledge as it has in recent years.

In any event, at least some of the alarm over America's rising trade deficit with China is misplaced. To a significant degree, the deficit's expansion reflects goods Americans might once have bought from Hong Kong, Taiwan, or Korea, which now come from China. The part of the trade deficit produced by imports of shoes, textiles, toys, plastics, hand tools, handicrafts, and consumer electronics items involves very few lost American jobs. These industries long ago moved manufacturing to low-cost labor centers in Asia and Latin America. China is cannibalizing jobs, but primarily from other Asian countries where labor is more expensive, *not* from the United States. "The number of U.S. jobs lost to Chinese exports is approximately zero," says Nicholas Lardy, a China expert at the Brookings Institution.[12] (One reason for this is the tendency for the China trade to create many more new jobs even as it threatens or eliminates some old ones.)

Perhaps the most important, if least understood, benefit of the China trade is the impact of cheap imported goods from China on American living standards. Despite the strength of the U.S. economy during the 1990s, the real income of the average American family has barely improved. The availability of cheap Chinese imports, from running shoes to CD players, makes a significant difference in how much a household can buy. By some measures, the entire increase in average American consumption in this decade can be attributed to the difference between the prices of products made in China and the prices those products would have had if they came from other markets. As a bevy of prominent economists and policy experts have noted, the first negative impact of Washington-imposed sanctions on China would be rising prices for American consumers.

3. The Great Global Game of Go

In several important industries, the China market represents such an outsized chunk of total future growth that companies wishing to maintain global competitiveness are essentially compelled to compete for access. China is so critical to Westinghouse that *Business Week* declared it to be "key to survival" for the proposed spinoff of the company's $3.2 billion industrial group. "With a strong foothold in China,

The global game of go: "This is the most competitive market in the world. . . . Every major competitor AT&T has in the world is here; we don't face that anywhere else on the globe. And if you are not successful in China, you cannot be successful in the world market."

—WILLIAM WARWICK
 CHAIRMAN AND CEO,
 AT&T (CHINA)

Westinghouse could carve a niche for the twenty-first century. Without it, look for the giants [i.e., its major competitors] to gobble up what's left of George Westinghouse's old empire."[13]

Companies that build power plants, dams, and airports know very well that China could account for as much as $1 trillion worth of international-class infrastructure projects in the next ten to fifteen years. China wants 16,000 megawatts of new electric generating capacity alone each year through 2000; this project will require at least $20 billion in foreign capital. More than half a dozen agreements for private power projects were signed with foreign investors in 1996, even after earlier investors had been subjected to strict limits on their returns.[14]

You can't be in any business, it seems, and not stake a claim in China. Analysts predict the pharmaceutical market will more than triple in size for foreign companies to around $20 billion over the next seven years. Intel reported that personal computer sales in the mainland in 1998 were helping offset the effects of a slowdown in the rest of Asia. Even Levi Strauss & Co. resumed production in China after a five-year absence. Peter Jacobi, Levi's CEO, told reporters he felt that violations of human rights, the issue that caused the company to make a high-profile exit from China, had lessened. "We think that in Asia it's crazy to be operating in this environment and not be engaged with China," said Jacobi.[15]

In 1996, the city of Shanghai had some 2,000 major construction sites, with more cranes at work than in the whole of North America.[16] That makes China the center for the world elevator business, as well as a huge market for window glass, air-conditioning systems, and everything else that goes with such a building boom.

"China is the center of a great global game of go in the automobile industry," says Kenneth Courtis, a Deutsche Bank economist based in Tokyo:

> North American, European, and Japanese production of vehicles is relatively flat . . . because these are mature, saturated markets. Almost *all* the growth in the world auto market is going to come from the emerging markets, with China the leader. China can add the equivalent of the entire annual European market every decade for several decades to come. If I am an automobile company executive, I *need* to be in China in order to get access to that

growth to drive my global cost curves down, to amortize my R&D costs across a wider base, and to have a growth market that is uncorrelated with the cyclic rise and fall of auto sales in the developed countries.

Currently, the American Big Three automakers are way out in front of the Japanese in China. Every U.S. auto company has a major project in China, as do the leading European companies. The Japanese giants, on the other hand, are involved mostly in auto parts, motorcycles, and other peripheral areas of the business. This reflects the Chinese preference for doing business with American companies, which are much more willing than the Japanese to transfer technology and operate joint ventures. It also reflects the timidity of Japanese companies, which prefer to export (this has been a very good business for them), rather than localize production in China.

Although American automobile companies have not had an easy time in China, the fact that they are outcompeting the Japanese has very significant long-term implications for sustaining American competitive prowess on a global basis in the future. "If you are not in this market, it basically means that you are not going to be one of the top three players in the world," GM's general manager for China, Rudolph Schlais, told us. European firms are also getting a new lease on life thanks to their strength in the China market. Volkswagen's joint-venture factory is the leading producer of cars in China, making models for taxi fleets and the masses as well as a popular upmarket Audi for newly prosperous Chinese who don't wish to pay for (or who find it politically incorrect to be seen in) expensive ultraluxurious imports. Nevertheless, the world's second largest market for Mercedes-Benz S-class luxury cars (after Germany) is no longer the United States but China. Even severely challenged European companies like Peugeot are looking optimistically to China. Currently, Peugeot has just 8 percent of the stagnant European market. Winning new markets is a life-or-death matter. Says Jacques Calvet, Peugeot's chairman, "China is incontestably the market of the future."[17]

The competitive proving ground of the twenty-first century is likely to be China. American, Japanese, European, and Asian corporations will compete with each other (and with the local Chinese giants) for access to and control of

A car for every garage? "China is such a potentially huge market that if 1 percent of Chinese people could afford cars, that would be 12 million. That's roughly our market size for Europe."

—MICHAEL G. MEYERAND GENERAL MOTORS

93

key industries and markets. Even though profits have proven elusive for many and the landscape is increasingly studded with competitive threats, few major companies can afford to turn their backs on China's promising future. They need the growth. What's more, they cannot surrender the market to their competition.

Regardless of trade policies adopted in Washington, regardless of the exhortations by the China Threat school to avoid doing business with the Chinese, American corporations cannot resist either the temptation or the imperative to dig deeply into the China market.

4. Piracy of Digital Bits

A serious Washington-Beijing skirmish has flared on and off over intellectual property rights and the Chinese tendency to pirate American computer and entertainment software. This is a recurring and at times tense issue. Twice the Clinton administration has gone to the mat threatening trade sanctions. Twice Beijing agreed at the last moment to do something. And some of the worst abuses have, in fact, been cleaned up. Big state- and army-owned corporations are no longer flagrantly cranking out pirate CDs. Yet the problem is by no means solved. Especially as China's installed computer base soars, the demand for pirated software is growing by quantum leaps.[18] In the back streets of Chinese cities, one is more likely to be approached by someone offering CDs for sale than illicit drugs or sex.

Since agreeing to U.S. demands that China clean up its software business, Beijing authorities have made several big, well-publicized shows of closing pirate factories. For the benefit of the cameras, tractors are seen crushing cloned CDs. Yet every time one plant is closed, another sprouts up. China may still be responsible for up to 60 percent of the 200 million CDs pirated worldwide each year.

All through 1996 and 1997, even as Washington was trying to curtail software piracy, European companies were busy selling the stamping equipment needed to mass-manufacture pirate CDs to Hong Kong middlemen, who were surely reselling the equipment in China. The Europeans are taking a "see no evil" attitude, complains U.S. Trade Representative Charlene Barshefsky; they benefit from brisk

More than meets the eye on piracy: To China's claims that it is difficult to shut down makers of pirate CDs or videos because the factories are beyond their administrative reach, a senior U.S. trade official responded, "If these plants were turning out videos for dissident groups they would have been closed in two days."

sales of their stamping equipment and don't care about the longer-term implications of rampant piracy.

Pirated intellectual property is a complex issue particularly because it involves the clash of cultures. American experts on the new economy have long expected that the export of U.S. services—including royalties and licensing fees—will eventually begin to offset the huge deficit in manufactured goods with global trading partners.

Moral justifications wash over software piracy in ways that make uniquely compelling sense on the domestic market in China: Pirated goods are "needed" to start businesses, earn money, and catch up to the West. The West never paid the Chinese royalties on China's great ancient inventions, from gunpowder to paper. Software copying is a victimless crime. Piracy is not like stealing because all the real "work" (i.e., the duplication and distribution) is being done locally in China. And so on.

Listen to the angry rant of Sang Ye, a young Chinese computer hacker:

> Foreign devils have been ripping off the Chinese for ages. What's the basic element of computing? Binary notation! That's the theory of yin and yang. Everything in the universe is made up of yin and yang, and the Chinese discovered that. What about electricity and magnetic fields? Who discovered magnetism? Pardon me, it was the Chinese! Without Cai Lun [the legendary Chinese inventor of paper], those foreigners would still be writing on parchment. Foreigners can't face up to the fact that they owe *us* for copyright infringement.[19]

But there is another important side to the story. First, some companies, including Microsoft and Disney, are having success in getting their Chinese customers to understand the legal and moral necessity of paying licensing fees and royalties, however minimal. Even as these companies continue to be victimized by pirate factories in one part of China, they are expanding their *paid and profitable* market share elsewhere. Piracy could even be said to build brand-name awareness, making people want the real item. Disney, Microsoft, and other companies have been successful by promoting corporate policies of "engagement": lowering the royalties to make it easier for the Chinese to pay, providing "site licenses" with very broad coverage for one low, fixed price,

Putting the shoe on the other foot:
Microsoft has complained long and loud about the way Chinese companies violate its intellectual property rights and clone its software at will. But in March 1997, a Beijing court ordered Microsoft to pay a $24,000 fine to a Chinese advertising agency. It held that Microsoft had commissioned some artwork, declined to pay for it, but then used it anyway in newspaper ads all over China. The court also ordered Microsoft to apologize.

providing technical cooperation, and giving the Chinese back very significant opportunities to create jobs and promote their economy. This works considerably better than angry demands from outsiders that Chinese factories stop copying their software.

A different way of looking at who is stealing whose intellectual property: An American official negotiating the problem of software piracy in China opened the meeting by declaring that "We are talking to thieves." A Chinese trade official immediately countered that the American side was not exactly a paragon of respect for intellectual property rights. "Look at your museums," he said, "aren't they full of articles looted from China and other countries?"

Second, this is one of those areas where some influential Chinese acknowledge that they could actually *benefit* from American pressure. Piracy, such a problem for foreign companies, is an even bigger problem among Chinese firms, which are currently stealing each other's brand names, copyrights, logos, trade secrets, and designs right and left. "We can use the high standards the United States wishes to impose on us to clean up our own problems in this area and promote the rule of law," acknowledges a Chinese foreign-trade official.

At the heart of this struggle is a key twenty-first-century question: If extraordinary amounts of value, information, and creativity can now be stored in various software media in the form of easily replicable digital bits, what is to stop the digital Have-Nots of the world from stealing and pirating their way into the realm of the Haves? Software piracy, incidentally, is not confined to China. More of it takes place unprosecuted right inside America's borders.

5. It's Not Just China: Here Comes the New G-7

If China is successful, it will do more than change global commerce. It will pose new challenges to the Western way of looking at the world. The China challenge will remind all concerned that history is not "over," and that the Darwinian struggle of social and economic systems continues.

With its callous disrespect for the free flow of information inside its society, China will challenge the widely held belief in the virtues and inevitability of an "information economy." With its different view of intellectual property rights and its propensity for software piracy, it will challenge the notion of a future economy where intellectual property becomes more valuable than real property.

China will challenge the growing perception that flexibility and mobility in an economy are more important than size and scale. It will, of course, challenge the relative importance the West places on individual rights and liberties. And it will challenge an article of faith at the heart of 200 years of Anglo-American economic leadership in the world: that there is a high correlation between democracy and economic success.

Contrary to the opinions of many sages of the "new economy," moreover, the rise of China will also challenge the premise that nation-states will disappear any time soon. In fact, the reemergence of China, one of the world's oldest nations (and one of the most self-conscious and most zealous about safeguarding its nationhood) is a hint that we may be in for a new era of twenty-first-century realpolitik in which nations and national economies matter very much indeed.

Such systemic differences will remain with us for a very long time. Even if the U.S.-China relationship improves, the fundamental differences will remain. They are dry tinder in a world of fiery economic, political, and military competitions. Unless they are handled with great delicacy, they could catch fire at any time.

In a world that has been moving toward increasingly globalized markets, eradication of national borders, and diminished power for the nation-state, China can be expected to buck all these trends and to encourage other emerging-market nations in a similar direction.

China, of course, is not just any country experimenting with a new development path. It is the world's most populous country, which will someday be the world's largest economy, situated at the center of the world's fastest-growing region. It represents (metaphorically, if not politically) the whole power shift now taking place in the world from West to East and from the developed countries to developing ones. It is, in Singapore Senior Minister Lee Kuan Yew's apt phrase, not just another player, but "the biggest player in the history of man."

The rise of China is among the most compelling of all the leading indicators telling us that we are moving out of an era in which first a British and then an American-led club of rich, advanced, democratic countries, whose cultures derived from Europe, enjoyed political and economic supremacy and hegemony. The era ahead is one in which wealth and power will be much more widely held and wielded. Never before in history has the world's leading economy been one in which the per-capita income and living standards were not

"The conventional expectation, frequently proclaimed by boosterish books on the Asian economic miracle, is that China's burgeoning market of new consumers will solve the global system's fundamental problem of overcapacity—mopping up the surpluses of industrial goods. This assumption is an illusion. If China succeeds in its plans, it has the capacity to become a nightmare for the global system, a dynamic cornucopia of low-cost output that wrecks other economies and destabilizes the multinational regime."

—WILLIAM GREIDER
ONE WORLD, READY OR NOT

also world leading. Yet this is precisely the future for China, which just thirty years from now will be hugely powerful in the economic aggregate, yet still quite poor and backward on average.

For the last 200 years, world economic leaders like the United States and Britain have promoted free trade, free investment, globalization, human rights, and an open, democratic world order. These are *not* China's ideals, nor are they particularly in the geopolitical and geoeconomic interests of a country that is still poor and backward.

We can expect to see China using its ever-growing economic clout (coupled to some degree with its military strength) as a bargaining tool to get what it wants from the rest of the world. Foreigners have less leverage than we think with the Chinese, and they have more with us than we know or understand. The Chinese have convinced themselves that if they can't get what they want from America, they can get it from Europe and Japan. And if they can't get it there, they can do without.

If there still is a "G-7" grouping of the world's leading economies three decades from now, current members like Canada, Italy, Britain, and France will no longer qualify for this elite club. China would be number one in this G-7 hierarchy of the future, followed by the United States and Japan. Germany will still be on the list, and the rest will be made up of some combination from among India, Indonesia, Brazil, Mexico, a unified Korea, and Russia. Although today more than half of total economic output is generated by the rich industrialized countries, the World Bank estimates that by 2020 some two-thirds of total output will be from countries that are not today considered rich or developed. And China will be in the forefront.

China, moreover, symbolizes the possibility that ancient empires and once-great civilizations can reintegrate themselves with the modern world. "The next century will belong to China, and it will become the first ancient culture to rise, fall, and rise again," notes Justin Yifu Lin, founder of the China Center for Economic Research in Beijing.[20] As a result, China may at times play a role even bigger than its enormous size would suggest in determining the shape of new global trends, politics, and institutions.

The awakening of the big Chinese dragon, together with the other dragon economies of Asia, whose dynamism and

The estimates may vary but the end result is the same: In 1992, World Bank economists helped set off the China investment boom by arguing that China's economy was already bigger than those of Germany and Japan and that, should then-current American and Chinese growth rates stay roughly the same, Chinese total output would exceed American total output in 11 years. In 1996, the World Bank issued a revised estimate: not only was the Chinese economy 25 percent smaller than earlier estimates, the country would take 20 years longer to become the world's largest economy.

vibrancy are already economic legends of the late twentieth century, is a turning point in modern history. Asia, with China at last having reclaimed its historic place at the continent's heart, may well shape the next century much as the rise of the United States shaped the one we are leaving. But this process does not fit neatly into the world order as it has been developing. In many ways, it is at odds with recent developments. It is therefore necessary for American leaders, strategists, and decision makers—and ultimately the American people—to prepare for a roller-coaster ride ahead.

6. Eating Big Macs Doesn't Make It McChina

The explosion of entrepreneurial energy all over China and the promise of the booming China market of the early nineties brought with them a corollary, in the view of most Americans: China was eager to become as fully market oriented as any other emerging country. The Western news media fueled that notion by running breathless stories of newly minted millionaires swilling cognac by the gallon and dancing the night away at trendy discos. Perhaps it should be no surprise, therefore, that one of the factors most aggravating the relationship at present is the American side's intense disappointment that the Chinese are not turning out to be the full-tilt, hard-charging privatizers, protocapitalists, and supply-side wannabes we imagined they would become.

In a 1994 cover story, *Business Week* framed the issue this way: "China: Will a Freer Economy Lead to Social and Political Reform? There Are Signs That It Is Starting to Happen."[21] But two years later, in another cover story, the same magazine recognized that the earlier analysis looked deeply flawed:

> After decades of hostility and conflict [Americans had hoped] China would open to the outside world and embrace at least some Western values. Businesses would be able to tap the Middle Kingdom's vast market, creating wealth at home and in China. Gradually, as the Chinese tasted the fruits of economic progress, they would obtain greater political freedom, easing both the Communist Party's iron grip and any possible threats from the People's Liberation Army.[22]

"When you introduce Western concepts into China, be it Christianity, Marxist-Leninism, or free markets, in many cases you are going to get something that is unrecognizable coming out the other end. You may have wishful thinking about what you want China to be, but you may also end up 'jilted' or disappointed."

—JAMES R. LILLY
FORMER U.S.
AMBASSADOR TO CHINA

But that was not the process reporters in the field saw happening by 1996. The magazine ticked off the assumptions of the past and contrasted them to the realities of the present. A small sample suffices to illustrate the dissonance Americans were finding between the path Western economic and political theory would have China take, and the very different path it was actually on:

Assumption: With market forces set loose, China's socialist economy would crumble. Privatized companies would replace the state-owned sector. Foreign companies would be able to enter the market aggressively, selling their export products profitably and creating jobs at home.

Reality: China is privatizing little while keeping its old State-Owned Enterprise behemoths afloat. Rather than using foreign investment to promote competition and efficiency, Beijing is actively pushing industrial policies that pressure foreign companies to transfer technology and manufacture locally—thus encouraging the export of manufacturing jobs from the United States to China.

Assumption: Economic reform in China would lead directly to political liberalization.

Reality: The Chinese are using new opportunities opened up by economic reform to focus on "getting rich rather than on politics." The Communist Party "remains in control as it cracks down on dissent and the media."

Business Week's conclusion: "Yes, it's a huge market. But it's also emerging as a key competitor, demanding Western technology and building its own sophisticated industries. Meanwhile, the military is rattling its saber, and Beijing's political grip remains tight." In short, it was time to "rethink China."

For most of the last twenty years, since Deng Xiaoping began implementing his post-Mao reforms, Western pundits have referred hopefully to what the Chinese are doing as constituting some kind of frontier, gold rush–style "capitalism." Indeed, when Deng Xiaoping died, the epitaphlike subhead under the main news headline announcing his death said, "Chose Capitalism."[23] But it was not capitalism Deng chose. Deng himself was clear on this; during his 1992 southern tour he reportedly said: "A market economy is not capitalism, because there are markets under socialism, too."[24]

Nor was it just a semantic anomaly that the Chinese

themselves refused to call the new economic system they were building a capitalist one. They know perfectly well what capitalism is. They opposed it zealously for fifty years. In the last two decades, they have studied it, in almost all its variants, in order to see what they could appropriate or learn for the cause of China's development and modernization.

At the senior level of officialdom, however, and even in think tanks and liberal freethinking circles, the Chinese have never wavered in their belief that unbridled, Adam Smith–style capitalism is *not* what their country needs now. They have been completely candid with the outside world, announcing over and over again to all who would listen that China is trying to build "socialism with Chinese characteristics"—a new system that tries to combine institutions of socialism with elements of the marketplace.

China will continue for many years to move further toward the marketplace in its economic system and toward greater elements of consumerism and democracy in its culture and politics. More middle-class consumers will eat more Kentucky Fried Chicken and Big Macs. More Chinese youth will watch MTV on technically illegal satellite dishes. More will surf the millions of World Wide Web sites the Beijing authorities have not tried to block—and many will find their way onto the handful that have been forbidden. More overnight millionaires will be minted as privatized businesses grow and go public in burgeoning financial markets. But no matter how many Big Macs are eaten, no matter how many hours of MTV are watched, no matter how much illicit democratic argument seeps in from Chinese dissidents abroad, the Chinese political economy will not end up where many American observers (and a few Chinese liberals) hope or expect it will.

7. Toward the "Confucian Social Market"

If not laissez-faire capitalism, then what? At bottom, China is creating a fundamentally new political-economic paradigm that is neither a traditional statist-Marxist-Maoist model, nor a liberal-democratic-capitalist market model. Call it a third road, market socialism, or state corporatism. Or call it by our favored label: the Confucian social market.

By "Confucian" we mean that China will draw much

The Wild East: "The West is assuming [China] is going to be capitalist. Now, that's a very big leap in faith. I'd say that that's probably not going to be the case at all. I think it's going to move to a system of even more personal connections and a 'Wild West' style of cutting deals than ever before."

—ROBERT BROADFOOT
 MANAGING DIRECTOR
 POLITICAL & ECONOMIC
 CONSULTANCY, LTD.

from other Asian governments that are highly authoritarian with respect to certain basic political issues and that actively mold the morals and institutions of the citizenry. Lee Kuan Yew's Singapore is, of course, the most notable model—one often praised by Deng Xiaoping as far preferable to the chaos of laissez-faire Hong Kong. Lee and his colleagues have actively sought to resurrect Confucius and his teachings on stability and order as relevant guidelines for Asia twenty-five centuries later. Some other Confucianist values are a high-quality bureaucracy, a strong educational system, and a historically based sense of national and cultural pride. Reliance on family rather than on government largesse is another hallmark of the Confucian approach.[25] The Confucianism of the next century may reclaim aspects of the philosophy now buried by those using it in the name of strict obedience, hierarchy, and social order. The tradition also includes rule by moral example and such teachings as "Without the trust of the people, no government can stand."[26]

"Social market" refers to Germany's description of its own political economy as a system in which the state leads certain core areas of society, while the market leads others. Although coined in Germany, the phrase could apply to political-economic philosophy throughout the European Union and Scandinavia, and in some of the emerging economies of Eastern Europe. In all these countries the state owns considerable portions of industry directly, employs very large numbers of people, takes responsibility for extensive social welfare systems, sets parameters for private business, and determines economic ground rules in ways that make America's own problem with governmental "over-regulation" seem trivial by comparison.

Yet while the European economies lack the dynamism and verve of the more laissez-faire Anglo-American model, they are more able to look after social problems and intervene based on their social agendas than are the more purely based market economies. In that, China sees virtue. "If you study the rise of Germany, France, and Holland many years ago, there are long periods of time when it is very hard to tell what is public and what is private," says Hu Deping. Hu, the head of an organization devoted to entrepreneurship, is the son of a former Communist Party leader and reformer, Hu Yaobang. Even in modern Europe, Hu Deping notes, there have been times when state-owned industry has represented a higher percentage of total economic output than it does in China today. "If you look at examples all over the world, we can see there is no one way to manage a market economy. So it is only logical that China will incorporate the market in its own way."

That is always the view, even from reformers and liberal-leaning thinkers like Hu: *incorporate* the market; *use* the market; *allow* the market to work in some areas. But never resign the key functions of the state to the market alone. No shock therapy for China. No radical privatization. No sudden love affair with Adam Smith.

One way or another, the Chinese state will be retaining most of its powers for a very long time. Power is very gradually devolving to regions, localities, and, ultimately, the marketplace and the private sector. But the process is slow and gradual. For some time to come, the dominant form of the economy will be governmental agencies and entities—especially local governments—slowly commercializing themselves, not a large-scale private enterprise boom welling up from below.

When the current leadership transition is finally over, China will have settled on a system that is more democratic than any it has known in the past, yet that still remains far more authoritarian and opaque than anything Westerners would recognize as truly democratic. In economic terms, the system of the future will be more decentralized, privatized, and entrepreneurial than any socialist state of the twentieth century. But agencies of state power—national, regional, and local—will still play a very powerful agenda-setting role. They will still have at their disposal an extensive web of control mechanisms, including industrial and trade policy tools that advocates of big government the world over have favored from the birth of European social democracy, through the heyday of John Maynard Keynes and the post–World War II statist economies of Europe and Japan.

"In the next twenty-five years, I believe that China will do to Japan what the United States did to Great Britain in the last century."

—ANTOINE VAN AGTMAEL WORLD BANK

These days, Western economists tend to disparage such policy interventions as distortions of free trade that are also ineffective and domestically anticompetitive. But even as they begin to disappear from North America and Europe—and even as the Japanese begin to deregulate in earnest—government planning and interventionism will remain central pillars of the Chinese economy.

8. "China Could Be Like Japan on Steroids"

As we have argued, a U.S.-China cold war will be less all-encompassing and less virulent than the U.S.-Soviet superpower rivalry of the last half century. Perhaps, a U.S.-China conflict might more likely resemble our recent trade conflict with Japan.

Like Japan in the past, China already has world-leading growth rates and exploding trade surpluses. And like Japan, too, Beijing encourages or at least condones nationalist-protectionist-mercantilist practices that go against the grain of Washington's vision of open markets, free trade, and free investment. But more like the former Soviet Union—and most emphatically unlike Japan in the 1980s—China is not to be trifled with militarily or politically.

Dealing with China in the next thirty years, therefore, could be a bit like dealing with a combination of the Soviet Union *and* Japan over the last thirty years. Japan is the more relevant comparison, however. It is the only great power of modern times to become a serious all-around economic competitor to the United States and to do so on the strength of an economic system at odds with the American practice of capitalism. And China is headed into similar terrain.

The clash of the American and Japanese models led to the past twenty-five years of bilateral trade wars, currency wars, auto wars, semiconductor wars, and many other kinds of business wars. True, there was no shooting war, but then, there hardly could have been, given Japan's lack of military power. Yet the relationship between the United States and Japan has been tantamount to a *cold economic war,* one that has only recently begun to show signs of abating. (One reason the U.S.-Japan cold economic war is dying down is the rise of China and the growing sense in Washington that the United States has much more to fear from China than from Japan.)

Consider, for a moment, just how powerful the Japanese challenge to American business has been in recent years, and how widespread the resulting economic and political dislocation—including all the Japan-bashing, alarmism, protectionist legislation, and high-level Washington debate of the 1980s. Now consider that

- China is destined to become a bigger economy in aggre-

China's destiny as seen from Japan:
"While I am not an alarmist over China, I believe that in the bottoms of their hearts, the Chinese regard themselves as the true leaders of Asia. For centuries, China was the 'middle kingdom.' During periods of strength, it exercised some kind of loose hegemony over its neighbors. The Chinese today believe that since the collapse of the Soviet Union, China is the only country in Asia or the world that can deal with the United States as an equal. And this results in Chinese thinking that China eventually needs to be equally strong as the United States."

—Koichi Kato
  Secretary general,
  Liberal Democratic
  Party (Japan)

gate than Japan, with a bigger long-term trade imbalance with the United States and other countries;

- China already has the military and political clout Japan has always lacked. The safety net that always lay beneath the surface of U.S.-Japanese trade acrimony—the military security agreement and other explicitly defined mutual interests—is, as yet, entirely lacking in the Sino-American relationship.

- No one in China's political leadership class is arguing for a close interdependency with the United States, as the mainstream of Japan's Liberal Democratic Party always did, at least on certain matters. Beijing does not have what the Japanese LDP bosses could always count on: a U.S. State Department ready to moderate the influence of American trade Hawks with overriding arguments about global political strategy.

- American political and business attitudes are not as open and expansive as they were when Japan was a rising economic superpower. Politicians know how trade deficits can bite. Japan, Inc., first ate into the soft underbelly of the American economy at a time when much of American business was too fat and happy to notice. China has no such opportunity. Americans are already ringing alarm bells.

- China's integration with world markets and the global economy has been likened to a gorilla picking up a Stradivarius. He is likelier to smash it, even if only by accident, than immediately to figure out how to play it. This was and is a danger with Japan's lack of transparency as well. World financial markets are still nervous about the Japanese banking system, seven years into its crisis. But Japan has at least become translucent to outsiders. China remains utterly opaque on key matters foreigners need to know to assess risk and investment allocations. With China more and more important in world commodities and financial markets, but not yet fully integrated in terms of regulation, disclosure, and risk control, the chance of an "accident" is magnified.

- Japan at least espoused many of the same goals as the United States and actively sought to be accepted by the West as a "normal" member of the club of advanced democracies. China does not espouse those goals nor does it seek such acceptance, so the West has much less leverage than in dealing with Japan.

Not the yen but the yuan: "Looking at least 50 years ahead, it is not impossible that the Chinese yuan will topple the dollar as the world's leading currency."

—*THE ECONOMIST*

In sum, China's values, belief systems, and economic forms diverge from the United States' much more than even the Japanese do. No wonder analysts, such as Gerald Segal at London's International Institute of Strategic Studies, say, "China is even scarier than Japan."[27] Adds a former U.S. trade official, "China in 2010 could look like Japan of 1988 on steroids." That fear may be overstated. But then again, most fears of the unknown are.

Prophetic words? "We are creating a competitor of extreme proportions," argues a senior U.S. official. "But we don't have the tools to deal with that threat."

9. A Different Kind of "World's Largest Economy"

Japan's rise a decade ago came so fast and furious that Americans began to fear becoming an economic colony of Japan. From trophy real estate to U.S. government bonds, Japanese companies grabbed a big, disproportionate, and sometimes alarming share of American markets. Some Japanese businesspeople even began to act like neocolonialists, talking of buying California to reduce America's debts and setting up factories to take advantage of cheap American labor.

As Washington became increasingly critical of closed Japanese markets, Tokyo's negotiators eventually began to respond in kind. During the Structural Impediments Initiative, the American side griped about objectionable Japanese trade practices, while the Japanese side chastised Americans for high budget deficits and low high-school test scores.

Could something similar happen with China? Trend spotter John Naisbitt thinks so. He says there may come a day when an economically empowered China threatens "to withhold Most Favored Nation status from the United States unless it does something about the slums in our big urban centers (or improves its SAT scores!)."[28]

We have already started to see Beijing use some of these tactics, at least in its rhetoric. Taking a cue from the State Department's annual review of objectionable human rights practices, the Chinese now issue similar reviews of human rights in America, criticizing instances of racial discrimination and the poverty and squalor of America's underclass. A few other signs may seem familiar to those who recall the American alarm about Japan in the 1980s: Chinese investors showing up prominently in the U.S. bond market (but nowhere near as forcefully as the Japanese), buying a few chunks of real estate (but often low-end and middle-market motels, not yet the trophies that captured the Japanese fancy), and even trying to buy a decommissioned naval facility in California to use as a home port for transpacific trade. The latter has aroused the concern of many citizens, but nothing like the outrage that was expressed when Japanese companies bought Pebble Beach and Columbia Pictures.

China is not likely to induce the kind of economic fear and trembling Japan did in the 1980s—at least not for a very long time. Back then, Japan was coming on so strong that it seemed likely to close in on the United States in total economic output by the year 2000, with a population only *half* America's. Even today, after the many Japanese setbacks and strong American gains of the 1990s, Japan's per capita economic output is greater than America's, and average wages are higher by some measures as well.

By contrast, if and when China surpasses the U.S. economy in total output (and we think this is at least three decades away, not in the next decade as some economists have forecast), that output will be produced by a population five times greater than America's. Chinese workers will certainly have moved up the living-standard ladder—from the 4 cents they are paid today for every dollar an American worker earns, to about 20 cents on the American dollar.

These differences matter a great deal. Being the largest economy in the world will certainly give China enormous political and trading clout. It will also give China the resources to make the vast investments it needs in infrastructure and communications, as well as to pursue some higher-end economic activities in technology and advanced manufacturing. On average, however, China will remain a backward and inefficient economy well into the next century. China will expand its pockets of excellence (it already has some now). But without a high-tech, high-quality, high-output, high-productivity base like that Japan enjoyed in the 1980s, China will not easily become supercompetitive in the high-value-added businesses and product lines now dominated globally by American, Japanese, and European companies.

What's more, since China is not yet even close to embracing the knowledge economy, the gap created by the difference between American living standards and China's may

The global impact:
What happens when China contributes millions of workers to the global labor market? "A colossal depressive force upon the real wages in the richer countries," says Paul Kennedy, a Yale history professor who wrote the 1980s bestseller *The Rise and Fall of Great Powers*. "Wages may tumble in some economic sectors by as much as 50 percent over the next two or three decades."

actually widen. Even given the ineluctable logic of compounding high growth rates, China, with its "brawn-based" economy, may be a long way from competing with the West on an across-the-board basis in the "brain-intensive" economy. And if China's underlying growth rates continue to moderate, the gap will widen further.

It is not our intention to dismiss China as an economic competitor. For example, many experts believe that dominance of the semiconductor memory chip business has already begun to migrate to China. The Chinese may replace the Koreans as the world leaders in this field over the next decade. (The Koreans, of course, dethroned the Japanese, and the Japanese took the business away from the Americans.) Similarly, in the course of building up a big domestic automobile industry, China may produce some successful low-cost export models that make it a major global force in that business. In fields from steel manufacture to cellular phones, the size and scale of the domestic Chinese market should enable Chinese companies (or joint-venture companies with foreign partners) to become world-class competitors. But this will happen only in selected industries and with certain kinds of globally traded products.

Even when China is "the world's biggest economy" thirty-plus years from now, most of its economic activity will be taken up with feeding itself, building its own infrastructure, sourcing the energy to keep this huge machine running, and providing what will then be a billion and a half people with modestly improved housing and a modicum of consumer goods.

Most rising powers in modern history (Spain, Holland, Britain, the United States) have been keenly interested in extending their economic reach all over the globe. But China is comparatively uninterested in global issues that don't have a specific bottom line for Chinese interests. Almost all of China's efforts to throw its weight around come when vital Chinese interests are perceived to be at stake *close to home,* such as in Taiwan or Tibet.

"China is too diverse and too focused on its internal development to carry out highly targeted export campaigns such as Japan used in the past years," says Victor Fung, who ran Prudential Asia and heads the Hong Kong Trade Development Council. In Japan, economic planners decided to develop an excellent automobile industry and to make auto-

There's no choice but to notice: "China is an existential threat. They're just so damn big."
—JONATHAN POLLACK
RAND CORPORATION

mobiles a major export item. In China, the automobile industry will develop to serve domestic transportation needs, and only as a secondary goal will it become an export business—maybe.

"We are too busy with our own internal challenges to threaten other countries economically or militarily," says Zhang Haoruo, who became head of the powerful State Commission on Economic Restructuring after serving as governor of Sichuan province and minister of internal trade. And if China masters those challenges, what then? "I wish I could say our current agenda will take us only a few years to solve. But realistically, China will be occupied with its internal domestic reforms for half a century."

What if China fails or faces grave difficulties domestically? Doesn't history show that leaders frequently try to shift attention from domestic problems with nationalism and aggression across borders? "Such a habit is really not in our culture," says Zhang. To a large degree he is correct. But past performance is no guarantee of future trends. That is one of many compelling reasons why it is in the West's interests to help China succeed economically.

China will be constrained for decades by its relentless focus on the huge and knotty problems it faces domestically. Bringing the vast peasantry out of its backwardness, modernizing the national infrastructure, moving the coastal prosperity inland and to the hinterland, coping with the side effects of globalization—these are China's highest-priority goals at the twentieth century's end. All are seemingly inward-looking; none inherently threaten others. Nevertheless, as China accumulates economic and other kinds of power, there will inevitably be concern in many quarters.

CHAPTER 5

Threat or Challenge?

Of Divas, Tenors, and Peking Opera

"Great Powers tend to arrive on the stage of history like great opera divas, commanding and demanding the attention of everyone in the theater," observes Fareed Zakaria, the managing editor of *Foreign Affairs*. Zakaria writes from his post at the Council on Foreign Relations in New York, an institution that is evolving out of the Cold War–industrial age mentality, but which (for good reason) is not yet about to forget the understanding of power and realpolitik gained through the epoch-defining conflicts and tragedies of the twentieth century. And in Zakaria's view, "The defining international political event of this era is the rise of China to world power."

Unfortunately, the world has had a poor history of accommodating new "divas." No accepted procedures exist for adapting to the necessary rearrangements of wealth and power. Over the last 500 years, most new great powers have claimed their place in the world's hierarchy to the accompaniment of revolution, armed conflict, or even all-out global war.

As economists, historians, foreign-policy specialists, and journalists have watched China's rise in the 1990s, they have invoked ominous parallels with Bismarck's Germany and Europe between the wars. Even more ominously, they talk of analogies to Hitler's Germany and imperial Japan. The

Hawkish spin is that China is an aggressive power whose drive for dominance in Asia could trigger the next world war. Unconsciously echoing Lenin, Hawks suggest that China, as a latecomer to the feast of great powers, is *compelled* to be aggressive to elbow those already at the table out of the way. Engagers take a different tack, reminding those who will listen that Europe and America handled the rise of Germany and Japan poorly and that the world should not make the same mistake with China.

Have we, in the latter part of the twentieth century, become more "reasonable" about sharing world power with rising countries? The reascendancy of Germany and Japan as great powers after World War II was largely a peaceful process and is cited by some as cause for optimism in this regard. Unfortunately, the experience cannot be generalized to mean that the modern world has found a way to welcome new powers into its bosom without military conflict. In fact, the circumstances were entirely unique.

For reasons specific to Cold War strategy, the United States actually nurtured postwar Japan and Germany economically—even when doing so posed a competitive threat to American economic interests—in order to create regional bulwarks against the perceived threat of Communism, not to mention markets for American goods and services during the long postwar expansion. As a victor in World War II, the United States also neutered Japan and Germany militarily, just to be sure these reascendant powers posed no future military threat.

The truth is that in the second half of the twentieth century American policymakers have had to deal with competitors and rivals that were *either* strong economically (Japan, Germany, and others), *or* strong in a political-military sense (the former Soviet Union). But as the first new superpower of the twenty-first century, China will hold both types of power assets to some significant degree.

Compared to Japan and Germany in their miracle growth years, China's economy is just as dynamic. But it will be bigger in aggregate and may therefore make a much bigger footprint in the overall global economy. And whereas Japan and Germany were virtual American vassal states in political, military, and strategic terms for much of the last fifty years, China is highly independent and has the capacity to become a very challenging political-military-strategic rival.

Can the rise of China be compared to the rise of Germany a century ago? "There are huge differences, but China shares with turn-of-the-century Germany the sense of wounded pride, the annoyance of a giant that has been battered and cheated by the rest of the world . . . [and] now it is undergoing an industrial revolution and arms buildup that within a decade or two will allow it to avenge these wrongs."

—NICHOLAS KRISTOFF
FORMER CHINA
CORRESPONDENT
THE NEW YORK TIMES

A contrast is presented by the former Soviet Union, which descended from economic weakness to all-out basket-case status during the Cold War. The Chinese dragon already breathes far more competitive fire than the Russians ever did. While China lacks—and currently does not desire or plan to create—client states and the weaponry necessary to project military power as the Soviets once did, it packs enough military punch to be taken seriously in the great global game, and certainly in Asia.

Thus, when we speak of China we are speaking of the rise of a new great *all-around* power—a "comprehensive" power—with its economic might matched by plenty of political clout (especially in Asia but also globally, through its United Nations veto power and other means), and military muscle (China is in the nuclear club and maintains the world's largest standing army).

If one had to forecast the future based only on the basis of the past practices of other great-nation divas, one would have little choice but to anticipate a major military clash surrounding the rise of a new power as significant as China. And that is precisely the forecast some are making. If, on the other hand, one could believe that the twenty-first century will be ordered by economic efficiency, free trade, zestful consumerism, and a borderless global market, then perhaps China could develop simply as a melodious fourth voice joining the (relatively) harmonious three tenors (North America, Europe, and Japan) already onstage. That view, the conventional wisdom until a few years ago, is still popular in some quarters, especially among proponents of the "new global economy," who think that talk of war between great nation-states is an anachronism in an era when economic power is what the competition is all about. We find this optimistic view unrealistic, but as a low-probability scenario it deserves as much weight as all the theories about how China might launch World War III.

Like all attempts to generalize about China, metaphors only go so far and are ultimately culturally constrained. China and the West share a tradition of "opera." But Peking opera differs extraordinarily from Puccini. And so, too, do the behavior, roles, and styles of the divas.

The new China is fundamentally different from the leading global powers of the last 500 years. China is inward-looking, having no need to colonize other countries to fuel its growth in the current era, even if some traditional Chinese impulses push Beijing to seek de facto political and military control over its border areas.

China is hugely populous, as everyone knows. This may make it economically strong in aggregate but poor and backward on a per capita basis. As we pointed out in chapter 4, there has never been a "world's largest economy" that was not also a world leader in per capita wealth and living standards.[1] If and when China again becomes the world's largest economy, its continued internal backwardness will make it a very different kind of actor on the global stage than Britain and the United States have been in similar world-leading roles.

The United States is also a very different kind of superpower than any that has come before. While American policy is (and should be) self-interested, its goals are set more openly and their pursuit (at least in the last quarter of this century) has been more benign than any other great power's. The United States is not trying consciously to build or maintain a wholly-owned empire, which makes it reasonably good at partnering and power sharing, as well as a genuine believer in a multipolar world.

The United States is unique in another way. It may be the first modern great power to enter a significant downward spiral, then beat the disease of decline. Because the United States is no longer a declining power (as it appeared to be through much of the 1970s and 1980s) and China is inwardly focused on its own development, it is possible to believe that America and China can design a modus vivendi based on a positive vision of a common future. This will be in contrast to the negative, zero-sum view that accompanies decline—and has historically tempted nations to go to war in defense of the status quo.

We must learn from history, but we must also be careful about making analogies that are too facile, misapplying the lessons of history—or, worse yet, drawing the wrong conclusions altogether.

The Cold War with the Soviet Union had a compelling raison d'être. One can argue with the manner in which the United States pursued its side of this conflict, but the evidence of Soviet expansionism, aggression, and subversion in every corner of the globe was incontrovertible. Although much less alarming, the cold economic war with Japan was

"We formed our joint venture in 1985. Things were very fuzzy. There was no Chinese legal system to guide us. But in an environment where you expect change, you cannot wait for things to settle. That day may not arrive for a long time. And if you wait until then you will be too late."

—LEE S. TING
VICE PRESIDENT,
HEWLETT-PACKARD ASIA PACIFIC

justifiable, or at least rationalizable, given how the Japanese economic juggernaut for a time assaulted basic American industries and threatened to destabilize the world trading order.

But China is different. It could eventually emerge as a Soviet-style geopolitical threat. As we have indicated, we doubt this is likely; in any event, Americans will have many years to wait and see if this scenario obtains. China could also come to represent a Japan-like economic threat, but as we have also indicated, this is not only far off but is offset by positive opportunities for American economic interests.

It would be tragic indeed were we to let slip a historic opportunity to engage China, benefit from a strong relationship with it—and perhaps in some modest ways even influence it in a positive direction—all because we were busy making the cold warrior's fist. As economist Robert J. Samuelson has observed, "The Cold War's moralism remains a false reference point." Vilifying the Chinese and beating our breasts may make us feel good, he says. But it is bad—even dangerous—policy. "Treating China as an implacable adversary could become self-fulfilling."[2]

The "China Threat" Reconsidered

Our belief that the United States and China can step back from a new cold war and develop a positive partnership for the future is very much conditioned on our assessment of what kind of power China is today and what kind of superpower it will become in the next century.

In our view, there is little doubt that China will be a nationalistic superpower that looks after its own national interests first. Its legitimate pursuit of those interests will pose numerous complex challenges for the United States and others. China will become neither fully democratic nor fully capitalistic at any time in the foreseeable future. Its economic, political, and military relations with other countries will be driven by a political economy, a cultural history, and a belief system sometimes at odds with our own. This will inevitably lead to differences and clashes, but these need not turn into overall antagonism or constant friction. China will be a challenge, and be seen as such. But that does not mean it must become a threat.

We believe China is mainly concerned with its own internal economic development and political order, not with expanding its empire abroad or projecting military power on a global basis. China's inward focus results from deep forces in its Confucian heritage and its long history. Zheng He, the legendary Chinese admiral of six centuries ago, had at his disposal the skills and naval technology to make China the world's leading maritime power a century before the rise of Portugal and Spain and three centuries before Holland and then Britain played that role. But China turned away from global projection of its power and remained focused on its Asian empire.

We believe that fact is more than a bit of interesting history. It reflects a pattern that will be seen again in the twenty-first century. The Chinese will generally be uninterested in *global* force projection. Inside Asia, however, China will project its power and its clout—subtly most of the time, overtly when it deems necessary. Fundamentally, however, China is likely to become a modern, responsible power, not a rogue state. There is a very strong basis to believe that if the United States embraces rather than isolates China, extensive benefits can flow to American business and the American people, including the benefit of minimizing possible long-term conflict with China.

In these assessments, as we have indicated, we differ very strongly from the Hawks of the China Threat school. But since the Hawk view has come to such prominence—and has at times threatened to become the mainstream view—we must analyze at least some of its major arguments. We have picked a few key issues to illustrate how our judgment of some tough questions about China differs significantly from the Hawks'.

The issues troubling the Hawks are almost never made up out of whole cloth. Many of the trends and incidents they cite trouble us deeply, too. It is rarely the Hawks' facts that we question. Rather, it is the interpretation of those facts, the context, the balance, and ultimately, the conclusions. With that caveat, let us consider a few of the specific arguments made by the China Threat school.

China as Military Threat to the United States

As alleged by the Hawks, China is engaged in a massive arms buildup. Militarization is said to be the central fact

Setting the record straight: "The rumor of a so-called China threat as spread by some foreigners is a complete fabrication."

—LIU HUAQING
CENTRAL MILITARY
COMMISSION, CHINA

about China today. Again and again in Hawk literature, the statement is made that China is "bound" to become America's long-term adversary. Several prominent Hawks imagine a hot war between the United States and China, initially arising over the Taiwan issue.

There is no disputing that China's annual military expenditures have been increasing lately, with the 1996 budget reportedly about 11 percent higher than the year before, and the 1997 budget 13 percent higher than 1996's.[3] Several years in a row of double-digit budget increases is part of the *official* Chinese account of their military spending; certainly, the Hawks are right that the total military budget is far higher than the paltry $9 billion officially reported by Beijing in 1996. But it is certainly not as high as the $87 billion alleged by Richard Bernstein and Ross Munro in *The Coming Conflict with China*.

Many problems get in the way of calculating a real Chinese arms budget. The Chinese don't account for military R&D in their budgets as the West does. Some of China's more advanced equipment comes in barter deals with Russia, so it doesn't "cost" anything and is therefore treated off-balance-sheet. Where and how the profits from the PLA's 20,000 civilian enterprises are recycled—or how the losses are subsidized—is a maze that even the Chinese Politburo would like to understand better. Labor costs next to nothing, so China can have a standing army almost three times the size of the U.S. armed forces at less than a tenth of the cost in salaries.

When all these cross-cultural factors are reconciled and purchasing-price parity is adjusted, Pentagon experts think the Chinese may be currently spending about $24 billion to $36 billion a year. Even if one assumes the high number of $36 billion—a figure that infuriates the Chinese as ridiculously inflated—China's budget would still be only a sliver of the U.S. military budget: about one-seventh of it.

To put that in the Asian context, China spends less on its military than Japan does. And Japan is constitutionally supposed to be a pacifist state, forbidden to maintain offensive armed forces.

Some of China's recent military spending represents catch-up after years of budget slashing inspired by Deng Xiaoping when he was trying to free up every available resource for investment in the civilian economy. All through

And don't forget the PLA, Inc.: "Today, a decade and a half into China's great economic awakening, a loose network of some 20,000 [army-affiliated] companies—a virtual PLA Inc.—operates as an integral part of the nation's military, and the People's Liberation Army has become the ultimate brand name in China."

—*INSTITUTIONAL INVESTOR*

the 1980s, China's military budget was falling in absolute terms—and nose-diving as a percentage of GDP. According to one reckoning, Chinese military expenditures have fallen from a high of 16 percent of GDP to 3 to 5 percent more recently. To the degree expenditures have edged up in absolute terms in the last three years, China is a bit like the United States, whose military budget is also starting to rise again after years of heavy post–Cold War cuts.

President Jiang Zemin, who lacks Deng Xiaoping's credibility with the army, may well find it necessary to reward commanders with the new procurement and spending programs Deng promised them would someday be the return on their years of sacrifices for the sake of the civilian economy. But the armed forces Jiang is adding to are already sharply downsized. Over the last decade and a half, the regular standing forces of the PLA have *declined,* from a high of over 4 million troops to 2.9 million. And at the Fifteenth Party Congress in September 1997, Jiang vowed to cut the total troop count by an additional 500,000.

The increased Chinese military capability may also be a defensive response to the changing regional power balance. Spending levels are rising throughout Asia as a regional arms race accelerates. Although the Hawk view sees a China that is growing economically and matching its new wealth with higher military spending, the reality is that China's spending as a percentage of the total military spending in Asia has *declined* precipitously, from 54 percent in 1980 to 34 per cent in 1994.[4]

Almost every military expert believes the PLA is extremely backward in terms of hardware. Observes scholar Robert S. Ross, an expert on China-related security issues, "The gravest danger posed by China's 1996 missile tests was their obsolescence: the missiles were so primitive that they could have veered off course and hit Taiwan."[5] Ross further argues that China's projection of power off its coast relies on "1950s and 1960s generation aircraft. While China is working to develop modern planes, its most advanced domestically-produced fighter, the F8-11, is the equivalent of a late 1960s warplane. Even this primitive plane has yet to enter fully into production."[6]

Yes, China has obtained more advanced SU-27 aircraft from Russia in barter deals that also have potentially frightening implications for Americans concerned with the possi-

Lessons in strategic thinking: "The highest realization of warfare is to attack the enemy's plans; next is to attack their alliances; next to attack their army; and the lowest is to attack their fortified cities."

—SUN TZU
THE ART OF WAR

bility of a new incarnation of the old Sino-Soviet alliance. But so far, the best of the Russian equipment is of 1970s vintage—less advanced than what the United States sells to Taiwan, and far less advanced than what Japan coproduces for its defense with the United States. Two Kilo-class submarines that China purchased from Russia in 1995 were laid up in the harbor two years later with serious problems stemming from poor maintenance. "Just buying a submarine or a destroyer or a fighter airplane doesn't mean you have the ability to use it properly," says Robert Karniol, Asia-Pacific editor for *Jane's Defense Weekly*. A news report added, "The possibility that the Russians sold China defective subs can't be ruled out."[7]

The Hawks imagine a hegemonic plan by China to rule the sea-lanes of Asia; at whim, Beijing could block the flow of oil to Japan and other countries. This is an interesting scenario, considering that China has never been a naval power. At the moment, its naval prowess is dwarfed by Japan's. It is true Beijing has recently indicated that it plans to develop a more serious blue-water naval force. Some may find cause for concern in this. Others will argue that any great power in China's position, facing the many tensions and conflicts in North and East Asia—and with nearly 40 percent of its GDP now involved in world trade—would inevitably have to move to develop a modern navy.

Military-minded Beijing watchers believe China is also moving to develop an aircraft carrier. A significant carrier group would be absolutely necessary to control Asia's sea-lanes. But developing and outfitting even a single 1970s-vintage aircraft carrier is a ten- to fifteen-year undertaking. And developing a carrier *group* is a twenty- to twenty-five-year project. Such time horizons allow cooler-headed experts—while not dismissing China's potential to destabilize Asia militarily in the near term—to believe that the United States has the luxury of a decade or two to observe how China progresses and modernizes before determining if we need to treat it as a long-term adversary.

China's occasional use of force—such as the provocative live-artillery tests near Taiwan, and its seizures of disputed islands (discussed below), obviously discomfit its neighbors, who have to live near this sometimes unpredictable and increasingly powerful country. But for those of us far away, trying to understand the long-term implications of these

China's ambition to build a blue-water navy is running into obstacles. China sources so many different components from different countries that there is poor integration. "Even the newest destroyer, the Luhu class, must be a maintainer's nightmare. It is equipped with Chinese-made 100 mm guns, French surface-to-air missiles, Italian torpedoes and U.S. engines."

—JOHN DOWNING
  INTERNATIONAL INSTITUTE
  OF STRATEGIC STUDIES,
  LONDON

force projections, it is important to remember that *every* case of Chinese projection of military power to date, disturbing as it may be, has involved disputed territory, border areas, and what China perceives to be its strategic interests of security and territorial integrity along its borders. We may disagree with Beijing's perceptions of the level of threat to its national security; we may not like to see the use of force in any case. But it is important to recognize that every such activity has been very specifically directed. None has spilled into wider conflict.

The Hawks like to play a game of straight-line extrapolation. These suggest that if China continues its current economic growth and military spending patterns year after year into the distant future, it will become a bigger economy than the United States and will support a bigger military. Such straight-line extrapolations are almost always unsustainable, however.

The Hawks are probably right that at least some strategic thinkers in China envision, over the long term, trying to edge the U.S. military out of the Asian-Pacific region. The Hawks are also right to argue that the American fleet and other armed forces ought to plan to stay in Asia, as they represent a critical piece of the balance of power that provides some constraints on China's most dangerous tendencies. But *right now there is no active campaign by Beijing to oust the United States from Asia.* Indeed, many experts believe that despite occasional veiled swipes from Beijing at "outside forces" that should leave Asia, mainstream Chinese strategic doctrine favors a continued U.S. presence at least for the next decade or so, as a check on Japan's remilitarization and other trends Beijing finds dangerous. The role of American military forces will be a major issue of the long-term future, but it is not currently a significant problem in U.S.-China relations.

The United States is going to continue developing its formidable military prowess and continue spending on the most advanced weapons systems imaginable. We don't need the bogeyman of an institutionalized Chinese threat to stir such spending. The many possible dangers in today's world, including the small risk that China will turn into a rogue nation and threaten its Asian neighbors or the West with its nuclear capabilities, are enough to keep Washington focused on this course.

Given the extraordinary American strengths in high-tech

Newt to Beijing: "You're not the enemy after all": After his March 1997 visit to China, Newt Gingrich said, "I don't think people should exaggerate either the size of the Chinese market, the threat of Chinese economic growth, or the size of the Chinese military. It will be many, many, many years before China is a first-class military power or a world economic power."

warfare and the related power-projection mechanisms, the reality is that the world has probably never been so thoroughly dominated militarily by a single nation. China's increases in arms spending are worth watching, to be sure, but they represent the efforts of a 1950s military force to get itself into the 1970s. American military R&D, on the other hand, represents the development of the definitive military capability of the early twenty-first century. We feel confident in predicting that even in the 2010–2025 period, there will be no comparison between China's global military reach and capability and America's.

"The United States will not be able to force the PRC to spend itself into bankruptcy in a competitive arms race. Unlike Gorbachev's economically imploding Soviet Union, Jiang Zemin's China is growing at a 10 percent annual rate. And given the fact that the United States and Europe are no longer the world's center of economic gravity— the bulk of the PRC's trade and investment is within Asia—the cold reality is that the United States cannot isolate China economically."

—JAMES SHINN
   WEAVING THE NET

True, China is a nuclear power and, as the Hawks like to point out, its nuclear warheads are now the only ones pointed at the United States. However, while a handful of Chinese missiles have the range to reach our western coast, the Chinese nuclear missile program is not the major area of Beijing's arms buildup. Very few military experts believe that China now, or even in several years' time, would present an aggressive threat that could not be adequately checked by American defensive technology.

"It is only a matter of decades before China becomes the other military superpower on earth," runs one Hawk argument, "so it's best to prepare now." But, retorts Owen Harries, editor of the *National Interest,* in a well-reasoned article refuting the Hawk case, "a matter of decades is a long time in politics. By the time those decades have passed, the United States itself will have made further vast technological advances."[8] The world will be a very different place. And we will all have a much clearer idea of China's intentions. If China emerges as the kind of threat the Hawks have warned of, there will be plenty of time to prepare.

China Has Declared the United States Its Enemy

Bernstein and Munro cite ominous comments from senior Chinese military men who believe the United States is China's enemy. Their book opens with this particularly alarming comment by Lieutenant General Mi Zhenyu: "It will be absolutely necessary that we quietly nurse our sense of vengeance. . . . We must conceal our abilities and bide our time" until some presumed day of reckoning with America in the future.[9]

But the fact that some people think this does not make it

official policy. In this era of increasingly diverse voices, other influential Chinese thinkers and interest groups have different views. We don't always hear them in this country—indeed, we often drown them out with our "simplistic neo-containment strategy," as Harvard professor Alastair Johnston puts it.[10] Many Chinese we know have actively worked behind the scenes in facilitating their country's increasing involvement in international norms and institutions. These involvements have to some degree constrained (and arguably even moderated) the Chinese impulse toward aggressive behavior.

Moreover, most of the Chinese who believe the United States is their enemy do not start by designing a strategic plan for Chinese power and then concluding it would be a good idea to challenge America. Rather, they conclude that America is hostile because of what they see as U.S. efforts to do China harm in recent years. Their thinking is reactive, not proactive. Widespread as it may be—after all, Hawks are ascendant in both countries—it is subject to change if American policy toward China becomes more constructive.

China as an Expansionist Power in Asia

Another article of faith among Hawks is that even if China does not directly threaten American military strength now, Beijing is an irresponsible, adventurist military power, eager to dominate Asia. Already, it is said to be more and more intimidating toward its Asian neighbors. According to the Hawks, China seeks "hegemony"—an ironic play on the Marxist term for dominance, which was Beijing's code word for Soviet intentions in the 1970s. The very process of seeking hegemony in Asia will bring China into conflict with American interests there. The conclusion is that if the United States doesn't contain China, China will eventually dominate Asia and, by so doing, threaten America's long-term global interests.

If the Hawks define Chinese "hegemony" to mean that China is going to become the heart and soul of Asian economics, with many neighboring countries bending to its wishes because of its economic power (as countries all over the globe bend now to American interests), then they had better get used to it, because this is likely to be the case over the next twenty-five to fifty years. If the Hawks have in mind

Look who's watching whom: In the 1996 edition of their annual defense white paper, the Japanese downgraded Russia as a security threat and added a paragraph that for the first time put China on the "watch" list.

that China's very public flexing of its military muscles in the Taiwan Strait and South China Sea is meant to deter others from challenging China's self-defined sovereignty, they have a point. But if the Hawks envision a militarily expansive China bent on making Asian conquests, then the evidence for such a future trend is thin.

China's recent threats and provocations against Taiwan, as well as its military intervention and subsequent "occupation" of Tibet, are often cited. Of course, Chinese policy in both cases is anything but new. The determination to reincorporate Taiwan is almost fifty years old; the "liberation" of Tibet took place forty years ago. China's claim to sovereignty over these areas and its assertion that these are internal and not international matters are persuasive to many independent-minded Westerners.

The next most often cited evidence of China's military provocativeness is its claims to the contested Paracel (Xisha) and Spratly (Nansha) islands, and its occasional use of military force to assert its sovereignty over these islands against counterclaims by Vietnam, the Philippines, Malaysia, and others. In 1974, even when China was still nominally allied with North Vietnam, it seized one of the Paracels and dislodged North Vietnamese troops in a minor skirmish. In 1988, sparks flew between Chinese and Vietnamese forces again over the Paracels.

Then, in 1995, the Chinese erected a reconnaissance station on the aptly named Mischief Reef in the Spratlys, also claimed by the Philippines. Tipped off by a fisherman (and not, interestingly, by intelligence reports from the United States), Manila reacted with shock and indignation: "We are a David in front of a Goliath. Only this David doesn't even have a slingshot," said Philippines Chief Advisor General José Almonte.

When Manila formally protested, China dispatched a naval group to back up its claim. China also surprised the members of ASEAN (the Association of Southeast Asian Nations) by unilaterally asserting its sovereignty over the Spratlys. That caused deep consternation in Southeast Asian capitals and was met by a rare collective ASEAN response, rejecting China's approach and calling for negotiations. China's actions in the South China Sea are widely seen in Asian capitals as a clear indication of Beijing's long-term intentions. "The course of the dispute can be considered an

The Asian perspective: "China has been around here for 3,000 years," an Asian elder statesman told *New York Times* columnist Thomas Friedman. "The United States has been out here in Asia for about 50 years. We figure you're maybe good for another 20 years. But after that you'll be gone, and we'll be left here alone with China. We can't afford a confrontation."

indication of trends in regional relationships in the post–Cold War era," said Mark Valencia of the East-West Center in Honolulu. "Will China be a cooperative, benign neighbor, as it claims, or will it seek to dominate?"[11]

Actual legal claims to the islands involve a welter of confusing and ambiguous historical facts, documents, agreements, surveys, and charts. China essentially claims all of both the Spratlys and the Paracels, although it has been willing to participate in discussions and negotiations with its Southeast Asian neighbors. Never mentioned by Hawks is the fact that Taiwan generally concurs with Chinese claims that these islands are, in fact, Chinese territory. (Indeed, Taipei agrees in principle with Beijing on most Chinese territorial issues.)

There are important long-term issues of possible offshore oil and control of sea-lanes. But much of the argument over these particular islands is more symbolic than strategically consequential. It is part of the give-and-take of negotiating the new order in Southeast Asia—and all claimants understand it as such. The Hawks would like Americans to deem the fall of an obscure atoll in the Spratlys the moral equivalent of Hitler's annexation of the Sudetenland. But the Spratlys are not likely to become that type of question. Some are underwater much of the time, and none is big enough to support naval operations and the deployments necessary to defend the islands. "The military reality of the Spratly Islands is that they are easy to occupy but difficult to hold," notes one commentator. "Defending them would drain, not enhance, China's power projection capability."[12]

On a few occasions, China has shown a willingness to let might make right and to cling to the proposition that possession is nine-tenths of the law. However, these island seizures are far from the active, aggressive expansionism the Hawks portray. China sits idly by every day of the year while Vietnam occupies several of the Spratlys. Even in all the conflict over Taiwan, China never bothered to challenge Taiwan's occupation of the largest island in the Spratly chain. Nor has it shown upset over Malaysian construction of tourist facilities on another.

Make money *and* war? Twenty percent of the tanks Iraq lost in the Gulf War in 1991 were Chinese.

Southeast Asian political leaders are rightly nervous about what China will do next. "China is like an infection in the Spratlys," says a Philippine naval officer. "We have to develop enough antibodies to check the infection."[13] Through

ASEAN, quiet diplomacy is having at least some impact on keeping the Chinese from making another island grab. In March 1997, for example, when Vietnam protested the erection of a Chinese oil rig in disputed waters, negotiations, rather than military action, ensued. In May of that year, when the Philippine government protested China's activities on another small disputed island, China pulled down the hut that had caused the controversy. Such negotiation and cooperation may not last. But these indicators are just some of the small, daily signs from the great body of China's behavior toward its neighbors that suggest at least an inclination to become a reasonably responsible, normal superpower.

That the Chinese are not so weak and prickly that they feel compelled to respond militarily to every provocation against their claimed territory was confirmed again by the case of the Diaoyu (Senkaku) Islands. These specks of Pacific sand are claimed by both China and Japan. (Taipei sides with Beijing on this issue as well, and is even more vigorous in pursuing it.) In 1996, a small group of Japanese rightists erected a hut and a Japanese flag on one of the islands. This bid to claim Japanese sovereignty flew in the face of a joint agreement to preserve the status quo while Tokyo-Beijing negotiations worked toward a permanent settlement.

One can imagine an extremely energized and enraged Chinese response to what must have seemed a provocative action by much-despised Japanese rightists and militarists. In the past, volcanoes of Chinese anger have spewed forth over the way Japanese atrocities in China during World War II are depicted in Japanese school texts. To say China is extremely sensitive to (and critical of) Japan's actions toward it would be one of the great understatements of the second half of the twentieth century.

The Chinese quickly denounced the incident in the Diaoyus, which (unlike past, government-manufactured campaigns against foreigners) touched a deep nationalist nerve at the grassroots. In this situation, Chinese students and others were ready to march on Japanese diplomatic facilities and Japanese-owned stores and businesses. The prairie fire spread quickly to Hong Kong (where a man died accidentally in an emotional demonstration) as well as to Taiwan (where parliamentarians actually called for Taiwan to be ready to go to war with Japan).

China could have landed a symbolic detachment of forces

and reasserted its claims. Given Tokyo's embarrassment over the bravado of the right-wingers who had erected the hut, the Japanese government could have been shamed into accepting this consequence. But that is not what happened. Suddenly, Chinese officialdom moved to rein in the mass protests. It was announced that the problem would be solved through bilateral discussions with Japan. Very quickly, passions died down in China, although they remained very much alive elsewhere in Asia.

One explanation of China's action was that the authorities feared that if students had a state-sanctioned excuse to mobilize and demonstrate, such actions could quickly lose their focus on the Diaoyu problem and become generalized protests on the order of Tiananmen Square. And perhaps that was part of it. But there was a more strategic explanation as well. China was making some progress in its relationship with Japan and did not want to end up in a two-front war of words with Japan on the Diaoyus and the United States over Taiwan. Whatever the reason, the disappearance of the Diaoyus from public discussion in China reflected the leadership's priorities in picking worthwhile battles and weighing them against the likely consequences to strategy and national interests. Contrary to the Hawk view, Beijing is not a dangerously maniacal regime eager to lash out in all directions. It is a rational, deliberative, careful, and conservative power, at least most of the time.

China Behaves Aggressively and Provocatively Toward Taiwan

Yes, it does. But even this bedrock element of the Hawk case should be looked at much more carefully. China's recent threats to Taiwan consist of the provocative military tests and bellicose statements of the 1995–96 period. Stunning and disquieting as those were, they account for a small portion of the new cross-strait relationship built before, during, and since that crisis.

First of all, it is important to understand the role of the Taiwan question in Beijing's perception of its national security. As one China expert has eloquently noted, the American public discussion about China's motivation for its fierce stance toward Taiwan encompassed every conceivable hypothesis—"historic resentment, antipathy to Taiwan's

Chinese boxes: "What if China won't listen, if our every attempt to court its leaders falls flat? After all, their behavior so far has been anything but reassuring. We grant them MFN status, and they arrest Harry Wu. We sign a trade agreement with them, and they pirate all our movies. No matter what we give, they consistently characterize American moves as 'hostile.' Quite simply, the junta in Beijing has more to gain by vilifying the United States than engaging it."

—*THE NEW REPUBLIC*

democracy, febrile nationalism, the internal power struggle. Every hypothesis, that is, except that in trying to gain control over an island 100 miles from its shores . . . China might be pursuing its national interest."[14]

One doesn't have to agree with China's perception of its national interest in order to recognize the intensity of Beijing's belief that reunification with Taiwan is its right, its duty, its destiny, and vital to its national security and national interests. Yet for all Beijing's threats against Taiwan, for all its statements reserving the right to "liberate" Taiwan by force, Pentagon experts say that China lacks the modern gear necessary to carry out a quick, efficient conventional invasion and successful occupation of Taiwan. Only if China were prepared to accept immense numbers of casualties could it use its comparative advantage in manpower to carry out what otherwise would require sophisticated amphibious landing craft, air power, and well-targeted missiles. A U.S. Naval Intelligence study of China's most advanced military training exercise so far for an invasion of Taiwan indicated that "logistics and amphibious lift capability will need to be improved" to carry out a "real-world operation along the lines of the Taiwan invasion scenario."[15]

Colonel Karl W. Eikenberry, a respected American expert on Asian military affairs, has watched the senior leaders of the various service branches of the PLA up close, traveling with them on tours of U.S. bases and visiting them in China. He believes that their strategic and tactical coordination is still far too undeveloped to sustain an aggressive, modern military campaign of attack and occupation of Taiwan, let alone similar campaigns against other Asian countries.

While Hawks in Washington scream about protecting Taiwan from an aggressive China, one hears far less of such concerns in Taiwan itself. There, China is more often viewed as a strategic business opportunity than as a strategic threat. More than $20 billion in direct investment by companies and individual investors flowed into China between 1990 and 1996. More than 20 percent of Taiwan's vast exports now go to China via one means or another. Some 40 percent of all companies listed on Taiwan's stock market have mainland operations.

A Taiwanese instant-noodle company is considered a model for the success of direct foreign investment in China. China and Taiwan are major trading partners, and China

Time heals all wounds: "By the year 2000, the mainland will probably become our biggest trade partner and the most important region for investment, the major source of foreign-exchange surpluses, and the heartland for economic development."

—LIEN CHAN
 PREMIER OF TAIWAN

enjoys a significant inflow of technology and managerial know-how from Taiwan. Indeed, Taiwan is a crucial ingredient in the economic melding that Western experts have taken to calling the creation of a Greater China. (Also included are southern and coastal China proper, Hong Kong, Macau, and the Southeast Asian economies dominated largely by ethnic Chinese businessmen.)

Much of the Taiwanese shoe industry has moved its operations to China in search of lower wages (just as this industry once closed up in America and moved to Taiwan and other low-cost Asian labor markets). In Dongguan City, a Guangdong province foreign-investment boomtown, an incredible 1,350 companies belong to the local Taiwanese Association. With the complete acquiescence of local Chinese authorities, Taiwanese managers in Dongguan City impose strict discipline and almost boot-camp-like conditions on thousands of workers—most of them young peasant women from the Chinese countryside—who make many of the Reeboks, Nikes, and other running shoes that will eventually show up in American stores.

With on-the-ground cooperation working well, it is perhaps not surprising that the Chinese took no punitive economic action against Taiwanese businesses in China even at the height of the 1995–96 political wrangling over Taiwan. "We assumed we might become targets," says a manager of a major Taiwan-owned enterprise in China. "But even as we read the newspaper articles every day denouncing our government, nothing happened."

Lee Teng-hui has urged Taiwanese businesses to curtail investments in China. And on more than one occasion in the last three years, the Taipei stock market has crashed in response to fears of an aggressive Chinese threat. But the bottom line for Taiwan's biggest businesses is that China is simply too attractive to pass up. By the end of 1996, Taiwanese companies were continuing to make important new investments, helping China up the high-tech ladder in everything from cellular phone software to biotechnology. Taiwan's largest company, Formosa Plastics, proceeded with a huge $3.2 billion power plant investment in China's Fujian province, even after the Taipei government encouraged the company to stop. For leading-edge companies in particular, the China market offers a scale unobtainable in Taiwan. "In Taiwan, we haven't entered the biotech field at

The world's largest shadow economy: Estimates are that the 51 million "Overseas Chinese"—ethnic Chinese now living throughout the world, including some of the fabulously wealthy *taipans* of Southeast Asia—now control $700 billion worth of annual sales. This is roughly the size of the GDP of their 1.2 billion brethren on the mainland. Their liquid wealth (cash, gold, shares) may run to as much as $2.5 trillion, more than the combined GDP of France and Germany.

all," says Jeffrey Wang, an executive with the Taiwan-based China Chemical & Pharmaceutical Company. "The Taiwan market is too small. It's not worth it." But in China, the company is constructing a $50 million biotech facility.[16]

Another sign of growing cross-Strait commerce is a direct shipping agreement that went into effect in 1997, allowing mainland and Taiwanese ships to call at each other's ports (although only for transshipment of goods) for the first time in forty-eight years.

Reading how the Taiwan-China situation is covered in our media, Bankers Trust's William Overholt laments the fact that Americans "know every detail of missiles launched around Taiwan, [but] have no knowledge of China's generation-long, largely successful peaceful initiatives toward Taiwan, initiatives that have turned the relationship from one of mutual isolation and military shelling to one of dialogue, trade, investment, and exchange of tourists."[17] If anything that resembled the developing cross-strait economic relationship existed among former enemies in the Middle East or the former Yugoslavia, American politicians would be hailing it as an enormous victory for the peace process. Yet the Hawks instead focus the discussion on aggression by China and the possibility of war over Taiwan.

We would not want to dismiss the possibility of another Taiwan crisis breaking out—if, for example, Taiwan declared independence and China responded militarily. But a balanced look at all the facts suggests that the big story of the 1990s might be that normalcy and peace are breaking out in China-Taiwan relations, despite some extremely troubling moments in the past few years.

China Is a Rogue Nation That Refuses to Play by International Rules

A pattern of Chinese behavior in recent years has horrified thinking people the world over: selling nuclear weapons-related equipment and material to Pakistan; helping Iran develop a nuclear reactor; selling chemical warfare components to Iran; smuggling AK-47s into the United States for sale to California street gangs; and committing an assortment of nonlethal economic sins from running up a giant trade surplus with the United States to operating state-owned factories whose main business is pirating American intellectual property.

Certainly, Chinese behavior that falls far outside the bounds of international acceptability should be criticized, condemned, and punished. (Trade sanctions against the Chinese entities selling chemical warfare materials to the Iranians are thoroughly appropriate, for example.) But perspective has been lost amid the din of criticism over these issues. China is a country that has gone from near-total diplomatic isolation twenty-five years ago to being an active, respected, and responsible member of the United Nations. In Security Council votes, China has used its veto power extremely rarely. In fact, it has sided with the United States more often than not and has politely abstained rather than use its veto when it did not wish to endorse U.N. peacekeeping missions it judged too interventionist.

China is a member of forty-nine other international governmental organizations, as well as over a thousand international nongovernmental organizations, ranging from the International Monetary Fund, the World Bank, and the Bank for International Settlements (China has accepted the Basel accords and follows them in terms of the capital-adequacy ratios of its banks) to APEC (Asian Pacific Economic Cooperation forum) and other regional bodies. These affiliations weave it into a vast network of international rules, most of which it follows. Beijing has also become a signatory to numerous global environmental agreements and even to nine international human rights agreements, although its compliance is obviously mixed and subject to interpretation.

Yes, China is, unfortunately, a significant arms merchant. Some of its weapons are highly competitive in global markets and some of its foreign-policy objectives can be bolstered through arms sales. Overall, of course, China is a very small-scale arms trafficker compared to the United States; its total sales volume runs at about 10 percent of American arms exports. China's sales are also considerably less than those of traditional arms merchants France and Israel. Yes, China has sold arms to countries with which Washington would prefer it not do business. But every country involved in the arms trade, especially the United States, ends up selling to rogue regimes. The story of how the United States built up Saddam Hussein's arsenal is well known. China in the 1980s

"I am not concerned about an aggressive, expansionist China. It is no longer a highly centralized controlled China able to devote its resources towards a single direction. In fact, China is becoming a more pluralistic and decentralized society. It is quite doubtful that any single leader could impose the kind of control over Chinese society that Mao Zedong once exercised."

—KOICHI KATO
SECRETARY GENERAL,
LIBERAL DEMOCRATIC
PARTY (JAPAN)

and 1990s has never come close to playing supply sergeant to a regime the United States deems dangerous.

In their compelling study of China's security policies, Andrew J. Nathan and Robert S. Ross write:

> Since the end of the Cold War, China's record on arms transfers and nuclear reactor exports has been relatively clean. In the early 1990s, China was negotiating to sell M-9 missiles to Syria, but canceled the agreement in 1992 after lengthy negotiations with the United States. . . . Following the U.S. decision to sell F-16s to Taiwan, Beijing undertook to help Iran develop a nuclear reactor. In response to complaints from the United States . . . China announced in 1995 it would suspend the agreement.[18]

While the headline-grabbing story may be China as arms merchant to terrorist states, Nathan and Ross stress the less well known bottom line: China has ultimately accommodated American interests and responded positively to pressure from Washington in some cases. Engagement, rather than confrontation, again appeared to be working when U.S. officials obtained a fairly specific agreement requiring Beijing to rein in sales of cruise missiles to Iran and curtail its nuclear assistance to the Iranian regime as well. This was part of a package of quid pro quos designed to make a success of Jiang Zemin's 1997 summit with Bill Clinton. One can object to the tradeoffs made by the American side (lifting the ban that has long prohibited American companies from selling nuclear power generating equipment to China) and one can question the enforceability of the agreement on Iran. But if ending Chinese missile sales and nuclear aid to Iran is an important goal—and most foreign policy experts would agree that it is—then this was a step in the right direction. Even this much progress could not have been obtained through confrontational means. Indeed, had the Hawks prevented the Jiang visit, or turned it into an embarrassment, one of Beijing's likely responses would have been to *increase* aid to Teheran.

According to Nathan and Ross, the big, glaring exception to China's willingness, eventually, to play ball with the United States on arms sales and nuclear issues is Pakistan, where the Chinese have abetted Islamabad's drive to develop nuclear technology. Pakistan, of course, is one of the most important countries in the world to Beijing, which sees it as a strategic counterweight to India, a link to the Islamic crescent in the Middle East, and a bulwark against Russian influence in the Asian far west. Beijing has had friendly relations with Pakistan longer than it has with the United States (which is why Kissinger chose it as the go-between for the historic rapprochement in 1971–72). Whatever aid China supplies to Pakistan is part of a well-thought-out long-term foreign policy, not a rogue state's opportunistic adventurism.

When it comes to the celebrated case of Chinese companies trying to sell AK-47s to street gangs in the United States, the issue seems to be not China's conscious policy goals, but the decentralized and highly personal fiefdoms created as the PLA has moved toward a market economy. At least eight profit-oriented Chinese corporations are now chartered to engage in various aspects of the global arms trade. Their executive ranks are often populated by relatives of senior Party cadres. This is a profitable business, and its practitioners are relatively free to profit where they can.

The FBI is still investigating the AK-47 case. But in the meantime, a Beijing court found four Chinese executives guilty of illegally exporting the weapons to the United States. The Chinese may well be using these four as the fall guys for a plan conceived and approved much higher up. Yet we very much doubt Beijing has any sort of official plan to profit from American gang wars or to destabilize the United States politically by running guns to gangs. Rather, this strikes us as resembling other situations in which China's central controls have broken down: units that were formerly part of highly planned economies of scale are now told to fend—and profit—for themselves.

That competing power centers can do as they please—and that some of them will test the limits or abuse their new freedom—is a natural by-product of the marketization of the Chinese economy. Americans should seek the punishment of Chinese individuals or companies that violate U.S. law. But that is very different from imposing economic sanctions on all of China because Americans are displeased with Chinese domestic politics. The Rand Corporation, a generally pro-defense industry think tank, even argued in a 1997 study that the United States should allow PLA-linked companies to operate on American soil (while monitoring them closely).

Point counterpoint: Former secretary of commerce Mickey Kantor on why the trade deficit is high: "Closed market, discrimination, failure to live up to trade agreements, inability to get rid of tariff and nontariff barriers." Rubbish, counters William Overholt, of Bankers Trust in Hong Kong. He contends that China is much less closed than South Korea and Japan were at comparable stages of development, citing 120,000 Avon Products, Inc., salesladies in China, Kodak's commanding China market share, and Coca-Cola's 25 percent chunk of China's soft-drink sales.

The profits of their trading activities are generally not used for weapons purchases, according to the study.

The nuclear issue is another that has troubled policy-makers. China always opposed the U.S.-Soviet nuclear monopoly and has been reluctant to participate in the post–Cold War nuclear arms limitation process. Beijing believes that its nuclear weapons are a source of power in the world and it is not about to give them up to an American-designed disarmament process. The solution to this problem has to do with getting the Chinese to participate in designing the disarmament framework. But in the meantime, the image the Hawks paint of nuke-laden Chinese leaders swaggering about, threatening the world, is grossly overstated. China has actually greatly curtailed its nuclear testing program. It is steering most of its increased military budget into conventional weapons systems, not nuclear ones.

On the trade front, there are certainly many foreign complaints about China's practices—but many fewer than there were about Japan a decade ago. China's market for trade, and especially for investment, is far more open than the Japanese market was then. Unlike Japan in the past, which sought to have a positive trade balance with all its partners, China runs a trade *deficit* with some other major trading partners (such as Japan) and only a small surplus with Europe.

China has gone from almost no participation in the world trading system to $300 billion a year of import and export trade. Total trade now represents a stunning 50 percent to 60 percent of the country's annual GDP, making the Chinese economy proportionally far more integrated with the world's than either the American or the Japanese. All this has happened in just twenty years. Foreign investors have been able to invest in companies, buy assets, and even arrange LBOs and other Western financial vehicles that are to this day virtually impossible in Japan owing to the protectionism of its investment market.

The debate over China's accession to the World Trade Organization (WTO) is an extremely important one. China wants to retain the special conditions and exemptions of a developing country; the United States wants it to be treated like any other developed country. What is interesting is that China is arguing its case, not seeking to join the WTO under false pretenses or trying to assert its right to special exemptions after the fact. In short, it is taking a principled position

Just who is creating the American trade deficit with China?

"Foreign companies control about three-fourths of China's exports. Half come directly from foreign-owned factories. Only one-fourth of China's exports consist of Chiense goods made by Chinese-owned companies . . . and that share is shrinking."

—*The Wall Street Journal*

on the terms of its membership from the point of view of its own interests.

American and Chinese interests diverge on several key points. When such situations arise, China will generally assert its own interests. This does not make it a rogue state. This is what makes it an independent great power on the road to becoming a superpower. It would be naïve to expect a superpower such as China to simply follow all the rules already written by preceding great powers. China will want to be an insider to the process of global rule making. And American interests will be best served by making it possible for China to become that insider, rather than allowing it to follow some of the more extreme impulses mentioned above.

China Is a Fascist Dictatorship and the World's Leading Human Rights Violator

Ironically, the true picture of human rights, broadly defined, has grown much brighter in China even as the country has become the subject of ever-greater criticism by Americans and other outsiders. As William Overholt has observed,

> Americans hear the intricate details of Chinese abuses of human rights, as indeed they should, but are completely ignorant of the extraordinary improvements in freedom of speech, freedom of movement, freedom of employment . . . that impress any close observer of China. American politicians and [the] press define human rights almost exclusively in terms of the fate of about 2,000 dissidents and ignore improvements in the freedom . . . of a fifth of the human race.[19]

Both sides of Overholt's equation may be overstated, but a basic political truth underlies his sweeping statement. The actual number of dissidents in jail is small—2,000 to 3,000. Of course, thousands more are under house arrest or are closely watched. Many more have abandoned their dissent because the climate is too repressive. Thousands have gone into exile. But even if one added all those who face one form of repression or another, the number of people persecuted for their political statements or beliefs today is the lowest it has been since the 1950s.

Among the Hollywood films released for the fall 1997

"**Companies have a moral obligation**, a duty to raise human rights issues and put the suffering and oppression of Chinese people above or at least equal to their own profits."

—REPRESENTATIVE CHRISTOPHER H. SMITH (R-N.J.)

More intellectual freedom than is generally thought? Li Dawei, a rising young writer whose latest novel features a talking cat that goes to Hollywood, believes the government concentrates its censorship efforts on television, newspapers, and magazines. "If you write a book," he says, "I think you can write just about anything."

season was *Red Corner,* starring Richard Gere, the actor who is America's best-known champion of the Dalai Lama and Tibetan independence. The film had nothing to do with Tibet (although Gere called it a political statement about Tibet, anyway). Instead, it told the story of an American entertainment executive wrongly suspected of murdering a Chinese woman on a visit to China, and the juridical process that ensued. Although the film sought to expose the absurdities of the legal system and the brutality of China's jails, Gere's character was eventually found not guilty, largely through the relentless efforts of a young Chinese lawyer, played by a Chinese actress, to force the court to hear the truth. Ironically, some American reviews of the film criticized as "fantasy" this very real-life portrayal of the early shoots of democracy and rule of law piercing the authoritarian bureaucracy, while finding plausible the brutalizing of the American media mogul played by Gere, something for which there is no precedent in recent Chinese history.

The Chinese people are far more relaxed about self-expression than they have been in their entire cultural history. The media have burgeoned, with a recent count of over 10,000 publications now in circulation, compared to the sparse handful of officially approved magazines and newspapers twenty years ago. About 90 percent of the new publications are neither launched nor controlled by the Communist Party.

Academic freedom has been enormously expanded. China's think tanks—which grow increasingly independent of the government as they become more self-supporting through consulting and other private-sector work—publish respectably independent studies and papers. Books that are out of favor with the government are published anyway and even become best-sellers (for example, *China Can Say No*). Protest lyrics are heard in Chinese rock songs. Village Party leaders are unceremoniously dumped in free local elections. For the most part, people in China can live comparatively freely, so long as they do not openly challenge the central premises and personalities of Communist rule. That is, of course, a huge speed bump in the middle of this march of progress. It leaves China far, far short of genuine democracy and freedom.

Nevertheless, no one who visited China in the late sixties or early seventies can go back today without remarking on the enormous diversity of personalities and lifestyles that was simply invisible in a prior era. This has happened largely because of the breakup of the "snitch dynasty" (as the Canadian journalist Jan Wong so aptly labeled it[20]) and the old *danwei* (work unit) system. Until recent years, the Communist Party controlled the country down to street level, creating "Neighborhood Party Committees" to keep track of everything from individuals' loyalty to the Party to their cooperation with family-planning policies. Workers were overseen by the Party committee of their factory or work unit as well, which controlled their work and residency permits and compiled dossiers that would have made the East German Stasi blush. The loosening of the iron grip of these institutions has brought immeasurable relief to hundreds of millions. Yet it is a story we hear very little about.

Yes, there are religious believers who are persecuted; and, yes, genuine freedom of religion is far from the reality in China. But there are more people practicing Christianity, Buddhism, and folk religions today than at any time since the 1950s. Christianity officially has 10 million adherents; researchers in Hong Kong and the United States claim the number to be between 12 and 65 million—and perhaps even as high as 100 million.[21] Billy Graham's movement and other American evangelical organizations active in China believe that opposition to MFN will only "strengthen the official Chinese perception that Christians are a threat, which will likely result in greater persecution."[22]

Yes, there are cases of dissidents denied the due process rights that have recently been enacted, cases that call into question the very nature of law in China. But a Chinese courtroom today operates in a way at least somewhat closer to Western practice than to the kangaroo courts of the previous era. The law is being used every day by the man on the street to get redress from local government, manufacturers, and even foreign companies.

The scholar Merle Goldman, who has been active in championing human rights in China, observes that in spite of all the current and continuing abuses

it should be remembered that there is a qualitative difference between the human rights abuses of the Deng and Mao Zedong . . . eras. Whereas Mao attacked whole classes of people—such as the Western-oriented intellec-

One man's perspective on the human rights issue:
"This is one of the mysteries that I find very difficult to solve: Why do your human rights and civil liberties groups believe they can admonish China as if she were a colony in Africa or in the South Pacific? This is absurd. China has fought her way up. She wants to find her own feet, and when she does, she wants a place at the main table. I would not go around baiting them and provoking them."

—LEE KUAN YEW

tuals in the 1957–1959 antirightist campaign and millions of bureaucrats as well as intellectuals during the Cultural Revolution, not to mention causing the death of more than thirty million peasants during the course of his utopian Great Leap Forward (1958–60), the Deng [era's] repression of dissidents is directed against specific individuals, not against their families, friends, and the class to which they belong.[23]

Goldman goes on note that Mao's prisoners were often tortured and died in captivity, whereas today's dissidents usually reappear in public after some jail time. The most famous of those dissidents, Wei Jingsheng—who coined the notion of democracy as China's badly-need "fifth modernization"—was released in 1997 after spending nearly sixteen years in jail. His release and resettlement to the United States for "medical treatment" was the direct result of pressure brought to bear by the Clinton administration. It was another of the quid pro quos of the engagement policy surrounding the visit of Jiang Zemin. Obviously, it should not take presidential intervention to get a political prisoner released. Nevertheless, Wei's freedom could only have been obtained in the atmosphere of renewed engagement with China that Clinton introduced in 1997. It simply never would have happened in response to Hawk-style confrontation.

By any objective measure, the human rights situation in China has made progress. That argument is made more compelling still if one accepts any part of the Chinese definition of human rights. To the Chinese, the human rights to food, clothing, shelter, economic development, and security, as well as the right of individuals to live in a stable society, are paramount over traditional Western-style individual political liberties. Judged by this standard, China in the last twenty years is a leader, not a laggard, in promoting the human rights of its people.

Again, Owen Harries, editor of the *National Interest*:

> True, there will be some terrible occasions when the violations of human rights will be so horrendous that the absolutist moral approach becomes—or should become—compelling. Such was the case with the murderous regimes of Hitler and Stalin. . . . China today does not constitute such [a case] . . . the best estimate of the number of

---

China in the 1990s— gridlock at rush hour: "I jokingly say that if you want to see a microcosm of China, look at an intersection. It's utter, constant chaos. Yet the presence of law is sufficiently there to try and keep things under control. Sometimes there are fender-benders, but somehow everyone gets through the intersection."

—RICHARD LATHAM
   PRESIDENT, UNITED
   TECHNOLOGIES CHINA

political prisoners in China currently is 3,000. In a population of 1.3 billion, this amounts to 0.00023 per cent, which is hardly the equivalent of the Gulag or Nazi concentration camps. Ironically, back in the early 1970s, when most Americans, liberals and realists alike, were enthusiastically applauding the U.S. opening to China, the Maoist regime *was* in the same league as the Hitlerite and Stalinist regimes.[24]

Harries goes on to make the point that while the human rights situation in China is not good by American standards, it is not unlike that in Indonesia, India, or Saudi Arabia, for instance. Yet in most of these cases, the United States is able to have normal and even close relationships that are not overwhelmed by the human rights agenda.

The Hawks are wrong to judge the violations of human rights as so severe and the Chinese regime as so odiously undemocratic that China should be shunned rather than engaged. But there is a deeper question here as well. Is the attainment of Western-style democracy and American-style respect for human rights even an appropriate set of goals or expectations for China?

We believe that such expectations will provide American policy with an unnecessary exercise in frustration for many years to come. Neither China's leaders nor the vast majority of its people have set political democracy as a goal or demand. They are clearly focused on a better economic life and a higher standard of living, which most (although not all) are getting. Even China's intelligentsia has few conscious democrats in its ranks, not because they have been cowed into quietude, but because they are mostly consumed with the national project of modernization and economic development and see the campaign for democratic political rights as a diversion. As scholar Thomas Metzger puts it, despite the dramatic entry of Chinese dissidents and democrats on the world stage during Tiananmen Square, most Chinese, *and quite possibly the vast majority,* "have been either unaware of these Chinese demands for democracy, uninterested in them, ambivalent about them, or critical of them as impractical and irresponsible."[25]

Americans like to believe that the desire for political liberty and human rights as we know them is absolute and universal. But what if the Chinese people don't desire

Was there a larger meaning? In the same week that China charged "rightist" dissident Wang Dan with crimes against the state, the "ultraleftist" hard-liner Yao Wenyuan, one of two surviving members of the Gang of Four, was freed after serving a 20-year prison term for his role in the violence and destruction of China's Cultural Revolution.

Western-style human rights as passionately as Americans like to think they should? Indeed, there is an immense gap between American expectations of what the Chinese people should want, and what they actually do want. A good illustration of this was provided by data from a public opinion poll on the eve of China's takeover of Hong Kong. When asked whether the takeover was desirable, only 4 percent of Americans thought so. But an astounding 62 percent of Hong Kong Chinese thought it was desirable to be reunited with China.[26]

In a seminal 1996 article, Harry S. Rowen, a professor emeritus of management at Stanford's Graduate School of Business, asked the question: "When will China become a democracy?" His answer: "2015."[27] The explanation for this seemingly facile conclusion was research marshaled by Rowen to show that "stable democracy correlates with mean incomes between $5,000 and $6,000, and becomes impregnable at the $7,000 level." According to Rowen's assumptions about its growth patterns, China should have the requisite per capita income to sustain a democratic system by 2015. Like a number of other scholars, Rowen shows that several other Asian countries that seemed to be intractable dictatorships—notably South Korea and Taiwan, as well as Spain, Portugal, Chile, and Argentina—all made the transition from dictatorship to democracy when they reached annual per capita incomes in the $5,000 to $8,000 class.

Since economic setbacks along the way could delay this timetable, Rowen argues that those who really believe in bringing democracy to China should hasten it with favorable U.S. trade and economic policies. "Washington should therefore stop holding trade relations hostage to an array of current political disputes. The United States should instead make MFN status for China permanent, and impose no extra obstacles to its admission to the WTO."[28]

In our view, Rowen may be too optimistic. Democracy could well take much longer to arrive in China, and its development there is likely to be much less full-blown than Rowen assumes. Nevertheless, his key point is the right one. Democracy of the type Westerners would like to see in China requires a material basis not yet present there, as well as a philosophical basis and a set of institutions that are still undeveloped. To use trade and economic leverage to punish the Chinese for being undemocratic works against the goal

Crossfire: "China exploits conscript and slave labor to produce goods for export. It maintains a one-child-per-couple population policy, enforced by coercive abortion, that has led to widespread infanticide of female babies. There are now more Christians imprisoned in China for their faith than in any other country on earth. It has sold missiles to Iran, nuclear technology to Pakistan, and has launched rockets at the ports of Taiwan to disrupt a democratic election. All this is financed by a burgeoning trade surplus built on the backs of American workers. Our trade deficit with China [in 1995] . . . killed at least 700,000 jobs."

—PAT BUCHANAN
U.S. PRESIDENTIAL CANDIDATE

of making China prosperous enough to have a fertile climate for democracy.

Thomas Metzger goes further still, urging Americans to look beyond the simplistic, binary view that all movements for democracy are moral and all regimes that resist democratization are immoral. Drawing on the work of sociologist Seymour Martin Lipset, Metzger says: "In some cases, nondemocratic, authoritarian rule may be advisable during periods of transition." The paradoxical and unpleasant fact is that some "instant"-democracy movements can destabilize society to such a degree that its long-term trend toward democracy can be set back. Metzger questions whether we should support such movements in China. What is equally paradoxical and unpleasant, "a government working to realize the social requisites of democracy may have to maintain political stability by forcibly restraining dissenters whose efforts to quicken democratization threaten instability."[29]

For the reasons given by Rowen and Metzger, although today's Hawks appear to be the champions of democracy and human rights in China, they may well be contributing to the delay and even the prevention of democratic developments, by insisting on unrealistic and arbitrary degrees of progress as preconditions for good American trade and political relations with China.

Alternatives, Anyone?

The curious thing about the China Threat school is that many of its leading proponents, while full of sound and fury about the dangers China poses, have precious few policy alternatives to propose. The most extreme and concrete proposal— to deny MFN status to China until it meets the Hawks' criteria on political change—has a growing constituency in Congress, but probably not enough to override the president, as long as he remains in favor of MFN. What's more, as Newt Gingrich's 1997 about-face on this issue shows, even many of the Hawks have realized that denying MFN to China would hurt Hong Kong's economy, as well as stunt the growth of the new Chinese entrepreneurs who depend on exports to the United States for their companies' success.

If Hawkish logic continues to predominate, it is very possible a future American Congress could override Bill

An old Chinese sport—playing the barbarians off against each other: "Based on their experience with U.S. partners, Chinese businessmen have concluded that their cooperation with European partners is less politically charged than it is with the United States, which frequently claims it will exert sanctions on China, thus politicizing trade and economic ties [and] resulting in their losses."

—Premier Li Peng

Clinton and deny MFN to China. Or that a post-2000 President Dick Gephardt or Pat Buchanan or Ross Perot could pull the plug on MFN to fulfill a campaign promise. But let's look for a moment at what would happen if MFN were ended. First, bear in mind that although the United States absorbs a disproportionate share—40 percent—of China's exports, the Chinese have other markets for their goods. In the event of an MFN denial, Japan and Europe would undoubtedly curry momentary favor with Beijing by moving to absorb more Chinese imports. American business interests involved in importing Chinese goods into the United States would lobby and sue for exemptions to keep certain goods coming on a preferential basis. Some Chinese goods are so cheap that they could withstand the high tariff structure of 44 percent without MFN and still sell competitively in the American market. Certainly, China would suffer a net export loss, but not a 100 percent loss.

Between the market share the Chinese would pick up in Europe and Asia and what they would retain in the United States when all the lobbying and repricing were done, MFN denial *might* represent a net loss of 10 to 20 percent of total Chinese exports. Would that be enough "pain" to force China to learn its lesson and behave as American Hawks wish it to? Undoubtedly not, because that is not the way the Chinese think. Here is what Foreign Minister Qian Qichen had to say on the point: "For 23 years before President Nixon opened the door of relations between China and the United States there was no trade whatsoever between us. I think you lived quite well. And so did we."[30]

Moreover, China would retaliate, almost certainly shutting down American imports and canceling contracts with U.S. companies. The factories cranking out pirated American CDs and videos might step up production to full throttle and resupply the rest of Asia. But that's not all. There would certainly be some measure of political retaliation. China might sell a few more missiles to the Iranians, fire a few more shots across Taiwan's bow, or otherwise push Washington's hot buttons. It might round up a few prominent dissidents and jail them in order to show it will not be intimidated by the American Congress.

Some American Hawks like to believe that denial of MFN could slice 10 percentage points off the Chinese GDP and that such a loss would cause the economy to implode. Their expectation is that if the Chinese growth machine faltered, a political revolution against Jiang Zemin would be the next step. In our view, just the opposite is the more likely case. Jiang would rally his own people more tightly in support of the government, telling them to tighten their belts and redouble their efforts. All of China's economic problems would be blamed on America. In the wake of this heinous new American betrayal, the mood in China would become more nationalistic and more anti-American. Most Hawks are keenly aware of this possible outcome, which is why they rail about MFN but, when pressed, support it anyway.

Another frequently invoked Hawk idea is to keep China out of the WTO. Dick Gephardt favors using this lever, as do many on the Right in Congress. But again, there are problems. First, China is not desperately enthusiastic about joining WTO in the first place. It wants the prestige and acceptance that come with membership in the world's premier trading club, but it has already indicated that it is very reluctant to make the changes in its internal market demanded by membership. A Hawk-led boycott of China would give Beijing the definitive excuse it needs to stay happily out of WTO and avoid its rules and responsibilities. Without China, the WTO becomes a much less effective body over the long term.

Upgrading relations with Taiwan is another idea from the Hawk corner. Invite Lee Teng-hui more often, sell Taiwan more advanced weapons, recognize Taiwan's independence before it is even declared. But even the Taiwanese do not want Washington to set off on such an irresponsible and provocative road, because they know China would respond with military action against them.

Pressing China harder on human rights is another old chestnut of the Hawk approach. But denunciations of Chinese human rights violations do not seem to bring results at all. The Hawks frequently argue that Engagement does not work, yet every time in this decade when the Chinese have quietly released a dissident or two (or terminated a weapons-sales program the United States found objectionable), it has been in the context of Engagement policies. Since the Taiwan crisis of 1995–96, when the American approach began to drift from Engagement to confrontation, the Chinese have been singularly unaccommodating.

As it turns out, the Hawks are ready to ring the alarm bells

Are we too easily distracted? "Today, as we talk about peace plans in Bosnia, elections in Haiti and hostages in Chechnya, there is a danger of neglecting the defining international political event of this era—the rise of China to world power."

—FAREED ZAKARIA
MANAGING EDITOR,
FOREIGN AFFAIRS

about China, but the more thoughtful and responsible among them usually back away from radical proposals because they know these won't work. The Hawks' discussion of China is more "spleen-venting than policy," says Robert Manning of the Progressive Policy Institute. The *Washington Post* columnist Paul Blustein observes that Hawks' policy prescriptions are sometimes surprisingly "tepid" and "moderate" considering the clear and present danger the Hawks suggest China presents. Bernstein and Munro paint a frightening picture of China, but even Bernstein has expressed concern that American Hawks may have missed his message that China cannot be "bludgeoned into submission" through "a policy of punishment and condemnation alone."[31] Similar examples abound, notes Paul Blustein. "Although some of the recent bashing literature advocates dropping engagement in favor of a containment-oriented policy, the reluctance of so many ostensible hard-liners to go that far speaks volumes about the pitfalls of trying to corner the Chinese."[32]

In chapter 18, we outline our policy prescriptions for handling the U.S.-China relationship. We specifically do not guarantee that they will change China from 800-pound gorilla into docile pussycat. American policymakers must come to understand that the very fact that China is becoming a superpower means, by definition, that no made-in-America vision can shape its destiny—except, perhaps, at the margins. The rise of China is not a threat of the kind envisioned by the Hawks, at least not yet. But it will certainly prove an enormous challenge to the United States. We think our proposals, conceived with a view to working from a basis of *shared* interests and *common* concerns, and trying to cope with challenges rather than trying to eradicate threats, stand a considerably better chance of working than those advanced by the Hawks.

The Myth of the Allies

Hawks and Engagers alike have a fondness for one particular policy prescription: Get "the allies" to do more. Indeed, if there is a single most frequently cited corollary to Washington arguments about containing, restraining, taming, and democratizing China, it is that America's allies should vigorously participate in this effort.

And another problem with containment:
"The main problem with a containment policy," says a senior American official, "is that unlike our approach to the Soviet Union, when we had a large number of good allies, we'd have not a single ally in Asia to help us carry it out. You'd cause great strains with Japan, Korea and all of Southeast Asia, let alone Australia."

—*THE NEW YORK TIMES*

The argument goes like this: Japan and the other countries of Asia are the frontline states with the most to lose if China grows up to be a belligerent seeker of economic and political hegemony. Europeans, too, have significant direct interests in China, and even greater interests in maintaining the stability and order of the world trading system. Besides, no one set of bilateral relations seems able to make a substantial dent in China's realpolitik outlook; by multilateralizing such issues as human rights, security, and nuclear proliferation the world stands a better chance of restraining the fearsome dragon.

Learned policy groups and symposia frequently try to square the circle of American policy on China by introducing the theme of the allies. Point one: If Europe and Japan will make common cause with America, the Chinese will have to listen or risk total isolation. And then, inevitably, point two: Perhaps Japan and other Asian countries can somehow translate America's message into the Asian cultural context so that it makes better sense to their fellow Asians in Beijing.

America's allies, unfortunately, show little interest in accepting this Mission Impossible. Partly, this is the coat-holding syndrome at work. As Winston Lord complained when he was the top State Department officer for Asian affairs, the administration's efforts to force China to respect trade accords and halt the spread of weapons were exploited by Europe and Japan, which were happy to "hold our coats" while they "gobble up our contracts."

Certainly, there is plenty of timidity and hypocrisy among America's allies. And, if this were the nub of the problem, then some greater efforts at boosting the allies' self-esteem, empowering them, and encouraging them would be in order. But differences of policy, philosophy, and interests, not cowardice, are the real issues. Most Europeans and Asians do not believe that American policy—at least as shaped by the Clinton administration until now—has much hope of bringing about the liberal, democratic China it envisions.

Europeans face their own trade problems with China, although they are much milder than America's. The European Union as a whole suffers a $1.2 billion trade deficit with China (compared to almost $40 billion for the United States). Yet even this mild deficit is enough to spur European officials to put in place scores of quota programs and other import controls. Europe plans to stave off the flood of Chi-

Some words on China from the hard-headed Dr. K: "If hostility to China were to become a permanent aspect of our foreign policy, we would find no allies. Nationalism would accelerate throughout the region. Just as American prestige grew with the opening to China, most Asian nations would blame America for generating an unwanted cold war."

—HENRY KISSINGER

nese textiles, toys, glassware, consumer electronics, ceramics, and footwear that has inundated the United States. European countries are, on the whole, far more protectionist than America when it comes to the micro-level issues of keeping goods out of their market. They believe that this will work better for their interests than pursuing Washington's macro-level agenda about China's overall political-economic policy direction.

Coming to every neighborhood soon: In 1996, Matsushita, Japan's biggest consumer electronics company, had 100 shops in China; over the next three years it planned to open 3,000 more.

Always ready to benefit from poor Sino-American relations, Europeans from Germany's Helmut Kohl to France's Jacques Chirac have annoyed Washington with their habit of arriving in Beijing just when American policy is trying to isolate and punish China. This approach has been very, very good for European companies, which end up getting the plum deals U.S. firms were bidding on.

China is thus able to see Europe as an alternative business partner to the United States. Europeans are more than willing to play that role, even if, as *The Economist* says, it requires their senior politicians to "kow-tow for contracts" and make "distasteful compromises" with their own political beliefs. The leading Western journal of free trade goes on to expose the philosophical flaw in the American approach: "By persistently threatening sanctions . . . America has encouraged the notion that trade should be the plaything of politicians." In fact, "America and Europe should agree to keep trade and politics apart except in times of crisis."[33]

At the heart of America's problem with getting the allies to go along with Washington's moral-political crusade is not Europe but Japan. Like the rest of Asia, Japan is caught in the middle of this emerging conflict. On the one hand, there are great benefits for Japan in allowing itself to be seen as America's reliable ally. The incessant U.S.-Japanese conflict over trade, which utterly dominated the bilateral relations for most of the last twenty years, is winding down, even though the trade imbalance is still massive. This is so in part because American policymakers and strategists today fear China far more than Japan.

But while the appearance of being America's ally in Asia benefits Japan, the reality is far more complex. American geostrategists who expect Japan to help implement American policy are dreaming of a course of events that will never occur. Most Japanese leaders have little interest in Washington's campaign to foist its vision of human rights on the Chinese; indeed, when American companies pulled out of China after the 1989 Tiananmen Square incident, Japanese companies stayed behind to build and grow.

When urged by Washington to play a significant role in deescalating the Taiwan issue America's way, Tokyo politely demurred, not wishing to follow a course it believed would only further bait an already volatile and incensed Beijing. "Those are *their* damn oil and shipping lanes—why won't they step up to the plate and tell the Chinese they've got to cool it on Taiwan?" was a typically frustrated remark from a senior White House official. "We don't think antagonizing China is the right way to protect Japan's interests," responded a Japanese journalist.

Throughout its post–World War II development, Japan resisted thinking of itself as a quintessentially Asian economy and sought to involve itself with North America, Europe, and the world economy. But now that the action has shifted so dramatically to Asia, Japan's corporations and economic planners are refocusing their attention on Asia—and on China in particular. For years cautious and reluctant to invest on the ground in China, the Japanese now regularly outinvest Americans.

Some Asia hands have always sensed a possibility that Japan and China would overcome their profound antagonisms and troubled history to build an Asian economic network together. Right after Pearl Harbor, with Japan and China fighting a vast and bitter war with each other, the American novelist Pearl Buck wrote FDR a letter in which she made an extraordinary prophecy: China and Japan, as well as other Asian countries, would come together after the war in a grand anti-Western alliance.

Asia experts of the 1970s saw similar possibilities. But the assumption was always that Japan would lead and China would follow. Japan would play the role of metropolitan center while China supplied cheap land, labor, and resources. Japan would bring China out of the dark economic age of Communism and into the modern age. It would earn rewards in the process similar to those the United States reaped from defending and developing Western Europe after World War II. In the late 1990s, that proposition sounds quaint. China is an emerging superpower; it is not going to become a neocolonial appendage to the Japanese empire. Instead, Japan

What a difference some distance makes: In a recent poll commissioned jointly by *The Wall Street Journal* and Japan's *Nihon Keizai Shimbun*, 34 percent of Americans surveyed said that China posed the greatest threat to peace in Asia (the other choices were North Korea, Russia, Japan, and the U.S.). In Japan, however, only 19 percent of respondents listed China, while the North Koreans got 54 percent.

must now adapt itself to the power of the Chinese dragon, just as it did many centuries ago.

Fatalism has crept into Japanese thinking about China. Six years of a constrained postbubble economy, combined with the vibrant spectacle of double-digit growth just across the sea in China, has humbled Japan and sapped some of its visionary verve. Where once our Japanese futurist friends imagined a new, benevolent, economics-led "coprosperity sphere" in Asia, with Japan at its center, now some worry about how long Japan can remain independent of the powerful force of a rising China.

"Westerners think democracy will cure China's problems," notes Kenichi Ito of the Japan Forum on International Relations. "Even if China became democratic internally—which is doubtful—it would still have a self-interested, big-power, undemocratic view of Japan and other neighboring countries. We Japanese are destined to live in China's shadow, and we must cope with that as best we can."

Yukio Okamoto, a senior advisor to Japan's foreign-policy establishment, says that the United States must continue to play a strong military role in Asia. If it does not, he predicts, "Japan will have to become a subject of China," with its "political agenda dictated" by Beijing.[34] But even Japan, which has been the strongest supporter of the American military presence in the Pacific, may not always side with the United States. Domestic political pressure is increasingly turning Japanese opinion against the U.S. military presence. This was seen particularly strongly in the 1996 case of a rape of a Japanese schoolgirl by American servicemen. Much of the Japanese public was far more concerned with ending such abuses by terminating America's role in Japan than with the implications that exit would have for Japanese security.[35]

As for other Asian countries, it is worth noting that when push came to shove and the United States dispatched warships in the Taiwan crisis of 1996, *no Asian government openly supported the move,* not even those known to be most fearful of Chinese expansionism. Not a single Asian government openly criticized China's provocative military exercises. Most countries, even those swimming in Taiwanese investment, reluctantly concurred with Beijing that its treatment of Taiwan is China's own internal affair. The Philippines, the country most concerned about Chinese land grabs of contested islands, effectively expelled the U.S. Navy from its huge Subic Bay base in recent years, and has not invited it back.

Asian countries are getting ready to live with China as an ever bigger dragon in their midst. Some face that prospect by focusing on the regional economic opportunity China presents. Others are more fearful. But no Asian government is inviting or encouraging Washington to press the new cold war with Beijing. Most Asian nations want the United States to stay involved militarily in the region as a counterweight to Chinese power, but few have the courage to say so openly. To the degree Americans choose to confront China directly, they should be aware they are doing so essentially on their own. And *that* fact should give Americans pause.

PART II

BENCHMARKING CHINA

Amid the turmoil and tumult of battle, there may be seeming disorder and yet no real disorder at all.

—Sun Tzu

Nothing could be more fallacious than to judge of China by any European standard.

—Lord Macartney (1794)

The Shanghai Allusion

Beijing. A bitter cold day in November 1995. We have been invited to interview Qiao Shi, one of the most powerful men in China at the time. His position as chairman of the Standing Committee of the increasingly activist National People's Congress made him the Chinese equivalent of Newt Gingrich. But he was much more powerful than Gingrich—and much subtler in his use of power. Although in his early seventies, Qiao was then sometimes mentioned as a dark horse candidate to lead China should President Jiang Zemin stumble. Few foreign experts had met Qiao; he was a low-key and shadowy figure. Yet some China watchers hailed him as a pragmatist who was building a more independent People's Congress and championing the idea of the "rule of law" in China. Others saw him as an old-style, backroom party operative who rose to power as head of China's internal security apparatus, yet was reportedly clever enough to abstain from the Politburo vote that led to violent imposition of martial law during the Tiananmen demonstrations in 1989.

Our questions, carefully drafted and redrafted to elicit insight without causing alarm, had been submitted well in advance. We sought answers not about China's convoluted past (Qiao is one of the last living party veterans who know what really went on at key moments in Chinese Communist history), but about the future: the role of the National People's Congress; the balance between national and regional interests; and what major economic and legislative changes he foresaw in the next twenty-five years.

We arrive early for the appointment. The fully armed PLA soldiers who guard the entrance to the Great Hall of the People tell our young escort (who is armed with a constantly ringing cell phone) that we are to wait in the car. It is parked on the concrete apron immediately adjacent to where Changan Boulevard opens into Tiananmen Square—a few hundred meters from where Mao Zedong proclaimed the People's Republic of China in 1949. It is also near the spot where PLA tanks pushed their way violently into the crowds of demonstrators in 1989.

After much back and forth over the parking space—a classic quotidian "power struggle" of China in the nineties—the time for our entry into the Great Hall arrives. We walk up the long flight of cold concrete exterior steps,

Is this the good news or the bad? In 1997, some influential Chinese leftists began circulating a letter warning against the deep penetration of "bourgeois liberalization"—the code words for Western influence. Among its disdainful points: "Some provincial governors have suggested that we must give more promotion for a privatized economy. They even strongly advocate preferential treatment for private enterprise. Some municipal secretaries have urged government departments to give the green light to facilitate 'unconventional' high growth for privately owned enterprises. They hope their cities can give birth to more millionaires and billionaires. Many of these senior cadres believe only capitalists can save China."

then through the imposing entryway and into a time warp. In a carefully orchestrated scene redolent of the long traditions of Chinese statecraft and protocol—and incorporating the modern demands of court photographers and scribes who will note every utterance—we are rushed into the doorway of an ornate meeting room, guided through the receiving line, arranged in ritual order into overstuffed chairs, and, after a few pleasantries, asked what it is we want to ask. But before you begin, says Chairman Qiao, let me tell you about the history of socialist construction.

How to fathom China:
"One who does not employ local guides cannot gain advantages of terrain."

—SUN TZU
THE ART OF WAR

An extended monologue follows. It starts with the famous Tsunyi meeting in the 1930s when Mao consolidated his leadership of the Communist Party, and goes on to the success of the revolution and the old socialist economic model first adopted and then adapted from the Soviet Union. Qiao then traces Chinese Party history from the 1950s, revisits the Sino-Soviet conflict and the Sino-Indian border clash, and goes on to the colllectivization movement in the countryside. When he comes to the Cultural Revolution, he pays very focused, particular attention to the activities of the "Shanghai clique," the ultraleftist Gang of Four that was reputedly responsible for the Cultural Revolution's worst excesses and then tried to seize power after Mao's death. In sharp detail, Qiao reviews the personal history of each member of the Gang—people whose names are rarely even mentioned in China these days—and stresses the connection of each one to the city of Shanghai.

Not once does Qiao touch seriously upon the submitted questions. A couple of careful efforts to interrupt and shift the conversation are brushed aside like a few pests on the hide of a dragon. Our scheduled appointment is nearly over when he finishes and invites a question, "as time allows." Once again we try to press him about the future. But Chairman Qiao is brief and noncommittal. A "comfortable" life for most people can be reached in ten years, he says, and in fifty China will be a middle-level economy. But "it is not easy to reach a relatively comfortable standard of living." Aides start to shuffle. Notebooks have already closed.

Exiting to smiles and handshakes, the Middle Kingdom once again safe from divination by inquisitive Westerners, we repair to a restaurant nearby to evaluate it all. Clearly Qiao Shi had important things to say. Obviously, his monologue wasn't without a hidden logic. But what was it? The roads to interpretation could go in several different directions or nowhere, each option being equally valid. Our quandary is, in itself, a perfect metaphor for China.

Qiao had given us a talk that was part Party history (did he have it on his mind simply because he had an appointment on the same morning with the head of Vietnam's Communist Party?), part cautionary tale (he stressed Mao's fallibility at the end of his life and the problems that accompany "rule by man" instead of "rule by law"), part paean to Deng Xiaoping (was there deeper meaning behind Qiao's pointing out Deng's willingness to learn from mistakes and his support of the rapid evolution of law?).

But most important, we decide, were Qiao's comments about the "Shanghai clique," their efforts to usurp power, and the damage they did to China in the 1960s and 1970s. Today's preeminent leader, Jiang Zemin, was born in Shanghai and served as mayor in the 1980s before being recruited by Deng Xiaoping to work in Beijing. In recent years, Jiang had been accused by critics of overstuffing key ministries and departments of the central government with loyalists and supporters from Shanghai. Qiao and Jiang were rumored to differ on several major policy questions. How serious these differences were at the time—or even what, specifically, they were over—no one who knew would say definitively. In the months leading up to the Party Congress in September 1997, it would become increasingly clear that Qiao and Jiang were political opponents and rivals. At the congress itself it was revealed that Jiang had succeeded in muscling Qiao off the Communist Party Politburo's Standing Committee and thereby out of the leadership. But in November 1995 there was no public evidence of such a rivalry, no overt policy disagreements (just, perhaps, some difference of emphasis), and no directly critical public remarks by either leader about the other. Was Qiao, in his talk with us, carrying on the long Chinese tradition of criticizing opponents without naming them? Was he taking the veil off the current debate, but doing so obliquely by invoking historical experience?

Later, a Chinese friend with good connections to the senior leaders listened to our report on this meeting and said she got a "chill down her spine." It was clear to her that Qiao's remarks would only have been made if very severe

Views on government from the ancients:
"Ruling a large state is like cooking a small fish."

—LAO TSE

153

differences had developed with Jiang and Qiao's position was being threatened. That prospect itself was unsettling to some Chinese.

Objections to our interpretation of what we had heard of a Jiang-Qiao rift could be made on several counts by other well-placed sources who either hoped to see Qiao stay in power because of his enunciated "rule of law" views or else wanted to believe in the myth of a unified post-Deng leadership. First, Qiao Shi, too, hailed originally from Shanghai, where he was a student revolutionary organizer in the 1940s. Although he wasn't part of the recent crop of Shanghai people whom Jiang has brought to powerful posts in Beijing, his own connection to Shanghai arguably made his criticism of Shanghai people murky. Perhaps, some might have said, Qiao's comments about Shanghai should be viewed as no more than the sort of remark Ross Perot might make about how too many people from inside the Beltway run the American government—a view that would be consistent with the long-standing rivalry between Beijing and Shanghai and the penchant people from each city have for finding fault with people from the other.

Second, to link someone to the Gang of Four, even eliptically, would go beyond the expected bounds of expressing some policy differences, especially if done in front of foreigners. The Gang of Four are associated with themes of treason, betrayal of the Chinese revolution, illegitimate usurpation of power, corruption on a vast scale, political extremism, torture, murder, and dictatorial abuses of power. One Chinese leader certainly wouldn't compare another to the Gang of Four lightly.

But that seemed to be the point of the Shanghai allusion. Qiao Shi *was* trying to communicate a warning about Jiang Zemin and some of the high-ranking party and state leaders around him. The reference to the Gang of Four *was,* in all probability, carefully chosen.

That we could come away from a lengthy meeting with a senior Chinese leader and have only tantalizing tea leaves to read and no clear, hard facts about what he meant says much about China today—and in the future. Even after thirty years of a radical Communist revolution that sought to break all ties to China's feudal past, and then twenty more years of reform and opening to the world, China is still very much a

Views on government from the ancients:
"The ruler does not try to work side by side with his people and they accordingly respect the dignity of his position. He does not try to tell others what to do, but leaves them to do things by themselves. Tightly he bars his inner door, and from his room looks out at the courtyards; he has provided the rules and the yardsticks, so that all things know their place. Those who merit reward are rewarded; those who deserve punishment are punished."

—HAN FEITSE
  (280–233 B.C.)

154

society unto itself. Only the most powerful insiders truly understand the political dynamics.

In these respects, the China of the 1990s is still a traditional Chinese society, just as Qiao Shi was a traditional Chinese leader expressing himself in traditionally opaque ways. For years to come, China will be conditioned by the experiences and traditions of the past, many of which reside so deep in the people's collective unconscious that neither wars nor revolutions nor the tumult of modern markets can alter them much—and certainly not quickly.

The result is that China has many contradictory notions about itself. It wants to be treated as a great power, but still expects special considerations normally reserved for poor, developing nations. It keeps an iron grip on dissent, but tolerates a surprising degree of freedom in social and economic spheres and has launched "open" elections at the local level. It has taken active steps to promote the rule of law, but still carries out show trials to convict those who have antagonized the powers that be. Some of the late twentieth century's most powerful films and novels have been created by Chinese intellectuals, but what can be read or shown varies with the political temper of the times. In one period, leaders promote the slogan "Let a hundred flowers bloom," and then in another insist that art must follow the government's dictates and the leaders' current view of "spiritual civilization." At one point China seems to be lunging forward toward American lifestyles, prosperity, and consumerism; next, America has been declared the enemy, China's nationalistic back is up, and nearly everything American is suspect.

Clearly, outsiders who wish to understand China's present and future had better leave their own cultural assumptions at the door. What's more, they had better start through the entryway with a high tolerance for ambiguity and an appreciation of the many layers of Chinese reality. China's overall development cannot be categorized as "either/or." Envision, instead, a Calder mobile, with planes of history, geography, ideology, culture, and more, pivoting loosely around each other. Over time, one or another of these elements will move into the foreground; their various colors and sizes will influence the overall shape and balance as well as the viewer's perception of them. In effect, Chairman Qiao symbolically

Politics, a Confucian perspective: "A gentleman allies himself with individuals, but not with parties."

—CONFUCIUS

reminded us that being preoccupied with one aspect or another of the future is to take too static a view. China didn't simply appear, tabula rasa, in the last quarter of this century, ready for modernization. There is no blank slate simply awaiting our good instruction.

A successful American relationship with China depends on understanding the ups and downs of the short term in the context of the longer-term process at work. China now has a two-decade track record of striving toward modernization. It is a messy process, with no clear vision and no leadership that Americans are comfortable with; it is replete with contradictions and setbacks. The way the Chinese have pursued modernization is probably not the way a representative group of American politicians, businesspeople, and economists entrusted with the task of modernizing China would choose to proceed. Nevertheless, in our view, the Chinese process is working, despite the challenges posed by geography, history, and culture and in circumstances for which Western theory has never had to provide an answer.

By "benchmarking" where China is in its modernization process, we can get a better understanding of where it is likely to go. Throughout Part II, we offer insights and ways of looking at a variety of historical influences, current realities, issues, and problems that illustrate two basic themes: One, how different the Chinese experience is from what Americans are conditioned to expect because of our own history, values, and experiences of a liberal democratic capitalist system in action. Two—and critically important in the current policy debate over U.S.-China relations—how the system China is evolving, while very different from our own, is not *necessarily* incompatible with American interests and the general interests of the global economy in the next century.

To make intelligent policy toward China, one first has to understand it. All too many policy tracts from the Hawk camp, as well as the overly optimistic assumptions of the Engagers, reflect only a superficial understanding of the Chinese experience. We cannot provide a comprehensive assessment of every important issue, but we can look through many of the lenses of the past and present that we have found worth keeping handy in examining the work in progress that is China.

Understanding China:
"China today may be too big, too varied and changing too fast to allow more than blurred snapshots. One can only conclude that everything one hears about China is true, but none of it is reliable."

—JOHN FRANKENSTEIN
UNIVERSITY OF HONG KONG

156

CHAPTER 6

Of Bulls, Bears, and Being Moderately Bullish

Contemplating China's long-term future is a bit like taking a Rorschach test of your own thinking about the great issues of our time. As various experts stare into the enigmatic inkblot that is China and try to extrapolate a vision of conditions ten, twenty, or thirty years from now, the commentary they produce will tell you more about their own beliefs—about business, economics, politics, history, society, and culture—and about their relative confidence in the future of the West than it does about China.

In the current policy debate, the Hawks and Engagers who take the Chinese Rorschach test have come up with polarized interpretations. The Hawks worry about what effects China's success will have if not moderated early on by American influence. The Engagers believe that by contributing to China's success, Americans can influence what kind of superpower China becomes. But for the most part, both camps believe China will be successful.

However, a great divide does exist in another dimension of the China debate. This is the argument over whether China will, in fact, become the new superpower Hawks and Engagers expect, or whether the weight of its burdens, contradictions, and unaddressed problems will eventually abort its success, diverting it from the path of modernization and prosperity into disintegration, chaos, a hardline restoration, or a new revolution.

The Bulls Have Their Run

The debate between Hawks and Engagers largely concerns politics and policy and is conducted chiefly by nonexperts on China. But the debate over whether China will succeed in its long-term modernization drive *is* conducted chiefly among experts and has significant practical implications for businesspeople and global corporations as they consider whether, how, and where to invest in China.

At one end of this spectrum are "China Bulls." Even after the bursting of the early-nineties investment bubble, even after the intense wrangling with the United States over Taiwan, the uncertainty of the Hong Kong transition, the death of Deng Xiaoping, and the slowdown of Asian economies, Bulls remain optimistic. They point out that China continues to prosper and retains its status as the world's fastest-growing economy: some 300 million people are approaching middle-class status; new wealth pushed consumer sales an astonishing 20 percent per year during the first half of the 1990s in major coastal cities; China continues to be one of the leading markets for foreign direct investment, with annual inflows in the 1990s averaging close to $25 billion; whole sectors of manufacturing industries (toys, watches, garments, compact disk players, cellular phones, and even personal computers) are relocating to China; and the nonstate sector of the economy is now larger in total output than the troubled state sector—and growing much faster.

Among brokers and bankers throughout the Pacific Rim, one finds a strong contingent of Bullish experts. William Overholt, managing director of Bankers Trust in Hong Kong, developed an optimistic scenario, recording all the positive fundamentals of the Chinese economy, in his 1993 book, *The Rise of China*.[1] More recently, he argued that China after Deng "will remain more unified, stable, and secure than at any time in the last two centuries."[2] Jim Rohwer, formerly with *The Economist* and now chief economist for Asia at CS

Capturing all things small: "A few years ago, plans were hatched at MIT and in Paris to bring computers to Africa to help close the gap between haves and have-nots in the information age. The plans came to nothing. The Chinese, however, have come with pens. Pens costing three to five cents. The poor person in Africa has virtually no money. He has a small plot of land on which he grows some tomatoes, some cherries. He takes them to the market and sells them for 50 cents. And for that 50 cents he can buy some small necessity made in China. In Africa the French are gone. The British are gone. The Chinese have arrived."

—Ryszard Kapucinski, NPQ

First Boston, believes the nerve center of Asia is inexorably moving from Hong Kong to Shanghai and that, despite the problems, there is basically "no stopping China," whose experiment in economic reform has been "vastly more spectacular than anyone dreamed it could be."[3]

The same expectations are held by a good number of journalists, academics, futurists, and other pundits who see China enjoying a far brighter long-term future than even Beijing's optimistic officialdom tends to forecast. "What is happening in Asia is by far the most important development in the world today," comments John Naisbitt, adding that a modernized Asia, with China at its center, will "become *the* dominant region of the world: economically, politically, and culturally." China, and the Overseas Chinese business networks, will soon overshadow Japan and emerge as the most dynamic economic force in the world, according to Naisbitt.[4]

And some of the staunchest Bulls can be found within the international business community. Despite the negative experiences of some, the Chinese market already has produced big winners. Procter & Gamble has captured around 60 percent of the Chinese shampoo market, even though its products cost three times as much as some local brands. Sales of all P&G brands in China have hit about $500 million on their way to an anticipated $1 billion by the year 2000.[5] The head of a chain of European fashion boutiques notes, "There are 300 million people who live in the coastal areas around Shanghai. That's larger than the European Common Market. If only one percent can afford to buy European fashions, we will be happy."[6] Chris Nelson, the chairman of Dairy Farm, a Hong Kong–based chain of small supermarkets, believes, "We're going to look back in 20 years' time and say the promise of China's mass market, which has been so talked about since Lord Macartney's trade mission in 1793, actually materialized in the 1990s."[7]

Those who offer the bright scenarios construct a future with few major political shifts, no sharp veering off from the present road of economic reforms, and certainly no violent spasms. In this vision, the economy continues to race ahead, averaging double-digit annual growth for a generation. On the strength of such compounding numbers and extrapolations, some have envisioned China as a new kind of global juggernaut. Economist Larry Summers, then with the World Bank (he subsequently became undersecretary of the Trea-

Unparalleled nation building: "The only thing comparable to what's going on in China is the reconstruction of postwar Europe under the Marshall Plan."

—RAJENDRA NATH
BEIJING GENERAL
MANAGER
GE AIRCRAFT ENGINES

sury), stunned the world in the early nineties when he forecast that China's total economic output would surpass that of the United States as early as 2011—a position from which he and other experts have now retreated somewhat. Today's Bulls suggest that it will take China until the 2020s to match the United States in GDP. Even so, that would be one of the most spectacular and rapid surges of economic growth the world has ever seen. It is often pointed out, for example, that Britain's first doubling of GDP after the industrial revolution took almost a hundred years. America's took nearly fifty. China has collapsed that phenomenon into a single decade.

Bulls frequently anticipate that China will continue to evolve a civil and commercial code and that democratic rights and the rule of law will be increasingly institutionalized. Some believe that the grassroots of Chinese society will not rest until they have gained the "fifth modernization"—political democracy—and that a democratic system will be the vehicle both for resolving China's major challenges and for turning the whole country into a vast free-enterprise zone. Experiments in direct elections now taking place in the countryside will spread, many hope, to the central organs of state power. Perhaps a suggestion raised in a long-running dialogue on the Internet in 1995 will be taken up: Beijing might establish "Special Political Zones" to test political reforms just as it set up the Special Economic Zones as laboratories for free-market reforms in the 1980s. Even the formerly authoritarian and repressive governments in Taipei and Seoul, which thrived on tight political control for a long time, have now liberalized. China, the reasoning goes, can't be far behind.

The Chinese themselves are more cautious than many of the foreign Bulls. Madame Wu Yi, the minister of foreign trade and economic cooperation, observes, "China is a typical developing country. There is no possibility in the short term that it can catch up with the level of developed nations."[8] In interviews with us, other senior officials have ventured statements that are variations on a theme first expounded by Deng Xiaoping: by the middle of the next century, China will have attained the economic level of a "middle developed country." No one uttering this phrase can be pinned down to what it means exactly, but we might surmise the leaders think that China will have become something on the order of a giant Spain by the year 2050.

Better too soon than too late: "China is a market where if you wait until everything is perfect, you'll never start."

—PHILLIP DAVIS
VICE PRESIDENT
ANHEUSER-BUSCH ASIA

China Bulls sometimes think Beijing deliberately under-estimates its future in order to bolster its desire for continued preferential treatment as a "developing" country for WTO and other purposes. Or perhaps, in order not to scare or shock the rest of the world, the Chinese leaders want to avoid going on record as convinced that theirs will be the most powerful economy of the next century. High-ranking officials have even become publicly argumentative in dismissing asser-tions they think too Bullish. An assistant foreign minister, Chen Jian, criticized *The Economist* for "exaggerating China's economic development" and reporting that "in a very short period of time China would be the second biggest economic power in the world, and then the biggest." Chen went on to suggest the subtext for this unusual Chinese modesty about growth statistics: "These predictions ... have led people to conclude that the rise of China will inevitably unbalance the region. Such arguments don't hold water. China is not a superpower. It is not at present. And it will not be one in the future."[9]

Bulls often compare China to Japan to show what happens when double-digit growth rates are compounded over a long period of time. Just forty-five years ago, the average Japa-nese worker was earning less than one-twentieth as much as his American counterpart. Today, the worker in Japan earns about 20 percent *more*. And that stunning achievement oc-curred on the strength of average annual GDP growth rates in Japan a little *lower* than China's recent torrid perfor-mance.

The Bulls also know that supercharged growth—the kind that changes a nation from backward to modern in a single generation—is not just a Japanese anomaly. From Seoul to Singapore, East Asians seem to have figured out how to breathe fire into GDP growth, productivity, and savings and investment rates. All of these statistics stand in sharp con-trast to the developed West, where most similar measure-ments are now low if not downright anemic. If the "little dragon" economies can do it, why can't the Big Dragon do it even bigger and better and on a grander scale?

China's assets, after all, are quite remarkable: the world's biggest labor force, ready to work for extremely low wages and conditioned to work hard, respect authority, and com-plain little; universities churning out tens of thousands of engineers every year, highly skilled by world standards in

Explaining China:
"What is happening in China today is unprecedented, but there are analogies . . . : the American West in the nineteenth century, with some areas functioning in an orderly fashion and some utterly lawless; France in the Fourth Republic; Italy today; a yacht race before the gun goes off."

—RICHARD MARGOLIS
  MANAGING DIRECTOR,
  SMITH NEW COURT
  (CHINA)

161

areas crucial to the development of high-tech industries; abundant natural resources of the type Asia's other dragon economies always envied but had to import from elsewhere; a population that has endured incredible hardships and privations but is now driven with a passion rarely seen in the West to improve its lot and bring family, factory, and community up to modern standards; a central political authority that can, if it chooses, focus the nation almost entirely on economic construction, free (as of now) from the kind of intrusive environmental regulations, tax burdens, and other bureaucratic fetters so often accused of constraining growth in the United States; foreign corporations and governments from every part of the world ready to invest, transfer technology, train Chinese counterparts, and otherwise shoulder some of the heaviest lifting involved with modernizing the country; and a culture generally regarded by outsiders as one of the most respectful of education and advancement, and one of the most enduring, pragmatic, materialistic, self-organizing, and adaptable on the planet.

"Look at it this way," says one Bull, "China is simply reclaiming its natural place in the world order. For two thousand years China always was the world's largest economy. It's only the last two hundred years that have been the aberration."

Some Bulls lean toward the Hawkish view, imagining that China will abuse its future position as the world's largest economy, together with its military strength, to achieve Asian and even world domination. Most offer a more benign forecast: an Asian century, perhaps, but one in which the spending power of Asia's—and China's—emerging middle class offers "the West, and especially America, some of the most extraordinary business and financial opportunities ever," as Jim Rohwer of CS First Boston puts it. Companies need growth to remain competitive and, as Rohwer notes, "The lion's share of worldwide demand growth will come from Asia, much of it from China. And, because Asia's markets are so new, most of that chunk of extra demand will be up for grabs by anybody. That is why Asian markets should prove so vital to any Western company that wants to grow fast."[10]

The Bears Have Reasons to Growl

At the other end of the spectrum dwell the Bears, who see nothing but trouble ahead for the world's most populous nation. In their view, China might have fallen apart already were it not for the way Deng Xiaoping skillfully (if ruthlessly) held the pieces together. But Deng was the last Chinese leader cut from the remarkable cloth of the Long March; there are no more great Chinese leaders on the horizon. Some Bears wonder whether Jiang or those who follow can hold the country together at all, or whether China will be returned to a new era of "warring states," as happened in the past when dynasties collapsed. The University of California scholar Jack Goldstone sums up this view when he warns of a "terminal crisis within the next 10 to 15 years" because "China shows every sign of a country approaching crisis: a burgeoning population and mass migration amid flattening agricultural production and worker and peasant discontent—and all this as the state rapidly loses its capacity to rule effectively."[11] An infamous study commissioned by the U.S. Department of Defense in 1994 had a majority of its expert participants from the military, universities, and think tanks signing on to a scenario in which there was a 50–50 chance of a Soviet-style breakup in the wake of Deng's death.[12]

Name the ill and China is afflicted with it: bankrupt state enterprises, metastasizing corruption, and the growing economic gaps between rich and poor, urban and rural, coastal and interior; a ruling Communist Party that faces a crisis of credibility and legitimacy, while no viable institutions exist outside it to provide alternatives; an economic reform process that has raised expectations immensely but cannot continue delivering the goods without a political reform, which Beijing refuses to launch; intellectuals and dedicated civil servants becoming impoverished or outcast, or leaving the country in the continuing brain drain, while the crass, brutish, and corrupt climb to the top of the new oligarchy created by the free market; rich southern provinces and ethnic minorities in western ones seeking to go their own way, while fiefdoms are carved out and modern warlords arise; a "floating" population of 100 million unemployed, traveling the country in search of work, creating increasing social chaos and even the seeds for revolution; increasing nationalism that might drive China to invade Taiwan and establish military hegemony over Asia (depending on which Bear you talk to), either because the nation is made arrogant by economic success or because it is so desperately fearful of

Not yet ready to ride the "third wave": "We are contributors to the food chain and ready only for technology niches that don't require massive industrial development. Breakthroughs require capital and accumulated knowledge; we have neither."

—Liu Chuanzhi
President, Legend Group

failure that it conceals its shortcomings by focusing public attention on military campaigns.

From prostitution to gambling, from violent crime to street begging, every ill of old China, frozen in the ice of the 1949 revolution, is coming back to life as the heat of the marketplace melts the constraints of Maoism. And if all this is not daunting enough, the Bears will remind you that China's limited arable soil is eroding, deforestation is rampant, and some forecasts suggest the Chinese will be unable to feed themselves twenty years from now. Smokestacks continue to belch pollution no longer tolerated in the West, while the true environmental impact of new industry and energy projects is routinely ignored in the mad rush for development. Just reading the index entries under China in the Worldwatch Institute's annual *State of the World* report for 1997 is scary: "alcohol abuse . . . aquifer depletion . . . biodiversity depletion . . . carbon emissions . . . CFC use . . . chronic disease . . . desertification . . ." et cetera, et cetera, et cetera.[13]

The arguments of the Bears are often based on the assumption that unless the government gets itself out of the economy and the lives of its citizens, the country will inevitably decline and even collapse. In his article "After Deng the Deluge," for example, the Naval War College and Brown University scholar Arthur Waldron writes, "The root problem in all these [disastrous] scenarios is the anti-democratic character of the Chinese government and its consequent inability to deal with rapid, large-scale change."[14]

A meta-Bearish argument has also come to the fore recently: Some experts believe that all the economies of Asia are running out of steam, and that China will not escape the slowdown. Even before runs on the Thai baht and the Malaysian ringgit triggered the wave of financial and banking crises in Asia in 1997, a number of experts were arguing that most high-growth Asian economies were running out of steam. Now they point to the continuing muck in which Japan, the senior success story in Asia, has found itself, the South Korean miracle grinding to a halt, and the little dragons of Southeast Asia that have been accumulating problems for years—from political succession to excess debt—they can no longer conceal with spectacular growth. The Asia China is joining, say the meta-Bears, is itself a deeply troubled economic region and those who see cracks in the fa-

Views on government from the ancients:
"Look at a small boy herding chickens and you will learn a lesson about governing the people. When the boy presses the chickens too hard, the chickens will become alarmed; when he herds them too gently, the chickens become unresponsive. When their minds are at ease, you can approach them; when they stagger and become unsettled, you should feed them. The best way of herding is by not herding."

—HSÜN YUE (A.D. 148–209)

çades of Asian miracle economies now find troubling similarities in China. A variety of new statistics and new ways of quantifying what's going on in the Chinese economy have recently begun to suggest that poverty is far more widespread than outsiders have generally thought, with as much as a quarter of the country now dwelling below the poverty line. Overall GDP growth is said to be significantly slower than has been assumed, and is no longer in double digits. Foreign investment is slowing as even the ever-naïve foreign businessmen come to realize that Beijing will never let them have real access to those 1.2 billion consumers.

One argument advanced by Bearish economists is that China has already accomplished the "easy part" of economy-building, by decommunizing agriculture and establishing a market basis in other sectors. Further growth will come hard and will require the kind of innovative policy initiatives the Chinese have been reluctant to launch. Removing Communist dogma is easy; sustaining near double-digit economic growth over a long period of time is not.

Economist Paul Krugman, the world's leading expert on productivity, believes China is not seeing much growth in what he calls total factor productivity, which is the main engine for the long-term economic improvements that show up in rising living standards and increased competitiveness internationally. To Krugman, this is a problem not just with China but with all the formerly high-growth dragon economies of Asia. What is needed is not only the introduction of vast amounts of capital and expansion of work forces, but also efficient allocation of investment in both human and physical capital. That would enable economies to expand total output and also get more efficient output per worker.

The once rapidly rising annual growth rate of new foreign investment in China slowed down during 1996–97, which suggests that global corporations had become more cautious even before the stock market crashes that followed. Certainly, many foreign companies have become increasingly vociferous about their problems in accessing the China market even after they have built facilities and entered into joint ventures with prestigious Chinese companies.

However, even taking into account a dip from approximately $42 billion worth of new foreign direct investment commitments in 1996 to what may turn out to be less than $30 billion in 1997, global business interest in China remains

How not to treat foreign investors:
"The Chinese don't like to see investors make a good return on their investment. They see it as a case of foreign investors stealing money that rightfully should stay in China. They still don't really understand the role played by foreign capital, or what motivates foreign capitalists to invest."

—Gordon Y. S. Wu
Managing director,
Hopewell Holdings

165

massive. The figures conceal all sorts of unique Chinese anomalies. For example, significant amounts of domestic funds are exported offshore, only to be brought back as "foreign" investment and thereby freed from certain domestic regulations and taxes. Furthermore, "foreign" investment has always been led by Hong Kong, which the Chinese never considered "foreign" for political purposes, and which is now no longer foreign even in a technical sense. Yet despite all these asterisks on its foreign investment statistics, there is no doubt that China remains second only to the United States as the market of choice for foreign investment, a highly bullish indicator.

Toward the end of 1996, a confluence of the thinking of longstanding China Bears and newly minted Asia Bears emerged. As *Business Week* editorialized:

> Punch through the patina of optimism in Asia and realists will find severe problems. . . . While success has generated enormous profits, much of it has been invested in empty office buildings or in profitless overbuilding of auto, chip, and petrochemical plants. Corruption has mitigated the efficiency that comes with market forces. . . . Government-controlled banks and weak capital markets channel capital to state-owned companies. . . .
>
> To move to the next level of growth, Asia must give up the command economy and move toward one based on markets, merit, and innovation.[15]

All of the above comments could be read as criticisms not just of Asia's direction, but of China most specifically. As these ideas gained currency, however, the Bulls began to ask if they weren't just a lot of wishful Western thinking. Perhaps there *was* a cyclic slowing of Asian growth rates. But a China that is "only" growing at 7 percent is still growing more than twice as fast as the United States and other Western economies.

Within weeks of the *Business Week* article that adopted the Krugman thesis, *Forbes* shot back with a much more Bullish view, calling Krugman a Malthusian guilty of an unwarranted view of Asian growth trends as limited. "The Asian growth juggernaut will roll on," in spite of growing pains, *Forbes* declared. "China receives a qualified bravo. . . . [Its] nascent stock market turned in a stellar performance in 1996, beating

Before crying doom, remember the laws of economics: "We believe that Lester Brown [who predicts widespread famine and disaster as the result of rising demand for grain in China] underestimates the power of prices and markets on human ingenuity. At the right price, we strongly suspect, someone might figure out a way to grow corn on asphalt."

—JAMES GRANT
GRANT'S ASIA OBSERVER

the American S&P by a wide margin [even in a year when the S&P 500 index rose to record heights]. China's economic reforms bubbled along with growth in excess of 10 percent combined with falling inflation."[16]

Inflation, in fact, is an interesting subject to consider for a moment. It formed a prominent part of the Bearish case during an earlier part of this decade, when Richard Hornik, a former Beijing bureau chief for *Time,* opined: "The present regime is ... akin to the hyperinflationary Peronistas in Argentina. ... China's rulers will keep rolling the presses, printing an increasingly worthless currency to fuel a dangerously-inflated bubble economy."[17]

But China has confounded the Bears on this question. In the late 1990s, the consensus of foreign economic experts is that China has, indeed, done a credible job of slowing inflation to manageable levels. Inflation still could spin out of control in the future. But as of now, this particular crisis has been avoided.

Our Own View

We ourselves stand well between the extremes of Bulls and Bears—but not in the middle of the road. We take the Bears' arguments seriously. In the end, however, we reject many of their worst scenarios as unlikely. As for the Bulls, they are undoubtedly too optimistic, too dismissive of the dangers pointed out by the Bears, too forgetful of the drag imposed by culture, too willing to commit the biggest mistake in futurology: extrapolating present trends into the distant future. Nevertheless, we lean well into the Bullish wind when it comes to assessing how China will evolve in the twenty-first century.

You might say that we are cautious Bulls. We reject the idea that China will come to dominate the world as *the* great power of the twenty-first century. But we also reject the idea that it will it collapse of its own weight and fail to adapt itself to Western approaches to capitalism and democracy. China's emergence on the world economic scene will not be the gee-whiz success story that some businesspeople hope for. Nor will China be the exclusively negative force constantly undermining global peace, security, and the environment that some fear.

"**We are racing against the clock**, waiting to see which will grow faster, prosperity or the contradictions. If the growth rate falls below seven percent, and if a recession lasts more than a year, then the trend will be toward more and more polarization and fragmentation."

—ALLAN H. LIU
PRESIDENT, CHINA RETAIL FUND

Whatever number you choose, it's big— and will mean either boom or decline for your company: China will purchase more than 500 passenger planes by 2015 (Airbus, 1994). China will buy 1,320 aircraft with a seat capacity of more than 100 each between 1995 and 2014 (Airbus, 1995). China will need 800 new aircraft by 2010 (Boeing, 1995). China will spend $89.7 billion on 1,200 passenger planes by 2010 (Chase Manhattan Bank, 1994). More than 150 aircraft will be added to China's fleets by the year 2000, and 1,000 more by 2014 (China's aviation administration).

It is certainly legitimate to consider the possibility of extreme dislocation and chaos. China's modern history has witnessed radical systemic shocks and a tendency for the political-economic pendulum to swing more extremely and more rapidly than it does elsewhere. Recall, for example, that John K. Fairbank, the dean of American sinology in the latter half of the twentieth century, predicted with great confidence that no upheaval would follow the death of Mao in 1976, even as what amounted to an attempted coup d'état, a countercoup, and a seismic schism in the leadership were already happening.

The example of Fairbank makes us wary of forecasting that China will continue largely along the course already defined. In fact, we believe China *needs* (and we fully expect to see) a catharsis to sort out the errors of the past and establish the systems of the future. But such a catharsis need not set China back irretrievably. Indeed, it will make possible the continued push forward. We have witnessed with our own eyes and in our own experiences the process by which the new Chinese economic miracle has taken hold. Since our first travels, China has relentlessly and indefatigably pursued economic reform, developing at least some market mechanisms and opening to, and integrating with, the outside world. An argument could be made that Chinese economic policy has moved more steadily toward a distinct set of goals over the last twenty years than American economic policy has.

The fundamentals of the debate in China today, between what might be called a "conservative traditionalist" camp and a more "liberal reform" group, reflect public policy differences not much wider than those in the West. The substantive debate in China actually mirrors, to some degree, the arguments of the last two decades between Clintonomics and Reaganomics and between European social democracy and Thatcherism. In the West, of course, we have institutionalized peaceful methods of resolving these differences. The fact that China is only just now beginning to work on the rule of law, public participation in policymaking, and orderly transfers of power makes these relatively moderate political differences subject to inflammation at any moment.

The Chinese reform process has not been without alternations between overacceleration on the gas pedal and slamming on the brakes with a screech. But while we have seen veering off course, we have not seen 90-degree turns, let alone 180-degree turns. Instead, China has generally steered along the wide swath that constitutes the middle of the road forward.

For American business, and for foreign investors more generally, our view of the overall political-economic climate in China is cautiously optimistic. We would dissuade investors looking for a quick killing in China or for excess returns on investment. But for companies that are in China for the long haul, with sound strategies and good local partners and knowledge, the environment in which they are working is going to be relatively stable over the next few years. Although some American companies may continue to face political problems and the effects of Chinese nationalism, these factors will be balanced by the continued strong growth and maturation of the China market.

By the middle of the next decade, China's compounding growth numbers will start to be multiplied by an improved infrastructure for doing business, enhanced market access, a greater acceptance of WTO rules and other international norms, and an ever growing, better educated, more sophisticated middle class. The foreign companies that have stayed the course through the next few years of transition and turbulence will be the big beneficiaries.

CHAPTER 7

China's Burdens

CATEGORIZATION INTO "BULLS" AND "BEARS" is convenient but can't, of course, account for the depth of thinking or the various alternatives anticipated by those in each camp. China requires a perceptual shift away from easy categorizations and assumptions and toward a view of the country as a large, complex feudal castle unto itself, whose position, scale, history, and centuries-long habits of mind and heart inevitably shape it into a very different architecture than most in the West have preconceived for it.

In locating the benchmarks upon which China will construct its future—essential building blocks that will affect it not only domestically but also internationally—we must first consider a series of burdens unparalleled in development history that will constrain the hard-won progress made thus far.

The Burden of Scale

The most promising of China's characteristics is also the biggest threat to its very survival: scale. Everyone knows China is the world's most populous nation; currently its inhabitants number about 1.21 billion.[1] The dream of reaching some chunk of that vast consumer market is what keeps foreign companies willingly slogging through the otherwise overwhelming obstacle courses that China represents. And yet, many people fail to grasp China's dimensions or understand the limits and challenges this scale places on those whose job it is to try to pilot the most vast society in history through the often unnavigable waters of reform and modernization. It is therefore worthwhile to focus for a moment on just how vast China actually is.

Its ever-expanding population forces China to feed not just a quarter of the world's people, but an *additional* 13 million to 15 million mouths each year. In a single decade, China will add as many people as live in Japan today. Within a generation, it will likely have added the equivalent of a whole United States. Here are just some examples of what these population numbers mean in terms of people's daily life:

• Among China's State-Owned Enterprises there are 500 that employ more than 100,000 people—forty times the number of companies of similar size in the United States.

• Every year, China's economy must create 10 million to 15 million new jobs, two to three times as many as the miracle job machine in the United States creates. Amazingly, China's leaders have been doing just that.

• The "floating population" of peasants who have become migrant laborers is roughly the size of the entire United States workforce: over 100 million people. The government projects that in the next five years 137 million farmers (a number just 10 million short of the entire population of Russia) will become redundant.

• China has more cities of 1 million–plus population than the rest of the world combined. Thirty more are likely to emerge in the next decade. As Singapore's longtime prime minister, Lee Kuan Yew, notes when discussion turns to his country as a potential model for China, "Yes—but there are over one hundred metropolitan areas in China that have a population of Singapore's size or greater. The Singapore model may work if you can devote all your resources to it—but I don't know if even the Chinese with all their resources, all their cleverness, and all their determination can do it a hundred times."

• One province alone, Sichuan, would rank as the world's seventh most populous country, nearly as big as France and

"**Multiplying 1.2 billion** times anything is a lot."

—LESTER BROWN
 WORLDWATCH INSTITUTE

171

Britain together. Nine Chinese provinces would each rank among the top twenty of populous nations.

• The number of middle-class urban consumers in China is greater than the U.S. middle class. The number of paid government functionaries is greater than the entire population of Britain. The number of Communist Party members exceeds the combined total populations of California and New York. China has more peasants than the combined total populations of North America, South America, and Europe, both east and west. The preference for male offspring means there will be some 40 million more men than women by the turn of the century, the equivalent of the entire population of America's forty-seven largest cities looking for a date on Saturday night.

• China's energy appetite is equally outsized: the United Nations Development Program (UNDP) estimates China will burn 3.1 billion tons of coal annually by 2020. By then, it will be consuming more coal in one year than the United States has burned *since the Industrial Revolution.*

• Giantism takes its toll in every arena, including human misery and suffering. The number of disabled Chinese is greater than the total population of France. Floods have been known to create more new homeless people in a single year than live in all of America's cities combined.

• A great silver wave is about to envelop the country. China has 30 million retirees now; it is forecast to have more than four times that number by 2025, meaning it will have as many people aged 60 or more as the rest of the world combined.

Even China's entrepreneurs dream on a scale that might have made Robert Moses blush. Shanghai, already one of the world's biggest cities, has been the scene of the world's biggest building boom in recent years, with plans to complete the world's tallest skyscraper by 2001. Mou Qizhong, one of China's most flamboyant entrepreneurs, has proposed to blast a tunnel through the Himalayas to let warm, moist air from the Indian Ocean turn China's northwestern deserts into productive farmland. Millions of investment dollars aren't enough for him. With a mix of chutzpah and hubris, he declares: "I need billions."

Of course, China's vast scale has many virtues, from the

point of view of development strategies and economic growth. Just when in Japan, Europe, and North America the number of citizens outside the workforce is rapidly increasing the burden on government, there is a huge population bulge just entering China's workforce, ready to expand both savings and spending. Obviously, if China's market were not as huge as it is, it couldn't attract the kind of foreign investment needed to catalyze the modernization process. If the labor force were not so vast, China could not be the low-cost manufacturing center it is. Without the enormous captive domestic market to service, Chinese enterprises could probably not dream of becoming world leaders in higher value–added businesses. In short, it is the "big" factor that makes the Chinese dragon such a significant force in the world.

Still, scale is an immense burden to China. The sheer size of the population makes change, reform, and progress far more difficult and complex than they might otherwise be. When so many mouths must be fed, so many people clothed, so many jobs created, innovators can afford to take fewer risks in economic policy. To a person, Chinese leaders are deeply affected by the legacy of all the colossal policy failures in recent memory. They saw their people starve by the tens of millions during the Great Leap Forward. They have seen massive disruption in their lives from political travesties, chaos, and near civil war of the Cultural Revolution. They know what can happen when a wrong decision is made and then magnified by China's gargantuan dimensions. Thus, China's burden of scale figures prominently in the current atmosphere of caution. Big China dictates incrementalism, not more revolutions.

The Burden of Nature and Geography

Being big creates many problems, but perhaps none so delicate as trying to grow an economy of China's potential into a modern superpower on a highly constrained resource base. China is a good-sized continental nation—physically the second largest in the world—and is blessed with many natural riches. But no nation has ever undertaken so vast an economic and industrial revolution on so weak a resource and ecological foundation.

China must support one-fifth of humankind with less than

An environmental tsunami: Degradation of China's environment is taking place on a colossal scale. Half the rain in Guangdong province is now acidic; more than 14,000 people died from fertilizer and pesticide poisoning in 1994; the rate of lung cancer from atmospheric pollution is running near 20 percent; and about 40 billion tons of sewage and industrial waste flow back into the water supply each year— far more than the waste of the rest of the world combined.

one-fifteenth of the world's farmland. As relentless population growth and industrial progress continue, per capita arable land declines—a stunning 35 percent since 1978.[2] "Right there you have *the* key facts to know about China," observes Richard Margolis, a managing director of Merrill Lynch's Smith New Court unit in Hong Kong. Other resources are also in decline. In the past eight years, China's oil output has risen a mere 1 or 2 percent annually, while consumption has expanded 7 to 8 percent. And the economic boom threatens to literally choke the Chinese. Already, Chinese scientists say, industrial pollution contributes to respiratory ailments responsible for as many as a quarter of all deaths in China.

The shortage of arable land, dwindling natural resources, an inexorably rising population, and the black dragon of pollution create imperatives all their own, giving new urgency to the idea of sustainable development. It is a delicate balance that only a sound economic environment and stable political climate can help maintain.

The Hungry Dragon

Think for a moment about this statistic: four acres of rich, fertile domestic farmland support each American. Now consider China, where the arable land per person works out to be about the size of an American backyard. What's more, the size of that backyard is shrinking. Every year the country loses to urban development, erosion, and environmental degradation an area of arable land equal in size to the whole state of Pennsylvania—and gains half that state's population in the same period. The Japanese economist Susumu Yabuki estimates that China's existing arable land and resources cannot support more than 950 million persons optimally—and that is about 300 million people *less* than the current population.

The more prosperous China becomes, the greater will be the strains on its resources. So many people can now afford Big Macs in Beijing that beef consumption in the capital tripled in the year after McDonald's opened its first three restaurants. More meat in the Chinese diet means that the feed grain needed to raise more cattle, pigs, and chickens has gone up an astounding 50 million tons in the past four years, the biggest surge in world history. Estimates are that even if

Estimated impact on the world market price if China decides to supply just 10 percent of its domestic rice consumption with imports: +80 percent.

174

China could double its grain output in twenty years—and such a feat is generally considered unlikely—there still would not be enough to feed each Chinese as well as he or she eats today.

Chinese scientists estimate a food-grain supply gap of between 50 million and 100 million tons annually in the coming five decades. Lester Brown, director of the Worldwatch Institute, has made the dire prediction that China will need as much as 300 million tons of grain from world markets by 2030—demand that would be far greater than all the global stocks now available for worldwide export. A Chinese shortfall, Brown has suggested, could empty the world's cupboards and even cause global famine.

Such pessimism is probably excessive. Advances in agricultural science, increased productivity, and the expansion of new productive sources of supply, such as Russian croplands, will forestall this apocalypse. China—and the world—will adjust over time. Nevertheless, there is no doubt that Beijing's internal and foreign policies will be very much conditioned by the realities of China's soil and crop production.

The Black Dragon

Hanging over China's future is an appalling black cloud of pollution, giving credence to the notion that China is a candidate for environmental catastrophe. Professor Vaclav Smil of the University of Manitoba is one of the Western world's leading authorities on China's environment. He points out that even if China were able to *decrease* its annual economic growth rate from the current 10 percent to the Western average of about 2 percent (a decline that would likely create economic chaos and political rebellion), particulate emissions would still *increase* annually by an amount equal to what the United States spews out in a year. Output of acid-rain-causing sulfur dioxide would, even under that implausible growth-constrained scenario, "only" rise by an amount equal to the annual total in Germany.

China already has seven of the ten most polluted cities in the world, and forty-three cities whose air contains sulfur dioxide concentrations that exceed World Health Organization standards. Half the rain in Guangdong province is acidic; in the southern industrial city of Changsha, the figure

Not yet ready for the West's environmental standards: "You try to tell the people of Beijing that they can't buy a car or an air-conditioner because of the global climate-change issue. It is just as hot in Beijing as it is in Washington, D.C."

—Li Junfang
Energy researcher,
State Planning
Commission

175

is 90 percent. Already water poor, China finds its water table receding and its rivers and lakes fouled. In 1993, public water supplies in Jiangsu province had to be shut off for days to allow a sixty-square-mile "black tide" of poisonous effluent to pass downriver from factories upstream—and this was the country's eighth black tide in seven years.

Environmental degradation is likely to get worse. If, as projected by the Yale Center for Environmental Law and Policy, eight out of ten households in major cities have acquired a refrigerator by the turn of the century, that extra use of energy alone will double China's carbon dioxide emissions. Today China has only one vehicle for every 1,000 people, compared to the United States, which has 570 vehicles for every 1,000 people. Imagine the potential for pollution, let alone the unimaginable oil consumption, if China were ever to reach even half our ratio.

"Add the constraints of natural disasters—China has suffered some of the world's worst earthquakes and floods in recent memory—and one can easily envisage ecological collapse on an unprecedented scale," warns Douglas P. Murray, president of the Lingnan Foundation and an expert on China's environment. "That, in turn, implies the specter of mass migrations, floods of refugees crossing politically sensitive borders, appeals for international aid already stretched thin, and increasing reliance on the military as a means of control. Impossible . . . or just unthinkable?"[3]

The Difficult Balance

The combination of a shortage of arable land and a vast population to feed creates powerful forces that transcend ideology and politics, and drives China toward economic reform and closer integration with the world economy. As Richard Margolis points out, "China has become a net oil importer, it is a net staple crop importer, and it has over $100 billion of net external debt. Any leader who wants to maintain growth and prosperity in China has to recognize that there is no going back to self-sufficiency and autarchy. China *must* participate in the global economy."

Skeptics argue, however, that China's shortages of food and resources could just as easily encourage it to become an aggressive power, seeking to obtain what it lacks through military force. But this theory is somewhat melodramatic. It

Your threat is my threat: "At their brief summit meeting in late 1995, President Jiang Zemin of China asked President Clinton bluntly, 'Are you trying to contain China or not?' Replied Mr. Clinton, 'No, no, I'm trying to engage, I don't want to contain you. But it might surprise you to know what I think the greatest threat to our security you present is— that all of your people will want to get rich in exactly the same way we got rich. And unless we try to triple the automobile milage and to reduce greenhouse gas emissions, if you all get rich in that way we won't be breathing very well. There are just so many more of you than there are of us, and if you behave exactly the same way we do, you will do irrevocable damage to the global environment. And it will be partly our fault, because we got there first and we should be able to figure out how to help you solve this problem.' "

—THOMAS L. FRIEDMAN
THE NEW YORK TIMES

is hard to imagine China marching into Vietnam, occupying it successfully, and exporting its rice crop back to China, for example, in a throwback to the past empire's feudalism and colonialism. It is easier to imagine China and Russia striking up a twenty-first-century alliance that involves trading Chinese manufactured goods for Russian wheat and other crops.

It is the environmental problem that may present the most danger. From the viewpoint of those of us in an advanced economy, the solution is straightforward: rein in China's economic growth and follow sounder, more environmentally conscious development policies. As rational as this logic may be from an outsider's viewpoint, it will always be hard for the Chinese to accept. That should not be surprising. After all, as the United States drove west in the nineteenth century, Native Americans warned that we were depleting and destroying the environment. We not only ignored the message, we killed the messengers. Even today, when American society has become so ecologically aware, we still continue to operate the most resource-consumptive and wasteful economy in the world.

The Chinese have some strong environmental laws and programs in place and cannot be said to be uninformed or unconcerned. However, they are underfunded and lack consistent means of enforcement when dealing with large State-Owned Enterprises that pollute. Still, hundreds of factories have been closed down, many because of strong, local grassroots lobbying. And Beijing is assiduously trying to reforest, fight soil erosion, and develop clean new industries. The government is also exploring solar power, methane gas, and other alternative energy sources more actively than the United States is. Some of Beijing's policies most disliked by Western human rights activists are, ironically, of direct benefit to the environment; these include population control and measures to prevent migrants from flooding into the cities as has happened elsewhere in the third world.

Chinese leaders must play a constant game of environmental chicken, trying to grow the economy as much as possible without triggering ecological disaster. That is going to be a very difficult balancing act indeed, considering that there are no parallels in history with the scale, scope, and intensity of China's modernization. And it's just one of the many challenges any leadership group must face.

Finding the key toward a new and better environmental policy: "Environmental protection is a priority at the highest level of government because it is seen as a critical part of the need to maintain social stability, and everything here ultimately boils down to whether it contributes to social stability. That is why I am hopeful that some of the worst scenario prophecies will be wrong."

—ARTHUR HOLCOMB
CHINA REPRESENTATIVE,
UNDP

The Burden of History and Culture

Powerful as the constraints of size and resources are, the constraints of culture may be even more potent. Customs and beliefs chosen or rejected over several millennia have shaped China as it now is. Even modern China is more a civilization than a "nation" or a "government."

Although the changes of the last twenty years have been enormous, there are many core areas in which Chinese culture insulates itself from change. There is, for example, the centuries-long dominance of a single set of values, and the accompanying intolerance toward rival, incompatible views of society, politics, and the world. These tendencies, in turn, are magnified by the persistent legacy of China's long feudal past. This is particularly important for Americans to understand, especially since we have so little history of feudalism in our own national background. In China, feudalism was only yesterday, and its thick sediment slows and distorts the onrushing swirl of modernization. History dominates in the Middle Kingdom, as it always has. No society in the world has so much of it, nor such dramatic, complex, and persistent themes, nor so many echoes and influences from the past on the present.

The autocratic methods of leadership, the one-way relations of people with the state, the powerful forces of clannishness, the problems of an institutional framework that lacks deeply rooted democratic impulses, the importance of pride and "face." The role of intellectuals, the distrust of entrepreneurs, the propensity to nationalism and xenophobia, the contradictions between the cities and the countryside. The role of women; the deep conservatism and provincialism that gridlock action on pressing problems. All these factors and many more derive in large part from China's long feudal past, accentuated and bolstered by the Maoist experience, which often meant feudalist policies with Communist rhetoric. Emperor Mao and even Emperor Deng were, after all, the true last emperors of China.

Time

The influence of the past begins with a sense of time. In some areas China is racing ahead, compressing into the space of a decade changes that took place over a century or more in other parts of the world. That kind of wildfire growth creates many pockets of advancement alongside the ancient backwardness. For example, the world's biggest network of pagers and mobile phones is being rolled out in China, even while basic land-line telephony remains woefully inadequate.

In other areas, China appears to plod on, almost unconscious of the time it is taking to put certain reforms in place. Westerners are frequently frustrated when they see officials dragging their feet on a policy decision or a license approval where quick action would appear to be very much in China's own interests. Chinese leaders, on the other hand, generally do not perceive themselves as being in a race with time or with any other force. Unlike Japan of the 1960s and 1970s, where policymakers furiously optimized national development strategies, urged on by the stated goal of catching up to the GDP of one country after another, China is more concerned with maintaining order and stability—or political advantage—than with achieving any specific development goal in the short term. The preference in China is to make only those changes buttressed by an appropriate consensus, changes that will rock neither the political nor the social boat.

We in the West like to think that time is on our side because we are adaptable, flexible, and change-loving. But we may turn out to be hares competing with the Chinese tortoise. Back in 1898, when the British signed the ninety-nine-year lease on Hong Kong's New Territories, no one in their ranks gave much thought to what would happen when the ninety-nine years was up, because ninety-nine years of Anglo-American/European time is an eternity. One might as well have asked what the earth will do when the sun burns out. But to the Chinese, ninety-nine years is a blink of the eye. Now the tortoise is patiently, ploddingly marching forward to absorb all the fabulous wealth that many hares built over the years in Hong Kong.

Emperors, Intellectuals, and Bureaucrats

One can read the history of Western politics as the story of an effort to find an effective way to balance the power between ruler and ruled. The West is full of organizations and institutions that provide checks and balances: supreme courts,

Views on government from the ancients: "In the government of the Sage he empties their minds and fills their bellies; he weakens their ambitions, and strengthens their bones."

—LAO TSE

179

congresses, churches, mass media, labor unions, and other organized interest groups. No such tradition exists in China. Few autonomous institutions ever emerged to limit, much less share, the emperor's power.

In modern China, the "emperor" is the Communist Party. Though it is weaker and less influential than it once was, it is still the most powerful institution in the country. Even the armed forces, arguably the only institution in China with any independence, are still led, for now, by the Party. All the checks and balances on the Party's power are internal to the Party, and invisible to the outside world.

This arrangement grows out of Communist history only in part. In larger measure, it arises from the tenacity of a traditional system in which autocrats and bureaucrats shared control over the machinery of state and key levers of the economy. As the Singapore-based cultural historian Wang Gungwu points out, the extraordinary continuity of the imperial system was made possible by generations of intellectuals whispering to the sovereign in power: "Ruling a country as complex as China is a difficult job, so better let us run it for you." By agreeing, the emperor earned the virtual blind loyalty of the administrative elite. The quality of China's "mandarins" and intellectual policymakers—along with their abject loyalty to rulers both good and evil—defines the periods of China's greatest achievements as well as its darkest hours.

Mao tried to shatter this cozy arrangement, but Deng Xiaoping returned to the old convention; he believed that growth—and stability—had to be engineered *through* a trained bureaucracy, not by trying to go around it. Made indispensable once again, and able to serve a reformist government, hundreds of young, energetic, educated people in the late 1970s and the 1980s became government functionaries, professionals, academics, scientists, engineers, writers, and artists. They began work in think tanks and in business and financial institutions. Some were appointed mayors or given top-level provincial posts.

They may be very capable, talented, and educated in the new knowledge of the global economy. They may aspire to help develop the rule of law and a more pluralistic society. They may be critical of some government policies, and even openly cynical about the party's shortcomings. But if they have stayed in important posts, they have generally become like their historical brethren: offering loyalty and cautious gradualism to the rulers of the state, favoring stability and incremental change within the system.[4]

Most Chinese, even sophisticated, middle-class urbanites, now accept the traditional view: spontaneous politics is destabilizing and should be avoided. Disagreement on moral principle is an honorable tradition. But organizing outright political opposition has almost always been seen as leading to chaos, and is now—after the brief Tiananmen spring—seen that way again.

The historical dominance of narrow, hierarchical Confucianist thinking often makes even Chinese baby boomers and Generation X-ers more supportive of the system than outsiders might at first assume. Because of the younger generations' consumerism and their desire for better living standards and freer lifestyles, foreigners seem to think it axiomatic that they will be outspoken supporters of a more Westernized political future. But while the desire for genuine political democracy may exist widely in latent form, it rarely takes any specific, programmatic shape. Outside the country, a handful of visionaries articulate substantive programs of political change. Inside the country there are brave individual voices. In universities, think tanks and study groups, there is discussion. But it is muted at best. If there are Thomas Jeffersons, Alexander Hamiltons, and James Madisons among today's Chinese intellectuals—people who can see beyond today's political realities and project an entirely different system *in the detail necessary to implement one*—it is certainly hard to find them.

Even among those whom foreigners would expect to be able to articulate a democratic vision, the results can be surprising. "I don't disagree with socialism," a thoroughly modern "new capitalist" tells us. "We just have to reform it, not make revolution against it." When a reporter interviewed Song Qiang, one of the young, brash neonationalist authors of the 1996 best-seller *China Can Say No,* he continually repeated the major theme of the book: to just say no to "American culture, ideology and value systems." So, asked the reporter, to what did Song want to say yes? "Traditional values taught by Confucius and Taoism: Submission, obedience," came the reply.[5]

The continuity of tradition: "For 50 years there were almost no good private restaurants in Shanghai. All the great chefs of the pre-Communist era left China or died off. But go to Shanghai today and you find they are cooking just like they did 50 years ago. That's the power of tradition. The Chinese have not lost the talents that come from having once been a great culture."

—JIMMY LAI
CONTROVERSIAL HONG
KONG ENTREPRENEUR

900 Million Peasants

"But have you been out in the countryside to discuss China's future with the peasants?" The question, asked toward the end of an elaborate lunch held to discuss the future of China's banking system with one of the country's most powerful financiers, would seem a non sequitur if we had not been hearing the same message for the past twenty years. After talking about the problems of the State-Owned Enterprises, China's emerging markets, and mergers-and-acquisitions business in the West, why is our host asking us this question? And why is it asked over and over again by the senior Chinese officials who talk to foreigners?

Deference to China's 900 million peasants is an acquired characteristic of all Maoists, even lapsed ones.[6] Mao developed his sinicized version of European Marxism on the basis of his understanding of Chinese feudalism and the Chinese peasantry. Later, he made the theory work in real life by leading the modern world's first successful peasant revolution. Forever after, "the wisdom of the peasants" was a phrase stamped into the thinking of Chinese intellectuals and officials whose natural habit, given the legacy of feudalism, would otherwise have been a kind of noblesse oblige or, more likely, condescension. Chinese elites for thousands of years have known that how the peasants are governed makes the difference between a prosperous and successful China and a hungry and rebellious one. But only in Mao's time did the peasants become glorified political heroes.

In recent years, however, restiveness in the countryside and growing income disparities have told the leadership that it may have tilted too far in improving the lives and opportunities of city and coastal dwellers at the peasants' expense.

The one thing Chinese leaders are certain of is that they cannot afford a restive peasantry. (Which is why, for example, the government said it would not raise taxes or impose new ones on farmers before the year 2000.) Nor can they allow the conditions that would create an all-out dash for wealthy cities like Beijing, Shanghai, Guangzhou, and Chongqing. They know that in the blink of an eye, these cities could have the kinds of urban slums that mark Rio, Mexico City, and Lagos, where peasants have swarmed off the land in a fruitless search for opportunity in the cities. With 100 million Chinese peasants already turned into a potentially volatile pool of floating migrant labor, and with the gap between the richest city dwellers and the poorest peasants becoming a shocking social divide in a country that has known nominal egalitarianism for fifty years, new solutions must be found.

In aggregate, the peasantry is an enormous stumbling block to China's development. Anyone with a flair for economic theorizing can imagine how to turn China's 300 million urban and coastal dwellers into a new "Asian dragon" economy akin to Singapore, Hong Kong, or Taiwan. But as for the 900 million peasants and rural dwellers, no one has a good answer. Their land could be used more productively for other purposes. But if too many peasants lose their roots to the land too quickly, there will be no jobs for them elsewhere.

Knowing that a Herculean job lies ahead to promote peasant productivity growth and enhanced living standards, the Chinese leaders long ago dropped the prediction made popular during Deng's initial stages of reform in the early 1980s: that China would be a modern nation and catch up with the rest of the world by the end of the century. Because of the peasantry, its poverty, backwardness, and highly constrained future, China *as a whole* cannot catch up to the West any time soon—if ever—in terms of living standards, per capita output, or other such measures.

Blades of Grass—China's Entrepreneurs

The business press is full of breathless stories of China's new capitalists, always on their cell phones making deals, tooling around in their Mercedes, frequenting trendy boutiques and glitzy restaurants. Shanghai's most dashing elite now own Ferraris, even though there are few places to drive them. In a Zegna menswear boutique in Beijing we ask the shopkeeper: "Who buys these two-thousand-dollar sport coats?"

"Businessmen," she says.

"Foreigners?"

"No!" she says. "Rich Chinese businessmen. From here!"

The Western media seem to be saying that these wheeler-dealers personify the future of China. But if entrepreneurship and the private economy are to define China's future, then that future is much further off than casual observation in

Left behind on the farm: Women now constitute half the agricultural workforce; the local men have joined construction crews and pools of day laborers in cities.

the lobbies of China's international hotels, upscale restaurants, and roaring nightclubs would suggest. Once again, the feudal tradition places considerable drag on the modernization process.

In history, merchants occupied the lowest rungs of the Chinese social ladder, below peasants and far, far behind the scholar elite. Not that commerce wasn't important; the fabled Silk Road, the ancient traders' highway between Europe and Cathay, dates back to the second century. Economic expansion during the Sung Dynasty in the twelfth and thirteenth centuries was so great it could be called a "commercial revolution." But what did *not* happen is the relevant point. The imperial bureaucracy not only looked down upon merchants, but utilized its power to tax, issue licenses, and grant privileges to stunt the growth of a real merchant-business class. When businesses (such as the salt trade, or the lending of money) became too successful, Chinese officialdom simply appropriated these businesses for its own profit, turning them into state-run monopolies.

In Europe, the rise of the merchant class led to its accumulation of wealth, the growth of the cities, and the eventual realignment of government: once oriented toward agriculture and feudalism, it became oriented toward commerce and capitalism. No such social movement took place in China. Merchants did not emerge as a class; towns remained seats of bureaucratic power; no industrial revolution took place; and feudalism remained intact into the twentieth century.[7]

It is an open question how much China has changed in this respect. A tale of two cities makes the point. Dongjiao, a rural township near Guangzhou, claimed in 1995 to have achieved the remarkable per capita income of $1,600 per year (the national average for rural areas is $145). The town did it by selling outsiders shares in its major farm enterprises. Chinese national media were prohibited from reporting on this success, however, and told instead to lavish praise on towns like Nanjie in Henan. The reason? They have grown richer by pooling their *own* resources rather than selling stakes to outsiders. Nanjie is being touted as a paragon of market success *and* recollectivization. Its citizens have incomes far above the rural average. It has eschewed the Dengist "responsibility system" and erected a thirty-foot marble statue of Chairman Mao. In this back-to-the-future

Who's important to China's development? Not entrepreneurs but peasants, says a Chinese poll. A 1994 poll asked respondents nationwide to rank various social and professional categories in terms of their importance to China's economic development. Private businesspeople and entrepreneurs finished sixth, well behind peasants, peasant-workers, ordinary cadres, senior cadres, and entrepreneurs in state and collective enterprises. Ironically, the same poll taken in the early years of the reforms ranked entrepreneurs first.

enclave, "socialist spiritual civilization" is taught in the schools, as are the quotations of Chairman Mao. The Party secretary, responsible for this economic renaissance within a socialist framework, tells a reporter, "We urge our people to be round on the outside and square on the inside."[8] See, China's leaders seem to be saying, we can use all the key aspects of modernization—competition, entrepreneurship, new technologies, advanced management techniques—while still putting the group first.

The recent rise of entrepreneurs has been officially encouraged in China, and some of these people have become incredibly wealthy. But while the system can utilize the energy and economic benefits of entrepreneurs, it doesn't champion them. After all, their potential as an independent power base is threatening. Zhang Yapei, the head of Shanghai's Federation of Industry and Commerce, makes this clear:

> The state will retain ownership of the major share of the city's economy *forever*. Private enterprise will always only play a supplementary role. We can't have a system in which private companies play the primary role. The private sector is only useful for handling the activities that the state sector cannot handle.[9]

This means that, for now, the most vital growth and innovation must continue to occur outside the system rather than within it. This is an irony that touches even the most successful companies. Consider the case of a company like the Stone Corporation, founded in 1984 by four friends with little more than pocket change and a software program that allowed a Japanese computer printer to print out in Chinese characters. Today Stone is China's biggest "private" high-tech enterprise, with sales of over $700 million. It boasts joint ventures with Panasonic, Compaq, and Mitsui, has a division listed on the Hong Kong stock exchange, and dabbles in everything from pharmaceuticals to baby food, industrial controls to furniture and chocolate pies. It also has divisions handling real estate, securities trading, and merchant banking.[10]

Yet its success depends almost entirely upon the government. While Stone describes itself as "private," it is actually registered legally as a "collective" enterprise, meaning it is outside the state system but still accountable to it. Moreover, after a number of Stone executives and employees joined the

It may be "glorious" to get rich, but it is still not esteemed: In a 1994 poll asking people nationwide, "How many people have reached wealthy status through 'normal' means?" nearly 50 percent checked the answer "Not too many," and 11 percent more said "Virtually none."

—*WEN WEI BAO* (HONG KONG)

1989 antigovernment demonstrations in Tiananmen Square, the People's Liberation Army occupied Stone's offices briefly and three members of senior management fled the country. Stone, which has been synonymous with innovative private enterprise, was suddenly the target of ideological scrutiny and attack. Today, Stone's chairman, Shen Guojun, waves this painful memory off by saying simply, "We had some difficulties caused by the June fourth incident, but that is something out of the past."

Even now that the company is once again in political favor and thriving commercially, some part of Shen Guojun remains wary. He offers a telling analogy: "Between the concrete curb and the sidewalk itself is often a crack, and sometimes some grass grows out in between. But it is not nurtured by good soil and water. It is more fragile. And when the wind blows . . ." Shen's voice trails off, leaving only the hum of the air conditioner to fill the silence.

CHAPTER 8

Impossible Problems— and Possible Solutions

THE BURDENS CHINA CARRIES into the next century are not just physical and cultural but social and institutional. Two decades of growth and enrichment have unleashed forces that threaten to pull the society apart. Many of them are caused by the contradictions that have plagued China historically and that Maoism had once sought to eradicate forcefully. The sharpest of these are between the Haves and the Have-Nots, between the cities and the countryside, between the central government and the increasingly powerful provinces, and between the still-dominant state-controlled economy and the emerging market economy.

These rips in the fabric of society produce unemployment, corruption, and a wide unraveling of social values. Each in its own way poses a significant risk of widespread social upheaval. Taken together, and if allowed to widen, they could certainly create the basis for the disintegration and chaos that the China Bears imagine. At the same time, as Mao might have said, these contradictions carry within them the seeds of their own solution. The Chinese leadership must be able to make at least some progress toward solving these problems to prevent systemic breakdown. But it will clearly be a challenge.

Whoops, he spoke too soon:
"Economically, the contradiction between town and country was an extremely antagonistic one in capitalist China. But in a socialist country this antagonistic contradiction has changed into one that is nonantagonistic; and when communist society is reached it will be abolished."

—MAO ZEDONG

Haves and Have-Nots

Mao's revolution swept to power partly because it promised to do something about the terrible wealth disparities of pre-1949 China. True to its ideals, the Communist Party managed to establish a peasant-based economy that enforced egalitarianism in income and status. Workers, soldiers, bureaucrats, and intellectuals were no better paid or more respected than peasants—often less so, in the case of bureaucrats and intellectuals. Inequality, of course, existed even at the high tide of Maoism. Senior Chinese leaders lived a good and even luxurious secret life through some of China's harshest times. But considering the size of Chinese society, wide disparities were remarkably absent in the Maoist days. Egalitarianism was real, even if everyone stayed poor together.

In the go-go 1990s, however, there are millionaires driving fancy cars and living lavish lifestyles, and there are homeless beggars in the streets of Chinese cities. Domestic services, illegal during the Cultural Revolution, is a huge new job category. Class and privilege have returned with a vengeance, and the country's social polarization is beginning to approach the extremes of American and other capitalist societies, which the Chinese have historically deplored.

At Beijing discos and nightclubs like NASA, Paradise, Top 10, and Apollo, the new elite soak up French cognac, watch the latest foreign videos, join in drunken karaoke singing, and swap tales of real estate investments and public offerings of their companies' stock. But millions have been left behind, a concern that weighs heavily on the mind of Yan Minfu, vice minister of civil affairs. Yan is pensive as he tries to convey the mind-boggling extent of China's social welfare burden. While the urban nouveaux riches swill the most expensive wines, some 80 million people in the countryside cannot afford tea and are chronically short of drinking water. "What is the true dimension of the challenge?" we ask Minister Yan. The stunning answer: an average of 120 million to 150 million people a year need social welfare just to survive. If Yan had to help everyone in China whose income falls below the international poverty line of a dollar a day, he and his government would have to reach some *340 million* people.[1]

Another ominous counterpoint to the new prosperity can be heard in the streets, which echo with the footsteps of millions of workers fired or "temporarily" furloughed from the cash-strapped State-Owned Enterprises. Talk about downsizing: Shanghai mayor Xu Kuangdi reported that 870,000 in his city had been laid off between 1992 and 1996 as the result of economic reform. Of these, 190,000 are still looking for work. Officially, China's national urban unemployment rate is 4 percent, or 8 million workers—a number lower than the comparable U.S. figure. The United Nations, however, estimates the rate to be 18 percent and pessimists argue that up to 50 million may be idle inside China's cities. And that number doesn't reflect the tens of millions of state workers who stand to lose their jobs if sweeping SOE reforms go ahead as planned. Nor does it count the floating population *outside,* who lack work and the residency permits necessary to get in. And this situation will get worse. Even a government think tank predicts that about 54 million urban workers—including an estimated 36 percent of the entire state payroll—will be forced to find other jobs in the final years of this decade.[2]

Cities versus the Countryside and East versus West

The gap between Haves and Have-Nots is echoed in the disparity between rural and urban China. In the early days of reform, during the late 1970s and early 1980s, Deng Xiaoping made the successful decision to focus on the countryside, where the mere freeing up of the land from the commune system and the return of some rudimentary market principles understood by farmers everywhere could generate big productivity and economic gains, quickly. Farm income rose 18 percent annually during that time. However, once the government began to concentrate on industrial reforms in the cities, much of the countryside was left behind.

City income has increased by double-digit percentages annually in recent years, but rural incomes have risen an average of just 4.5 percent. The discrepancy between city and farm income has become more extreme than in Indonesia or even Bangladesh. Peasants now typically earn only 40 cents for every dollar their urban cousins pull in—a

"If different social strata appear, they will have difficulty living with each other, and the struggle between them will very likely be a savage one. This would be a disaster for China and the rest of the world."

—WANG SHAN
LOOKING AT CHINA THROUGH A THIRD EYE

189

dangerous ratio in a time when television and mass communications make many peasants keenly aware of the higher living standards in the cities.

The problem is exacerbated by excess labor. Out of the existing pool of 450 million rural workers, agriculture itself can provide a living wage for about 200 million. And that number is falling owing to mechanization, even as the rural population, which is more traditional and less accepting of birth control and small families than urbanites, is growing. Rural industry and business absorb an additional 100 million, which leaves up to 150 million people—more than half the U.S. population— "floating," either unemployed and roaming the countryside and migrating toward the cities, or underemployed where they live. Ten million are on the road in Sichuan province alone; about half of them are going beyond their provincial borders to join the human flood into eastern China.

In Shanghai, city fathers estimate the number of *mingong* ("floaters," or migrant workers) to be 3 million, or one-fourth the city's population. The city has now flatly refused to provide housing for migrant workers for the first year they are in Shanghai. "It's not that we don't care about them," says a city official, "but we cannot keep expanding our city. Otherwise, the whole country will come to Shanghai. We risk utter chaos."[3]

Urban and rural disparities are aggravated by those between China's eastern and western regions. There is widespread jealousy in the inland and the far western provinces of the richer coastal areas, where average income is between two and four times greater. Because the disparity continues to increase, western regions have formed a special alliance to lobby Beijing for additional aid. The government has begun to address the issue, but many feel the new initiatives are window dressing. Complained one delegate publicly at a special government-organized 1997 East-West Trade Forum, "These are just empty words. Beijing has not injected any capital into the inner provinces. The State Council has not announced any concrete measure to encourage foreign investment in our areas."[4]

Protests and spontaneous worker strikes have reportedly already numbered in the thousands—a phenomenon one scholar characterizes as "China's moral equivalent of off-year elections."[5] In just one incident in 1997, thousands of disgruntled textile workers beseiged a city hall in central China for thirty hours.[6] Even Premier Li Peng, who rarely comments candidly on domestic problems, acknowledges that "The social order in some areas is not good."[7]

What It Means

Resentment is clearly building in the hearts and minds of those left behind by reform, modernization, and growth. For perspective, however, it is important to understand two facets of the problem of poverty in the countryside. First, most of the difficult conditions in the countryside and remote areas are difficult primarily by comparison with the enrichment of urban and other more rapidly developing areas. There *is* some absolute descent into poverty in China; there are people who are actually worse off than they were twenty years ago, before the reforms began. But this is the case for only a small percentage of China's population. For the vast majority, things are better, even if not as good as they would like.

As in all societies, living standards, necessities, and poverty lines are socially defined. With Haves and Have-Somes having done so well in the last twenty years, the Have-Nots stand out more sharply by contrast. In other words, although economic polarization in China is an important problem, it is properly seen as a problem created by the success of reform, not as an indicator of its failure. In the 1950s and 1960s, famines and government dogma combined to starve and cause the deaths of tens of millions, even as Beijing claimed that China had eliminated poverty and hunger. That China now acknowledges a huge problem with poverty is a sign of increased political realism and modernization.

Second, there is a very important silver lining to what is seen by skeptics as only a massive social problem. The same rootless, disenfranchised rural poor who present a threat to the social order can also be seen as an important force propelling needed economic and social change. Some officials speak admiringly about the *mingong* as people of high ambition, who seem as motivated and strong as any nineteenth-century American pioneer. Moreover, these workers tend to float to where the jobs are. Young peasant women from remote areas stream into the electronics factories of Guangdong province, making many of the household

A shocking statistic in a country whose government came to power through a peasant revolution: According to Chinese press reports, at least 830 incidents of rural rebellion involving more than 500 people each were recorded in 1993, including 21 cases involving crowds of more than 5,000.

products that will ultimately end up in American homes. Thousands of men search the country for jobs in construction and road building. Thus, much of the migrant flow is a rudimentary market mechanism, adjusting labor supply and demand and also laying the groundwork for the eventual emergence of the still-underdeveloped service sector.

Once peasant migrants find stable work, they usually contribute indirectly to the improvement of the rural or interior economy by sending home some of their salary. When they return to the countryside—and many do—some start businesses and reinvest their savings in the local economy. Yasheng Huang, a Harvard research fellow, believes the income gap separating China's richest and poorest areas is significantly moderated by this process.

Breaking the iron rice bowl: Before 1979, when all agricultural workers worked for the state economy, 100 percent of them were covered by medical insurance; now, as independent workers in a "socialist market economy," only 20 percent are covered.

Still, like Banquo's ghost, China's out-of-work peasants hover over the minds of China's urban dwellers and Beijing's policymakers. A banned (but widely read and discussed) book entitled *Looking at China with a Third Eye* likened these peasants to a "volcano that could erupt at any time." Every Chinese with an elementary education knows, after all, that the most successful rebellions in their history—including Mao's Communist revolution—found their initial strength among poor, dislocated peasants in the countryside.

"The Center Has Its Measures . . . but the Provinces Have Their Countermeasures"

Few questions are more important to China's stability in the twenty-first century than this: Can authority be properly allocated among the center, the regions, the provinces, and the localities? Historically, China thrived when there was a strong sense of central authority that could make itself felt down to the remotest hamlet in the Middle Kingdom. Whenever the central government was weak, disunity, economic catastrophe, chaos, and revolt followed. Such periods of turbulence have marked almost half of China's 5,000-year history.

Under Mao Zedong every test of the lines holding society together was ideological. There was no room for slack. But neglecting economic growth and material well-being for the greater cause of center-directed ideological rectitude exacted an inordinate price from the Chinese people, even as Mao built a true wonder of the modern world in embroidering and updating the Confucianist way of using a small elite at the center to control the lives of a billion people.

On their return to power, Deng Xiaoping and his colleagues realized that the country would have to allow, and even encourage, decentralized economic decision making. Only then would provinces and cities have the flexibility to make the most of their own resources and to experiment with the best ways to promote productivity and growth. As Kenneth Lieberthal of the University of Michigan has written, the new bargain reversed the old: the center would allow flexibility at all levels of the political system as long as growth and stability were the outcomes. This new "flexibility" quickly became a euphemism for the provinces' finding ways around Beijing's administrative control.[8]

A good example is the problem of collecting central government revenues. As a percentage of GDP, government revenues have shrunk dramatically: from 31 percent in 1978 (the year the reforms started) to a measly 12 percent in 1996, about a third of the level of other developing countries. That steep decline might warm the cockles of Steve Forbes or Jack Kemp's heart. However, especially after a dramatic revenue-sharing agreement was reached with the provinces, Beijing is now seen by many experts as too weak financially to meet many needs that the central government alone is suited to handle.

When the government tried to find ways to raise revenue, the provinces and cities shifted assets into tax-free zones, fought for rebates and postponements, and found ways to collect "off-budget revenues" such as arbitrary fees. Taking into account tax breaks, evasion, and the revenue-sharing arrangement that leaves the provincial governments with 40 percent of the taxes collected, Beijing's share is only about 5 percent of the country's economic output, compared to roughly 15 percent for India and 20 percent for the United States.

Every time China's top leaders talk about reestablishing central control over the tax system and raising taxes, they have to face powerful local interests and constituencies. Here, too, is an ironic duality. Beijing still appoints provincial governors and top local officials. Many are not even natives of the areas they are sent to manage, and that theoretically keeps them beholden to the center. However, they must collaborate with the indigenous power structure if they are to get things done. This has made them power brokers,

A cautionary perspective on politics: "Those who once had power want to go back to the past. Those in power now want to remain as they are. Those who have not yet had power want reforms. This is a general rule."

—LU HSÜN
NOVELIST (1881–1936)

and has created a new stratum of elites that will be highly influential in charting China's future.

The "open door" policy, which has brought in foreign trade and investment as an alternative to central government investment, has also helped the provinces gain the economic power with which to exercise their newfound political clout. World Bank figures show that some provinces trade more with the outside world than with other Chinese provinces. Guangdong's engine for growth is no longer Beijing but Hong Kong and the provinces to its west and north. Fujian's economy has become closely tied to Taiwan's; Shandong's to Korea's. With as much as 75 percent of China's exports of manufactured goods arising from foreign investment and joint-venture businesses,[9] the question of which province and which city will attract foreigners produces intense internecine struggle—and a battle to keep a large portion of profits and taxes for the local economy.

This push-pull relationship is often characterized as a struggle between the provinces collectively and the central authorities in Beijing. But there is also conflict between and among the provinces and regions themselves. Emboldened both by the devolution of authority at home and by international economic forces that ignore national borders in favor of regional nodes of growth, the provinces have begun feuding with one another as well. Over a thousand internal border incidents have been documented. Provinces have set up protectionist barriers against each other, prohibiting entry of commodities or products that might compete with locally produced goods. Freight traffic is often taxed as it moves across provincial borders. Nontariff barriers such as expensive permits or "quality control" inspections are also rife. At least three provinces have attempted to use their own currencies. Guangdong actually used army units in a "rice war" with Hunan, carried out to assure itself of cheap rice.

Why Things May Not Be As Bad as They Seem

Two analysts at the Chinese Academy of Social Sciences wrote a report in 1993, warning that regionalism was getting out of hand and that unless drastic action was taken, China would break apart like Yugoslavia. There are, however, compelling arguments to be made against such a worst-case scenario. These have to do with the fact that Beijing continues to hold the key levers of power over the economy, the political system, and the army. There is also the homogeneity of the population, and the historical impulse to unity. The recent fragmentation of nation-states (particularly Yugoslavia and the Soviet Union) has been driven by ethnic, religious, linguistic, and cultural differences. China also has such differences in Tibet and Xinjiang, where strong independence tendencies run parallel to the religious beliefs of Buddhist and Muslim leaders. Organized separatist groups exist, including some with arms and some favoring terror tactics. But away from these sensitive and geographically significant border regions, the bulk of religious and cultural differences fall within the same Han Chinese majority family.

Perhaps most important, and in contradistinction to the former Soviet Union, economic growth is helping pull China together. Although interior provinces are poorer and growing more slowly than their coastal neighbors, their growth is rapid from their own baseline. Sichuan, for example, is China's most populous province (100 million plus), but also one of its slowest growing. Still, its per capita income jumped by 50 percent in only six years.[10] The boom is also headed west. In 1995, China's fastest-growing province was Anhui, which benefited from the booming economy far downriver in the Yangzi delta. The poorer provinces may be vigorously lobbying Beijing for greater help, but they are not trying to secede.

The current bickering and brokering are likelier, in our view, to lead to China's integration than to its disintegration. In the end, the pushing and pulling will lead to a kind of decentralization that can help ensure China's survival as a unitary state (even though areas like Tibet and Xinjiang may eventually break away). A modern economy cannot exist without institutionalized, interdependent power centers. At some level, Chinese leaders know that brute force alone won't hold China together. There is some evidence that they are consciously—not haphazardly—working toward a more equitable balance of central and regional power. Slowly, haltingly, messily—but palpably nevertheless.

Southern China's building boom: "There is more construction going on here [the Shenzhen–Guangzhou corridor] than in the whole of the eastern seaboard of the United States."

—GORDON WU
MANAGING DIRECTOR,
HOPEWELL HOLDINGS

Socialist Dreams, Capitalist Nightmares

Once touted as showcases of Maoist industrialization, many of China's 100,000-plus State-Owned Enterprises now appear to be economic dinosaurs, stuck in socialist ooze, blocking the emergence of a vibrant enterprise system that can take China into the next century. Their notorious inefficiency and high debt load sap the treasury and help fuel inflation. Their reliance on government-mandated "policy loans" keeps banks from putting money into more dynamic sectors of the economy and delays badly needed financial reforms. And their low productivity creates bottlenecks and stokes unemployment, underemployment, and resentment.

State-Owned Enterprises employ huge, concentrated numbers of workers—about 125 million of China's 170-million-strong urban workforce by recent count—and dominate essential industries and technologies. They account for more than one-third of gross industrial output, but rack up about two-thirds of all official losses. Even what is produced often finds no market. There was a national stockpile of $65 billion worth of unsold state enterprise–produced goods in 1996.

Many experts consider the issue of the SOEs *the* critical Chinese challenge. Even twenty years into the process of reform, no agreed-upon course of action has been implemented for these bloated behemoths. The Deng-era approach was to encourage some basic shifts away from central planning and toward the market, while leaving untouched fundamental issues of SOE ownership structure, profits and losses, and commitments to employees. Understanding just how knotty and politically complex reform of the SOEs would be, Beijing chose to focus first on the comparatively easier problem of building up the nonstate-owned sector, which includes everything from the booming Township and Village Enterprises (TVEs) and other collective forms of worker-owned businesses to the small shopkeepers, restaurateurs, and fix-it men who are truly in business for themselves.

The success of this emphasis on a second engine to drive the economy speaks for itself. Most of the new economic growth and almost all the creation of future-oriented businesses has taken place in the areas that are most market-oriented, or where privatization in some form has been a notable factor, or where foreign investment has been significant. While the industrial output of SOEs has been expanding at only about 8 percent, the nonstate-controlled sector has been growing by 15 percent. The World Bank estimates that the SOEs' share of total industrial output fell from near 70 percent in 1985 to around 35 or 40 percent in 1996. This, plus the ongoing reforms within the SOEs (several hundred have been cleaned up and put into good enough financial shape to be publicly listed on the Shanghai or Shenzhen stock exchanges, and even in Hong Kong, New York, and other global markets) has given the government necessary breathing room.

Still, Chinese economists as well as foreigners doubt that Beijing can get away forever with trying to solve the SOE problem silently through the comparatively painless attrition and shifting of priorities that it practiced in the eighties and thus far in the nineties. For one thing, the hope that the SOEs could somehow become more productive and efficient without a change in their basic social contract and ownership structure has largely been frustrated. Thousands of SOEs *are* profitable and successful; some have become legendary for their management turnaround stories. But most SOEs have failed to make the turn toward the market. Operating losses are rising, reaching $7.2 billion in 1996, nearly 40 percent more than in 1995. Fan Gang, an influential economist at the Chinese Academy of Social Sciences, estimates that 40 percent of the SOEs have chronic deficits. Depending upon who does the accounting, 10 to 30 percent more could be considered hidden loss-makers whose ostensible profits are wiped out by crippling debts on their books.[11]

Evidence is growing that the Chinese leadership is at last taking the issue very seriously. At the Fifteenth Party Congress in September 1997, Jiang Zemin's speech dealt at length with the SOE issue. His injunction to Party cadres to solve the problem through aggressive use of tools ranging from stock offerings to bankruptcy proceedings was called "bold," "groundbreaking," "visionary," and "revolutionary." This vocabulary was used even by foreign observers normally inured to the frequent rhetorical heights of Chinese official oratory. "After years of squirming away from its most intractable problem, Beijing is finally ready to face state-enterprise reform," reported the *Far Eastern Economic Review*.[12]

The boldness of Jiang's speech was in its argument, both

We'll do it *our* way, thank you: Defying assumptions, China is becoming less and less dependent on foreign money and technology to build its telecommunications infrastructure. Big foreign telecom companies such as AT&T, Alcatel, and Siemens are providing the technology components China lacks, but in doing so, they are helping China move up the ladder on its own. "We keep waiting for them to open up; they keep becoming more self-sufficient," says Louis Witters of Alcatel Alsthom (France).

stated and implied, that all but a small core of the biggest SOEs would somehow be moved out of the state sector. Considering that China has over 300,000 SOEs of all types and more than 100,000 industrial ones, a plan to scale down to only a few thousand and let the rest move toward various forms of marketized ownership is obviously huge in its implications.

But Jiang's speech was extremely vague as to the means that would be taken, the timetable, or the degree of privatization—as Westerners might understand the term—that would be allowed. Just as many experts have underestimated the degree of reform that has already been in process—and which Jiang in some ways simply was endorsing and officially urging on—so many may now be overestimating the impact the speech may have in the short term. As one Chinese official told us privately, "Now the real debate begins. Everyone knows SOEs must be reformed. But who should own them? Do they have to keep their commitments to retired workers? Can they lay off unnecessary workers? Who should benefit from the sale of stock in these companies? These are questions that have no answers yet."

Some Western experts forecast and hope for a huge wave of SOE sales to foreign interests, the world's biggest mergers and acquisitions boom, and fat underwriting fees from tens of thousands of IPOs. Realistically, however, the more appropriate set of expectations is that some hundreds of SOEs will be sold to foreigners over the next decade—not thousands, and certainly not tens of thousands. The same is true for IPOs. A relatively small number—a few hundred, perhaps, over the next five years—will qualify for international listings. In China's domestic equity markets there may be thousands of IPOs to come. However, even after stocks are listed, companies will continue to face significant questions about who really owns them and about the relationship between stock ownership and control. For tens of thousands of SOEs, however—perhaps for the majority—there will simply be no easy way out.

Jiang Zemin is undoubtedly serious about SOE reform, as is Zhu Rongji, who has studied the issue in depth for years. It is likely to be Zhu's central task throughout his tenure as premier. But how much Zhu and Jiang—and even the reformers in key departments and ministries—can do, and how fast, is not yet known.

Shanghai's public works planners work overtime: In addition to the subway, Shanghai has completed two river bridges and two major tunnels within the last five years. "The pace is something akin to building the Brooklyn and Manhattan Bridges in New York and the Lincoln and Holland Tunnels to New Jersey all in five years."

—*THE NEW YORK TIMES*

The recent economic turbulence in other East Asian economies, combined with slowing GDP growth rates in China, is giving Zhu Rongji less room to maneuver. Experts have often said that if China's growth slows from its double-digit pace of recent years to "only" 4 or 5 percent per year, it would be the equivalent of a recession, even if the same 4 to 5 percent in the mature economies of the West would constitute a boom. We may soon find out if the experts are right, because China's growth is almost certain to moderate in the next year or two.

A slower-growing China might deny its leaders the luxury they have had up until now of using the expansion of the total economic pie to delay a serious reckoning with the country's long-term social and economic disparities. It might make it nearly impossible to generate much traction for the urgently needed reforms of China's state-owned industrial behemoths. Alternatively, however, it could create the crisis conditions that would allow Zhu Rongji to cut through bureaucratic resistance and insist on a scale of privatization in the state sector that might otherwise have taken a decade to achieve.

Many would argue that if the Chinese draw the right conclusions—particularly if they tone down the role of state-directed policymaking in economics and allow more vibrant, flexible, and truly private market mechanisms to work—their growth dynamic will be renewed on a sounder, more sustainable footing. It is not clear, however, that the economic pain of the next few years will be sufficient to lead to those radical conclusions. And even if the pain is great, there is no guarantee that China won't draw the opposite conclusions. In Malaysia and Indonesia, for example, an attempt is already under way by government leaders to blame the turmoil of 1997 on the intrusive influence of international capital. Some of the solutions proposed involve *more* government control, not less. One could certainly imagine Chinese leaders having similar reactions, or at least using the crises elsewhere in Southeast Asia to justify their go-slow approach to marketizing, privatizing, and internationalizing China's economy.

Our guess is that progress over the next few years will be real—but slow, and deliberately so. Kenneth Lieberthal, a University of Michigan China scholar, puts it well:

The changing mandate: "The Chinese Communist Party is no longer about the expropriation of private property or the redistribution of wealth. It is only out to stay in power," said Jesse Wong, a Hong Kong–based correspondent for *The Asian Wall Street Journal.*

We have seen repeatedly in the past that China has muddled through on issue after issue without doing what foreign scholars and business have said they "must" do to avoid catastrophe. In China, as in the U.S. and other countries, there is almost no such thing as a national political-economic issue that cannot be delayed, reshaped, fudged over, neglected or whatever.[13]

There are those who disagree with Lieberthal and believe that on *this* issue, anyway, if China does not submit itself to quick, sweeping change, the results could be disastrous. The scholar Jack Goldstone, for example, warns that the SOEs are "bankrupting the regime" and will almost inevitably cause a system-wide collapse if thoroughgoing reform doesn't take place quickly.[14]

But one reason Beijing may not rush to put out the fire of the SOE crisis as fast as Westerners imagine necessary is that it may not be quite as big a crisis as is widely supposed. From the point of view of China's overall political economy, the SOEs may be more of a bargain and less of a basket case than they appear—at least in the near term. The SOEs have always been mini–welfare states, providing everything from pensions to child care for workers. Shuttering them abruptly would leave tens of millions of people jobless without support. Consider this: The $7.2 billion in SOE write-offs in 1996 represents less than 1 percent of China's GDP ($818 billion in 1996). In the United States, our various social security and welfare assistance programs run to about 12 percent of GDP.

Reverberations

Although the SOE debt burden seems more tolerable to us than to the China Bears, the government cannot go on forever infusing SOEs with subsidies and cheap loans. The growing problem is with the soundness of a banking system that needs to modernize its operations but has been hamstrung by the imperative to make "policy loans" to SOEs with little chance of being paid back.

Perhaps 80 to 90 percent of all loans by state banks are made to SOEs. The total of outstanding loans to SOEs went from $86 billion in 1993 to $120 billion in 1996.[15] "How can anyone expect a bank to operate efficiently if it is forced to lend much of its money at low rates to state enterprises that

An inside joke: The Chinese, who are as good as Americans at finding ironic humor in the midst of adversity, have been passing around this jingle in face of the many layoffs now occurring at State-Owned Enterprises: "Chairman Mao told us to go to the countryside, Deng Xiaoping told us to go into business, and Jiang Zemin tells us to leave our jobs."

are not good credit risks?" asks the blunt-spoken Wang Qishan, president of the powerful People's Construction Bank.

There are signs of change; state banks are no longer being required to throw good money after bad to SOEs. But bad loans and deficits are also starting to pyramid within the economy. Unable to get more from the government or its banks, many State-Owned Enterprises have simply chosen to "borrow" from each other (by not paying for raw materials, for example).

Some Western pundits unceasingly advise shutting down the state sector altogether. "Shock therapy" is what these Chinese dinosaurs need most, say the fiercest free-marketeers, to avoid the continuing drain on resources that one senior government official told us bluntly was "as useless as putting cosmetics on a corpse." China, it seems, faces a classic no-win situation: "If we don't allow companies to go bankrupt we will face difficulties . . . but if we do allow them to go bankrupt we will face even more difficulties," summarizes Zhang Daogen, an economist at Shanghai's Academy of Social Sciences.[16]

The "Big Dragon" Bottom Line

In the next few years, China will be prompted to take more vigorous measures to reform the SOEs just as Jiang Zemin signaled in his 1997 speech. State control will be loosened in areas previously thought sacrosanct: the export trade, retail business, and some infrastructure projects.[17] More SOEs will be permitted to diversify their ownership by taking on domestic institutional investors, issuing stock, or allowing foreigners to acquire stakes—usually minority stakes, but sometimes even more than 50 percent (though not, in most cases, the voting control that normally accompanies a majority interest). State banks are gradually being freed of the obligation to give lines of credit to loss-making enterprises, which will be left to sink, swim, or merge with sounder ones. The rush to bankruptcy will continue and thousands of money-losing companies will compete to take part in a state program that has already set aside $3.6 billion to pay off debts and provide help for surplus workers.

But one should be careful about any facile argument suggesting that there will be sweeping, wholesale privatization.

"**The Chinese government is getting less socialistic than some Western European countries,**" says Robert Mundell, an economist at Columbia University, commenting on the fact that while just under 40 percent of China's GDP is accounted for by government, in Denmark and Sweden it's 60 percent, and in France and Germany, 50 percent.

To Western economic sensibilities it seems irrational for the Chinese to continue to bear this burden and absorb these losses. In the Chinese view, however, it is radical privatization that would be the irrational course. Indeed, the Chinese see the SOEs as more than a colossal problem. They are also integral to the solution.

Whether the Chinese economic policy makers are right or wrong—and we believe that they are more right than outsiders generally think—it is important to understand how they look at this critical issue. First, it is essential to recognize that the SOEs, especially the biggest ones, are de facto governments. They serve as the welfare system not only for their workers (who frequently receive housing and healthcare benefits through their place of employment) but, more important, for retired and disabled workers as well. Only very recently has China begun to experiment with funded pensions and social security–type programs for retired workers. Until those programs are scaled up and can incorporate millions of SOE retirees, it makes economic as well as political sense to leave the burden where it is. "SOE debt is really just invisible government debt," says Guo Shuqing, a leading economist. "The state has many assets to sell to pay down this debt. For example, urban landholdings of the state are worth five times the total of SOE debt."

Defenders of the SOEs point out that without the massive burden of retired workers' pensions and benefits, many more SOEs would be profitable or at least not as loss-making. This is the key reality most casual observers miss: while bad debt associated with the SOEs is skyrocketing, the total cost to the state is probably no more than the cost of deficit-financing a full-fledged national social welfare system. In fact, says Wu Xiaoling, an economist who specializes in banking issues, "The SOE debt burden is high, but the government has comparatively low accumulated debt. So the SOE burden can be managed for some time."

The SOEs are also producing jobs for millions of workers who are not really needed according to any strict bottom-line view of business. Were these people jobless, the cost to the state—in unemployment benefits and political problems—would be a dangerous double whammy. "In some ways, the state system is like a holding pen for excess workers until the private economy can absorb them," notes the Hong Kong–based economist Pan Ming.[18]

Second, while economic policy makers have grasped the importance and value of marketplace competition and market mechanisms, they believe that SOEs, if well managed, can not only become profit centers but also remain a value-added economic form. The value added is the political power that goes with controlling these central institutions of the economy, as well as the ability to use the size, scale, and prestige of the SOEs as large participants in the economy. Even Premier Zhu Rongji, considered among the most eager to tackle SOE reform, has observed, "The difficulties in the sector come not from the concept of [state] ownership per se, but in bad management."

Currently, about half of SOEs bring profits into the state coffers. Combined with Beijing's need for revenues, the fact that so many are profitable whets officialdom's appetite for turning around many more. If Beijing can get a higher percentage of SOEs running profitably, a major portion of the government's financial woes will be solved. Moreover, by keeping them state owned, the central government retains control over the most important parts of the economy. It will then be the Communist Party that decides how SOEs should be reformed and made more competitive and efficient, not the chaos of the marketplace. Finally, state ownership of profitable enterprises will mean that the interests of tens of millions of workers will continue to be aligned with those of the state that employs them. This is the meaning behind statements such as this, which appeared recently in *China Daily:* "At present, the role of the State enterprises is not simply economic and it is irrational to judge them solely on this basis."

In sum, no matter how nightmarish the SOE losses seem from the outside, it is imperative to remember how the Chinese look at this problem. They do not share Western assumptions about the best government being the one that governs least. They do not see anything inherently wrong with government having a major footprint in the world of business. A hallmark of the "third road" solution China seeks is the belief that government does know best. Government—led, of course by the Party—is virtuous and should apply its virtue to reforming and stimulating business and industry.

"Corruption is a virus that has infected the party's healthy body. If we ignore this phenomenon, it will bring down our party and our system."

—JIANG ZEMIN

Corruption: Back Door to Modern Capitalism?

China today is neither a free market nor an authoritarian state. It is instead more like a network, "a kind of Chinese six degrees of separation," as one sinologist has called it. Everyone who counts works through links to everybody else who counts. In Chinese, that's *guanxi.*

Guanxi ("personal connections") has always been an important fact of life in China, socialist or dynastic. For most of the 1950s, 1960s, and 1970s, when everyone was more or less poor together, *guanxi* was used for relatively minor purposes—extra ration coupons, a better job for a child or relative. Now that the economic stakes have been raised so dramatically, so have the give-and-take of "connections." These days *guanxi* is about the ability to divert government loans for state enterprises into speculative private investments, getting an automobile, starting a joint venture, buying a telephone, or getting tariff relief. Whatever you want to do, you have to have contacts. Life becomes an endless search for the right person, followed by continuous negotiation. One might update Deng Xiaoping's famous aphorism "It doesn't matter whether a cat is black or white, as long as it catches mice" to say that in today's climate, it only matters whether the cat pays a fee, kickback, commission, or other consideration.

Every sector of the economy is affected. Funds raised in the stock market are "just a way for companies to get money and say good-bye," we were told by a former official who helped create China's fledgling stock market. In each day of 1994, an average of 10,000 metric tons of oil, or 77,000 barrels, entered the country illegally. Roughly 150 luxury cars per week were being smuggled into China from Hong Kong in the early 1990s—Benzes and Lexuses swept off the streets of Hong Kong by criminal gangs and delivered by high-speed boat to Chinese officials in the mainland within hours. Flood-relief money is squandered on officials' work banquets. Reporters demand payments for covering news events; sources demand compensation for being asked questions by journalists.

In one of those staged media events only Chinese officialdom can create, the Beijing government held an "auction" of confiscated luxury cars in August 1995. The intent was to demonstrate to the citizenry Beijing's determination to crack down on the excesses of officials even at the highest levels. But there were only ten cars, nearly all of them with over 100,000 miles of obvious wear and tear on them. One can be sure that any late models netted in the crackdown found new homes before being considered for the public auction block.

While corruption, of course, saps China's moral fiber, crime is beginning to threaten order and stability. Gangs of bandits roam the countryside, hijacking trucks and setting up roadblocks to collect "toll fees." A kidnap ring in Anhui province gang-raped hundreds of women before selling them off as wives or prostitutes. Drug addiction, the scourge of nineteenth-century China, has reappeared, particularly in southern China. In 1992 Communist Party authorities declared a border town near Burma to be in the grip of "representatives of evil forces" and sent in 2,000 troops to break up the thriving heroin trade. Security forces in these border areas routinely confiscate bombs, land mines, and grenades. Gunfights over drug deals have occurred in Kunming, the capital of Yunnan province, which is, after all, only a short distance from the infamous Golden Triangle opium region of Southeast Asia.

Another typical nineties story concerns the strange case of a dynamite explosion in an apartment house in central China. The resulting inferno killed at least 95 people, injured more than 400, leveled 40 buildings, left a 2.5–acre crater, and shattered windows for miles around. Deadpanned a Western wire service report, "Officials were not able to explain why such a large amount of dynamite was stored in an apartment building. The state-run Xinhua News Agency said workers had been handling the explosives in a way that violated regulations."[19]

But the same media that gladly tell lurid tales of crime and corruption in low and remote places are often silent on the biggest acts of corruption in the highest places of government and party leadership. In 1995, Beijing mayor Chen Xitong received the dubious honor of becoming the first Politburo member to be sacked for what seems to have been a massive scheme of favoritism, kickbacks, and cover-ups. Many of his ranking cohorts have also been arrested for "serious economic crimes." But although Party insiders knew about Chen's outrageous behavior for years, the media

To write heroic novels you need heroes: Responding to government complaints that his novels were "low-class and coarse," the famous Chinese novelist Wang Shou responded, "How can I write moral novels? How can I write about beautiful things? I have no reference point."

never even hinted at it until the Politburo moved against him and ousted him.

Long ago the military strategist Sun Tzu warned against corruption: "The Commander must stand for the virtues of wisdom, sincerity, benevolence, courage, and strictness." Confucianism is all about the moral rectitude of officials. In calling for a new "spiritual civilization," today's leaders are implicitly acknowledging the depth of corruption. Indeed, Jiang Zemin has said corruption was the evil that could topple nearly fifty years of Party rule. As premier, Li Peng warned against "money worship, ultra-individualism and decadent lifestyles," saying such problems are "a matter of life and death for our nation."[20] And with what was presumably unintended irony, the *People's Daily* used the seventy-fifth anniversary of the Party in 1996 to editorialize that the scourge of corruption was largely due to "the concentration of power in a few hands."

Of Princelings and Eunuchs

All this high-minded invective is falling largely on deaf ears, however. "China today is reexperiencing an old theme from its history—the battle between the 'princelings' and the 'eunuchs'—and corruption is a weapon for both sides," says Zhai Zhihai, a distinguished intellectual formerly associated with the People's Liberation Army and now a business consultant and advisor to foreign firms.

The "princelings" are the sons, daughters, and other relatives of China's senior and powerful leaders. Many have lived a highly privileged life of late: education abroad, postings to Hong Kong, San Francisco, and London, and top positions with some of China's biggest companies. Through their role with these companies, some are amassing significant fortunes—not just to live the good life now, but to have the financial tools necessary for a power base in a very different China of the future.

On the other hand, there are the "eunuchs"—the secretaries and advisors to powerful leaders. Although these individuals are scarcely known in the West, they are extremely influential. They help determine what their bosses will and won't put their "chops" (signatures) on in the formal decision-making process. But they are also the point men for the informal process, arranging all the many approvals, fa-

Be careful about wishing for the rule of law—you might get sued! Consumers can now go to court for redress against companies selling shoddy products, including foreign ones. A wholesaler of Coca-Cola in Henan province sued the company for $2.4 million for ostensibly selling him 14,000 bottles of rancid cola. And a disgruntled buyer of a Sony CD player in Sichuan not only complained to the local press that Sony "was trying to cheat the Chinese people," but also demanded that Sony buy him a million-dollar life insurance policy because, he alleged, the company hired thugs to threaten his life.

vors, permissions, licenses, and funding for most of what happens in China. They are the ones to whom the adage currently popular among those who try to subvert government bureaucrats best applies: "Swap my money for your power, and then use your power to earn me even more money."

China and Western societies are often contrasted this way: In the West, everything not specifically forbidden by law is permissible. In China, it is the opposite—everything not specifically permitted is forbidden. Forbidden, that is, unless one has informal approval from on high. Providing those informal approvals is frequently the province of the eunuchs. They also keep close tabs on the corrupt practices of others. It is as if hundreds of J. Edgar Hoovers were running around Beijing with their own private files, which could be used at any moment to embarrass or condemn powerful individuals. (And the man with the most, and most damning, files wins!) As some Chinese insiders will tell you, President Jiang Zemin's ever-firmer grip on power during the mid-1990s was not disconnected from the diligence of aides in collecting such files on all others who vied for power.

Respecting the rules of this game means using this leverage rarely, and always privately and quietly. To engage in constant public exposés would be tantamount to launching a war of mutually assured destruction. But Zhai Zhihai believes the rules of this game might change in the post-Deng transition era, as princelings and eunuchs compete for power and control of key positions.

The Mother's Milk of Market Economics?

Western skeptics see corruption as a deadly affliction that is increasingly poisoning the economy and at the same time ravaging the already weakened sinews of the overstressed society. The Chinese leaders themselves acknowledge the dimensions of the problem and fight it actively, in part because they want to maintain their grip on power. Jiang and his allies certainly understand how destabilizing it is to try to build an economy and maintain public faith in public institutions when everything gravitates toward a system of informal bribes and favors. It would hardly be surprising, however (and not all that different from Democrats and Republicans in the United States on matters of campaign financing)

Yes, Confucius could have made it in modern China: "Wealth and rank are what every man desires. . . . Poverty and obscurity are what every man detests."

—CONFUCIUS

to point out that Jiang and Company are first and foremost interested in the corrupt practices of those not fully supportive of their leadership.

But look at corruption from another angle. Some aspects of activities classed as corrupt may only represent the development of an informal economy. A contributing factor to China's phenomenal growth of recent years has been the ability of the more entrepreneurially inclined companies, state agencies, towns, and individuals to seize the day, start making and selling products, building up distribution channels, putting up buildings, hiring workers, and so on. If the appropriate regulatory framework for all these activities had to be put in place first, and if everyone had to wait for laws, regulations, and licenses, China's growth rates in the last decade would not have been what they were. That cash and favors have had to lubricate the system should come as no real surprise. What, concretely, was or is the alternative? How could anyone expect that a transition from a socialist planned economy to a market-influenced one could take place without extreme instances of what Marxists like to call uneven development—where the base of the economy is moving much faster than the superstructure of regulation and governance?

"Graft and the loosening of controls allow the entrepreneurial spirit of those with ability to flourish," observes Yin Xiaohuang, a student who left China after Tiananmen to study in the United States. On a visit to his homeland he was impressed by the role that "extra income" (achieved through less than fully permitted means) had contributed to allowing the Chinese people to "display their personalities and reclaim their private lives."

In Hong Kong today, one can find several budding taipans, assembling diverse empires out of investments in trading companies, import-export, real estate, restaurants, and much else while cruising around in Bentleys and Rolls-Royces and talking of global investments. They are young, hail from the PRC, and are increasingly respected. Where did they get their money? How did they get their start? It is usually difficult to learn the details, but over enough food and drink the story eventually turns to some *guanxi* connection they had in China that enabled them to get hold of Chinese commodities free or at state-subsidized prices. They then turned around and sold them at market prices in Hong

Trouble ahead:
"Whoever succeeds to power in the post-Deng era will face a truly daunting problem: while breathing life into the old Communist order seems virtually impossible, it seems no less difficult to forge a new order from today's confusion, whether by democratic means or strong-arm tactics."

—LIU BINYAN
   CHINESE WRITER

Kong. Or there was a piece of property on which they obtained a sweetheart option just before the run-up in real estate prices. Or they carried out what we in the West would consider insider trading in a Chinese stock offering.

But however "gray" or "black" the original source of capital may have been, these young taipans are now investing back in China, launching companies, factories, and real estate development, contributing to economic growth. A certain amount of corruption therefore has to be seen as the mother's milk of market economics in China and the inevitable outcome of the transition from the past structure to the future.

The question then becomes, Is this robber-baron aspect of Chinese society just a stage in the transition to a modern market economy, or is corruption becoming so deeply embedded in the system that it will undermine the modernization effort? There are optimists. Fan Gang, for example, thinks massive corruption sets the stage for a modern legal and regulatory framework:

> Gradually, people are bound to find out that all this cheating and protecting yourself from being cheated consume too much time and energy, and that the best way to do business is playing by a set of mutually respected rules. New rules and laws will be passed, and people will be ready to abide them. Maybe we will *cheat* out a new system.[21]

CHAPTER 9

The Impulse Toward Unity: The Geopolitical Meaning of the "Middle Kingdom"

CHINA IS UNIQUE IN world history for having transformed itself from an ancient empire to a twentieth-century nation-state almost entirely intact. As an astute anthropological commentator recently observed:

> While modern American history is the story of how our continent's expanse became American, and Russia's history is the story of how Russia became Russian, China's history appears to be entirely different. It seems absurd to ask how China became Chinese. China has *been* Chinese almost from the beginning of its recorded history.
>
> China was unified politically in 221 B.C. From the beginnings of literacy in China over 3,000 years ago, it has had only a single writing system, unlike the dozens in use in modern Europe. Of China's billion-plus people, over 700 million speak Mandarin, the language with by far the largest number of native speakers in the world. Some 250

million other Chinese speak seven languages as similar to Mandarin and to each other as Spanish is to Italian.[1]

Although China has many significant minority groups (fifty-six, by official count), most dwell in peripheral and border areas. The minorities make up only about 7 percent of the population. Han Chinese make up 93 percent. This is not to argue that China isn't diverse. It is filled with regionalisms and cultural contradictions of all kinds. The minority areas, which include Tibet and Muslim-majority stretches of central Asia, may be small in population, but they pose vexing long-term challenges in the evolution of Chinese politics and to the very issue of national unity. From rain forests to deserts, from coastal modernity to hinterland backwardness, from the wheeler-dealers of Guangdong to the industrialists of Shanghai and the political elite of Beijing, Chinese society is subject to significant variation.

The point of distinction is really this: China is less diverse than many nations. Chinese homogeneity, however, is anything but a spontaneous state of affairs. For about half of its history, China has had multiple governments. There was, for example, the period of the Three Kingdoms; there were Northern and Southern Sung dynasties. The Ming emperors (the last dynasty to be led by Han people) ruled over an area about one-third of the size of China today. It was the Manchus, a small minority, who established the Qing Dynasty (1644–1911) and expanded the empire to its present size. Unification was always tentative, a direct product of policies implemented by strong, autocratic Chinese leaders from Emperor Qin in 221 B.C. to the Communists in 1949.

Challenges to China's unity and territorial integrity are a major theme of its history. In the ninth century the disintegration of central leadership and the lack of coordination among provincial authorities spawned a major rebellion led by one Huang Chao. He started in central China in 875 and reached Guangzhou in 879, by which time he already commanded close to a quarter of a million men. His demand for the military governorship of the province was rejected by the Tang court. Some sources hold that in a fit of pique he slew 120,000 Muslims, Jews, Christians, and Persians. Forced to turn back, he went with 600,000 men to Xian, which he held for two more years, until forced to flee eastward. He was finally caught and beheaded in 884 in Shandong

Nationalism as old as Confucianism: "If you can rule your whole country, who dares insult you?"

—CONFUCIUS

province, having led one of the most far-reaching rebellions in Chinese history.[2]

Another great challenge was led a thousand years later by Hong Xiuquan, whom the historian Jonathan Spence has dubbed "God's Chinese son."[3] Hong considered himself to be the younger brother of Jesus Christ after he had a vision of the Heavenly Father (attired in a black dragon robe and high-brimmed hat) commanding him to slay the demon devils who were leading the people on earth astray. From 1851 to 1864 he led the Taiping rebellion, which managed to overturn the authority of the ruling Qing Dynasty throughout a large stretch of southern China. Until overcome by a combination of Qing and Western forces (led by the British general Charles "Chinese" Gordon of Khartoum fame), the Taiping rebellion caused the death of some *20 million* Chinese.

The rebellions of the 800s and the 1800s were both extreme manifestations of an enduring Chinese dilemma: "While an efficient central authority is very expensive to maintain, the lack of it increases the potential for dire consequences."[4] Their culture may make the Chinese people predisposed to conformity, homogeneity, and unity. But if leaders do not actively cultivate the unity of China (and suppress attacks on it), the bonds of unity run the risk of unraveling—violently and chaotically.

Maintaining Territorial Integrity

Chinese leaders continue to display inherited traits of insecurity, knowing that they, like their forebears, will be judged by future *Chinese* largely on how well they hold the Middle Kingdom together. One of Mao's enduring accomplishments in the minds of the Chinese was that he united the country for the modern era. No one wishes to betray that particular part of his legacy. From both the feudal and the Communist past, today's leadership has inherited the belief that national unity is something that must be constructed daily and defended constantly. It is a belief as visceral as it is practical. No one in leadership has any desire to find out through experience whether they are right or wrong about their vigilance.

The specific agenda of defending China's territorial integrity fuses with an intense nationalism that is both arising spontaneously and being creatively stirred by a leadership looking for tools to keep the society highly unified. This is just one reason why the reunification of Taiwan with China—which the Chinese believe to be their inalienable right and destiny—is such an important, overarching, and emotional issue in a country that would seem to face so many more important challenges. Taiwan is the litmus-test issue, but other difficult questions and potential flashpoints abound: Tibet, the Muslim areas of Xinjiang Autonomous Region, and the territorial conflicts with Vietnam, the Philippines, Japan, and others over the islands in the South and East China Seas.

Keeping the Barbarians at Arm's Length

China's sense of nationhood will play a big part in how it defines its interests and arrangements with other countries as well as in how it develops its military forces and positioning. China shares borders with fourteen countries, including several "emerging markets" of the future—Korea, India, Vietnam, Russia, Mongolia, Kazahkstan, and Myanmar, just to name a few. In examining all these relationships, Chinese strategists are more concerned with long-term themes of history and geography than they are about the policies of current governments.

One might think, for example, that China and Vietnam would be highly cooperative, given that both are emerging from the economic shackles of socialism and trying to reform their economies. However, history and geography have taught them to mistrust each other and seek alliances and balances of power that keep each other at bay. China says it wants "normal" relations with countries like Vietnam. The only problem, in the words of sinologist Gerald Segal, is that "China often defines 'normal' relations with certain neighbors . . . as ones where China is dominant."[5] But China's zeal in what it perceives as the self-defense of its borders and border areas is mirrored by a long history of being uninterested in projecting power much *beyond* its own borders, and unwilling to do so. In ancient times, Chinese emperors could have gone on the same path of conquest across Asia and into Europe that the Mongols eventually took. But this never tempted them.

"Middle Kingdom" is the literal translation of the Chinese characters that mean "China." By "middle" the ancients did not mean that China is simply sandwiched between one kingdom and another. Just the opposite. It meant then, and still means to some degree in the Chinese mind, that China is the center of the world and the highest

The essentials of national strategy:
"The ancients who excelled at warfare proceeded from the spiritual employment of strategic power. Those who attained it, flourished; those who lost it, perished."

—*Six Secret Teachings*

civilization of all. All nations, of course, like to think of themselves as exceptional. But none has so willfully nurtured its sense of superiority for so long. In well-known historic incidents such as the eighteenth-century Macartney mission (see chapter 2), one can already see the idea forming that the world needs China more than China needs the world. Even today China continues to display strength and loftiness in encounters with others, even when admitting to itself that it is behind, backward, or out of touch.

Boeing, the American aircraft maker acknowledged as the world leader in manufacturing a product China wants and needs, is one company that must wonder how far the West has really come in dealing with China 200 years after Macartney. When its board of directors met in Beijing in June 1996, Premier Li Peng lectured them for forty minutes on the pitfalls of U.S. trade policy toward China. The board, which had gathered in Beijing as a way of demonstrating the importance of China to its future, also heard Li warn that American moves were causing China to question the reliability of Boeing as a business partner.[6] What gave Li's lecture a particular sting, of course, was that just two months before, China had passed up Boeing in favor of Airbus in placing a $1.89 billion order for thirty-three planes. "I don't think you can ever separate politics from business," commented Philip M. Condit, Boeing's CEO.[7]

One particularly galling aspect of Chinese "Middle Kingdom" arrogance is found in Beijing's attempts to insist that foreigners who want to be well received in China follow its dictates on how matters relating to China should be discussed or portrayed. For example, when Chinese cultural authorities learned that Disney was involved in the making and distribution of *Kundun,* a movie that would lend support and credibility to the current Dalai Lama's struggle for an independent and religiously free Tibet, they had no qualms about publicly threatening the company with economic retaliation against its burgeoning China business. "We are resolutely opposed to making this movie," said a representative of China's official Film Bureau. Chinese authorities reportedly told Disney executives that "other business could be affected" if the film was produced.[8]

Sony and MGM faced similar kinds of threats in regard to other film projects that authorities did not find to their liking. Disney ended up proceeding with *Kundun,* just as the others did

"Unfortunately, China is very hard to change. Just to make a table or overhaul a stove probably involves shedding blood; and even so, the change may not get made. Unless some great whip lashes her on the back, China will never budge. Such a whip is bound to come, I think. Whether good or bad, this whipping is bound to come. But where it will come from or who it will come from, I do not know exactly."

—Lu Hsün
   Novelist (1881–1936)

with their films. As of this writing, no specific retaliatory steps have been taken. Either the Chinese authorities have become more statesmanlike and recognize the futility of threatening the free speech and artistic expression of Hollywood filmmakers, or else they have determined that the more appropriate course is to retaliate in subtle rather than overt ways. If the Chinese authorities live up to their threats, they will probably do so quietly—simply not approving the next expansion of Disney stores in China, or slowing down Disneyland theme park discussions (even though Shanghai's mayor continues to insist he wants a Disneyland as soon as possible). William A. Brent, publisher of the periodical *China Entertainment Network,* summarizes the situation in a way that is apt with respect to many matters, not just films about Tibet: "The Chinese have absolutely no ground to stand on, except that they have all the leverage. And they're very good at using it."[9]

Nor is it only Americans who are forced to choose between doing what China wants or incurring its wrath. In the same month that the Disney issue made front-page news, Nelson Mandela announced the severance of South Africa's diplomatic relations with Taiwan. In an extremely candid statement, Mandela acknowledged that he preferred to maintain the relationship with Taiwan but simply could not owing to pressure from China.

German president Roman Herzog visited China around the same time and was greeted by the sudden expulsion of a German priest who had allegedly stirred up underground religious movements. The embarrassed Herzog "smiled for the cameras, made a few noises about human rights and focused mainly on trade."[10]

Japan is frequently warned by Chinese leaders and official newspaper editorials to change its ways. Every time Japanese rightists try to tone down the wording in school textbooks about the country's brutal occupation of China during World War II, Beijing denounces the move, throws a fit of anger, and demands an apology. And nearly every time Japan seeks to upgrade its military capabilities, or discusses even the slightest changes in its security arrangements with the United States, Beijing denounces Tokyo as warmongering.

The Chinese belief that they can define reality by declaration and shape the terms of a debate by threat is evident even in normal business discourse. When we interviewed Shang-

Picture, picture on the wall: In 1995, the 10 U.S. films permitted into China—including *The Bridges of Madison County* and *The Lion King*— accounted for 40 percent of all Chinese movie theater receipts.

hai's vice mayor, Zhao Qizheng, he declared that Americans were losing out in the race for future influence in Pudong, the new business and financial district of East Shanghai:

> I received a letter from a big American businessman, telling me that because of the state of U.S.-China relations and China's abuse of human rights he would withdraw the company's investments from Pudong, at least until relations improve. I wrote him back telling him I would wait for him and welcome him back, but that Japanese businessmen won't wait. That German, Singaporean and Australian businessmen also won't wait. We know which countries have a positive attitude toward investment and which don't. Even the emperor of Japan, who never pays attention to business, brought one hundred businessmen with him when he came to China.

Keeping foreigners out of certain business areas, playing them off against one another, threatening to deny business opportunities to those whose governments harass Beijing—none of these are new policies of the Chinese government. Rather, they are part of highly evolved and generally successful traditions.

Nationalism with Chinese Characteristics

The corollary to the expressed conviction of China's ascendancy is the belief that other countries will fall behind, at least relatively. Listen to a young policymaker in Beijing: "The United States is a declining power, relatively speaking. Europe is fine, but they have too many problems. Russia will not be an economic giant, at least within the next decade or so. So China will push up relative to all those." A fast-rising entrepreneur in Shanghai serves up the same lesson in more colorful terms: "While the United States will remain strong, it will nevertheless get comparatively weaker. In the future, the United States will be behind China in areas of technology and science, just like they are in garments now."

A Chinese studying in the United States used an online news group on the Internet to express this glowing burst of nationalism: "Today's technology makes the rich Chinese heritage more powerful than ever! Think about it; our past tools with today's paradigm. In the 21 century, Chinese based languages will replace the European based culture of today." Such nationalist commentary stems essentially from pride and rediscovered self-respect. It is understandable, given how far and how fast China has come. What is interesting, however, is how much of it comes from leading-edge Chinese, who may be quite skeptical about the Chinese Communist Party and the government while absorbing uncritically the nationalism promoted by these same forces.

China's nationalism also has a darker side, which traces its lineage to the view of China as a celestial empire surrounded by barbarians. It is defensive, strident, exclusive, and sometimes even racist. An intellectual who studied for several years at a major American university and is now a senior official in a Beijing think tank told us this popular parable: "A son who works in the United States is called by his father. 'I know you have to work miserably hard in a restaurant, son, but stick it out and come back when you have a degree. You can then make Americans become your servants instead.' "

Combine such nationalism with a dose of paranoia and you have an extremism whose implications are not only cultural but military and geostrategic as well. General Xu Yimin presides over the China Institute for International Strategic Studies. He is a veteran of the anti-Japanese war in the 1930s and of all the Communist Party's military and ideological battles. He has agreed to talk to us about China's foreign policy and strategic positioning in the world of the twenty-first century.

He is one tough old general, and powerful too. He puts the institute's private dining room at our disposal—a cavernous space two stories high, with an entryway that includes an indoor miniature garden complete with running brook and bowed bridge. In the middle, set on the marble floor like a museum piece and at least twenty feet from the nearest wall, is a perfectly set table for six. The meal is one of the best we've had in some time, but it is served with great heapings of virulent neonationalism.

General Xu's briefing style takes us right back to the Cultural Revolution era, with its equal doses of triumph, certainty, and intimidation. His is a zero-sum view of the world, utterly without nuance. China is at the center of the world, and the United States can have no possible purpose in its policy of "engagement" with China but to attack, destroy, and dismember the Chinese nation. The United States is pulling out of Europe so as to be in a better position to enter Asia and surround China. The Pentagon, Congress, and the president may be discussing cutbacks in the American mili-

The rhetoric of nationalism isn't always uplifting in the U.S., either: "It is astonishing that today's Chinese, heirs to one of the world's greatest civilizations, should find themselves embracing a hollow form of nationalism—one devoid of ideals or inspiring principles—that is little more than racist passion."

—LUCIAN PYE
PROFESSOR EMERITUS, MIT

tary presence in Asia, but General Xu dismisses this talk with a wave of the hand: "The day the U.S. withdraws from Asia is the day the sun will rise in the West." General Xu then gives us his global vision:

> Chairman Mao said a long time ago that Americans were stretched too far. You still want to be the policeman of the world; you still want to control the world as the sole superpower; you still want to spend your money to solve all the problems of the world. But even if you're the richest country you can't look after everything. The center of world gravity has shifted to Asia. So you are trying to create an aggressor in China to justify your troop presence in the region. When you write your book, tell the American people not to try and control everything!

General Xu is not just an out-of-touch octogenarian longing for the good old days when Maoist guerrillas battled the Japanese. Almost the same moment he was delivering his uninterruptible bombast to us, President Jiang Zemin was arguing that "Western hostile forces have not for a moment abandoned their plot to 'Westernize' and divide our country." Leading political figures and scholars had, as many visitors to China reported, reached the consensus that American policy was designed to "divide China territorially, subvert it politically, contain it strategically, and frustrate it economically."[11]

Think Local, Act Global

Several prominent Chinese thinkers are working on developing the theoretical basis for the new nationalism they believe the Chinese government should actively promote. China's own "neoconservatives" advocate, among other ideas, raising the "volume of state-sponsored propaganda featuring nationalistic love of country and the Confucian ethic of respect for authority."[12] These neoconservative intellectuals see nationalism as a cure for the country's spiritual malaise and loss of direction as the Maoist past wanes and no new clearly defined set of values arises to take its place. To jumpstart a more fervent brand of nationalism, Shanghai professor Xiao Gongqin believes, the government should bring back to life the "profound sense of humiliation" at the hands of foreigners that took place in the last century, and target overbearing foreign influences today for eradication.

Such cultivation of nationalism is not just political rhetoric. In Hangzhou, for example, a "Just say no to foreign tea" campaign was organized after Lipton tried to post a prominent advertisement near the city's tea museum. In Tianjin, the local media criticized Sara Lee when the U.S.-based company acquired a local trademark to help sell its shoe polish brand. "A famous Chinese brand" was being "driven to the brink of extinction," declared the editorialists, looking for hot-button nationalist issues to feed to their readers.[13]

When the system doesn't thwart their success, foreigners can outcompete indigenous Chinese companies in their own market, fueling the protectionist reactions. "Our country faces an embarrassing situation," the *Worker's Daily* moaned. "Our leading companies have been shoved into a corner." In 1995, deputies to the National People's Congress briefly considered a motion to "appropriately restrict" the Coca-Cola Company and PepsiCo. "We should protect traditional beverages and help them get on their feet. . . . The market share of Coca-Cola and Pepsi is too big," said Chen Bixia, the deputy who introduced the motion.[14]

Even in the wake of Deng-era reforms, when China's door is more open to the outside world than ever before, the inward-looking nationalist view remains entrenched. China has not invested in these long-standing efforts to develop a cohesive nation, defend its territorial integrity, throw out foreign colonialists and imperialists, and build up nationwide control systems only to suddenly lose interest in the nation-state as an entity. Other parts of the world may be speeding toward supranational organizations such as the European Union or the North American Free Trade Area. There may well be a strong international consensus for supranational rule-making organizations like the WTO. But while China is willing to play by international rules much of the time, it is unwilling to cede power on issues that it believes affect its sovereignty. Nor is it willing to join without having a say in the rules. As the experience of the European Union, the world's most advanced supranational institution, has demonstrated, it is only when national governments cede some of their sovereign powers that borders truly fall.

Changing Chinese views on these kinds of issues requires long-term Engagement policies and mutual trust building. China bashing by the West, on the other hand, will only strengthen the neonationalists and encourage them to take more extreme antiforeigner positions.

Misplaced hubris: "Outsiders must be wary of imagining they can have much influence over a place like China. That is a mistake that Americans seem especially prone to make."

—*Newsweek*

CHAPTER 10

"Crossing the River by Feeling the Stones"

CHINA, THE MEDIEVAL CASTLE, long isolated by geography and custom, its people garbed in the cloak of feudalism and ready to defend its ramparts, is now prepared to open itself to the colorful but tumultuous process of modernization. But as it looks at long last across the moat, what is coming? And what will the kingdom look like once transformed and integrated into the world surrounding it?

Within China itself, there are very few people who have a vision of "where China is headed" in any way that can be clearly articulated. That they no longer engage in comprehensive blueprinting of their own future is probably a positive sign of how far the Chinese have moved away from state planning and toward the market. Even though China still makes five-year plans and from time to time issues other comprehensive blueprints, these have been dramatically deemphasized. To use an old Chinese expression, quoted by Mao and carried forward by Deng, China is in the process of "crossing the river by feeling the stones." Its leaders have no master plan for how to ford the raging currents. They cannot even see the other side clearly through the fog. And the river has begun to rise dangerously.

Careful, controlled experimentation—messy and uncertain though it is—has been judged preferable to instant decisions concerning the best way to reverse thousands of years of culture, a couple of centuries of chaos, and four decades of central planning. When things work, expand them. When they don't, cancel them. Prune the excesses only when they get too far out of hand. Gradualism has worked; shock therapy is feared.

In one of the many ironies that surround the China trade, Westerners have been known to develop a nostalgia for the old Communist days, when China seemed so "organized" and when the power of the central authorities and institutions was unquestioned. Those who did business in China fifteen years ago or more remember a time when an important official could, with a wave of the hand, change a policy, implement a deal categorically, or say authoritatively how the Chinese market would respond to a foreign business venture. No more.

Look at today's China at any given moment in time, or look at any single piece of the reform process, and it is easy to become frustrated and discouraged. Everything is being done wrong, or at best, partially. Everything is being built on uncertain foundations. The Communist belief system has never been deeply or officially criticized, yet on this rock a market system is being constructed. China is the "muddle kingdom," with its hybridized and contradictory "market socialism."

Any Western CEO, economist, politician, or intellectual can tell the Chinese a thousand and one ways to improve their reform process. But for every suggestion, the Chinese have a particular reason, valid in the context of their development, why it wouldn't work or would incur unintended and undesired consequences. A Hong Kong businessman recounts this story: In a candid and informal dinner meeting, a senior Chinese leader was decrying the state of China's rural backwardness, illiteracy, and lack of educational opportunities. The Hong Kong businessman offered to provide 10,000 free satellite dishes to a remote area so that a distance-learning experiment could be established. The Chinese leader reflected on this, but politely declined. The introduction of satellite dishes would cause the rural poor of the province to see too much of the outside world, raise their expectations, and thus cause "too many other problems." Better to do nothing than invite such difficulties.

A classic description of the Chinese: "A great people, the most numerous people on earth, a race in which the patient, laborious and industrious capacity of the individual has, for thousands of years, compensated for the collective lack of cohesion and method, and has constructed a very unique and very profound civilization; . . . a state older than history, always bent on independence, constantly striving toward centralization, instinctively withdrawn into itself and disdainful of foreigners, but aware and proud, unchangeable, perpetual—such is eternal China."

—CHARLES DE GAULLE

Similar stories are repeated dozens of times every day. As a result, the "micro" picture can be endlessly frustrating; China's decision makers can seem hopelessly inactive and inept. But if you take a larger view, you can't help but be impressed by what now appears to be the inevitable force of history unleashing the economic energies of a quarter of the world's population.

From the ancient concept of yin and yang to Mao's philosophical work trying to "Asianize" the dialectic of Hegel and Marx, Asian thought systems are much more at ease with ambiguity and with the confluence of ideas and realities than are Western ones. Neither Chinese policy nor the reality of Chinese political or economic systems is ever as sharply "either-or" as comparable systems in the West. For a very long time, China will be neither completely totalitarian nor fully democratic. Its economy will be neither a command economy nor a free market. And in terms of its relations with the United States, Japan, other countries, and the world institutional system as a whole, China will be neither just a great economic opportunity nor just an ominous regional or strategic challenge. Long into the future, the answer to the question "Which?" will still be "Both."

Yin, yang, and the trinity: "China today can be described accurately only by self-contradiction. . . . China's paradoxes may be more than a feature of transition. They may be constitutive of a system in which power is so all-encompassing yet decentralized that the trinity of state, society and economy have become one. This may just be the way China works."

—ANDREW NATHAN
  COLUMBIA UNIVERSITY

The Yangzi Is Not the Mississippi

One thing is absolutely clear, however. The river the Chinese are trying to cross by feeling the stones is not the Mississippi. It is a Chinese river, with Chinese stones in it.

It has become historical habit to impose upon China *our* dreams, interpreted according to our psychic and political makeup; often they have little in common with Chinese reality. A young Chinese friend of ours once brought tears to the eyes of a delegation of hard-driving American political and business leaders at the conclusion of a *mao tai*–fired farewell banquet in the early 1980s by reciting, movingly and in excellent English, Lincoln's Gettysburg Address (which President Jiang Zemin has also been known to recite). It is doubtful that any of these sentimental Americans could imagine that a few years later, this seemingly still-gentle Chinese would show little sympathy with the students demonstrating in Tiananmen Square. He believed the demonstrations, not the crackdown, were bad for China's image, bad for business, and potentially bad for all his government connections.

We assume that people who have learned to talk in the same terms as we do will direct their society in the same direction. Anything else is simply "irrational." We have been told, after all, that we have reached the "end of history," that rationalist Western thought, mirrored by the West's liberal political democracies and free market economies, is *the* way forward, naturally selected by the social Darwinism of the last several hundred years. What we fail to take into account is what China's history demonstrates: That from a Chinese perspective, the goal is not to have a democracy, but to move a huge society forward cohesively. That it is not capitalism that China's leaders seek, but modernization. That it is perfectly rational to believe in both markets *and* socialism; in more "openness" and certain kinds of freedom *as well as in* the suppression of political dissidents; in world peace and stability *as well as in* the foreign policy of maneuver, manipulation, and Chinese interest above all.

Looking in the Mirror

When one inventories China's major problems, the list is daunting. But so, too, is any country's, including the United States. Indeed, the problems both our societies face are one of the most interesting areas of commonality between us:

- They have corruption in high places and a serious social problem with crime—and so do we.
- They have a society that until recently was largely egalitarian and is now increasingly polarized between Haves and Have-Nots. We have a society that until recently had the largest, strongest middle class, but now has the widest gap between rich and poor of any advanced economy.
- Their state-owned enterprise system is virtually bankrupt, in large part because of its commitments to the health care and pensions of retired workers. Our Social Security and Medicare programs are headed toward bankruptcy for the same reason.
- Their social fabric has been fraying ever since Communist ideology lost its hold. Our social fabric is also fraying as a result of the breakdown of major public institutions from church to neighborhood to the public schools.

"Different values should be permitted in the world today. You use knives and forks in the West. We have 5,000 years of history and a quarter of the world's population. Let us use chopsticks."

—Xu Kuangdi
Mayor of Shanghai

- They are experiencing the repercussions of becoming more efficient by "breaking the iron rice bowl," while we have to deal with similar problems caused by downsizing and with the increased uncertainty and risk that accompany new opportunities.
- They face a serious challenge in dealing with their minority peoples and keeping them integrated into China. The challenge of integrating minorities into our society remains America's number one social problem.
- Their current senior leaders, such as Jiang Zemin and Li Peng, are considered ineffectual and weak compared to the great leaders of China's recent past and the nation's founding fathers from Sun Yat-sen to Mao and Deng. Similarly, American leaders like Bill Clinton suffer from comparison with FDR and America's founding fathers.
- They have no blueprint for the future, and neither do we. They are following Deng's advice and "crossing the river by feeling the stones," while we are building the equally amorphous "bridge to the future" that was a regular feature of Bill Clinton's stump speech in the campaign of 1996.

Countries—especially those in rapid transition—are frequently treated in lay discussion as if they were human beings, who will get sick, have heart attacks, or "die" without the right policies. But as economist Paul Krugman has recently reminded lay commentators on economic matters, nation-states are not really all that much like human organisms. True, their economic wealth and global clout rise and fall, and they experience healthy and sick periods. But, with certain exceptions, they generally don't "die."

China has a higher risk than many of falling into chaos or experiencing the breakup of its current structure. But we don't believe those are high-probability scenarios. The probability we foresee is, in fact, just the opposite: a stronger, growing China for decades to come. Almost all scenarios, however, assume that there will always be a China. Whether or not the leaders implement the right policies, whether or not China becomes the world's leading economy, whether or not some provinces or regions spin off from the core of the Middle Kingdom, China will nevertheless be a force to reckon with in the twenty-first century, as it was not in the twentieth.

An Explosion Still Ahead?

Yet it is legitimate to ask how sustainable China's growth may be in the absence of a more clearly articulated political-economic model. "Crossing the river by feeling the stones," and other vintage Dengisms ("Development is the most important theory," or "That which works we'll call socialism, and that which fails we'll call capitalism," or the famous "Black cat, white cat, so long as it catches mice") can only take China so far. Important as these aphorisms have been as powerful polemics *for* pragmatism, markets, and real-world solutions—and as arrows in the heart of the old Maoist ideology—they have grown less and less useful as guides to solving China's present problems. As Hong Kong journalist Willy Wo-lap Lam observes of the recent track record of the Deng-led Chinese Communist Party: "It's way past midnight" for this "Cinderella with advanced-stage Parkinson's disease." Since 1994, the Party's mainstream faction has not only demonstrated that it has "run out of new ideas" but has even stopped trying to suggest that it is capable of "novel solutions."[1]

There is a gathering crisis ahead in what Maoists would call the contradiction between China's "base" and its "superstructure." The base—the fundamental economic foundations of the society, the economic relations between people, and the system of ownership—is undergoing vigorous, if uneven, change. But the superstructure—the governmental institutions, laws, ideas, values, managerial methods, belief systems, and moral philosophy—is creaky and atrophying. Classical Marxist-Leninist-Maoist theory holds that such circumstances create the conditions for revolution.

We are of the opinion that this gathering crisis will eventually come to a head. That probably will not happen in the immediate future, but is more likely in the early years of the next decade. The form of the explosion is unpredictable, but in all likelihood, it will include an element of spontaneous public demand for change as well as some leadership from elements of the party capable of responding positively to such demands.

The explosion need not be total and apocalyptic. We rather doubt, in fact, that it will be a replay of Tiananmen Square. And the outcome we expect will not necessarily be an extreme departure from the status quo. But whatever form

Message from a pro-mainland Taiwanese professor: democracy is dangerous. "On behalf of China at this point in history, I dare to proclaim, Down with democracy, Down with freedom! Freedom and democracy are not at all absolute goods; for China they are relative 'evils.' For freedom can only cause China to fragment, and democracy can only cause it to collapse. . . . Japan and Germany are again considered powers. Is that because their democracy and freedom so exceeded those of America and England?"

—Yan Yuanshu
China News Analysis

225

the explosion takes, it will be a convincing message that the leadership must begin to put a premium on innovations that can reform the superstructure. China *may* be captured by the gravity of the world market and the Western approach to democracy and personal liberty. We would not rule that out for the far future. "Democracy" was one of the three principles laid down by Sun Yat-sen (China's George Washington, say some) in the early 1900s, and the democratic impulse remains present, if usually vague, among intellectuals and other segments of the population. Nor would we disagree with those who would like to *hope* for a faster curve of political change and a democratic awakening in China.

But hope is different from belief. In our view, China is more likely to follow the imperatives of its own—different—culture and history. After all, Sun Yat-sen was pushed aside by a military strongman vowing to restore order and maintain stability. The banners of democracy were raised again over Tiananmen Square in 1989, but "democracy" was more a slogan than a deep belief, at least among most demonstrators.[2]

The present government's own attitude toward democracy is that it was tried, but failed. "In the 1960s we already tried so-called 'Big Democracy,' " Vice Premier Li Lanqing told us, referring, amazingly, to the Cultural Revolution—hardly an example of what Westerners would think of as an experiment in democracy. "At that time we had hundreds of thousands of parties, not like in other countries, where there are just of a couple of parties. This led China into big chaos and also cost China twenty years' time." Commented Wang Ruoshui, a former vice chief editor of the *People's Daily,* "The propaganda organs show fighting in the Taiwan parliament or they show poor Russian farmers and they tell the people: this is democracy. The people have been misled to believe that democracy equals chaos in the streets."[3]

For the next several decades, Chinese and Western systems will be notable more for their differences than for their similarities. Generational change will take . . . well, generations. It is better to come to a realistic understanding of this than continue the American dream of a China that will develop in our image and likeness. That realism is part and parcel of preventing a spiral of misperceptions and failed expectations that can only exacerbate conflict between the world's next two superpowers.

PART III

JUMPING INTO THE SEA

In the history of our country, there is only one such chance.

—ZHANG WEI, CHAIRMAN
EAST SHANGHAI HOLDINGS

The outstanding people create outstanding success.

—FENG LUN, CHAIRMAN
VANTONE ENTERPRISE GROUP

A Thousand Rivers

It takes a thousand rivers, says an old Chinese proverb, to change the sea. In the two-decade-old spring of China's market-oriented reforms, the Maoist economic glacier has begun to melt, unleashing roaring streams of entrepreneurial energy. These, in turn, have nourished the lives of hundreds of millions of Chinese, transforming them profoundly. We reflect on this historic shift away from the old refrains in doing business of *mei you* ("don't have") and *tai ma fan* ("too much trouble") to the new *xiang qian kan* ("march toward money") as we stand in the lobby of our sparkling, well-appointed joint-venture hotel in Shanghai, awaiting our ride to the offices of Zhang Wei, chairman of East Shanghai Holdings. Zhang is a fast-rising entrepreneur whose original stake of RMB 100,000 ($12,000) has multiplied 4,000-fold, to RMB 400 million ($48 million)—a percentage increase that would make him right at home among the top twenty-five on *Inc.* magazine's list of the 500 fastest-growing private companies in America.

Not all that long ago—back in the 1970s and even the early 1980s—we would have been waiting in a dowdy hotel or "guest house," with largely barren walls, ill-tempered "service workers," and as much dust in the lobby's red carpet as on the sidewalk outside. A Maoist ditty would have been blaring from a loudspeaker, instead of today's Mozart piece performed live by a string quartet. The escort coming to fetch us would likely have been a nondescript functionary from a government department, the car a standard-issue no-changes-since-the-forties Shanghai-brand sedan. A "model" factory would have been lined up, where the leading members of the department concerned would have been ready to spout a "brief introduction," demonstrating the unit's great leaps in productivity and ideological awareness.

Today, however, a melodious voice asks after us. It belongs not to some bureaucrat, but to Diana Shen, whose card identifies her as executive director of East Shanghai Holdings. Elegant and willowy, she is a vision in black: high-heeled black pumps, a short black dress, and a large, black leather designer bag from which she produces a matching cellular phone to summon the driver. A minute later, a luxury Chinese-made black Audi—the brand of choice among those wanting to avoid the eyebrow-raising effects of a

That was then, this is now: "Six months ago, China's deputy prime minister in charge of economy, Zhu Rongji, railed against outsiders who warned of financial problems. Such problems now occupy all of his time." So wrote *The Economist* in November 1997.

Mercedes or a Lexus in the current anticorruption drive—stands ready to whisk us across Shanghai. The car travels east along Yanan Road, named after Mao's revolutionary base in the 1930s, and passes just a few blocks north of the site that marks the founding of the Chinese Communist Party in 1921. The irony goes even deeper. During the Maoist era, when red was the color of political correctness, the worst insult imaginable was to be labeled black—as in vitriol like "Deng Xiaoping is a traitor and capitalist roader who is following the black line." Now, black is the color of choice among China's most daring and avant-garde entrepreneurs; the red is Revlon or some local brand, on the lips of people like Ms. Shen.

A trip through the new harbor tunnel takes us into Pudong, the area designated to become the heart of a reborn, world-class Shanghai—a Shanghai many Chinese hope and expect will become one of the key global financial centers of the next century. Unexpectedly, the car turns left against oncoming traffic in the middle of a crowded, commercial street. It climbs the curb and pulls up in front of a downscale dress shop. Feeling like characters out of a spy novel (or perhaps the opening sequence of *The Man from U.N.C.L.E.*), we enter the store—two foreigners in suits with briefcases, wending our way toward the back stairs amid the throng of shoppers searching for a bargain. (We will later learn that this seemingly bizarre retail entrance to a suite of corporate offices was a way to get around the regulation against buildings devoted only to offices in this section of Pudong.)

Two flights up, we arrive at a glass entryway flanked by potted plants. The names of several of Zhang Wei's enterprises are etched into a brass placard mounted on a side door. After passing the reception desk and rows of modern cubicles occupied by graphic artists using the latest computer-aided design software, we find ourselves comfortably seated on a low-slung modern black leather couch in his office. There are bookcases along one wall, a black desk overflowing with papers and a computer, and more piles of paper everywhere, all speaking of many diverse projects, all ultimately controlled here. Bottles of Zhang's own brand of designer water are pulled by Ms. Shen from the corner refrigerator.

As we begin the interview with Zhang, catching up with the changes in the city since our last visit just a few months before, a phrase from an article in *The Economist* leaps to mind. In describing Shanghai's phenomenal growth and success—due in large part to the intelligence and energy of people like Zhang Wei—the newspaper quipped: "If all of China were like Shanghai, the rest of the world might as well concede defeat tomorrow."[1]

This change in how Shanghai and many other parts of China work began with some 25 million self-employed Chinese, most of them voluntarily leaving the state enterprise system, hawking factory-surplus goods along sidewalks, knocking on doors selling everything from AIG life insurance to Avon cosmetics, and running their own restaurants and shops.

It has continued with truck drivers, peasants, factory workers, and ex-bureaucrats who, through various permutations of hard work, connections, connivance, and speculation, have created some 435,000 "private" companies, turning some of these entrepreneurs into millionaires (at least, "RMB millionaires") virtually overnight. Hundreds of thousands of professionals have left government and academic sinecures to start their own companies or go to work in foreign joint ventures—600,000 of these people in 1992–93 alone.[2] Local party and government leaders now sport business cards identifying them also as directors, presidents, or advisers at trading and investment companies. And the cream of the rising young elite—China's best and brightest, tempered by the Cultural Revolution and dissuaded from politics by the 1989 incident in Tiananmen Square—have, like Mr. Zhang, turned their passion for system reform into genuine entrepreneurial zeal.

Of course, it is sometimes difficult to tell the true proto-capitalists with vision, skill, and drive from the lucky or corrupt, who were simply handed an opportunity or otherwise seized one during the madcap days in the late eighties and early nineties when real estate was being privatized, stock markets launched, and foreigners allowed to invest in Chinese companies. Not surprisingly, many members of the old Communist elite, as well as their children, dominate the new fortunes being made. But a multitude of ordinary Chinese are slowly emerging through this process into a new and dynamic group of true entrepreneurs and business-people; they are the forerunners of an upper middle class.

In whatever way these millions of Chinese have been able

Nouveau sophistication: China has replaced Japan as the world's second biggest market for brandy, which is successfully advertised as a prestige drink for the rich. One businessman in Hainan bested another in an evening's smash-the-bottle competition, breaking 17 bottles worth $25,000.

to express their entrepreneurial instincts, it is hard to over-estimate their courage or the importance of the tidal change they are creating. China's new entrepreneurs are often compared to the pioneers and frontiersmen of nineteenth-century America. But they face a singular hardship: centuries of bureaucratism and a culture that taught them "The first bird out of the nest will be shot." Choosing to give up the certainty of knowing one's place in the system, and forgoing the "iron rice bowl" that comes with it, are therefore doubly daring. It is uniquely uncertain psychologically as well as economically. It is a leap captured well in the expression the Chinese use for this switch in careers: *xiahai*—"to jump into the sea." The expression implies a level of risk hardly captured by the American equivalent, "starting my own business."

The people profiled in the chapters that follow—Zhang Wei, Chen Ping, and Feng Lun—represent some of the best of these "swimmers." Like many others, they recognized the shifting winds in China and consciously set out to get rich as soon as it became possible to do so. These three are particularly compelling, not only as exemplars with interesting stories to tell, but because they have set their sights higher, aiming to build great, institutionalized enterprises that can lead China into the twenty-first century. They are moving beyond the stage of simply being *political* entrepreneurs—those whose business is based almost completely on their *guanxi* with government bureaucrats and on the trading of favors—to being *market* entrepreneurs, taking more risks, building companies on their own strength, and acting independently of the system to the extent possible. In short, they are consciously building the Confucian social market of the future.

Intoxicating visions for multinational companies: In America, there is 1 car for every 1.8 persons, compared to 1 for every 1,093 in China. Telephones and TVs exist in an almost 1–1 ratio with people in the United States. China has 100 people per TV, 149 people per telephone.

CHAPTER 11

Zhang Wei: Finding Answers to the Question of Ownerhip

Some comrades do not like to think much about difficulties. But difficulties are facts; we must recognize as many difficulties as there are and . . . analyze them and combat them.

—MAO ZEDONG

WHEN ZHANG WEI SMILES, which is often, a boyish, quizzical look crosses his large, open face. His eyes come alive behind his gold-rimmed glasses. He has much to smile about, having taken Chairman Mao's saying about combating difficulties as good business advice. He has gone from being a "government researcher" to head of a 400-person company in a little more than three years.

Although he is one of Shanghai's rising entrepreneurs, Zhang is not among China's glitzy *nouveaux riches,* instantly wealthy and eager to flaunt it. He will not generally be found wandering through chic boutiques with a fawning claque at his side, or polishing off thousand-dollar dinners with a bottle of the finest French cognac and gold-flecked Belgian bonbons. He is, instead, a worthy example of the solid entrepreneurial skills and values at the heart of the next phase of China's economy.

On the surface, Zhang reflects many of the classic characteristics of go-go entrepreneurship familiar to Americans. He is a risk taker, ambitious and determined. Like many of the world's most successful businesspeople, from Bill Gates to the great taipans of Hong Kong, Zhang had no formal business training. "I just read some books about how people in the U.S. and Japan do business," he says. To start his company, East Shanghai Holdings—now a diversified group of companies in businesses from real estate to retailing to children's play centers—Zhang, like many young American entrepreneurs, had to convince a group of investors to believe in him as well as in his business plan.

What he also has in common with entrepreneurs around the globe is drive, plus a combination of talent, timing, strategic alliances, and a wide network of well-cultivated friends, colleagues, and government officials. These have brought Zhang to the point where East Shanghai Holdings earned RMB 25 million ($3 million) in after-tax profits in 1995 and has investments and partnerships in Japan, Australia, Europe, and the United States.

But despite these superficial similarities, Zhang has traveled a very different road. Indeed, his key talent may be his ability to understand and work within a system whose shape and function will not be found in any case study of American enterprise. His company may formally call itself a "corporation," but it does not much resemble those set up in Delaware or any other American state. It has "shareholders," but not in the way Wall Street would use the term. Nor does the company fit into a neat Western category of being "public" or "private." Indeed, as Zhang himself is the first to point out, "The system of ownership in China is not clear."

"I am not a businessman," he begins when asked the story behind his success. He once worked in the Shanghai city bureaucracy as an economist, assigned to help dress up local State-Owned Enterprises to make them attractive to potential foreign investors. By the early 1990s, Zhang had become vice general manager of a Pudong government company specializing in that task. To this day he remains a member of the Communist Party—not because of a firm belief in its

Labels without definitions: "Each country has its own way of defining its market system. There exists no market economic system that is the same. A German friend asked me to explain how to understand the 'socialist market system with Chinese characteristics.' I asked him a question: Can you explain to me how to understand the social market system in Germany? So I think there will be different systems around the world and China will be one with its own characteristics."

—VICE PREMIER LI LANQING, 1995

ideology, we suspect, but because cultivating good relations with the Party is for most Chinese businesspeople as essential as having good relations with regulatory agencies or the right local, state, or congressional officials is for Americans.

Zhang began entrepreneurial life by advising Chinese companies on restructuring. Soon, however, he moved to stage two: actively selling parts of these companies to foreign investors. "We made much more money selling companies than merely being consultants," he comments. Now he is well into a third stage: buying partial or majority interests in state companies himself, then using those shares as leverage to start new businesses. "I was the first domestic company in China to be able to buy state assets," he says.

Since then, Zhang has gone well beyond his core business. Indeed, East Shanghai Holdings has a catch-as-catch-can feel that reflects China's business world in general. As of late 1995, Zhang was deeply involved in at least half a dozen disparate businesses. Among them were real estate ventures (including what was slated to become Pudong's premier hotel), futures and securities trading, office-furniture manufacturing, automobile manufacturing in a joint venture with the Taiwan arm of a Japanese car maker, and a chain of gold and jewelry stores. (Zhang predicts that when the government liberalizes retail gold dealing, that business will be "bigger than telecommunications.")

Zhang is also the master franchise holder in China for the American company Fun World, which manufacturers children's playground equipment and sets up children's activity centers. He has centers already operating in Shanghai and Tianjin under the local names of Fun Dazzle. Two more are under construction; an additional thirteen franchisees are signed up. By the end of 1996, Zhang expects to have twenty more. The rate of return on investments in these centers is over 30 percent a year, he tells us.

But Zhang's company hasn't just pioneered the children's entertainment business—it has reached across the Pacific to pioneer the "reverse M&A" business as well, being among the first Chinese companies to buy an interest in a U.S. company. Zhang acquired a 50 percent share of the American parent of Fun World and is negotiating an arrangement that would shift the manufacturing of all the equipment for the centers to China. His long-term goal is to take over the U.S.

The Party line: Communist Party officials in Beijing explained why they won't allow entrepreneurs to join their ranks in this simple, clear-cut way: "If we allow them to enter the Party, this will rock the very class foundations of the Party."

company altogether, exporting the concept to other countries and selling the franchisees Chinese-made equipment.

What drives Zhang may surprise those who subscribe to the facile notion that Chinese entrepreneurs are out only for themselves, eager to adopt the most laissez-faire aspects of Adam Smith–style capitalism. East Shanghai Holdings has abided strictly by the intellectual-property rules laid down by Fun World, for example. Asked if it wouldn't be easier to just start the concept on his own, Zhang says: "I don't want to, for moral reasons." He himself has been a victim. Some of his original franchisees have stolen the company name, he says, and are opening their own centers. Here again, Zhang Wei is a pioneer, trying to use China's fledgling legal system to sue to stop the practice. But he is not suing the franchisees; instead he is suing the government. "So far there is no law protecting us against our franchisees," Zhang says, "so we are suing those government bureaus that let these people register in our name."

This streak of moralism runs throughout Zhang Wei's approach to business. He has devised a handsome profit-sharing plan for his employees and supports several schools in poor neighborhoods around Shanghai. He sees this attitude of "doing something for people" as a combination of traditional Chinese culture with the legacy of the Cultural Revolution. The Cultural Revolution may have been an unmitigated disaster on most fronts, but for many of the idealistic young people who went through it—China's "baby boomers," who are now in their forties—the experience left a distinct sense of the importance of social equity, egalitarianism, and similar values. So, although many new entrepreneurs are trampling over every vestige of traditional or Maoist values, for a solid number of them, like Zhang Wei, values still matter. "Business must be done on the basis of mutual benefit. This means you don't just exchange value without also some fairness being there. In fact, you have to go beyond that and make each side feel better that this has been done."

What sets Zhang most apart from his entrepreneurial brethren in other parts of the world, however, is the issue of ownership. In the West, ownership is a generally clear principle. To the degree any unclarities have arisen, these have been resolved and made absolutely crystal clear by volumes upon volumes of property law, securities law, corporate law, and so on. Questions may arise over who owns what in

Coke is it, now and tomorrow: Coca-Cola sales in China rocketed 76 percent in 1994, making it Coke's fastest-growing market by far. By 1997, Coca-Cola will have 23 plants—from Harbin in the northeast, to Wuhan in the center, to Xian in the northwest—representing a total investment of more than $500 million. "If you drink a Coca-Cola today, you still need to drink a Coca-Cola tomorrow," says Rick Yan, vice president of the Hong Kong consulting firm Bain & Co.

America or other market economies, but there are highly efficient means of answering those questions. In China, however, it is anything but clear who or what actually owns many of China's most dynamic companies, or what rights such ownership conveys.

In Zhang's story, for example, it is hard to find a clear dividing line between his old job as a Shanghai government employee and his new job as head of a "private" company. For some time, he passed out two business cards, an "old" one that presented him as vice general manager of the Shanghai government–owned "State-Owned Assets Investment and Management Corporation of Shanghai Pudong Area," and a new one identifying him as chairman of East Shanghai Holdings. "It was confusing, so I decided I would stop being general manager of the assets company," says Zhang.

Thus, while the casual observer looking for a good newsmagazine profile on the new taipans might seize on Zhang as an example of private enterprise in China, a closer look reveals that he doesn't *own* East Shanghai Holdings at all. "My company is not a state company, but it is also not a private company," he says, using "private" in the American sense. "It is a stockholder company."

So who "owns" East Shanghai Holdings? Ten percent is held by his old company, the city-owned Pudong Asset Management Company. A government oil-trading company, Sinopec, owns shares. So does a "private" travel agency. As do two "public" companies in Beijing ("public" here means the companies are listed on one of the Chinese official stock exchanges. Although their shares are now publicly traded, the core owners are still state enterprises). The permutations of who in the end "owns" what piece of East Shanghai Holdings become nearly endless.

At the same time, rules for share allocation, shareholder rights, and definitions of the powers of management are all evolving. No clear market mechanism exists for valuing, buying, selling, or trading the shares. Zhang's investors seem happy to allow him to manage the company however he chooses, even when making decisions about allocating profits and sharing dividends. There is no formal board of directors that can exercise control, even nominally. In that sense at least, East Shanghai Holdings acts as a "private" company.

Presumably, Zhang's investors could revolt and demand bigger dividends and different management. He must live

The new pecking order: "Investment bankers are more important than state officials in China today," said Zhou Yuan, son of Zhou Nan, China's top official in Hong Kong. The younger Zhou works for the Union Bank of Switzerland.

with that risk, constantly trying to keep them happy. And as long as the dividends flow, they do seem happy. The state subsidies such entities formerly received are dwindling, leaving managers to try and find more creative ways to shore up the enterprise. Companies like Zhang's offer the promise of much higher rates of return on assets than they can get from their own businesses. Moreover, this being China in the nineties, the investment may be funneled through a subsidiary of the investing company—a subsidiary in which managers may have a direct stake.

Over time, Zhang has been buying out some of his nine original investors. "We have no problem buying them out as long as we pay a high premium. Some holders have their own problems, so they are glad to get the money," he says. Thus proto-capitalist new companies help pump capital back into the old state-owned dinosaurs, staving off *their* crisis another year.

If the company's relationship with outside investors is murky, things are not much clearer when one looks inside East Shanghai Holdings. The shares bought back by the company are distributed to the employees—another characteristic of China's market socialism. Originally, the employees held 4.6 percent of the company (the government would not allow them more), but now the proportion is up to 15 percent. Zhang expects it will reach 30 percent within the next three years, but such a transition would be subject to a variety of local government approvals.

Of the employee group shares, 75 percent are owned by top management, including Zhang. Zhang has also given the employees the right to form a new company *outside* of East Shanghai Holdings. This company, which has its own set of "rights," can engage in other ventures and, indeed, is in the securities-trading business. The employees' company is connected to a third company with securities expertise, which also happens to have some ties to East Shanghai Holdings. And the circle goes on.

Such confusion, it should be noted, is fine with people like Zhang. Until the system as a whole changes, their success depends largely on their ability to move boldly through this foggy maze, gaining footholds wherever they have not been expressly forbidden to go. Unlike the United States, where mazelike structures like this often exist to minimize taxable income, these complexities arise in China as entrepreneurs try to find ways to maximize income, free from the still-constricting institutional setup and bureaucratic regulations.

As far as Zhang is concerned, the ultimate purpose of this game is not just profit, but survival. Competition looms and only the large and efficient will be able to meet it, he says. "No one person in our country has the necessary hundred million renminbi [$12 million] to create a solid foundation for enterprises like mine," he reminds us. "Now we face not only our internal market, but a world market. Even if we are good, we will not be able to compete if we are not also big. So, if we hold stock in each other we can build ourselves up to a more viable valuation of ten billion renminbi [$120 million]."

Ironically, messy cross-investing arrangements are also virtuous from the viewpoint of Beijing officialdom. They allow the transitional economic system to harness the capabilities of a Zhang Wei, while still keeping the entrepreneurial class part of a controlled, delicately balanced social and political infrastructure for as long as possible.

As he turns his gaze abroad, Zhang, like many other businesspeople of his stature, asserts a strong streak of cultural pride that spills over into political nationalism. He is definitely not part of what some pundits have tried to label a new, international elite whose education, management skills, and technical literacy give them a "supranational" identity with little allegiance to their home country. Not Zhang Wei. He is only bemused by the arguments of American Hawks who threaten trade sanctions and sometimes more. Neither the United States nor Japan dares threaten war with China, he feels, because "war would cut off their China market, which is essential to their economy. If China doesn't buy cars, airplanes, and such from the United States, it is bad for you; it is nothing for us."

Not surprisingly, Zhang Wei is optimistic about the future of his company and his nation. Personally, he expects that by the turn of the century he will control assets of RMB 3 billion to 5 billion ($357 million to $595 million), in great part through mergers and acquisitions. As to China's future, Zhang says, "Whether it is the economy, the political system, or our role in the world, it's a process of learning. But one thing unites us: it is the sense that we will be better off tomorrow than we are today. The years between 2000 and 2010 will be the decade of the fastest growth in our history."

No need to wait for the future, profits are now: Amazingly, given the need for long time horizons in China, major foreign enterprises are already profitable. According to a joint study released in 1995 by Andersen Consulting and the *Economist* Intelligence Unit, 65 percent of 47 large foreign ventures surveyed in China reported being in the black, with 1994 profits climbing as high as $10 million.

CHAPTER 12

Chen Ping:
The Adventurer

What is work? Work is struggle. There are difficulties and problems in those places for us to overcome and solve. We go there to work and struggle to overcome these difficulties. A good comrade is one who is eager to go where the difficulties are greater.

—MAO ZEDONG

HELLO, I'M CHEN PING. If I don't make any mistakes, I will become one of the wealthiest private citizens in China. I am trying to become the newly born bourgeoisie that the Chinese Communists have been trying to overthrow for almost fifty years."

It is in this provocative way that the ebullient Chen Ping, one of China's newly rich individuals, likes to greet foreign economists like Milton Friedman and other devotees of the free market. As Chen talks, the force of his personality seems to propel him far beyond his swivel-back black leather executive chair, set at the head of a conference table in his airy, contemporary office suite. Eyes flashing with enthusiasm, he fills the room with his booming voice. "People like me tend to be self-confident, with or without grounds," he tells us. "With this confidence and my 'three-inch tongue' I can be very persuasive." He uses his arms as punctuation marks, making ashes from the Marlboro in his ebony cigarette holder flutter to the floor with every exclamation point.

He gives the lie to the cliché that the Chinese people seek conformity; Chen brags that he always knew he wanted to be different. "As far back as 1973 I wanted to break the double bondage of human life: economic and political," he tells us. "But back then it really was not possible to go into business in a meaningful way." The few private enterprises tolerated were street peddling, repair work, and restaurants with a few tables for serving noodles and soup. So Chen remained, in his own words, "a modern-day version of the self-righteous feudal scholar-elite," working as a government economist.

He wrote reports on how China could use "ladder steps" and a "coastal belt of development" to jump-start growth and, in 1984, what he calls a "famous report" on the early success of Shenzhen, the special economic zone near Hong Kong. Chen also has a strong philosophical streak. In 1987 he wrote a book on "social ecology," exploring what kind of human habitat could serve as the basis for "human social existence" in the China of the future. Even today, this self-described "richest man in China" continues to keep a toe in the world of research and writing, much as generations of scholar-elites have done before him. He passes around not only his business card but a card identifying him as research director at the Peking University China Center for Economic Research.

It was the events surrounding the Tiananmen debacle of 1989 that finally pushed Chen Ping into the sea. Losing hope that he could have some impact on reforming the system, Chen first considered joining the many friends of his who were quitting the government and going to work for a foreign joint-venture company, which offered the chance to learn foreign business practices at first hand. But he saw that as a halfway measure. It would still have tied him to a system from which he wanted complete escape. Starting his own company was also not an option. Chen had no access to capital either from his relatives, his friends, or the banks (which at the time loaned only to state-owned or state-approved ventures). Instead, Chen made his way to Hong Kong, where he went to work as an import-export agent. The next six years were filled with adventures reminiscent of the old Horatio Alger stories, with a spot of Lee Iacocca thrown in.

On behalf of the Hong Kong company, Chen took train trips to various remote points along the border with Russia.

Rush Limbaugh would like this young Communist: "Today, if one person makes 3,000 RMB and another 300 RMB, then the second one feels angry and resentful. But one day that person making 300 RMB will say, 'I have to think; I need to do more. I can make 3,000 RMB, too, so I must start to work.'"

—LI ZHIPING
EDITOR, *THE YOUTH LIFE WEEKLY*

241

There he would take orders for clothing and textiles; returning with these goods, he would sell them at a commission of 3 to 5 percent. "In this period I was only beginning to learn the ropes of a market economy," he says. He reports earning about RMB 100,000 ($12,000) between 1989 and early 1991—a princely sum for most Chinese. But it wasn't big enough money for Chen, and he wasn't making it quickly enough.

At this point, the tales of Chen Ping's career begin to blur in the drama of their telling. At times he seems to be a candidate for Forrest Gump's Chinese twin. Like Gump, he finds himself in amazing places at historic times. Unlike Gump, however, he consciously exploits these coincidences of history to build his empire.

Scene one takes place in the wild northern borderlands of Burma, populated by bandits and drug smugglers. There, with a hired band of roving workers, he sets off in search of rubies and hardwoods. "I was like your American cowboys, armed and everything," he tells us, "except I rode elephants." Of the dangers, Chen says simply, "Money is more important than life."

He shipped the rubies and timber across the border into China and then to Guangzhou, where he lined up workshops to process them for the upscale jewelry boutiques and furniture stores of Hong Kong. The jewelry business did fairly well, but he learned that he been cheated on the wood—full of wormholes and rot, it was totally unsuitable for furniture. "I made several million, but I also lost several million, and by the second half of 1991 my loss was greater than my gain," he says of his first solo business adventure.

Scene two finds Chen in Germany, where he has entered into a partnership with a local friend to import Chinese furniture. This, too, failed. "In a month I found out I couldn't make a fortune in a Western country," he says. "The competition was fierce, and the market saturated. Nevertheless, I got a better understanding of capitalism, and I learned with my losses that success also had to do with the importance of quality."

By now it is August 1991, and the scene shifts to Moscow. Asked why, Chen explains, "There was a lot of change going on there and, as the old Chinese saying has it, there is opportunity in chaos." Also, Chen's biological father had been living there since the 1950s, ever since he got on the

These rules were made because these things happened:
Some of the instructions—spelling and grammar uncorrected—seen on an English-language "Notice to Guests" in a hotel in western China: "Wild drinking, disturbance, gambling, drug-taking, lecherous acts, prostitution, obscene and superstitious painting, calligraphy and videotape recordings disseminating and projecting are strictly forbidden.— Guns, Bullets, explosives, poisonous and radiative items (including inflammable chemical items) are not allowed inside the hotel.—The use of electric stoves, irons, ovens and other electric equipment is not allowed. Copymachines, telex and other office facilities can not be installed without approval.— Raising birds, poultry and livestock is forbidden within the room."

—THE WALL STREET JOURNAL

wrong side of an obscure Sino-Soviet Cold War diplomatic tangle known as the "two Wangs incident." The tale as Chen tells it is worthy of John le Carré, but suffice it to say that the double attraction of seeing his father (whom he had not seen since he was a small boy) and testing the waters for another business opportunity made Moscow alluring.

Soon after Chen's arrival, Moscow was thrown into the uncertainty of the attempted coup against Gorbachev. Chen says he was among those who climbed atop the tanks after Yeltsin stood down the hard-line plotters. Recognized on the streets by a TASS reporter he had known in Beijing, he was asked to appear on Russian television to give his perspective on the fate of reform in eastern-bloc countries. "But I didn't forget I was there to make money." Chen acquired surplus heavy winter jackets and took them to his next frontier: Czechoslovakia. There, he found the end of his first rainbow.

Through a chance encounter in which he helped an Overseas Chinese stranded without a visa, Chen found himself developing a friendship with one of Czech president Václav Havel's top aides, who happened to send him a greeting card. Chen appreciated the gesture but was surprised by the poor quality of the artwork on the card. Suddenly, inspiration struck: *Christmas cards*. Chen Ping, former Chinese Communist government official, would restore the true spirit of Christmas among Eastern Europe's Christians by importing Christmas cards from Hong Kong!

But not just any cards. To appeal to what he felt was Eastern Europe's pent-up demand for electronic gadgets, Chen's cards would combine traditional religious and seasonal themes with little flashing lights and music chips that played carols. Says Chen: "I ordered a million cards, and had them delivered by air. I then drove my car all over Eastern Europe to sign up agents, and sold all the cards in forty days, making a dollar each. But that is only part of it. I accepted payment in Czech currency, which no one else wanted at the time but which I felt would soon become convertible. It did and I immediately made a fortune."

This unlikely greeting-card king of Czechoslovakia, having made the transition from poor man to millionaire, next set his sights on the United States, where, Chen says, he was invited to become a visiting professor at MIT. Instead, he bought used and outdated computer equipment by the ware-

Plastic, plastic everywhere . . . : A study released in May 1995 by the People's Bank of China predicted that "about 200 million Chinese will have credit cards by the end of the century." That is roughly equal to the number of all Visa, MasterCard, American Express, Discover, and Diners Club cardholders worldwide in 1995.

houseful and then resold it into the distribution network he had earlier set up in Eastern Europe.

Also, Chen tells us, friends introduced him to a member of the Rockefeller family, with whom he entered a short-lived venture to make environmentally sound bathroom fixtures. "But," Chen notes ruefully, "it was very, very unsuccessful. I thought the process was patented, but no, they had not even finished experiments. And financial commitments were not met." Rather than embroiling himself in lawsuits and name-calling, Chen says, he followed the advice of his friends, avoiding any potential battle by paying back the initial Rockefeller investment and terminating the venture. One can easily imagine there being another side to this story. Nevertheless, when Chen tells it, he savors the notion that out of the goodness of his heart, he, a poor Chinese, paid back a Rockefeller money he did not owe.

By early 1992 Chen began to feel he had learned what he could abroad. Besides, "I had made enough money to return to China a rich man." What decided him was Deng Xiao-ping's famous *nanxun*, the January 1992 during which China's grand old man took every opportunity to urge the country to push ahead even faster with far-reaching market-oriented reforms. "My political sense told me it was time to go back for good; that now we would enter a period of great opportunity."

Like many of his fellow entrepreneurs, Chen found the quickest road to wealth lay in real estate speculation. There is, of course, great irony in a Communist government allowing the development of a real estate market. Just forty years before, the Party had seized all private land and property and placed it in the hands of the state to avoid exploitation. For most of the second half of the twentieth century, Chinese land still held nominal value, but only for accounting purposes: it was never traded. Suddenly, in the late 1980s, local governments were allowed to assess the worth of land and sell the rights to its use. Of course, there was no way of knowing what its true "value" might be, and in that fact, a huge and booming real estate market was born.

Those with insight, a stomach for arbitrage, and the right connections suddenly found a window of opportunity through which they could buy from sellers who rarely had a notion of the value of what they were selling, and then turn

On the critical importance—and great difficulty—of shaking the oppressive weight of tradition: "If we want to progress and not regress, we must have new ideas of our own all the time, or at least new ideas from the outside. With all these scruples, misgivings, and petty rules, this horror of offending our ancestors, this dread of behaving like barbarians, this perpetual sense of treading upon thin ice, this constant fear and trembling, how can we ever do anything worthwhile?"

—Lu Hsün (1881–1936)
Novelist

that purchase over to others wanting in on the boom. The technique was simple, the results often spectacular. The first step was to raise enough to buy an option on development of the property. Some, like Chen, had a little of their own money to put into a deal. Others had to raise it from relatives, friends, or Hong Kong investors. Sometimes a local bank would want in on the action and issue a loan for the down payment. Once secured, the would-be Donald Trumps had development plans drawn up, the grander the better. Then, usually on the renderings alone, they began to presell the housing, offices, golf courses, or what have you. With those deposits in hand, the buyer could begin to develop the property—or flip the investment over to someone else for a whopping profit.

The business was made for mavericks like Chen Ping. It was also made for the streetwise speculators, which is why many real estate projects collapsed like a house of cards. But the smart and the able have used these deals as the foundation of company structures that were to change the face of China. It is hard to overestimate the impact of the real estate boom in the takeoff of the Chinese economy. It created value and infrastructure from what had been thin "red" air.

So within a year of standing in Moscow's Red Square, Chen Ping had purchased twenty-nine hectares of property in Wuxi, at the edge of Lake Tai, one of China's most famous scenic spots. He saw, correctly, that the real estate market in the coastal cities had already reached its peak, and believed traditionally prosperous areas such as Wuxi—just over an hour from Shanghai but on the periphery of the action at the time—would soon provide the next stepping-stones in the surge of capital investment.

Thus was born the Li Hu Tide New Town project. It combined two of Chen Ping's greatest interests: making money and spinning philosophy. The land, a one-square-kilometer peninsula jutting out into the lake, cost him RMB 200 million ($24 million) and required a cash down payment of RMB 80 million ($9.5 million). Chen mobilized funds from his own projects, obtained a hard-to-get RMB 20 million ($2.4 million) loan from the Bank of China, and raised the rest by selling 28 percent of the shares in the project to friends in Hong Kong. By late 1995, 300 households were living in the development and it had a valuation

"We do things differently in China," said Li Yuan, the first Chinese entrepreneur to buy a bankrupt state factory, on the practice of keeping more workers but with lower salaries.

of RMB 900 million ($107 million). Chen Ping owns 78 percent of the project, either directly or through his company, the Tide Group.

Many made fortunes in Chinese real estate in the early 1990s, but few did it with as much style and marketing flair as Chen Ping. The Li Hu development, he says rhapsodically, will reflect the Chinese traditional sense of small-lane communities, "in which neighbors became kinsfolk, each helping supply what the other needs, all sharing the same glories and same faults which held the nation together for thousands of years." At the same time, it will "embody social ecological ideas, merge the quintessence of [Chinese] tradition and of the present day, put together the strong points of East and West and the cultural impulses of Chinese art."

Some of Chen's fine talk may just be clever marketing. But the underlying impulse of marrying the romantic past and the brave new future is one he clearly believes in. "If I end up making any contribution to China's economic strategy," he says, "it will be because I could bridge between Asia and Europe. There are defects in both Oriental socialism and European capitalism—I try to avoid both, and to bring about a marriage of the two sides."

Chen seems propelled by something beyond the ability to have a luxury high-rise apartment in Beijing, a fancy Japanese car in the parking lot below, and enough money to satisfy his whims. What drives him and many of his colleagues among China's emerging entrepreneurial elite is the desire for their companies and ways of doing business to be recognized and respected. Time and again Chen returns to the theme of entrepreneur as outsider, telling us, at one point: "Our company, like other private companies, is like a son brought up by a stepmother. We are within the system but do not have status. And the new marriage may be recognized in law, but it doesn't mean there is love. Such a child may die prematurely if it is not extraordinarily strong—strong enough to survive."

Also in this connection, Chen wonders why American business has not reached out to support and do more business with private entrepreneurs like him. "Why do Americans only want to do business with the state-owned sector?" he asks plaintively. "Why do business with officials, when you can do business with me?" This lament comes after he has

If we could sell one shock absorber to every car in China: In 1996, China had 1.8 million cars; by 2005 that number will double, to 4 million. Then, in the following five years, it is expected to quintuple to 20 million.

tried to interest us in helping him find a foreign partner for his fledgling effort to become a leading Internet provider in China. Ironically, one of Chen's main selling points was the assurance that relevant ministries and officials are supporting his efforts.

Can ambitious capitalists and big companies arise and thrive, even in the "new" China? Chen Ping is not sure. Dependent in great part on the blessings of officialdom and the manna of foreign capital, entrepreneurs like Chen are the stepchildren of China's reform, not yet guaranteed either permanent opportunity to practice their entrepreneurial instincts on a large scale, or the economic tools of bank lending and financial products. With resignation, he says, "My future? It is closely connected to China's future. I could live as a rich man anywhere, but I want to contribute, so I will stay here."

In that, China is fortunate. Because of Chen and a growing number of pioneers like him—large and small, all over China, in every sector—the country will find a way to carve out a true market opening in time.

CHAPTER 13

Feng Lun: Master Builder

It is not enough to set tasks; we must also solve the problem of the methods for carrying them out. If our task is to cross a river, we cannot cross it without a bridge or a boat. Unless the bridge or boat problem is solved, it is dreaming to speak of crossing the river. Unless the problem of method is solved, talk about the task is useless.

—MAO ZEDONG

FEW ENTREPRENEURS IN CHINA have broken more new ground—literally—than Feng Lun. In 1991 he and five friends started a company with less than $400 among them; just five years later the Vantone Enterprise Group was worth $600 million and its reach extended from some of China's most prestigious real estate developments to a pharmaceutical factory and a credit union. From the original six employees, Vantone's workforce has grown to 6,000; its offices stretch across China and internationally to San Francisco and Singapore.

When we meet, Feng Lun is under pressure to close on the financing of a new office complex in Beijing; at a time when the real estate market is bloated, Chinese banks have been forbidden to make loans to projects such as his, and Western investment banks have begun to step back from the euphoria of the early 1990s. Feng seems unperturbed by the financial vise that threatens his megaproject. He sits back on a small sectional couch in a very modest hotel suite at Beijing's Poly Plaza (a leading office and hotel complex, which Vantone helped develop). He has come dressed in the compleat Brooks Brothers look: elegant black-framed glasses; an open, understated pinstriped shirt with his monogram on the left cuff; wide-wale green-brown corduroys; and black tasseled loafers. A simple brown leather briefcase and a cellular phone are the only trappings of wealth and power—no scurrying aides, no fawning secretaries, no phone calls from princelings inviting him to golf or an afternoon of polo.

Feng Lun's original career track was far from the gritty world of real estate development. He started out as the very model of a young Communist Party scholar-official, one of the best and brightest, who rose from researcher to professor of Marxist-Leninist economic theory at a university run directly by the party's Central Committee. In the mid-1980s he was handpicked by then-Premier Zhao Ziyang to serve in the State Commission for Restructuring the Economic System, the most powerful think tank in working on the transformation of China's economy. Feng had arrived; he had no plans for the future except to fulfill the traditional role of intellectuals in "serving China"—in this case by doing comparative economic research and trying to reform the government from within, like generations of scholar-elites before him. Then came Tiananmen Square. Unlike Chen Ping, Feng did not choose to jump into the sea; he was pushed.

In early 1989, well before the spring demonstrations that would rock Beijing that year, Feng had been sent to establish a branch of the economic reform commission on Hainan island, where the most far-reaching experiments in economic reform were taking place. In mid-May, as the demonstrations at Tiananmen Square intensified and martial law was declared, Feng's boss, Premier Zhao, was sacked for showing too much sympathy for the students. Shortly after the June 4 tragedy, Zhao's (and Feng's) commission was "reorganized" and purged of the ex-premier's most visible followers. By the time Feng was able to return to Beijing in mid-June, he found himself without an institutional home.

It was a huge blow. At one level, Feng saw that his earlier assumption—that the interests of the nation-state and those of the governing party were identical—had been shattered.

A lesson on how different values can be in translation: As if the conspicuous consumption of cognac isn't enough, some Chinese wine drinkers have decided that a good claret or chardonnay goes down more smoothly when mixed with, of all things, Sprite.

—*THE ECONOMIST*

At an even deeper level, the loss of his position was a great loss of face in a society that had taught people like Feng to submerge who they were in what they did, intertwining identity with profession.

Feng left Beijing and went to work as an ordinary laborer in a factory in Xian whose boss he had come to know when he was sent down to the countryside during the Cultural Revolution. That experience had at least taught him strength in the face of adversity. Like many of his generation, he had learned the attitude that if one could survive that terrible period, one could do anything. Living like peasants, eating gruel, doing whatever menial tasks were needed, Feng and thousands like him developed a certain toughness, as well as persistence and hope. So in his spare time, Feng studied business principles. He also kept in touch with a group of close friends similarly cast adrift and investigating other opportunities.

Two years later, in 1991, Feng was ready to make his move. Together with five longtime friends he headed back to Hainan and started a real estate development company. They called it Vantone, meaning "ten thousand connections"—a wonderfully ambiguous Chinese phrase indicating both that they knew the right people and that they saw opportunity everywhere and intended to be the link between people and opportunities. A grand name indeed for a company capitalized with a mere RMB 200 ($24) from each partner plus RMB 2,000 ($240) scraped up from friends and relatives.

Why Hainan? "It seemed to us there were two conditions that made it similar to America," Feng explains. "One, it was like the American gold rush there—a new frontier that taught you how to overcome fear." The other reason was the partners' sense that in such a frontier atmosphere savvy and brains could count as much as connections. "If you put Beijing intellectuals in the frontier conditions of Hainan, then, like in America, you can overcome anything" was Feng's way of putting it.

A local banker also helped. In 1991, the state banks could still actively loan money to real estate developers, and Feng had befriended the local head of the Bank of China during the days when he was still a Beijing official on assignment. That loan, together with their minimal capital, was enough to make a down payment on a group of residential units. The Vantone six then rolled up their sleeves and began to reno-

Conundrum: Five of the top six personal computer companies in China are American based—Compaq, AST, IBM, Packard Bell, and Dell. The Chinese PC market is growing by 55 percent a year, more than twice as fast as the rest of the world . . . but none of these companies seems to be making much money.

—*THE WALL STREET JOURNAL*

vate the housing themselves. Shortly thereafter they were able to sell the complex to a new owner who wanted the land for office development. They were in the right place at the right time: Hainan proved the center of one of the great real estate bubbles of modern times. Their windfall profit put Vantone on the map.

Subsequently, Feng and his partners repeated the process several times, each time getting in and out quickly, and each time raising the stakes substantially. The early 1990s were true go-go years for the Chinese real estate market; it was in this context that Vantone—with its brains, guts, and ten thousand connections—rose to its present status. Within four years Vantone had become an RMB four billion ($476 million) company with offices in Shanghai, Beijing, and Xian and an RMB 1.1 billion ($131 million) fund to build shopping centers, office towers, and technology centers.

In 1995, Vantone had under development a wide range of projects: an office building complete with the latest intelligent high-tech functions set in the midst of a high-class shopping mall called Beijing Vantone/New World Plaza; an office project in Haikou, the capital of Hainan; Beijing Telecommunications Industrial Park, a 5-million-square-foot high-tech industrial park; and Lishan Plaza, a commercial development in the heart of Beijing's financial district. In addition, Vantone had acquired a pharmaceutical company and credit union in Nanning, the capital of Guangxi Autonomous Region, and a small commercial bank as well as an insurance company in Shanghai ("We intend to build a system similar to American investment banks such as Salomon Brothers"). There was a large chain of retail stores in China's northeast, and even a Chinese traditional-medicine factory.

To help him accomplish this, Feng has registered one of his subsidiaries—Beijing Vantone Industry Corp., Ltd.—as a "joint stock company." This allows him to sell shares to corporate interests (but not to the general public). By late 1995 he had sold shares worth RMB 800 million ($95 million), or roughly 60 percent of Beijing Vantone Industry, based on a 1994 valuation. Feng's shareholders are mostly state-owned corporations, a motley grouping looking to make profits in what has been a hot area of the economy. (Among them are the China National Stamp Corporation, the Accounting Center of China Aviation, and the Shenzhen

One man, in China's drama, plays many parts: In the 1970s Xing Chunhua was Party secretary of the model Red Star Commune on the outskirts of Beijing; he was known for his enthusiasm for Marxist dialectic. In 1992, he was prominently on hand as McDonald's opened its first restaurant in China. The reason? Xing had become chairman of the board of McDonald's China operations.

—JAN WONG
RED CHINA BLUES

Municipal Light Industry Group.) Like Zhang Wei, Feng intends to buy out these shareholders eventually so that he can regain full control. "Now we own forty percent," he tells us, "but as we gain strength we will buy back the other shares. Once that has been achieved we can offer it to the public, and get the company listed on the major foreign exchanges."

Reflecting on his rise from academic researcher to magnate of real estate, finance, and industry, Feng says, with characteristic understatement, "In the last four years, we have not only observed the economy, but managed to build a business." Like Zhang Wei and Chen Ping, he has managed to do all this without the slightest bit of formal business training. "Yes, I have read some general books on business management, both Western and Chinese," he tells us, "but I prefer Chinese traditional stories, like the Ming Dynasty adventure tale *Outlaws of the Marsh*. The main thing driving our success originally was not training, but knowing where the gaps were [in the system] and how to exploit them."

Feng cannot rest on his laurels. He has to keep growing simply to survive. "It is a difficult time for us," he says. "We are squeezed between two walls. On the one side is government control. State capital has its own privileges, and if they want to get something done they can do it the way they want. The other wall is the foreign enterprises and the changes they bring to our system, which will mean great competition and other threats."

Feng knows the bottom line: the government still holds the key to Vantone's future. For now Feng and people like him exist as a useful aberration, which is why Feng scrambles to give Vantone as much permanence as possible, diversifying by type of business as well as geographically, and working on projects that can sink their roots deep into China's development infrastructure.

As for the "wall" of foreign enterprise, Feng is referring to the considerable irony in the fact that the government is taking extraordinary measures to lure and nurture foreign companies on Chinese soil while doing little more than tolerating the country's own emerging enterprises. This policy, the quality of foreign products offered on the market, and the management expertise and marketing skills of foreign companies allow them to overshadow local Chinese rivals.

Feng Lun also knows he must innovate. He is therefore

The next Japan, Inc.?
"Within 10 years we'll see a significant number of internationally competitive Chinese firms."

—BARRY NAUGHTON
UNIVERSITY OF
CALIFORNIA, SAN DIEGO

determined to move beyond the traditional hub-and-spoke system of Chinese family enterprises and turn Vantone into a fully modern, transparent corporation. For Feng, that includes management training programs and motivational efforts. He also believes in inspirational messages. The company's newsletter includes quotations such as "It is an immutable law in business that words are words, explanations are explanations, promises are promises—but only performance is reality." Even a shopping bag sports the company motto: "The outstanding people create outstanding success."

Feng is not slavishly trying to follow Western concepts; instead, he says, "My goal is to follow China's traditional culture and find new ways of solving problems." For example, while he believes Western marketing skills are essential to success ("They allow you to establish yourself as a leader and stay there"), there are at least two other principles required for success that "must be found within our own culture: how to use the political system to your advantage, and how to deal with people."

Feng does not believe China should opt for laissez-faire capitalism. He is very unhappy with those who believe socialism should mean "Whatever works." That is too anarchistic for him, too opposed to what he believes leaders from Sun Yat-sen to Mao Zedong were trying to teach the society: that while it is important for the economy to become efficient, the society should remain fair and equal ("like the kind proposed by the northern European social democrats") and treat its people like one big family ("as in Taiwan and Japan"). In short, it would be socialism with Chinese characteristics. Asked what that phrase means to him, Feng tells us, "Socialism Chinese style means increasing the efficiency of production while at the same time advancing morally. It is a kind of idealism that combines good wishes with practical means to facilitate the changes that make our lives better. It creates harmony."

Feng admits that it will be difficult to implement this idealism in real life. In any event, it has earned him his critics. "Some old people think I am a capitalist, but the young people in my company tell me I am a Communist, and not strong enough to stand up to the government."

Trying to create an entrepreneurial spirit within a socialist setting is like trying to run on a precarious tightrope, under a

The new frontier:
"China right now is a free-for-all. I think we are more capitalist than you are. The government says: you recognize my authority, I let you be rich. How can you argue with that?"

—ZHANG HONG
SINO-AMERICAN
DEVELOPMENT CORP.
(BEIJING)

big top buffeted by strong winds that are severely straining its moorings. The balancing act requires great courage and agility; its outcome is far from certain.

The Lessons of Entrepreneurship

The dual drag of old culture and old politics: "The system is all too often still haunted by the old Maoist traditions: promote not the capable but the obedient; rule by personality and not by law; and reward the finger-pointers and punish the doers."

—ALLAN H. LIU
PRESIDENT, CHINA RETAIL FUND

The remarkable thing about China in the latter half of the 1990s is that there are hundreds of thousands of entrepreneurs who have Horatio Alger tales to tell. Zhang Wei, Chen Ping, and Feng Lun would stand out in any society. They and thousands of their colleagues are creating the entrepreneurial businesses of the future and laying the basis for a private sector.

These are complex individuals. Their lives and their businesses tell us much about the age of golden opportunity that has descended on China. Compared with the new stereotype of Chinese businesspeople as crude, corrupt, scheming, vicious, power-drunk Communist apparatchiks in ill-fitting pinstripes (the picture painted in Paul Theroux's novel *Kowloon Tong,* for example), those we have profiled are much more representative of the reality of Chinese business today.

These are the people the United States should be encouraging, both in the business deals American companies do on the ground and in the formulation of China policy. Zhang, Chen, and Feng are the kind of people who are driving the process of change in China by altering those all-important economic fundamentals and relationships at the base of the society. They may not see eye-to-eye with Americans on every issue, but their attitudes as managers and businessmen make them compatible partners for American business interests. They are the ones who will expand the space for markets and democratic rights in China, especially if they have a benign economic and political climate in which to work.

However, their stories also show that the capitalism being built by even the most entrepreneurial and successful Chinese is not necessarily of the type Americans might imagine. This is something those on our side of the Pacific must understand and come to live with.

The goals and values of the new business elite are more complex than simply the glory of getting rich. Similarly, the climate in which they must operate has certain "Chinese characteristics" that present constraints as well as opportunities—characteristics that foreign business ignores at its peril. We describe some of those factors below.

- *An environment in which the "system" and the "market" are not only hard to separate but remain inexorably allied and intertwined.*

Entrepreneurs who seek to stand outside the system or who can succeed in doing so are still the minority. As veteran China chronicler Ross Terrill puts it, "In the China of the 1990s it is not so much that capitalism has arrived, but that local and provincial government is commercializing itself." Directors, executives, and managers of "private" enterprises are often officials doubling as businesspeople; their success has less to do with breaking away from the system than with their ability to use it to their advantage, as a reward for service within it. This is what historians such as Columbia's William Theodore de Bary have called the "alliance of opportunity," the centuries-old collusion between government and business based not on ideology, or even mutual respect, but on shared self-interest.[1]

Even the iconoclastic Chen Ping has a problem breaking out. As we have recounted, Chen wondered one day: "Why do Americans only want to do business with the state-owned sector? Why do business with officials, when you can do business with me?" It is a good question, given the penchant of foreign companies to gravitate to state-run enterprises, which actively court the imprimatur of the highest state officials.

The entrepreneur-as-outsider is a remnant of a tradition of anticapitalism that stretches back to Confucius. But it is not just an old idea. An extensive 1992 national survey of young people—who are presumably receptive to new ideas—asked participants to say whom they most admired. Sixty-two percent chose revolutionary leaders; 45 percent chose scientists; 24 percent chose famous actors and singers. Only 4.6 percent chose entrepreneurs. Outsiders think of Chinese as "ethnically entrepreneurial." But that impression has been fostered by the success of *Overseas* Chinese—the ones who left, not the ones who stayed in China.

- *The leadership's attitude that large-scale private enterprise is supplemental rather than essential.*

Making the Nanjing scene, with fervidity, no less: From a flyer advertising the Red-Lip Nightclub in Nanjing: "Red-Lip Nightclub is a . . . place of entertainment which is present in the amusement world like a bright pearl, a gorgeous agate, and a glistening jadeite. . . . Entering this novel world, you can display your golden fancies to your hearts content. Downwards along the steps there appears in front of you a full-closed shooting range with five target positions. . . . Being here once, emotions of the old days will be traced back and the dreams of the childhood come into being. There is a world of dancing and singing on the second floor. In the Disco dance hall, the vigorous melody is rolling over and over. . . . Red-Lip Nightclub welcomes you with sincerity and fervidity."

—*Harper's*

China's leaders often view "private enterprise" as valuable only to the extent that it helps improve the efficiency and long-term viability of State-Owned Enterprises. Or to the degree that it sops up unemployment or meets social needs for new products and services. Hu Deping is vice chairman of the All-China Federation of Industry and Commerce, a nongovernmental organization representing private enterprise. If anyone would seem to be a cheerleader for emerging entrepreneurial companies, it should be he, especially as the influential son of former Party chairman Hu Yaobang. But Hu, understanding Chinese politics and culture, tells us the same thing we have heard from other officials:

> Yes, there is a role for private enterprise in China, because the state cannot solve all employment problems alone. And competition with private companies will help state enterprises increase their efficiency. But in China there will always be public and private enterprise. And the "private" part won't necessarily mean what it does in the West.

- *A concept of "ownership" that remains very cloudy but seems to work all right—at least in this period of transition.*

Assets may be under the control of entrepreneurs, but they cannot be utilized at will. The investors in entrepreneurs' companies are most often state-owned enterprises, looking to earn profits lacking in their own sector. At one extreme, some private companies are sometimes little more than legalized gambling outlets patronized by cadres from the state sector for their "private" ends. At the other, some are well-run emerging companies that are, nevertheless, faced with a constant drain on their free cash, which must flow back to the ministries and other government-owned entities that spawned them.

All over China, the quaintly philosophical "question of ownership" is being discussed. Who owns the assets and capital created by individual entrepreneurs, but with initial investment from state agencies? How tradable are capital assets? What can be bought and sold, and by whom? Often, there are no official answers. "Privatization" became a buzzword in late 1997—in terms of Western experts insisting on China's need for it, and Chinese leaders making sounds and speaking in euphemisms that, depending upon the interpretation, could sound an awful lot like it. Yet one thing is clear about privatization Chinese-style: it will be slow, complicated, and come in many flavors and forms.

The real answers to the question of ownership won't be known for some time to come. In the meantime, like the entrepreneurs profiled here, flexibility will remain the hallmark of those building vast empires, along with enough political astuteness so they can continue to reap the benefits of their own efforts.

- *A government that remains more willing to deal with big and powerful foreign companies than to risk the emergence of strong private—or even quasi-private—domestic Chinese ones.*

Foreign corporations are allowed to do all the things in China that individual Chinese entrepreneurs have so much trouble doing—from buying into major businesses to borrowing money. Dig into the success stories told by Chinese entrepreneurs like Chen Ping and you frequently find that to get to any significant size, they had to establish joint ventures with Hong Kong businessmen or other outsiders. This was not just because they may have needed financial or managerial partners, but because only a "foreign" business could get permission to do what they, as Chinese nationals, wanted to do in their own country.

It is irony enough that the nationalistically inclined Chinese would deny their own people the opportunities they routinely offer foreigners. But here is an even deeper irony in a society that places such a premium on virtuous role models: By making it so difficult to be a successful entrepreneur, the Chinese system has ended up rewarding and enriching what at times can seem like a motley crew of misfits. Some of the nouveaux-riches in China today are not particularly well-educated, not necessarily too visionary about running businesses, and not much like Zhang, Chen, and Feng. Some are merely people who were sufficiently on the fringe of society to have nothing to lose. They grabbed an opportunity when they saw one—particularly in the privatization of real estate—and have been leveraging their initial quick gains ever since.

Second thoughts on the virtues of state ownership: "When you stop to think about it, who has exploited workers more—the state, or those of us so-called capitalists who run private enterprises?"

—CHEN PING
  CHAIRMAN, TIDE GROUP

• *A bias toward entities, rather than individuals, as entrepreneurs.*

The government line on the development of large-scale individually-owned companies is that China is "not yet ready." True enough. But it is difficult to avoid the perception that the emergence of a strong business class is seen as a threat to order, stability and the maintenance of Communist power. Obviously, the system has little interest at this late-twentieth-century date in launching the bourgeois revolution China never really had. To do so risks creating a capitalist class that would ultimately have its own interests and form its own power base—exactly what many Americans hope to see in China.

• *The freedom entrepreneurs seek to expand their economic horizons does not necessarily translate into a desire to have political "freedom" in the way many Americans assume.*

Even those entrepreneurs who consider themselves outsiders and complain most about getting the government out of their business lives generally avoid getting involved with an overt agenda for changing China's *political* system. These businesspeople, many of whom may be among the next generation of leaders, do want a more open society, greater rights, new political institutions, and a set of laws that will protect them and their businesses. But even Chen Ping, the most freewheeling of our entrepreneurs, would undoubtedly agree with Feng Lun, who told us, "We don't disagree with the overall model. We just want to reform it, not make revolution against it."

Moreover, every major entrepreneur we have talked to over the years aspires to building a new kind of company—a *Chinese-style* company, not a Western one. There is an ownership pattern that suggests a kind of state capitalism, and a value system that attempts to integrate Western management techniques into an overall "Chinese" company model. As Feng Lun put it:

> We are not adopting the American model, where competition is everything and every relationship is a legal one [i.e., always governed by contract]. We want a different relationship between people, to keep a moral course, to

Mirror, mirror on the wall: The upscale Italian designer Ermenegildo Zegna prices his suits in China at 10,000 yuan ($1,250) and up—more than the average Chinese earns in a year. Yet, the company clearly is finding its target $100,000-per-year customers: Zegna has seven shops in China that account for 20 percent of its $500 million business volume in northern Asia.

find a natural balance between people and society. Efficiency must be stressed, but at the same time we have to care about quality and fairness.

All this is part of a creative if often awkward search to design a political-economic system that follows a "third road." Just as entrepreneurs want to see the pie bigger but still divided fairly, Chinese policymakers would much rather see the energetic and talented business leaders of the future emerge within municipal enterprises, TVEs SOEs, privatized collective university labs, provincial or national companies created with state investment, or even joint ventures with foreign companies. It is believed that in this way the good work those leaders do will enrich the many and not just the few. By making *entities* rather than individuals into entrepreneurs, a sense of economic cohesion can be maintained while the risks associated with the power of a true capitalist class of individuals can be avoided. At least that's the theory.

Similar experiences can be found in varying degrees in Japan, Singapore, Korea, Taiwan, and elsewhere in Asia. China's desire to have entrepreneurship without entrepreneurs, ownership without owners, and market economics without American-style democracy is not as oxymoronic as it may look to Westerners. Instead, it flows from the context of Asian values, Confucian principles, and Chinese history.

Whether Chinese entrepreneurs can have it all—a mix of Chinese culture, enlightened socialism, and an efficient, free-market economy—is an open question. For now the role of the market and the private sector is a capitalist riddle inside a socialist enigma; a straddling of history instead of a leap into shock-therapy capitalism. And most of all it is, as Zhang Wei says, a "once-in-history" opportunity.

There can be little question that their success is in America's interest. Even if their vision is not identical with a Western one, it is something foreigners can understand and live with far better than the mainstream vision in Beijing officialdom. But strengthening the hand of this emerging entrepreneurial group requires American engagement, not opposition. They deserve attention, respect, admiration, and support from American business—not, as the Hawks would suggest, the sting of moralizing, trade sanctions, and political restrictions.

Willy Loman would be proud: Deploying a small army of door-to-door salesmen, foreign and domestic insurance companies are booming in China. The industry estimates total life and nonlife insurance premiums will grow to between $19 billion and $25 billion by 2000. That's up from $8.5 billion in 1994—and door-to-door sales were introduced only in 1992.

PART IV

GEOMANCING THE DRAGON

China, by her resources and population, is capable of being the greatest power in the world after the United States. In fact, all the world will be vitally affected by the development of Chinese affairs, which may well prove a decisive factor, for good or evil, during the next two centuries.

—BERTRAND RUSSELL
THE PROBLEM OF
CHINA (1922)

China watching is the only profession that makes meteorology look accurate and precise.

—NICHOLAS KRISTOF
FORMER BEIJING
BUREAU CHIEF, THE
NEW YORK TIMES

Wind and Water

Feng shui, which literally means "wind and water," is the ancient Chinese art of geomancy. Its goal is to create harmonies and balances in life's physical spaces that will lead to the health, wealth, and good fortune of those who inhabit them. The practitioners of feng shui today are best known for their role in blessing, criticizing, or reconfiguring the layout and design of the homes, offices, hotels, and skyscrapers of Chinese Asia. They study angles and directions and harmonizing and contradictory forces in order to determine the optimal alignment of physical spaces with mental ones. They seek to balance wind and water, yin and yang, and to allow the all-important life force of Chinese cosmology, *ch'i*, to flow through unimpeded.

Feng shui masters prescribe rearrangements of physical spaces when things are going badly—when companies fall on hard times, when people get sick, or when other problems arise that can be diagnosed at some level as an imbalance of forces. Feng shui masters determine where to dig wells and where to bury the dead, taking careful account of the dragon that is the earth, the mountains that are the dragon's veins and arteries, and the water that is its *ch'i* flowing through its body.

Masters of this art are Chinese culture's original land surveyors, hydraulic engineers, environmental planners, alchemists, psychologists, faith healers, interior decorators, and New Age spiritualists. They are active in Hong Kong and other cities with large Chinese populations, including, now, Los Angeles, San Francisco, New York, Vancouver, and Sydney. Legends abound of extreme feng shui verdicts. Office buildings have been torn down at the suggestion of a feng shui master. Spectacular homes built by billionaires have never been lived in because a feng shui master said the owner would die in them. Executives of troubled companies have moved their desks into storage closets at the feng shui master's suggestion—and seen their company's stock price soar as a result.

For most of China's modern revolutionary history, the practice of feng shui was banned as superstitious nonsense. But when new buildings go up in China today, especially in Guangzhou and other southern cities, the feng shui masters are once again consulted.

"Those who deal with China should realize that today it is a frontier country, looking into the future while remaining rooted in the past. In any frontier society, nothing is certain and everything is possible."

—Franz Schurmann
WorldBusiness

263

In the art of Chinese geomancy, there may be an appropriate metaphor for our role in trying to forecast China's future. After all, we have studied the directional flows of the rivers that run through Chinese history. And we have surveyed the winds of change that are now sweeping over those patterns. On the basis of our studies, we have come to some clear—and, at times, provocative—conclusions about what lies ahead for this big dragon.

Like good feng shui masters, we are perfectly willing to be blunt in our forecasts and recommendations, even when they run against the grain of conventional wisdom. We have tried to be as specific as we can, winnowing down the multiple scenarios that *could* unfold to those we are most inclined to believe *will* obtain.

Unlike most feng shui masters we have known, we recognize a high degree of fallibility in our forecasting. We also understand just how much history can happen even in the short period between the time we write these words and when they will be read. Our forecasts are designed to give shape and definition to a *way of thinking* about China, its future, and our own. Even if we are wrong about specific events, we hope the approach we have taken here will have lasting value.

CHAPTER 14

The Next Five Years:
The Dragon at Home

Rites of Passage: The Post-Deng Succession Struggle, 1998–2002

What everyone wants to know about China's future right now is how the post–Deng Xiaoping transition will play out. What course will Jiang Zemin and other leaders take on the critical issues of politics and economics, and how will these affect international business interests and the global balance of power?

In reality, of course, the "Deng era" was over well before the "paramount leader" died in February 1997. A succession struggle had been going on throughout the 1990s among various leaders and factions in anticipation of Deng's death. Even today, after the Fifteenth Party Congress nominally put its stamp of approval on the current leadership lineup in September 1997, this struggle continues to percolate through the system. In the absence of a genuine rule of law and of transparent, institutionalized structures for debating and implementing policy, the succession struggle is, to a very large degree, the highest form of political debate. It is likely to continue in one form or another for several more years.

Although Deng was much more interested than Mao in assuring a stable succession after his death, he suffered a similarly low batting average in selecting the right individuals. In the 1950s Mao chose Liu Shaoqi as his second in command, only to turn on his successor-designate and castigate him as the enemy-in-chief a few years later. Liu was the initial target of the 1960s Cultural Revolution and was hounded out of office and to his death. Mao's next hand-picked comrade-in-arms was Lin Biao. But within a few years, Lin was accused of attempting a coup d'état. In 1971 he died, allegedly while trying to flee to the Soviet Union after this failed coup.

Deng's failures in creating his own succession team were less dramatic than Mao's. Nevertheless, the two successors he identified in the 1980s—Hu Yaobang and Zhao Ziyang—both ultimately proved too liberal and too far ahead of their times to stay in power. They were stalking-horses for the side of Deng's brain that was briefly attracted to a more democratic vision—a vision from which he himself subsequently retreated, leaving his successors out on limbs that the Communist Party summarily cut off.

Hu Yaobang was purged in 1987 after it became clear he was pushing too hard for political reforms, such as retirement for leaders of Deng's generation, that the rest of the leadership was unwilling to consider, then or now. Zhao Ziyang, Deng's other protégé, became prime minister after a successful stint leading the economic reforms in Deng's native Sichuan province. Zhao was arguably China's most modern, capable, open-minded, and experimental technocrat. Yet he, too, became a sacrificial lamb, willingly thrown by Deng to the conservative wolves in the aftermath of Tiananmen. His last public act was to arrive in the square shortly before the ultimate bloodbath. He expressed sympathy for the demonstrators and apologized to the students for having "come too late." It was arguably the most public act of personal political courage that modern China has ever seen. But it sealed Zhao's doom in the eyes of the growing conservative majority. In the aftermath of June 4, he was stripped of his positions and placed under what amounted to house arrest. Then in his early seventies, he was not even allowed out in public to attend the funeral of his onetime mentor, Deng.

Deng had somewhat better luck with the next dynamic duo of successors he selected: Li Peng and Jiang Zemin. Li, who followed Zhao as premier in the wake of Tiananmen, managed to serve out his two terms in that office, although he was always unpopular. Today he is seen as the dean of the minority faction of powerful conservatives who are tampering with Deng's legacy of boldly opening China up to the outside world and experimenting with new economic forms. But thus far, their role has been only to tamper, not to overthrow or stop. While Li and those allied with him must be appeased and assuaged, they are not the prime movers in defining China's direction.

Jiang Zemin has defied the initial odds and fared the best of all. Jiang was the mayor of Shanghai before Deng brought him to Beijing in 1989 to oversee propaganda work, just as the contradictions that would lead to the Tiananmen crisis were sharpening. Unlike Li Peng's, Jiang Zemin's hands are nominally clean of any direct participation in the bloodshed of the Tiananmen disaster. Although he seems to have been out of the direct decision-making loop, he certainly has shown no indication he disagreed with the political principle.

Few outsiders—and even fewer Chinese—believed in the early nineties that Jiang was up to the task of leading China and emerging as Deng's primary successor. One opinion poll purported to show that if a free election were held for president, the Chinese people would have voted for Nelson Mandela and Bill Clinton over Jiang Zemin by margins of ten to one. But, capitalizing on Deng's long, slow fade from the scene, Jiang consolidated a firm grip on power. He has thus directed a much more stable transition than many Western experts would have thought possible.

Measured purely by the titles he has collected, Jiang is now the most powerful Chinese in modern history, serving concurrently as president of the state government, general secretary of the Communist Party, and chairman of the powerful Military Affairs Commission. In fact, however, Jiang is not as powerful as his titles suggest. His very need for titles is a sign of his comparative weakness. Deng Xiaoping, by contrast, thrived on the canard that he was only a mere vice premier during his most active years. Later, he positioned himself as "retired," with no official title, even though he was still universally regarded as China's real leader long into his terminal illness.

Jiang's ability to build alliances and coalitions behind the scenes is probably the most successful result of Deng's

Deng Xiaoping's legacy: "All the common folk have tasted the benefits of his policies," said Zhang Baifa, vice mayor of Beijing. "It's like a fried egg. Once you've fried it, it tastes good, and if you wanted to make it raw again, you can't."

master plan for China after his death. Deng's experience through seven decades of twists and turns in the inner Party struggle had convinced him that the old single strongman emperorlike system was impractical for China's long-term modernization and even dangerous to it. His solution was to put in place two successors and an informal system of checks and balances within the inner circles of power. By leaving the right people in power—with the right adversaries—Jiang could ensure that any one leader's or faction's propensity for excesses was restrained, and China could be kept on a generally moderate course. The clearest evidence of all this is the example of Li Peng, who was seen by many pundits as not only deeply unpopular but as a serious rival to Jiang. The conventional wisdom had Li being shunted aside by Jiang during the Fifteenth Party Congress in September 1997. But, defying all predictions that he would be ousted, Li retained his high ranking in the Politburo and became head of the increasingly important National People's Congress in March 1998, when his term as premier expired.

So far, Deng's ultimate goal of stability has, indeed, been assured by this seemingly unstable approach. Jiang seems too woven into the fabric of the new consensus he has created to send China lurching down one road or another on his own whim. Even with his impressive collection of titles—and even within a system that the outside world readily identifies as autocratic if not fascistic—he must proceed with extreme caution, constantly building consensus within the Politburo, the State Council, and the Military Affairs Commission, and even with regional and provincial leaders. Although Jiang is considered by many an arriviste with neither charisma nor natural leadership qualities, "he is a good backroom operator, a Shanghai-style power broker," says Willy Wo-lap Lam, the Chinese-politics expert for the *South China Morning Post*.

It is possible that Jiang will prove so good at the new rules of the political game that he will slowly and subtly arrive at the kind of near one-man rule Deng sought to end. However, we find this outcome unlikely. Alternatively, it is possible that the cautious, go-slow balancing act required to keep the Chinese ship of state afloat will dictate so much moderation that a Jiang-led government will simply be unable to come to grips with China's major economic and political problems.

"The debates among senior leaders are not terribly different from those that have taken place in the West; the center of the British Labour Party 30 years ago was not far from the effective left of the Chinese Communist Party today."

—WILLIAM OVERHOLT
MANAGING DIRECTOR,
BANKERS TRUST CO.
(HONG KONG)

This could lead not only to the compounding and deepening of those problems, but ultimately to an anti-Jiang explosion.

We see this scenario as possible but less than likely. Jiang and his cohorts will be able to deliver the goods sufficiently, with respect to economic growth and continuous improvement of the quality of life, to continue this delicate balancing act for several more years. The evolution of an organized but tame opposition that seeks more dynamic economic policies and a more democratic political agenda is in process. But the need to come to grips with these forces—and the catharsis that will ensue—will probably have to wait until the middle of the next decade or later.

The right way to assess China's future is to focus on the process and the ultimate results, not the personalities. Political figures in any country can do spectacular flip-flops on issues. Sometimes, after they are elected, they end up implementing policies that are at considerable variance with what they espoused on the campaign trail. Chinese political figures are no different. The big difference is that the opaque nature of the Chinese system and the coded, nuanced vocabulary in which even the strongest leaders speak make it hard for outsiders to understand who's who and what they really stand for.

Just to offer one striking example: At the recent Fifteenth Party Congress, Jiang Zemin specifically singled out Standing Committee member Hu Jintao as a fourth-generation leader who should be given responsibility as third-generation leaders retire (at fifty-five, Hu is considered "young"). But who is Hu? And what does he stand for? Even the Hong Kong media's leading China watcher, Willy Wo-lap Lam, who normally knows who's who and what's what, said only that he was a "shadowy figure who avoids the limelight," a conservative thought to be "acceptable to most Party factions," having personal ties to both the left and the right.[1]

Jiang Zemin, under some pressure from critics to end his practice of stuffing the leadership with his colleagues from Shanghai, clearly gave the nod to Hu to bolster the notion that new leaders can come from various geographical areas and political factions—the principle of drawing from the so-called "five lakes and four seas." But whether Hu Jintao does, in fact, emerge as a senior leader, or whether that type of power remains largely in the hands of those who have

Dengism after Deng: "While it's true that wealth is not equally shared, at least there is wealth to worry about. And while many state-owned enterprises remain a heavy burden, the proportion of workers employed by the government continues to fall. In the tension between Dengism and purer forms of socialism, there will be conflicts over regional distribution of investments and the speed of reform. But one fundamental truth propounded by Deng is now almost universally accepted by all factions in China: the more economic freedom people have, the more economic advances they will make."

—*Far Eastern Economic Review*

been more directly associated with Jiang for longer, remains to be seen.

Our forecast is that most of China's current policy directions will remain more or less in force, even as the actual leadership changes to reflect the underlying reality of inner-Party struggle. Although there are substantive differences within the leadership today, and although increasingly clear camps of "conservatives," "centrists," "liberals," and others are visible, these camps are in general agreement on many of the issues outsiders see as the leading indicators of policy direction. No faction within the senior leadership wishes to close the door completely to foreign investment, for example. No faction believes it can shift China's focus away from economic growth and modernization back to politics and ideology and stay in power. Every member of the Chinese leadership class has come to realize that political power and stability now depend not on the barrel of a gun (or a mass political campaign) but, to a large degree, on delivering the goods economically.

The existence of these broad areas of agreement, however, does not mean that individual political leaders, their philosophies, and their personalities do not matter. In fact, they matter more and more now, when the range of acceptable views is widening, the issues to be reckoned with are unprecedented, and a "normal" politics of interest groups, perception, positioning, and spin is developing.

Chinese political successions in the twentieth century have often been chaotic, violent, and bloody. Indeed, from dynasts to nationalists to revolutionaries, the twentieth-century track record is unblemished by a single smooth transfer of power. To overcome this historical curse and maintain his grasp on the levers of power, Jiang will need to work continuously to minimize, marginalize, outmaneuver, or co-opt opponents, just as he has been doing for the last several years. The strongest groups currently vying for political power include:

The neoconservatives, mostly elderly senior party figures, but represented by Li Peng and urged on by a surprisingly wide group of hard-edged younger voices. They are often technocrats with a bias toward state control. They worry about how far today's leadership has strayed from traditional Communist beliefs and values. Longtime propaganda chief Deng Liqun is another good example. His acerbic articles

"Among [China's] 50 most prominent leaders, no voice argues that the state should retake farms, close off the economy from the world, or, like the Soviet Union, subsidize all state enterprises until the country goes bankrupt. All tendencies are toward market prices, development of capital markets, increased competition, an open economy, and reorganization of state enterprises."

—WILLIAM OVERHOLT
  MANAGING DIRECTOR,
  BANKERS TRUST CO.
  (HONG KONG)

and commentaries deride the cause of economic reform. Some neoconservatives have begun to refer more positively to Mao Zedong again. Li Peng has even argued that the Cultural Revolution still has validity and should not be dismissed entirely as a mistake. Some of the next-generation "neocons" have been educated in the West and are well positioned in government and policy institutions, eager to move into the front ranks of the power elite.

The "rule of law"-oriented gradualist reformers argue for greater use of the electoral process (within clear limits) and more transparency in politics and law. NPC chairman Qiao Shi had been their most prominent figure until his unceremonious forced retirement from the Politburo in 1997. But other leaders—such as Tian Jiyun—are also associated with this view. However, with Qiao out of the picture it is not yet clear who among the top leadership (if anyone) will assume the role of public spokesman for the critical task of building the institutions needed to make the laws work. "Rule of law" advocates are not always of one political faction. They can be found among "conservatives" as well as "liberals." The need for a law-based system is a particularly popular theme among those running financial and business organizations, from banks and ministries to small companies.

A diverse group of liberal reformers. These are the most direct counterweight to the neoconservatives. By and large, they were brought into power in the 1970s and 1980s by Zhao Ziyang and Hu Yaobang and now serve in various ministries, middle- and high-ranking political positions, think tanks, and academia. Many are savvy, Western-educated, and extremely capable. Some have made fortunes in business, but many would return to politics in a heartbeat if a more forward-looking leadership team came to power. (Some experts see Zhao possibly serving as a figurehead around whom a younger group of liberals might rally.)

Party elders still alive and able to play a role. Yang Shangkun, for example, is nearly ninety but is still active and has strong ties not only to the military but to some of the liberal reformers, including Zhao Ziyang. Slowly, the "immortals" are fading from the scene. Yet these octogenarians still command enormous respect and some influence, and a kind of veto power over certain changes.

The senior commanders of the People's Liberation Army.

Classic understatement: Hu Deping, head of the All-China Federation of Commerce and Industry, a nongovernmental organization representing more than 430,000 nonshareholding companies, had this take on China's future: "A certain part of the Communist old guard is worried that the future will not be what they have thought."

They have never played an independent, visible role in Chinese politics but might do so in any situation where they believed China was in danger of disintegrating politically or socially. While the PLA is generally conservative, it is not uniformly so, nor is it motivated entirely by typical military concerns of procurement and control of national security policy. After all, top PLA generals at first resisted the orders to move against Chinese citizens in Tiananmen Square, and the PLA has built one of China's largest business and economic empires, with a wide range of enterprises. Moreover, the military has benefited enormously from the moderate open-door policies, since they permit not only the transfer of technologies and the expansion of the profitable arms trade, but also the kind of high-level military exchanges with the West that allow firsthand evaluation of modern military equipment and doctrines.

Sophisticated senior technocrats with strong reform-oriented credentials and solid leadership track records. These individuals are best exemplified by Zhu Rongji. Deng Xiaoping once said Zhu was among only a handful of Chinese leaders who had a good grasp of modern economics. Ever since the 1950s, Zhu has been outspoken in the cause of economic reform. While most of today's leaders suffered during the Cultural Revolution, Zhu is almost alone among them in having been under attack for liberal ideas as early as the 1957 "antirightist" crackdown. Other prominent figures include Li Ruihuan and Li Lanqing. These people are generally sophisticated, modern, and forward-looking. Some are English-speaking and cosmopolitan. They are loyal to Jiang Zemin for now, but not necessarily closely identified with him. Separately or together, they could become impatient with the status quo Jiang seeks to maintain. One or several of them could seek to push for more decisive government action on key problems, just as Hu Yaobang did a decade ago.

The "princelings"—the sons and daughters of well-known leaders of the older generation—who have not only risen through the ranks but are now likely to be connected to business empires and the control of important economic resources. The princelings are scattered across the ideological map, but they represent a new kind of political force—one with its own wherewithal and alternative careers to pursue if political battles prove too overwhelming.

Outsiders from the senior leadership ranks have rarely

The sayings at Chairman Jiang: "I always say to our ministers: 'Go less to karaoke and learn more history and literature.' "

—PRESIDENT JIANG ZEMIN

272

played much of a role in Chinese history. Nevertheless, there are more visible, identifiable political voices outside the traditional party and state structures today than at any time in the last half-century. They run the gamut from democratic dissenters like Wang Dan to neonationalists and fundamentalists like the authors of *China Can Say No* to exiles like the Dalai Lama to secessionist minorities in Xinjiang.

Jiang Zemin's administration will be even more of a coalition than the governments of the Deng era. Some power and some voice will have to be allocated to several of the different trends of thought and power bases within the Communist leadership. Jiang's skill, apparently, is in brokering such deals and keeping the whole jury-rigged apparatus moving, even if not at maximum speed. In this sense, as in many other ways, China is becoming a "normal" country. Politically, it is (slowly) becoming able to tolerate and absorb some (modest) shades of difference in the leadership ranks, without triggering purges, mass criticism, or violence.

How "Jiangism" Will Shape the Next Five Years

If Jiang is unable to follow through on his vow to tackle major problems such as the SOEs, unemployment, and corruption, then he will only be continuing the other impulse deeply embedded in Chinese public policy: placing order and stability above the need to make progress on the rebuilding of the country's political and social framework. But this kind of "order" and "stability" could turn out to be a catch-22. China's problems could mount, its growth would be retarded, and the fruits of its prosperity would be less and less evenly distributed. Criticism, dissent, and opposition to Jiang would then swell. He would try to contain them with Band-Aid reforms and administrative changes and perhaps by pushing harder to rally the country around neonationalist, traditionalist, and at times anti-Western banners—hardly a recipe for genuine order and stability.

On the other hand, as Jiang becomes more confident and "presidential," he may be able to implement some of the bolder initiatives he has spoken about or hinted at—as in his appeal at the Fifteenth Party Congress to allow for much more flexible solutions to the SOE problem (including selling, spinning off, or otherwise privatizing thousands upon thousands of these entities). If he is paired with the more

Democracy belongs to him who can shout louder: Chinese President Jiang Zemin, speaking at Harvard in November 1997, was heckled by protesters outside the meeting hall demanding democracy for China and independence for Tibet. Asked about it, he said, "Although I am already seventy-one years old, my ears still work very well. So when I was delivering my speech, I did hear the sound from the loudspeakers outside. However, I believe the only approach for me is to speak even louder."

visionary Zhu Rongji, Jiang's lack of "the vision thing" might be less of a liability, and a bolder course on economic reform could be launched. Even as he grabs for the ultimate brass ring of recreating the post of Party chairman and taking it for himself, Jiang may preside over an extremely careful diminution of traditional Communist principles. This would include more of a voice for the provinces and various constituencies (such as business) and the wider use of elections at the village and local level.

We expect today's course to continue: on the one hand, positive, if incremental and gradual economic reform; on the other, some continued expansion of electoral democracy at the local level but very little willingness to face the need for political reform at the top. We believe Jiang can continue this balancing act successfully for some time. Our expectation is that he and his team will be able to maintain the status quo at least through the year 2000 and probably all the way to the Sixteenth Party Congress in 2002.

We anticipate that this period of transitional politics, from 1998 to 2002, will play out as a mostly peaceful process, without the kind of violent confrontation, civil war conditions, and de facto coups d'état that have characterized previous Chinese transitions. However, we *do* expect conflict over ideas and policies as well as personalities and power; most of that struggle will take place in smoke-filled rooms far from the prying eyes of foreigners. For example, it is likely there will be some process of "de-Dengification." Those who were closest to Deng are already finding their power and position under attack. In 1996, eight months *before* his death, his paraplegic son Deng Pufang (whose disability stems from a Cultural Revolution incident in which he was forced or thrown out a window by Red Guard critics of his father) gave an impassioned speech at a meeting of the Chinese Federation of the Disabled (of which he is president) defending his father's legacy against those who would "wholly negate the Deng Xiaoping line."[2] Subsequent official press statements criticized Western reporting of the event and attempted to deny the existence of any conflict over Deng's legacy, but it is obvious that Deng Pufang was speaking about a very real rift.

In addition to these high-level political arguments, some degree of public turbulence—strikes, riots, demonstrations—is possible, even likely. But our forecast is that there will be nothing on the order of the 1989 Tiananmen situation, let alone the upheavals of the Cultural Revolution.

In a historic sense, Jiang Zemin will get credit for bringing China successfully out of the dangerous waters of the post-Deng transition and for setting something of an example—albeit a problematic one—for the first peaceful, evolutionary political succession in modern China. The problems that pile up on his watch will also create the conditions for real and necessary changes when future leaders come into their own after 2002.

After Jiang, What? Generational Politics, Chinese Style

The kind of dramatic political and economic change that many in the West hope for, and that China ultimately needs to partake in to some degree, is closely linked to generational change. It will take more than a few political initiatives. It will take generations to change China.

Mao Zedong, Zhou Enlai, Zhu De, and their fellow revolutionaries who established the People's Republic in 1949 are considered the "first generation" leaders. These founding fathers started the Party, forged an army, went on the Long March, and were in Tiananmen Square in October 1949 when Mao declared the revolution victorious with the famous words, "The Chinese people have stood up." Like other powerful leaders of their era—Roosevelt, de Gaulle, Churchill—these men were powerful, charismatic, and larger than life. Battle-tested, tempered by war and revolution, they were the ultimate modern nationalists, focused on big, unifying visions of how to advance the interests of their country. Also like Western leaders of the World War II vintage, Mao and his contemporaries derived their authority from success in leading their people through the defining experiences of the modern era and the salvation of their countries. Their kind will not reappear in the near future.

Deng Xiaoping consciously placed himself in the "second generation" of Chinese leaders, even though in age and experience he had more in common with the first. This was partly out of respect for Mao (Deng was eleven years younger), but also because he wanted to distance himself from the chairman. He cast himself as the man destined to reform and

Like Mickey's brooms in *The Sorcerers Apprentice*: "The Chinese population doubled from 100 B.C. to about 1000 A.D. The next doubling occurred in the 18th century, then again over the next 150 years. And again in the 50 years since 1949. The next does not bear thinking about."

—W. J. F. JENNER
THE TYRANNY OF HISTORY

improve the system Mao had started. More the tough "uncle" than the beloved and charismatic "father," Deng was the first Chinese leader who was both in a favorable historical position *and* had a sufficiently open mind to contemplate seriously how to open China to the world and to modernity.

Jiang Zemin and his colleagues are the "third generation" of the leadership. They may have participated in China's 1949 revolution, but only as students or young adults. They are not war heroes but survivors of round after round of purges and intra-Party struggles—the last men left standing, so to speak. They have basic education and skills. Many, like Jiang, are university-educated engineers. But unlike Deng Xiaoping, who went to France as a young revolutionary student and forever after retained not only a love of croissants but a real understanding of the world outside, the seminal "cosmopolitan" experience of third-generation leaders would have been their Soviet training.[3]

They generally do have "active minds and can accept new things more easily," as a Chinese analyst commented in the newspaper *Guangming Ribao,*[4] yet their formative years were spent in a closed China where ideology was king. The only politics the third generation knows is the politics of Marxism–Leninism–Mao Zedong Thought. They understand that this legacy is largely irrelevant to China's future, but they have little vision of what to put in its place. Surviving the Cultural Revolution, "they have been trained to be cautious, looking behind their backs, stepping over each other to get up the ladder," as one Chinese observer puts it.

Westerners can easily fall into the assumption that the educated, technocratic third-generation leaders are "democrats and nascent capitalists," says China expert Kenneth Lieberthal. "But in fact these are individuals whose education and background do not predispose them toward any particular set of values and preferences."[5] Despite official rhetoric (for example, about building a "spiritual civilization"), the reality is that they inhabit a "spiritual wasteland," where "giving vent to anti-foreign passions" is one of the few unifying activities left, adds veteran sinologist Lucian Pye.[6]

By age and seniority Jiang and his contemporaries have come to dominate politics, but theirs is widely seen as only a temporary, "borrowed" leadership generation, lacking either a vision of their own or the authority to implement one.

Who are the real dissidents? Wei Jingsheng, one of China's best-known democracy advocates, who was jailed for nearly 16 years and then released for medical treatment in the U.S. following high-level diplomacy by the Clinton administration with Beijing, had this to say at a New York press conference: "I don't think it's quite right to call me a dissident. Most of the Chinese people want democracy. And the people who are different are just this little group of ruling elites of the Communist Party, so they are really the dissidents."

Some third-generation figures can and may play an important historical role now. Zhu Rongji has a sense of vision and has indicated the outlines of a plan for dramatic change. But even in his most senior position, he finds himself limited as to how far he can go. To visiting foreigners, Zhu has sometimes expounded much bolder economic ideas than any he has spoken about publicly in China or attempted to implement.

The "fourth generation" is the one that now runs banks and financial institutions and holds positions as mayors and governors. Its members are scattered through think tanks, government ministries, and innovative Chinese companies at home and abroad. These are people in their forties and fifties who will be taking senior positions in the power structure within the next decade. They tend to believe that political reform is crucial to China's future, yet they also know and understand the reasons for gridlock and gradualism. As young people, they were in the front lines of the Cultural Revolution, closing China's schools and institutions, wandering the country, "making revolution." They have seen with their own eyes how chaotic China can become in an atmosphere of radical change. They know better than to insist on radical change now. Yet they fear that without it China may not succeed.

The experiences of fourth-generation leaders have made them rugged, mature, sophisticated, and cosmopolitan. They withstood the harsh conditions of the countryside when they ended up living with the peasants in the Chinese outback during the Cultural Revolution. They fought passionately for what they believed was a righteous cause and made enormous sacrifices, only to have their belief system summarily shattered. As a leading banker told us, "We've been at the bottom, and it made us stronger. What have we to fear?"

This generation thinks more independently and critically than any previous Chinese leadership generation. Their formal education was, in most cases, interrupted by the Cultural Revolution, but many prominent figures finished their studies at leading Western universities when that became possible. Rebounding from the isolation of the Cultural Revolution, they seized the opportunity to learn new skills. Many embraced the democracy movement in the late 1980s. But after Tiananmen Square, most became convinced of the futility of political change and channeled their appetite for it into

Adding another Japan every decade: During the 1990s, even with China's slowing birthrate, the country will add at least 125 million people. That is the equivalent of today's entire population of Japan, or roughly half the U.S. population, in just 10 years.

—VACLAV SMIL
CHINA'S ENVIRONMENTAL CRISIS

business and economy building. Like American radicals and hippies of the 1960s turned into the yuppies of the 1980s, those Chinese who have gone in this direction have often been surprisingly willing to reaccept the old Confucian values of elitism, respect for hierarchy, and authority.

There is a curious duality in the fourth generation. They wish to see China prosperous, modern, and more democratic, but although they have shown themselves fearless in the past, they believe in biding their time. They are convinced that when their generation finally reaches the levers of national political power, they will launch a "golden era" of reform and progress for the twenty-first century. It may be, however, that in biding their time they are losing their nerve and falling under the sway of more traditional leadership patterns and beliefs.

We expect that the arrival of fourth-generation leaders in increasingly prominent positions over the next decade will usher in a variety of positive changes. But despite the hopes they have for themselves—and outsiders have for them as well—the ground for far-reaching change will still not be ready. The passage of the political torch from the third to the fourth generation will be a bit like the American experience of recent years, when the old, out-of-touch Reagan-Bush generation faded and a new, skilled, smart generation of Clintonites came to Washington: many new ideas, much new rhetoric, some important policy shifts, but in the end, nowhere near the kind of broad programmatic change that was expected from those who spoke of "reinventing government." Like Bill Clinton, China's smart, savvy, change-oriented fourth-generation leaders may well move back to the traditional center once they are in power.

If this is the case, however, they will still contribute along the way to changing the terms of the debate and laying the foundation for a more open society and a more responsive political system. But real transformation must wait for the "fifth generation" and even the sixth—China's version of Generations X and Y. These young people have lived almost all their lives in the post-Mao era. Reform, modernization, and change have been constants in their experience, while purges, inner-Party struggles, and extreme dogmatism have been almost nonexistent. They have no personal memory of the poor, backward, isolated, xenophobic, extremist China. They were never indoctrinated with Communist beliefs.

Growing up with "Confucian-Communist" values in the global classroom of MTV and Coca-Cola, these young people—at least the urban and coastal dwellers among them—are hyperlinked to the worldwide web of commerce and technology. Many are living middle-class, upwardly mobile lives. In the cities, most Chinese couples have followed government edicts on birth control and have had just one child. These only children are so doted on they are called six-pocket children, for the material things their two parents and four grandparents bestow on them. They are the first Chinese to grow up free of traditional family burdens—and free, as well, of political obligations. Thus, they are separating from their fathers and mothers—and from the paternalistic state and nation—in a way China has never seen. This is the group that will finally break up the old culture, the sense of *jia* (family) that kept society "safe" but held it prisoner; that unified it but choked its development.

There is a danger, of course, that like the American Generation X, this Chinese cohort will emerge rootless. Their freedom from the past may be too great and they may be insufficiently grounded in their own heritage to provide the kind of leadership China most needs. As the first generation of Chinese to be openly self-aware and full of self-esteem, the intellectuals and political leaders in this generation could emerge as too separate from the rest of the Chinese polity to be effective.

Our sense, however, is that the fifth generation will rise above these generational character flaws to be the force that actually transforms China into a thoroughly modern nation. They will design the value system that reconciles the impulses to be both Chinese and modern, and that develops political-economic institutions that successfully mix Asian and Western traditions. But the fifth generation will not even begin to take power for twenty years or more. And that is as good an indicator as any of just how far off, yet historically close, the ultimate transformation of China lies.

Mao Is Back!?!?

Another important theme of the next few years will be the incipient Maoist revival. The little news the West gets about Mao Zedong these days tends to further undermine whatever

Describing the future: "Here's a way to think about China's future: a giant Korean-style economy with a Taiwan-style political system."

—WILLIAM OVERHOLT
MANAGING DIRECTOR
BANKERS TRUST (HONG KONG)

reputation he had left as a towering figure of the twentieth century. A book by his personal physician caught a wave of American public attention in 1994 with its lurid stories of his sexual exploits and the Howard Hughes–like eccentricities of this supposed Man of the People.[7] A subsequent book documented his role in the great famines of the 1950s and 1960s, when he turned away foreign food aid even as millions of Chinese suffered.[8]

In China, however, Mao has been making something of a comeback. In the early nineties, taxi drivers in Guangzhou and other cities started adorning their rearview mirrors with Mao medallions for good luck. Mao statues that had been taken down in towns and villages started to reappear in some places. Sites around China devoted to Mao went into utter eclipse in the 1980s but are now starting to hum again. Those nostalgic for the Cultural Revolution can now eat in theme restaurants that hark back to those days. Even the revolutionary Peking operas created during the Cultural Revolution are being revived. And, of course, Mao's visage never left Tiananmen Square, even though the Chinese took down the portraits of Marx, Engels, Lenin, and Stalin that used to accompany his.

The Mao revival will grow, but only as one among many trends brought on by the breakup of the old single-minded ideology and dogma of Communism. As long as the new leadership is weak and uncharismatic, Mao will fill a political and even a spiritual void. He had godlike status in his lifetime, so it is hardly a surprise that people are turning back to him in more complex and challenging times, just as they are turning to Buddhism, Confucianism, Christianity, and New Age religions. He will never again be the unquestioned divinity he once was, but he may become a handy "kitchen god" for some Chinese.

Unfortunately, none of the current Mao revival is likely to address the real problem of Mao Zedong in Chinese history. China has managed to "move on" and break with Maoism in practice, while avoiding for two decades the political dangers of breaking with Maoism in theory.

By careful design, no new ideology has ever been elaborated, nor has any specific vision of the future ever been promulgated for China. It is certainly a relief for those accustomed over the decades to hearing false certitude from Chinese officials to hear, now, a healthy dose of agnosticism and

What would Chairman Mao have to say? On the occasion of the 75th anniversary of the founding of the Communist Party in 1996, an official in Shanghai was asked how the Party organizes itself in today's factories. "Our primary concern is moneymaking ability," he said. "Setting up a Party organization should be done in parallel with business functions. We will not get in the way."

280

admissions of uncertainty about the future. Many of these leaders are genuinely humble, modest, and open-minded in the face of China's unprecedented challenges. But there are also less attractive reasons why the Chinese, whose culture is so steeped in long-term thinking and strategy (for 5,000 years, not just for the fifty years of Mao's legacy), would maintain such a vague picture of the future.

To put forward a new, sharply framed vision of the future, China would be forced to confront the Maoist and Communist past directly. This would engender new questions about the fragile legitimacy of today's leaders, all of whom were originally disciples of Mao's revolution. To delve into the Communist Party's track record under Mao or the real meaning of its stated beliefs and goals would be to expose its outdated philosophy and its increasing irrelevance to China's current needs. Thus it is far easier to ignore the vestigial corpus of Communism underlying the Chinese body politic than to try to remove it.

If radical surgery is to be done on the Maoist core of Chinese political history, some new and specific vision would have to replace it. That would focus attention on politics and inevitably trigger a renewal of the 1980s argument that without the "fifth modernization" (reform of the Chinese political system and the introduction of genuine mass democracy), China cannot succeed. Jiang Zemin, like Deng before him, sees such a course as a poor use of the leadership's limited political capital and a miscalculated gamble that would surely disturb the surface stability China has managed to maintain for two decades now, in large part because debate was cut off on these issues back in the early 1980s. He has only to look to South Korea or the Philippines for confirmation of his fear that reopened debates about former dictators tend to endanger political stability and even economic success.

Even if the Mao revival proves to be merely a passing fad, the difficulties described above in coming to grips with the Maoist past will continue to frustrate the best intentions of fourth-generation leaders with respect to political modernization and democracy. Just like the United States at its birth, when slavery and Jeffersonian democracy coexisted, China faces a catharsis somewhere down the road.

Isms revisited: Sidney Shapiro, a lawyer from Brooklyn who has lived in China since 1947, explains today's China this way: "The great flaw of Chinese society has been recognized. It is not Socialism or Communism, but Confucianism. That means blind worship of authority, which has been used very much to the advantage and to the disadvantage of the Communist Party over the years."

"May You Live in Interesting Times"

Big democracy is a big mess: Li Ruihuan, generally considered to be among the most "liberal" of the leaders on the Politburo, is quoted as having said, "Do we still want more democracy? Didn't we get enough of that in the Cultural Revolution?"

Although we have attempted to identify many of the key issues that will define China's development over the next five years, some of the most critical issues of the future will certainly arise by surprise and without any obvious precedent.

Market forces, once unleashed, have a strange way of finding their own flow through history. It is incredibly ironic that for all the fear that Chinese political behavior might cause a financial panic in Hong Kong, the reality was that the market rose to new highs to greet the Chinese takeover and then fell into crash, pandemonium, and panic several months later for reasons that had everything to do with market forces and almost nothing to do with Chinese sovereignty. Market forces are like that.

The delicate balance of foreign investment, currency valuations, bad domestic debts, politically sensitive trade balances, and the atmosphere of impending Asia-wide financial crisis, could lead to any number of problems in China's fledgling financial markets, which in turn could lead to serious challenges to the government's credibility. Many experts have long worried that China has been (consciously or unconsciously) emulating the model of South Korea's chaebol-style conglomerates. With the once glittering South Korean economy having crash-landed in 1997 and been forced into the humiliation of begging the IMF for a massive bailout, the actual balance sheets of China's corporations, long ignored by outsiders who valued these companies' connections to power more highly than their actual assets, are facing new scrutiny.

As we have noted, China has resisted the path of radical privatization for many reasons, not the least of which is the perception that it has wreaked havoc in Russia. But what happens if, in the next few years, Russian privatization starts to pay off and the Russian economy starts to look better? If this happens, it could have a significant impact on the internal debate in China. Similarly, if Asia enters a prolonged period of recession and stagnation, and if China is caught in that vortex, a much sharper political debate over economic direction could break out in Beijing.

It is also possible that some specific dates or predictable events could trigger key countercurrents to the status quo.

For example, the death of Zhao Ziyang could bring his former supporters into the streets of Beijing again if Chinese officialdom tries to suppress public mourning.

In thinking about Tiananmen Square, it might be useful to keep an eye on what happens in Hong Kong on June 4, 1998, the first time Hong Kong citizens will try to commemorate this event under the Chinese flag. And the tenth anniversary, in 1999, will raise the ante for celebrations in Beijing as well as in Hong Kong.

The early part of 1997 provided a good lesson in the ironclad law of surprise that should be factored into any forecasting. Right alongside the death of Deng Xiaoping, an event futurists had been discussing, elaborating scenarios of, and drafting their op-ed pieces about for years, the scandal of Chinese involvement in the 1996 U.S. presidential election unfolded. Few forecasters could have imagined that while Clinton was dispatching U.S. warships to counter Chinese moves in the Taiwan Strait in 1996, he was simultaneously engaged in a special effort to raise campaign funds from Chinese sources. It only served to emphasize the fact that we are all living the ancient Chinese curse "May you live in interesting times."

CHAPTER 15

The Next Five Years: The Dragon Peers Out

Hong Kong: Life After 1997

Singapore's Lee Kuan Yew was once asked what would happen in Hong Kong after 1997. In a reflection of his confidence in the former British colony's future under Chinese administration, Lee quipped: "Nineteen ninety-eight."

The Western world is watching the post-1997 process closely. Because Hong Kong has historically been a beehive of free-market energy and the epitome of a free-trade outpost in a world of protectionism and mercantilism, foreigners believe they know and understand Hong Kong and its culture. In this one small bit of Asia, British, Americans, Europeans, Japanese, Taiwanese, Koreans, Indonesians, and others from all over the world have felt comfortable investing, living, doing business, trading, and making piles and piles of money.

In Washington, the issue of how Beijing handles Hong Kong has been put forward as a benchmark of "maturity," which will determine how favorably the United States should look on China itself. "We're not seeking to replace Britain as the guardian of Hong Kong," a senior Clinton administration official declared at the time of the transition. "But it's a role we cannot avoid. Since we are who we are, and we have so much business here, we will end up by being the first to cry foul."[1]

Meanwhile, congressional critics of Clinton administration policy have warned they are watching how vigorously the White House watches China. If Clinton does not defend Hong Kong from Chinese encroachments on democracy with sufficient firmness, they stand ready to attempt again to revoke MFN status for China, or to take other steps to police Beijing's behavior from Capitol Hill.

Far outside the Beltway, Americans more generally tend to feel that if Hong Kong goes well, China's future will go well; if Hong Kong doesn't go well, how can China possibly succeed? But this seemingly logical view may be another case of Western thinking that doesn't quite apply in Asia.

China's current attempt to square the circle—to absorb the world's most successful enclave of free-market capitalism into the world's biggest socialist country—has been a drama with almost two decades of planned buildup. When we started traveling to Hong Kong in the early 1970s, everyone in the know was already keenly aware that British colonial power had become an oxymoron and that the mainland now subtly controlled the key levers of Hong Kong's economy. China provided the colony's drinking water, food, electricity, and most other necessities. "We could send the PLA in and occupy Hong Kong any time we want," a Chinese Communist official observed in 1975. "But we choose not to do so. We can certainly wait for 1997."

In 1982, Margaret Thatcher went to Beijing, where she discussed the post-1997 future of Hong Kong. Her original intention was to negotiate some continued British rule. But in Deng, the irresistible force of the Iron Lady had met the immovable object of the Dragon Emperor. In a marvelously colorful rendition of their meeting, Paul Theroux has recently written:

> Spitting at intervals, Deng lectured her on Chinese sovereignty and repeated that it was not negotiable. And, looking ahead fifteen years, Deng specified a date for the handover: July 1, 1997. He never wavered. . . . Thatcher left the Great Hall flustered, lost her footing on the stairs, and fell clattering to her hands and knees, bobbling her handbag, her pearls swinging, and—with her arse in the air and her face flushed with embarrassment—she

Hong Kong's best days may be still to come: Referring to the "countdown" of months and days before the Chinese takeover of Hong Kong, David Li, chief executive of the Bank of East Asia, said, "When a countdown ends, a rocket takes off. How high will this one go?" His forecast is that Hong Kong's economy and that of the Chinese areas on the other side of the border will merge more and more, to form a "Pearl City," which by the year 2007 comprises 40 million people and has a per capita income twice that in South Korea today.

appeared to be kowtowing to Mao in his nearby mausoleum.[2]

Looking at the future of Hong Kong: "China does not cast a shadow over Hong Kong. It casts a bright light. Hong Kong is China's biggest asset. It may become the number one city in the world."

—ROBERT NG
CHAIRMAN, SINO LAND
COMPANY

With that for an opener, Beijing continued to outmaneuver London on almost every point of debate about Hong Kong's future. Deng made his bold proposal for "one country, two systems": socialist China would preserve Hong Kong's capitalist system and way of life as a "special administrative region" (S.A.R.) for fifty years, he promised. Before long, this improbable, unprecedented, and brilliantly Chinese formula was enshrined in the Joint Declaration and the Basic Law, the two key Sino-British agreements on Hong Kong's future.

Ever since those pathbreaking agreements, the West has watched very closely for signs of whether China really intends—or is able—to live up to this commitment. In the China boom of the early nineties, many Westerners were giddy with confidence that Hong Kong under Chinese sovereignty was going to create a win-win story for all, as the city's free market and democratic influences spread by example and proximity through other parts of China. Many a foreign expert in 1993–94 agreed with the summation of a senior economist for a major American brokerage house: "Hong Kong is taking over China, not the other way around!"

Few of those knowledgeable about the situation would make that statement now. "More and more, Hong Kong is becoming like China," observes the democracy-minded legislative representative Emily Lau.[3] The combination of Beijing's heavy hand and the Hong Kong elite's own desire to self-censor and please China is rapidly taking the steam out of Hong Kong's unique character.

With the hoisting of the Chinese flag on July 1, 1997, the departure of the feisty Beijing-baiting British colonial governor, Chris Patten, and the appointment of Hong Kong shipping magnate C. H. Tung as the first chief executive of the new S.A.R., the outside world can at last see the beginning of the actual results of Chinese rule, which had been debated so extensively for so long. One's opinion of Hong Kong's future depends on which of two conflicting premises one accepts about Beijing's thinking. On the one hand, it is clearly in China's material interest to maintain the status quo and continue to profit from a robust, successful Hong Kong.

On the other hand, when forced to deal with certain kinds of political issues, China has always been willing to forgo its economic interests in order to make a political point.

The conventional wisdom that has largely prevailed since London and Beijing agreed on the Basic Law for Hong Kong is that China will swallow hard and tolerate some degree of criticism, as well as political trends, lifestyles, and democratic behaviors it would not allow inside China proper, because it is in China's interests to do so. By keeping Hong Kong free, open, and confident, China knows it is simultaneously keeping open its principal source of inflowing investment. Since 1987, nearly $120 billion worth of investment has flowed into China from Hong Kong and from Overseas Chinese investing through Hong Kong–based vehicles—almost half the total from all "foreign" sources. Seventy of the leading enterprises in China had floated about $6 billion worth of stock in Hong Kong's public markets by the end of 1996, with 300 more in the pipeline seeking to do so. All of these companies are highly dependent on the confidence of Hong Kong investors to keep their share price high.

Just as important is capital flow in the *other* direction. Some 1,800 mainland Chinese companies have invested more than $45 billion in Hong Kong's economy in recent years. Huge China-owned conglomerates have spent much of their hard-to-come-by foreign currency reserves to buy assets in Hong Kong. Some of these companies are actually arms of Chinese government ministries, such as the sprawling China Resources empire, which is controlled by the Ministry of Foreign Trade and Economic Cooperation, and China Overseas Holdings, controlled by the Ministry of Construction. The seventy-story I. M. Pei–designed Bank of China building is the most visible element of the Hong Kong skyline. It cost over $1 billion to erect, and although many locals believe its angularities and conflicting glass planes have horrific feng shui, it dwarfs all the other banking towers of the city, a visual message conveying China's confidence in and commitment to Hong Kong.

Some of China's investments in the local economy are in businesses controlled by the sons, daughters, and other relatives of senior Beijing officials. Given not just China's general national interest, but these personal interests as well— and Hong Kong's extraordinary fit with China's overall

Worries about the Hong Kong financial markets: "The biggest test of Hong Kong's ability to separate the economic from the political lies in how it handles the red chips [Chinese companies listed on the Hong Kong Stock Exchange]. The companies come from a tradition of secrecy, and they bridle at Hong Kong's requirement that companies publish extensive financial data. 'Watch what happens the first time the Hong Kong authorities try to delist some stock that has plenty of connections,' warns the head of an American brokerage in Hong Kong."

—DAVID SANGER
THE NEW YORK TIMES

modernization needs—it would seem to outsiders the height of folly for China to do anything to undermine international confidence in Hong Kong.

Topping off the argument is the idea of the prestige and credibility China will gain in the world (for doing what is in China's own interests anyway). This prestige can be leveraged for even greater gain. If Hong Kong goes well, the chance that China can find a peaceful formula for reunification with Taiwan—a much bigger prize economically and politically—is greatly enhanced.

Joseph Yam, Hong Kong's respected senior official for monetary affairs, observes that he hopes Beijing will stop thinking that it has to work at making Hong Kong stable and prosperous. "I've been telling them time and time again if they do want Hong Kong to be stable and prosperous, leave it alone." It is a policy—"Don't just do something—sit there"—cleverly summed up by *The Wall Street Journal* as an inversion of the normal injunction.[4] On many matters, China has been following this advice since the 1997 takeover. Beijing has stood by and watched as the local government has shut down the Hong Kong operations of well-connected Chinese companies found guilty of supplying chemical weapons to Iran, for example.

Indeed, the main surprise produced by the first few months of Chinese sovereignty in Hong Kong was the degree of calm and normalcy that prevailed. As many as half of the 10,000 PLA soldiers who arrived to the indignation of many locals for the July 1, 1997, transition had slipped quietly back into China by September. U.S. Navy men are said to be more obvious in Hong Kong than PLA soldiers.

When Hong Kong's new chief executive, C. H. Tung, visited Washington in September 1997, even the most rabid anti-China members of Congress found it more productive to warn about all the dangers that might befall Hong Kong in the future, rather than attempt to make a case from the limited number of available anecdotes about negative incidents that had already come to pass.

An interesting test of China's commitment to Hong Kong's status quo occurred in the late summer and early fall of 1997, as indigenous economic problems, magnified by the swashbuckling negative bets placed by global currency speculators, drove several Southeast Asian currencies and equities markets into near free fall. With Thailand, Malaysia, and

Hong Kong to Washington: "Butt out." "This may sound simplistic," says Ronnie Chan, an American-educated businessman who believes Hong Kong will thrive under Chinese rule, but the best course for Washington is to "leave us alone."

Indonesia suffering currency depreciations ranging from 10 to 40 percent, several speculators were willing to make big bets that Hong Kong could not defend its linkage to the U.S. dollar. But the Hong Kong authorities persevered.

Asked how much of Hong Kong's $60 billion in foreign currency reserves he was prepared to spend defending the Hong Kong dollar, C. H. Tung said, "I think the question should be the other way around: How much are they [the speculators] prepared to lose to attack us?"[5]

China, with even vaster foreign-currency reserves, was also quietly intervening to defend the Hong Kong dollar. It did not have to do so—arguably, a depreciated currency in Hong Kong and China would be good for exports. But Beijing recognized that to let the Hong Kong dollar lose its mooring to the U.S. dollar would be to undermine confidence in Hong Kong. China may not permanently take that position, nor may it be able to do so the next time the global speculators try to drive down the Hong Kong dollar. In fact, many experts at this writing doubt that Hong Kong can continue to withstand the pressure to sever its link to the U.S. dollar and devalue its currency. Yes, Hong Kong and China have enough combined foreign reserves to take on all comers, but at a certain point it may become a foolish strategy to resist the will of the market so obstinately. Three months into the crisis, however, Hong Kong was continuing to defend its dollar linkage and the Chinese, as good as their word, were continuing to defend Hong Kong's economic status quo.

But China may not be congenitally capable of just sitting there and doing nothing over the long term. There are issues of pride and face that make it unclear whether China can really handle the kind of criticism and independent action a free society produces, or whether it will feel compelled to swat away the critical flies and quash the independent spirit.

Handling Golden Eggs

While we understand that China has material interests in Hong Kong's stability and prosperity, we disagree with the widely held Western belief that Hong Kong is "too important" to China for the situation to be mishandled. Hong Kong may be the goose that lays golden eggs, but as the well-known Asia hand Chalmers Johnson has pointed out, Chi-

An oenophile's advice to China on Hong Kong: "A confident wine maker would choose to be minimally interventionist, allowing the wine to make itself. After all, there is no way for the wine to escape the bottle."

—RAYMOND CHIEN
ECONOMIST AND
OENOPHILE

nese history is filled with incidents in which such geese were killed off anyway. Just as Mao once summarily expelled China's corps of thousands of Russian engineers and advisors, even though it was not in China's material interest to do so, Beijing will turn on Hong Kong if the experience there threatens it in any serious way.

This is what Hong Kong's democracy movement leaders, such as the lawyer Martin Lee, have been warning about. Without specific guarantees of democratic rights, the local people have nothing to cling to but the hope that China will retain a benign disposition toward Hong Kong. Given what Lee argues is already a long Chinese track record of broken promises, he wants world support—and particularly, Washington's. But although Bill Clinton agreed to see Lee just weeks before the takeover, and although he was willing to issue a statement indicating that the United States is watching Hong Kong's fate closely, few experts believe the Clinton administration, or any other world government, will intervene in any credible way to stop the erosion of civil liberties in Hong Kong.

Hawks in the West argued that Beijing was already tampering severely with Hong Kong's status quo even before the Chinese flag was raised. They believe that Beijing is so thin-skinned that it cannot tolerate any degree of free speech or democratic politics in Hong Kong. China must ultimately repress the democratic impulse in Hong Kong to keep the contagion from spreading, they say. Everything China has done both before and since July 1, 1997, is interpreted in that light.

Others argue that China's negative actions toward Hong Kong are minimal and even understandable. Beijing made it clear before the takeover that its idea of maintaining the status quo did not include allowing absolute freedom of the press and expression or supporting Patten's eleventh-hour efforts to install a semblance of local electoral democracy.

Outspoken officials such as Lu Ping, charged with overseeing Hong Kong affairs, told the world that China would not let Hong Kong be turned into a base for promoting Western-style ideas about human rights inside China. To advocate the breakup of China's territorial integrity, he argues, is to commit treason. This can be interpreted to mean that any argument for the independence of Taiwan, Tibet, or Hong Kong itself could be seen as a capital crime.

Shortly before the takeover, Foreign Minister Qian Qichen

was asked specific questions about what could and couldn't be done in Hong Kong afterward. Could people continue to hold demonstrations and memorial vigils on the anniversary of the Tiananmen Square incident, as they have done for the past nine years? "In the future, Hong Kong should not hold those activities which directly interfere in the affairs of the mainland of China," he replied. Will the media remain free to criticize China? The media, Qian said, could "put forward criticism, but not rumors or lies. Nor can they put forward personal attacks on the Chinese leaders."[6]

In a telling incident involving just such a personal attack on a Chinese leader as early as 1995, the brash Hong Kong businessman and media mogul Jimmy Lai called Premier Li Peng a "disgrace to the Chinese people" and "the son of a turtle's egg," which is the Chinese equivalent of the "m-f" word in English. Shortly thereafter, he found the popular Giordano jeans store he owned in China suddenly shut down by the authorities.

Questions about the future of Hong Kong's leading free press are exemplified by the evolution of the *South China Morning Post,* Hong Kong's leading English-language daily. Once owned by Rupert Murdoch, it was sold in 1994 to Robert Kuok, a legendary Malaysian-born Chinese billionaire with strong business and personal ties to China. Murdoch candidly admitted he didn't want anything the newspaper might say to upset his business dealings with China—a corporate position reiterated when one of his book companies clumsily axed the publication of a book by former Hong Kong governor Chris Patten that was highly critical of China (as Patten himself had been in his role as the last colonial governor).

Kuok never explicitly said he would turn the newspaper in a pro-China direction. But just ten weeks before the Chinese takeover, he arranged to hire Feng Xiliang, founder of Beijing's official English-language newspaper, *China Daily,* as a consultant. Journalists at the paper reportedly worried that Feng had come to serve as a sort of political commissar who would censor negative articles about China—a charge vehemently denied by the paper's editor in chief, Jonathan Fenby. Like much else about Hong Kong, this flap was more about perception than actuality. To date, the paper continues its often hard-headed coverage of China.

Such incidents, and many more like them, are certainly portents of the future. But they are more complex and subtle

The real worry is not political: "Hardly any expert worries much about Chinese authorities staging any kind of expropriation in Hong Kong. What people worry about is the insidious effect of Chinese management on the environment, infrastructure, and social structures. The biggest risk is that Guangdong-style corruption will erode credibility in Hong Kong markets and business practices."

—TIMOTHY MOE
SALOMON BROTHERS

than straightforward repression of civil liberties. China seems to have accepted the premise that money talks in Hong Kong. It is therefore in the process of buying out the opposition rather than trying to throttle it.

Democracy at Five Minutes to Midnight

The significance of several other issues in the runup to the Chinese takeover was hotly debated. For example, Beijing refused to recognize Hong Kong's Legislative Council (Legco). Chris Patten was instrumental in creating this legislature, whose members were elected in 1995 to four-year terms that would have run past 1997, even though China and Britain had previously agreed that both sides would have to agree on any elections whose results would span the transition. China did not agree to the Legco elections; it therefore announced it was setting up its own new provisional legislature instead. Not surprisingly, this body is made up entirely of members who see Hong Kong's future as best assured by a policy of cooperation rather than confrontation with Beijing.

The next landmark on this map was the selection of C. H. Tung as Hong Kong's first Chinese governor—or chief executive, in postcolonial parlance. Cosmopolitan, a thoughtful leader of the business community, well-regarded in Hong Kong, Beijing, and the United States, Tung emerged as the front-runner a year before his actual selection. But critics, mostly outside Hong Kong, chose to see him as a man in Beijing's pocket. Even though his family had fled the 1949 revolution to establish a shipping empire in Hong Kong, virtually every major American news article about Tung's selection pointed out that when his business became over-extended, it was bailed out by a loan provided in part by mainland Chinese sources.

Like much of Hong Kong's elite business community, Tung believes that Hong Kong has become "too politicized." Hong Kong is primarily about working, making money, and serving as an economic bridge between China and the West. It should not become the frontline city in the struggle to change China's political system. Just as his opponents charge, Tung has willingly supported China's desire to roll back some political freedoms only recently conferred on Hong Kong's citizens during the Patten administration.

As clever Chinese rhetoricians often note, Britain was

How the role of foreign businessmen will change in Hong Kong after 1997:
"Foreign business will certainly lose status here; their role will have to be redefined. Non-Chinese businessmen are going to have to come to grips with the fact that we will be a minority; we will become guests here and will have to start behaving like guests, aware that there are certain subjects on which we shouldn't make public expression of views."

—HANS MICHAEL JEBSEN
CHAIRMAN, JEBSEN &
COMPANY

never much interested in democracy for Hong Kong during its 150 years of colonial rule. If the British so cherished these freedoms, why did they wait until the waning days of their rule to grant them to the Chinese citizens of Hong Kong? One of the reasons Deng Xiaoping could propose the maintenance of Hong Kong's status quo with a straight face in the 1980s is that although the city was a center of free trade and free markets, it was ruled by a colonial government that offered almost no direct democracy to its 6 million citizens and solved most problems discreetly behind the closed doors of the elite. *That* system was compatible with the Chinese system.

Buying In

Some Hong Kong watchers suggest that since a certain reduction in political freedom is already built in to everyone's expectations, a more serious indicator is whether China induces Hong Kong authorities to make economic decisions in Beijing's interest. These might include investing more of Hong Kong's reserves in the Chinese government bond market, for example, or granting special tax status to Chinese corporations operating in Hong Kong, or relaxing stock market accounting rules for Chinese companies. Hong Kong can live without a vigorously independent press, argues this school of thought, but it can't thrive economically if its operational framework is compromised.

In this context, considerable controversy prevails over a spate of 1996–97 Chinese joint ventures, buyouts, and partnerships involving Hong Kong companies. In early 1997, for example, an unusual leveraged buyout of sorts took place in Citic Pacific, a Hong Kong subsidiary of China's leading investment company. In a sweet deal, the company's chairman acquired a huge block of stock at a discounted valuation of over $400 million. The chairman happened to be the flamboyant Larry Yung, son of Chinese vice president Rong Yiren (a pre-1949 Shanghai capitalist rehabilitated by Deng Xiaoping and given a mandate in the late 1970s to found Citic).

Larry Yung is everything Americans would want in a new Chinese entrepreneur: well-educated (at Stanford), a terrific deal maker, a man who professes independence from Beijing and says he wants only to make a great success of his

What, me worry? Says David Chu, Hong Kong property developer and pro-Beijing legislator, "I'm a patriotic Chinese, and I believe that patriotism must be unconditional, not just for personal gain. It must also be partial and biased toward China. Even if they are wrong, you must make up stories to defend them. We just have to learn to adapt and adjust."

company. He lives the life of Hong Kong taipans before him as a steward of the prestigious Jockey Club, a racer of horses, and a flashy gambler; he says he once won $5 million by making a mistaken $50,000 bet on a hundred-to-one shot.

Under Yung's leadership, Citic Pacific has been the best-managed and most successful Chinese company in Hong Kong, earning over $800 million in 1996 alone and enjoying a 70 percent climb in its publicly traded stock price. What's wrong with rewarding its chief executive with the highest CEO pay in Hong Kong ($26 million a year) and a huge chunk of the equity? Isn't that the American way? Absolutely. But questions linger. Where did Larry Yung get $1.24 billion of personal capital to put down for the stock that was worth $1.64 billion? No one knows. Does it matter? No one is sure. Indeed, it is rumored that back in Beijing, there are significant questions and criticism about how this deal was done.

Meanwhile, one Chinese company after another has become the partner of a traditional Hong Kong firm by acquiring stock, often at a significantly discounted price. In one sense, these deals are signs of China's commitment to and confidence in Hong Kong. Each deal ties Chinese material interests more closely to the successful performance of the Hong Kong economy. As even the *Wall Street Journal*'s editorialists admit, these investments are "a far cry from the crude nationalizations that have taken place in the past whenever a Communist party has taken over a country."[7]

Nevertheless, a troubling underlying concern accompanies each new stock purchase. What is the hidden political agenda that goes with China's financial investments? Will these companies operate differently as a result of their ownership structure? Will the local economy become a hive of corruption as money arrives from shadowy new owners seeking to use the companies for a variety of undisclosed purposes? Will every company feel compelled to do China's bidding, either because it wants to be rewarded with lucrative business partnerships or because it fears being frozen out?

On the other hand, some see the whole process going better than it is sometimes depicted in the United States. Journalist Frank Ching, a columnist for the Hong Kong–based *Far Eastern Economic Review,* argued on the eve of the transition in a tartly worded article that the loudest complaints about Chinese behavior were coming not from Hong Kong but from the American media and the U.S. Congress. Ching took *The New York Times* to task for its "Farewell to Freedom" editorial in which it declared that C. H. Tung and the provisional legislature had been selected "without the slightest accommodation to democracy." Ching fired back that the proceedings to select Tung—who was chosen over two other well-known and well-qualified candidates by a 400-member selection committee—"could certainly be criticized as elitist and non-democratic," but were "much more democratic" than the selection of Christopher Patten, who "was chosen by just one man, Prime Minister John Major." In fact, "all previous governors had been chosen with even less 'accommodation to democracy' " than Tung.[8]

In the spring of 1997, with the transition only months away, the Hong Kong stock market was at an all-time high, the property market was booming, 80 percent of local people expressed confidence in the future, and C. H. Tung enjoyed far higher approval rating than Chris Patten had ever had. The "red chip" stock listing of Beijing Enterprises, the commercial arm of the Beijing municipal government, was oversubscribed by a factor of 1,300 to 1.[9] Against this backdrop, Ching argued, it was a bit premature for the American media to be presenting Hong Kong's future as a dark scenario of repression and curtailment of freedom. "It's about time the United States stopped its funeral orations for Hong Kong," he concluded. "It's not dead yet, so please don't kill it."[10]

We suspect that a combination of pressure from taipans and civic fathers to avoid provoking Beijing with some willingness on China's part to turn a blind eye to some manifestations of local democracy will keep a lid on conflict so that the reabsorption of Hong Kong proves a generally peaceful process. However, we specifically do not rule out—indeed, we fully expect—some powerful initiatives from Beijing against those who don't otherwise get the message. Following that ancient rule of Chinese statecraft, Beijing will seek an opportunity to "kill the chicken to scare the monkey."[11] Exactly what form that will take—mass arrests at a demonstration, the closing of newspapers, or an attempt to charge prodemocracy forces with treason—remains to be seen.

The most real and probable threat to Hong Kong's future

Hong Kong's threat is not China: The biggest issue facing Hong Kong's business community is keeping its competitive edge. Local businesses are "as likely to face pressure from Benetton as from Beijing. It's capitalistic competition, not the imminent Communist takeover and the uncertainties over the rule of law and clean government, that is causing day-to-day heartburn in boardrooms."

—GARY SILVERMAN
FAR EASTERN ECONOMIC REVIEW

doesn't come from curtailment of its civil liberties, nor do we expect that the People's Liberation Army will march in, occupy it, and shut down its way of life. Rather, the threats are more subtle and longer-term. Even well before the takeover some local economists worried that Hong Kong was already losing its competitive edge in some industries to other Asian centers. And on the mainland, many in Shenzhen, Guangzhou, and Shanghai are jealous of Hong Kong's privileged position and believe their cities can do everything Hong Kong can. Indeed, much of Hong Kong's industrial, banking, and financial acumen derives from displaced Shanghainese who brought these skills with them in their post-1949 flight from China. Clearly, Jiang Zemin and the many colleagues he has recruited to the central government from Shanghai hope to make that city the dominant financial and business center of East Asia. The fact that they have that alternative in mind makes them just slightly less predisposed to the extra effort of maintaining the delicate balance of forces that underlies Hong Kong's success. As *The Wall Street Journal* quoted a senior Shanghai official as saying, "Shanghai will not be able to catch Hong Kong immediately, but Shanghai will be China's number one commercial city. This has already been decided at the highest levels."[12]

Shiu Sin-por, a Hong Kong–based advisor to Beijing, puts the issue in the starkest terms. Hong Kong is no longer needed as a "window" or a "bridge," says Shiu. "China doesn't need windows and bridges, and if they do, they have many of their own." Hong Kong, he warns, must change and adapt so as to continue to add value to the Chinese economy. Otherwise it will become a "second-rate, high-unemployment trading post early in the next century."

In our view, Hong Kong will almost inevitably blend into the megalopolis that is being created in the Hong Kong–Shenzhen–Guangzhou corridor. In this blending, Hong Kong may lose some of its edge of excellence, although it will remain a thriving center for trade and finance well into the twenty-first century. Eventually, Shanghai could become a more important Asian business center, but that is many years away. Hong Kong's fate may be to become just another one of several big, active, important Chinese coastal cities, albeit one rich in history, romance, and a special local character.

Blunt talk on Taiwan from Mr. Lee: "Taiwan is seen as a Chinese-Chinese issue. All countries in ASEAN accept the one-China policy and do not consider the cross-straits tensions as international tension. No leadership in China will be able to survive if Taiwan moves away and becomes separate. It's too big, too emotional a symbol of national unity."

—LEE KUAN YEW

Taiwan: A Contrarian View

Taiwan will remain a flashpoint of U.S.-China relations, and an important issue in Chinese policy more generally, for all the reasons discussed in Part I. Without revisiting all the complexities of this sensitive issue, we wish simply to suggest that the question of Taiwan may be *less* controversial in the next five years than it has been in the past three.

China's muscle-flexing of 1995–96 caused alarm in the United States and was assumed to be part of a new pattern of perennial Chinese aggressiveness and expansiveness. On our side of the Pacific, China was also judged to have failed and embarrassed itself with its military tests and threats against Taiwan.

The view in Asia is quite different, and in Taiwan particularly so. Clumsy as China's actions may have been, they had the desired effect. Beijing put Taiwan's president, Lee Teng-hui, in his place and weakened the incipient Taiwanese independence movement. Beijing may not feel moved to make this particular point again, especially if the Taiwanese leaders continue to "behave" and give China no need to respond to a provocative action. And although Beijing continues its negative invective against the Taiwan regime, the economic substance of the relationship with Taiwan is deepening.

Jiang Zemin, who reportedly came under intense criticism from the Chinese military for not reacting more forcefully to the first news of Lee Teng-hui's visit to the United States, has now amply demonstrated his willingness to join the hardliners on this issue and to rally the nation in support of a bellicose stance. Perhaps having demonstrated his mettle once, he won't need to do it again.

In Beijing's view, Lee Teng-hui continues to "fish in troubled waters," looking for ways to assert Taiwan's own identity and his administration's legitimacy. However, Lee's Kuomintang Party is, theoretically, opposed to independence and has historically favored "one China." The forces on Lee's flanks that are more explicitly committed to independence represent the greatest danger to the status quo. Should they start making noticeable gains again, the Chinese would certainly respond with another military jolt.

This issue is so sensitive—and American and Chinese views are so much at odds—that it could blow up again at

"In the last two decades who has used force in this region? China. We cannot take it for granted that there will be a benign China. We don't want to live under a Chinese nuclear umbrella; we don't want to become a vassal state to China."

—RYUICHI SHOJI
SENIOR RESEARCH FELLOW
JAPAN INSTITUTE OF
INTERNATIONAL AFFAIRS

any moment. Many experts expect continued triangular tension and contention between Beijing, Taipei, and Washington. But we take the contrarian view, forecasting a modest *deescalation* of the Taiwan issue in the coming years. There will be a return to the pre-1995 status quo, with growing cross-strait business, trade, and investment characterizing the Taiwan-China relationship, rather than political controversy and military threats. Taiwan will provide an increasing share of the "foreign" investment China needs. And the high-level political dialogue between Taipei and Beijing that began earlier in this decade might restart in earnest.

Tibet: The Next Taiwan

Even as the Taiwan issue loses some of its heat, a new and somewhat similar controversy is brewing over the future of Tibet. Like China policy more generally, the Tibetan cause has attracted an unusual political mix of those on the Right as well as the Left. In the last several years, a loose coalition of interests in support of the Dalai Lama's campaign for independence has emerged among the Hollywood entertainment community, Capitol Hill critics of China, religious and spiritual leaders in the United States, and a variety of other forces in American society. Prominent Americans from Richard Gere to Al Gore have befriended the Dalai Lama and taken up his cause. Taiwan is an issue of concern primarily for politicians and foreign-policy specialists; the problem of Tibet resonates with a much broader constituency, loaded as it is not just with issues of political independence but with romantic notions of a peaceable kingdom lost to time.

Tibet was the subject of two major Hollywood movies in 1997, *Kundun* and *Seven Years in Tibet,* with more films scheduled for 1998. (There is also a spate of books due.) These Hollywood extravaganzas provided plenty of impassioned argument in support of the view that China's role in Tibet is that of invader, occupier, and destroyer of Tibetan religious and cultural traditions—and that the Dalai Lama is the natural, traditional, and rightful leader of a Tibet that ought to be free of Beijing's yoke. These films also followed in the cultural footsteps of *Lost Horizon* and other depictions of Tibet as Shangri-la—a holy place of paradisiacal qualities—with the implicit argument that this out-

Would Einstein appreciate this confirmation of his theory? "The theory of relativity worked out by Mr. Einstein, which is in the domain of natural science, I believe can also be applied to the political field. Both democracy and human rights are relative concepts and not absolute and general. There can be discussion on the human rights issue, but I hope the West understands that our primary issue is to ensure that all Chinese people have adequate access to food and clothing." So said Chinese president Jiang Zemin in an interview with *The Washington Post* before his summit with President Clinton.

post of the earth closest to heaven has been destroyed by the heavy hand of Chinese Communism.

Although most Americans know little about the remote Himalayan land of Tibet, they believe they know enough to be outraged at China's treatment of the Dalai Lama and Tibetan Buddhists. Tibetan independence from China seems an appropriate and obvious solution not only to Americans and Europeans fascinated with Tibetan religion and culture but to many other friends of the Dalai Lama in India (where his government-in-exile is based) as well as in Japan and other Asian countries with significant Buddhist communities.

The Chinese see the issue in an entirely different framework. They believe the story they always tell about Tibet: That it has been a part of China at least since the 1300s. That the lamas and the Buddhist ruling elite of the past were vicious persecutors of the Tibetan people and treated them essentially as slaves; that China entered Tibet in the 1950s to liberate the Tibetans from this oppression and help modernize the region. That through a policy of "regional autonomy" Beijing has allowed for maintenance of traditional cultural and religious practices even while bringing modernization and some prosperity to an area traditionally feudal and poor. That although "excesses" occurred during the Cultural Revolution, contemporary Chinese policy has seen to the restoration of hundreds of temples and guaranteed religious freedom to Tibetan Buddhists. That the Dalai Lama has always been a tool of foreign enemies of China, from his flight from Lhasa with CIA help in the 1950s to the swelling movement he presides over today. And that the Tibetan independence cause has nothing to do with religious freedom and everything to do with foreigners who wish to destabilize China and dismember its territorial integrity.

Tibet has been of great importance to Chinese geopolitical strategy, serving as a buffer especially against India, with which China has a tense history including a mountain border war in the early 1960s and a long period thereafter during which China believed India was a vassal state of the Soviet Union and was being used by Moscow to "encircle" China.

Today's China, moving toward a modern, market-oriented society, could certainly do without the economic fetter of Tibet, which is extremely backward. And the old concern that an independent Tibet would be used to encircle or attack

Why Washington's threats of sanctions don't scare Beijing: Gary Hufbauer, a senior fellow at the Institute for International Economics and coauthor of a book on sanctions, notes that if economic sanctions weren't effective even against a tiny, impoverished nation like Haiti, they would be less so against a giant like China.

China is considerably less credible today, when Russia, India, and others in the region have also placed modernization and economy building at the top of their national agendas. So why won't China yield on Tibet?

First, because the sanctity of China's borders is a "motherhood" issue in Beijing, like Taiwan.

Second, there is general belief in Beijing that any move toward Tibetan independence could unravel much more of China and call into question China's commitment to other trouble spots, from Xinjiang to Taiwan. The anarchy and disunity that Chinese leaders fear so much could well be initiated by this trigger.

Third, the Chinese leaders believe their own story. They believe they have improved the lives of the masses of Tibetan people and have appropriately undermined the old slave and serf society run by the lamas. Especially because other important religious leaders (such as the Panchen Lama) have ultimately sided with Beijing, or at least entered into tacit complicity, the Dalai Lama appears to Chinese leaders as a rogue whose only strength is his foreign backing.

The issue of religious freedom, particularly for a people as apparently peaceful and noble as Tibetan Buddhists, is one that can capture the public imagination in the West as no ordinary economic or geopolitical issue can. Besides, in the Dalai Lama, the media in the West see a leader of the caliber of a Nelson Mandela or a Václav Havel: an individual through whom the cause of his people can be understood. "Hollywood's support for the Dalai Lama will make Tibet a far more important issue in U.S.-China relations than human rights in general, or trade disputes, or intellectual property, or any of the items on Washington's agenda," says one prominent American critic of Chinese policy. "With Tibet you have an issue that Americans care about."

With so many Americans caring about this once-obscure matter, Bill Clinton felt compelled to pay a brief courtesy call on the Dalai Lama during a Washington meeting between the lama and Vice President Gore in the spring of 1997, despite pointed Chinese warnings that even a presidential "drop-by" would undermine the new relationship Clinton was trying to establish with Beijing. "With only four million Tibetans and 1.2 billion Chinese, it is irrational for Americans to make this an issue," Jiang Zemin once confided to a former U.S. government official. Exactly such thinking shows how systemically different and at odds the American and Chinese ways of looking at the world really are.

Our forecast is for Tibet to become an increasingly hot political potato and for Beijing to continue to take a hard line despite growing public criticism. The surprise ending to this drama, however, will come in the next century, when the post-Jiang leadership has begun to tackle political reform seriously and new political institutions have begun to be created. Under those circumstances, it may be possible for a looser Chinese federalism to be established, especially for areas such as Tibet, Hong Kong, Taiwan, and Xinjiang. Policies could then be put in place and a compromise brokered that would allow the Dalai Lama to return to Lhasa at the end of his life, as the spiritual leader of a Tibet that was still part of the federal Chinese state, but that enjoyed genuine guarantees of religious freedom.

Japan Plays Its China Card

A central question about the coming Pacific era is the nature of the relationship that Japan will evolve with China. Japan is the already existing economic superpower in Asia. Its economy is seven times larger than China's, and even its military capabilities are more sophisticated in some respects. But almost everyone who counts in Japan knows that it is only a matter of time before China catches up in aggregate economic size and surpasses Japan in military firepower.

American Hawks and Engagers alike assume a fundamental identity of American and Japanese interests, hoping and indeed expecting that Japan will play a significant role to balance Chinese power in Asia and to participate in the fight for American economic and political values. It would certainly help the United States if the Japanese truly shared America's China policy. But as we saw earlier in discussing the "myth of the allies" (see chapter 5), this may well be a pipe dream.

The list of issues in the Sino-Japanese relationship is long and complex. "It is difficult to have a conversation with a senior Japanese policymaker for more than about thirty minutes before the conversation turns to China," reports a leading Asia correspondent:

Relations with Japan: "China and Japan can't afford aggressive competition. We are neighbors, and should be friendly. Still some hatred remains, and the Japanese look down on us. But if the leaders of the two countries cooperate and help each other, then it would be dangerous for the United States and the world would belong to China and Japan in the future."

—LI SANYOU
 CHAIRMAN, BEIJING HUI
 TAI INVESTMENT
 CONSULTING

The concerns in Japan run the gamut: A civil war in China could send tens of millions of boat people fleeing to Japan; a continued industrial revolution in China could raise global oil prices significantly and send acid rain and other pollutants across the sea to Japan; Chinese adventures against Taiwan or in the South China Sea could interfere with Japan's oil lifeline and cripple economies throughout Asia; an increasingly nationalistic China could seize Japanese islands and confront Japan militarily.[13]

The list could go, on with questions about the role China will play in the future of Korea and how increasingly close Chinese–Southeast Asian relations will affect major Japanese investments and trade relations in those countries.

Meanwhile, the "leftover questions from history"— Japan's wartime conduct in China, what politicians choose to say about that experience today, and Japan's current generation of school textbooks on this subject—all play a sensitive and easily inflated role in the intricacies of actual political and business negotiations, as well as in both sides' strategic thinking about the future of the relationship. In spite of this troubled political and military history, Japan is now the world's leading exporter to China and one of the few countries able to maintain a consistent trade surplus with the Chinese. Japanese business certainly understands the commercial implications of the China market. But even so, many in Japan retain a certain ambivalence about China.

Until fairly recently, Japanese companies were surprisingly slow to invest in China and to move Japanese domestic manufacturing to low-cost Chinese centers. Japanese executives resisted a full-scale plunge into the China market for many reasons. First, some felt unwelcome because many in China were nursing old wartime grudges (or at least manipulating those old wounds to seek greater benefits from Japan). Second, some Japanese businesspeople looked down on the Chinese and tended to doubt their work ethic, the quality of their work, and their integrity. Third, knowing China's turbulent history so well, many Japanese weren't yet convinced of China's long-term openness and stability. Fourth, some resisted the technology transfer Chinese authorities typically insisted on as part of joint-venture investments. (On this score, the Chinese found Americans much more willing to transfer technology and train Chinese managers in the United States, and therefore often held out for a better deal with an American corporate partner.)

When the rise of the yen became unbearable, Japanese corporate planners shifted gears and began moving manufacturing offshore. Even then, however, their first instinct was not to cost-shift right across the sea to nearby China, but to go to more docile countries hungry and thankful for the economic development (Thailand and Malaysia), or to America and Europe, where there was extreme political pressure to cut Japan's trade surpluses by doing more local manufacturing.

Japanese perceptions began to change in the wake of the tragedy in Tiananmen Square on June 4, 1989. With most Americans curtailing operations or scuttling investment plans as a result of Washington's condemnation of Chinese human rights policies, the ground shifted. Since neither the Japanese government nor Japanese companies have ever believed in imposing morality and ideology on business and commerce the way Americans have, it was convenient and comfortable for them to stay in China while many Americans packed up and left. The Japanese seized an element of comparative advantage over Americans in the race for China.

That watershed occurred just a few months before Japan's economic bubble of the 1980s was pierced. The postbubble economic strains in Japan have fundamentally changed its internal economic system and made its companies much more aggressive in seeking new opportunities and lower costs abroad. China is now seen as the natural frontier on both these points.

Today, the flow of Japanese investment into China is strong. New Japanese investment in China is now matching new American investment on a month-by-month level. Even with Japan's current fiscal and financial woes, outward investment to China remains strong. Eventually, Japan will likely be China's lead foreign investor and lead trade partner. One indicator of Japanese interest in China is that its officially registered press corps outnumbered even American media representatives at the Hong Kong transition ceremony in 1997.

Quality-conscious Japanese manufacturers that once mistrusted Chinese standards are now moving significant amounts of production to China. An electronics company

What's an army for, anyhow? In the rising tide of Chinese nationalism and anti-Japanese feeling that followed the Japanese building of a lighthouse on the disputed Diaoyu Islands in the East China Sea, Tsang Kin-shing, a Hong Kong legislator and leader of anti-Japanese rallies there, was quoted as saying, "The People's Liberation Army only attacks its own people. Why the hell don't they fight outsiders?"

that proudly insisted just a few years ago that its products were far too advanced to be produced in China now has more than half a dozen factories there. Areas in Guangdong province, Dalian, and other locations are beginning to resemble the industrial districts outside Tokyo or Osaka with their proliferation of Japanese corporate names. The Yaohan retailing chain, always an innovator, is moving its world headquarters to Shanghai.

Japanese companies, even if they are resented by the Chinese, are often better suited than their American counterparts for drilling down into the deep levels of doing business in China. Their time horizons for profitability are longer, their executives stay longer, and they are more willing to work in the remote areas where so much of the China market actually is. The cultures are not all that similar or harmonious, but much about China is more intelligible to the average Japanese businessman than to the average American.

The China trade is one of the answers to the question Japanese economic planners are asking themselves: How can Japan reinvigorate its economy? In Tokyo's Foreign Ministry as well as in the boardrooms of its companies, the talk is increasingly of China. Just as the United States has been perceived as the key strategic question for Japan in the last fifty years, so the agenda is shifting to China for the next fifty.

As Japan moves closer to China economically, it finds itself in multiple quandaries. The United States, for example, is constantly pressuring Tokyo to play a greater role in international peacekeeping and security affairs, while Beijing sees every Japanese step in this direction as a threat aimed at China and as a new sign that Japan has not changed its old militarist, imperialistic ways. In the near future, this issue will be a constant source of tension for Japan. Over the long term, Japanese policymakers will have to make some fundamental choices about whether they see their future as rooted geographically and physically in Asia in partnership with China, or in the virtual world of the developed Triad, with North America and Europe.

"In an unstable triangular relationship among Japan, China, and America, Japan will always seek to be in a twosome against a third," says Tetsuya Kataoka, a research fellow at the Hoover Institute who believes that

> **A fundamental lesson in political economy:** "Don't forget the possibility that the more organized and successful the Chinese become internally, the tougher bargain they will drive externally."
> —RICHARD MARGOLIS MANAGING DIRECTOR SMITH NEW COURT (CHINA)

American policies are helping to create a Sino-Japanese alliance.

In our view, the choice will not be black and white, all one or all the other. As Japanese business interests move deeper into China, the Japanese Foreign Ministry will be just as challenged as the United States is today to try to find a policy of engagement that doesn't come back to bite Japanese security interests with a dominant, aggressive China reared on Japanese investment and technology.

But Japan may well have to "tilt." We find it unlikely that Japan will see itself doing America's bidding in Asia. Rather, Tokyo's more natural tilt may be toward Beijing, where its greatest economic interests will lie. That would enormously complicate the task of making policy in Washington, as well as the business challenge facing American companies trying to compete successfully in Asia.

Food for Thought Provocation: When China's Military Is Modernized

In recent books about U.S.-China relations, several writers have described thought-provoking scenarios that ascribe a much greater likelihood to armed conflict and other apocalyptic confrontations than we think likely. Nevertheless, they are worth reviewing briefly.

Former U.S. secretary of defense Caspar Weinberger posits a nuclear-tinged U.S.-China conflict in his recent book, *The Next Hot War*. Weinberger extrapolates today's real tensions on the Korean peninsula into a highly improbable future war in which North Korea and China use nuclear and biological weapons to attack South Korea and American forces. In Weinberger's Hawkish tract, the Chinese–North Korean alliance ends up besting a no longer fully prepared U.S. military. Such a scenario is little more than futuristic fiction to prove Weinberger's thesis about lack of American military preparedness. Nevertheless, it reveals the fear and loathing that the idea of a strong China has evoked in American thinking.

Much more on point are the concerns raised by the Princeton University–based Asia expert Kent E. Calder, whose work has focused on economic-based conflicts, particularly over control of energy sources, and how these might interact

Warning bells: "In the Summer of 1995 the states of Asia have collectively seen something that most had considered a remote possibility: a China on the warpath. That vision will not be forgotten, no matter how many other things are smoothed over. Regional military budgets and military calculations will not be the same again. From now on the Asian security situation will increasingly resemble that of interwar Europe: a society of strong nation-states, increasingly well-armed and in possession of conflicting visions of the future, living in the shadow of an erratic and sometimes menacing power."

—ARTHUR WALDRON
NAVAL WAR COLLEGE

negatively with the trend toward arms races in Asia. Conservative estimates suggest that China's energy needs will double, at a minimum, over the next fifteen years as its economic growth and industrialization proceed. China has significant proven oil reserves as well as some promising fields in need of exploration, such as the remote and forbidding Tarim Basin. It is also a world leader in building hydroelectric power facilities and experimenting with alternative energy sources. The reality, however, is that China has become a net oil importer as demand races far ahead of domestic supply. This pattern will continue into the indefinite future. Extrapolate the trend, and, even adjusting for many variables and unknowns, you will quickly start considering the implications. Possible scenarios include:

- 1970s-style global oil shortages and price increases as China absorbs huge quantities of oil and bids up the world price.
- China's need to expand its production of nuclear energy, the most cost-efficient alternative to oil. That, of course, would entail serious global environmental and military considerations.
- A new set of military relationships might be fashioned between China and oil-producing countries in the Middle East. (Already, the Middle East is China's primary market for arms sales, aside from countries bordering on or near China.)
- More fiercely contested territorial battles over the Spratlys and other islands in the oil-rich South China Sea and over the shipping lanes of East Asia.

In Kent Calder's view, the dangerous equation that is unfolding in China looks something like this: Booming economies require more and more energy. China and other countries are only now beginning to see the growth of significant automotive industries and road building, which will add hugely to Asia's energy demands. As Asian economies grow and become rich—but also more desperate for energy—they will put more of their budgets into an arms race, perceived as necessary to control energy resources.

Just seven of these economies—China, Taiwan, North and South Korea, Japan, Russia, and Vietnam—have a total of more than 7 million men in uniform. Six of these countries

China's empty tank: A decade ago, China was a significant oil exporter, shipping nearly a quarter of its oil production abroad. By late 1993, however, it had become a net importer. Its dependence on world oil is likely to deepen: China's per capita oil consumption is still only $\frac{1}{60}$ of Japan's and $\frac{1}{180}$ of America's. Long-range projections show China may some day have 300 million cars on the road—which, if powered by traditional gasoline products, would need all of Saudi Arabia's annual production of oil to sustain.

—KENT E. CALDER
FOREIGN AFFAIRS

have nuclear technology already or else are close to being able to develop nuclear weapons. Observes Calder:

> The problem for Asian stability, growing with each barrel of Chinese oil imports, is now clear. It is the danger that China's attempts to safeguard its oil supply lanes and defend its historical "sovereignty" in adjacent seas poses for other nations of Asia, especially for Japan. China claims 80 percent of the South China Sea as territorial water; 70 percent of Japan's oil supplies pass that way.[14]

Calder's recipe of explosive ingredients is, indeed, a fearsome one. The reason we tend to fear the worst case less is that we anticipate these trends will unfold gradually, over the next ten to thirty years, with significant time for adjustment. Nuclear energy programs will expand, despite all the unfortunate dangers they entail. The Chinese and other Asians will learn to use energy as efficiently as the Japanese have over the last twenty years. (Japan, which has no domestic oil to speak of, now imports less per unit of economic output than the United States, a country blessed with rich energy resources.) New oil reserves will be found on Chinese territory and elsewhere. Technology for alternative energy will evolve.

During this time, we also anticipate that China will assert a gradually creeping hegemony over the region, a kind of Pax Sinica that will probably include a reluctant Japan within instead of outside its embrace. Eventually, it will include Taiwan as well. Armed-to-the-teeth opposing power blocs will therefore not be the long-term trend in Asia. This is not to say there will be no intra-Asian conflict over oil, territory, military power, or other issues. There already is, and there will continue to be. But on the whole, the military and security peace will be kept by the common bonds of a certain deference to China. This may not be what Americans would like, but it is the likely outcome over a long enough period.

We tend to agree with the way Singapore's Lee Kuan Yew has framed the combination of China's increased military strength with its minimal deployment. He once sketched this scenario:

> [By 2025] China has upgraded its armed forces, but still lacks the high-tech weaponry of the American Seventh

Oil, Japan, and China: "China is currently jousting with Japan for control over perhaps 100 billion barrels' worth of oil reserves in the East China Sea. Unless the United States backs Japan, China will score a dangerous victory, denying Japan the oil it will need to power its economy in future years."

—*THE NEW REPUBLIC*

Fleet. Its military-industrial complex, and research and development are far behind those of America and Japan. Although China knew that any significant increase in its ability to project its military might beyond its borders would alarm its neighbors, it could not resist the temptation to buy Russian arms in exchange for foodstuffs, textiles and footwear, and to hire Russian weapons scientists. Stalin turned in his grave. These weapons "encouraged" agreements of oil-sharing arrangements with ASEAN countries which claimed the Spratly Islands.[15]

In other words, Asia will be neither a zone of constant warfare nor an economic Eden free from military might. Instead, the continent will be at peace, but it will be a muscular peace with some of its terms set by China, and the rest set by balance-of-power politics that take into account American strengths as well.

The most provocative view among major scenario modelers is that offered by Harvard's Samuel P. Huntington, the architect of the "clash of civilizations" thesis. Huntington is both admired and vilified for his division of the postmodern world into groupings not by country but by ethno-religious and cultural "civilizations." In his cosmology, eight civilizations are challenging the West's vision of world order. The most significant and far-reaching challenges come from the Islamic and the "Sinic" civilizations (which, Huntington forecasts, will also grow closer together in the future).

For pedagogic purposes, Huntington puts forward a blow-by-blow account of how a global war among civilizations might break out in 2010, with the focus of this new world war being the confrontation between China and the United States. Like Calder, he sees the oil lanes of the South China Sea as the primordial ooze from which the next round of global conflict will arise. His world war will start over a move by China to assert full control over the South China Sea. Vietnam, backed by the United States, will lead in resisting China's hegemony. Some highlights from Huntington's 2010 scenario:

• As China invades Vietnam, Hanoi appeals to the United States for help. Washington agrees, calls for economic sanctions against China, and sends a carrier task force.

• The Japanese prime minister tries to negotiate a cease-fire. It fails. As the war escalates, the United States ignores

Japan's prohibition on using its bases for action against China; the Japanese then move to quarantine the bases.

• Chinese submarines, airplanes, and missiles launched from both the mainland and an already-integrated Taiwan inflict serious damage on U.S. ships and facilities in East Asia. As China scores these military successes, Americans begin to question the justification and expense of being in this war. Seeing which way the wind is blowing, the Japanese shift their position from neutral to cobelligerent. Washington withdraws all troops and establishes a blockade of Japan.

• Other powers are drawn in as well. Radical Islamic militants take over Persian Gulf countries and withhold oil from the West. India gets bogged down in a fight with Muslim Pakistan and Iran. Europe suffers strikes by Algerian- and Serbian-based missiles. Russia, afraid of total domination by East Asia, reinforces its troops in Siberia, which in turn brings on a successful Chinese invasion of all that was once the Russian Far East.

How would such a war end? Alternatives are mutual nuclear devastation, a negotiated halt as a result of mutual exhaustion, or the eventual march of Russian and Western forces into Tiananmen Square.[16] But Huntington's point in going to the trouble of depicting an extraordinarily improbable future scenario is not to forecast it but to prevent this particular conflict, or any similar "intercivilizational war," from happening.

While we find much illumination in the Huntington thesis, we believe it too extreme and too static in its separation of the civilizations. There will be huge conflicts ahead, but we don't believe the apex of the conflict trendlines will be a nuclear showdown or World War III. Wide, hot, world-threatening nuclear or conventional war could, of course, be a by-product of unsuccessful global accommodation to the rise of Chinese power. But in our view, it is certainly not probable.

The "clash of civilizations" we foresee between the United States and China, and between the West and Asia more broadly, is more complex, fluid, dynamic, and changeable than the vision depicted by Huntington. China is not merely rerooting itself as a great civilization around its Confucian core values—although, to an extent, that is happen-

China, too, has its Pat Buchanans: He Xin, literary critic turned futurologist and nationalist pamphleteer: "China should pay close attention to those countries either at odds with American interests or that could be potential strategic adversaries of the United States. We must understand that our enemy's enemy is our ally. China should try its best to find allies among countries and regions which could become the potential strategic adversaries of the United States, such as Germany and Japan."

ing. China is also absorbing much from the West and creating much that is new. On this point we agree with the China Bulls: the compulsion toward economic development, and the new interests modernity and prosperity will create, will prove sufficiently powerful to keep China's worst political and military instincts in check.

CHAPTER 16

Scenarios for the Twenty-first Century

The Overall Political-Economic Framework

The changes that will have the most impact on China, and will in turn lead China to have the most impact on the world, will *not* happen in the next five years. The real shape of China's new political-economic paradigm, for example, lies off in the more long-term future. "We are still in the very early stages of transition," says economist Fan Gang. "Five or ten years is not enough to make a comprehensive transition, not just in introducing the market but in culture, politics, and values." In the West, the new political and economic systems brought about by the industrial revolution took a century to implement and perfect in some places. "Even if we only take fifty years, it will be fast by comparison," says Fan.

As we indicated earlier, our long-term forecast is the creation and development of a "Confucian social market" (chapter 4). It will take at least twenty-five years to complete the infrastructure required for a comprehensive Confucian social market, although its embryonic forms are already visible now. The Chinese economic and political systems will become steadily freer and more modern over the next quarter-century. Both will evolve within carefully defined limits, however, and will not gravitate toward the full-fledged freedoms of the West.

On the continuum of "freedom" as Westerners think of it, the economic system will emerge as comparatively freer than the political system, although the economy will remain a mix of free-market, controlled-market, and nonmarket forces. The political system, meanwhile, will modernize in some key respects. But on the whole, it will remain an elite, authoritarian system that carefully keeps the most important levers of political and economic power in the hands of a single party's leaders.

Instead of an absolutist authoritarianism, China will evolve through a stage of what China scholar Robert Scalapino of the University of California–Berkeley has called a society of "authoritarian pluralism." As Scalapino explains:

> Under this system, although political choice will be limited and restrictions on various freedoms substantial, the perimeters of possibility will be repeatedly tested and will constantly shift according to circumstances. Increasingly, the state will share authority with other institutions. And the economy will evolve with an ever greater emphasis on the market, with the state's function that of planner and protector.[1]

This approach is not totally new. Within the picture just painted, one can imagine pieces that would be familiar in both Western and Eastern systems—part free-market, part corporatist, part state-planned, part democratic, part benevolent-despotic. The Confucian social market will have a strong resonance with Japan of the 1960s and 1970s, when government institutions set and tightly controlled the business and economic agenda.

Some of the Chinese state's intervention in the marketplace will resemble that of European social democracies. In pre-Thatcher Britain, in the France of de Gaulle as well as Mitterrand, in Germany and Scandinavia, governments have often believed in the ability of the state to own and run key industries. Although it would be easy to assert that China should learn from the mistakes of these European countries and leap to more market-driven systems à la Thatcher, the Chinese may need to pursue a lengthy transition, just as Europe had to do over the whole post–World War II period,

Which? Or both?
Consider these two headlines appearing on the same day in the two leading American print news publications: "China's Leaders Tighten Grip on Power," headlines *The New York Times*. "China's Communists Face Serious Threat: Creeping Irrelevance," says *The Wall Street Journal*. Are they irrelevant . . . or are they tightening their grip on power?

to arrive at similar conclusions—if indeed they prove valid for China at all.

Perhaps the Chinese vision of the future will draw the most inspiration from Singapore, which practices a highly advanced and particularly well-managed Confucian social market already. Singapore has a high standard of living, advanced technology, broad-based economic democracy (with almost 80 percent of its adults owning their own home), a skilled and educated workforce, global competitiveness, moral and social cleanliness, and big but efficient government programs. The tradeoff for all this is a one-party state, extreme official reactions to any opposition, and a muzzled media. In other words, Singapore's present is an attractive future for China.

Singaporean experts are currently building two massive new industrial parks from scratch in China, with Singaporeans consulting on everything from how best to layer the residential-industrial-recreational zoning to what health care benefits to provide the workers. Yet most Chinese understand that attractive as the Singaporean model may be, even this highly successful experience of a Chinese-majority society cannot be imported whole. Singapore is an island nation-state whose circumstances cannot easily be duplicated. Although Westerners never tire of criticizing the authoritarianism of Singapore's political system and the enforced orderliness of its society, both Hawks and Engagers would have to be delighted if the "worst" that could be said about China in the future was that it was a giant Singapore—a society that is enormously successful economically, threatens no one, and strongly supports many American ideals and goals.

The Great Wall in Ruins: The Search for New Values

It has become clear to most observers that a new political-economic framework cannot be put in place until a new set of values has taken hold. Marxism and Maoism have unmistakably outlived their relevance. Western values have relevance to some urban intellectuals but have also been the source of considerable disillusionment in light of how America's social system and American policy are perceived in

New values: "The replacement of authoritarianism by some form of democracy will require more than economic development. It will occur only after individual autonomy strengthens, the exaggerated sense of China's uniqueness breaks down, and today's youth become power-holders."

—ROSS TERRILL
FOREIGN AFFAIRS

China. National sovereignty and rampant materialism may be the only consensus values left. These, while useful, cannot be the basis—so everyone from government leaders to dissidents agrees—for guiding the fusion of the Chinese and the modern in the twenty-first century.

If China today is a group of players in search of a new morality play, there is as yet no convincing, powerful, unifying script, but its acts and scenes *are* being written, inspired by a mixture of ideas from Confucius to Toffler and Mao Zedong to Lee Kuan Yew. These ideas diverge as often as they overlap; all have "Chinese characteristics." Something of each will likely end up in the final draft.

Confucianism, as we have indicated, is coming back explicitly into official vogue. Never mind that the Sage has been seen by reformers and revolutionaries of the past 150 years—Mao Zedong chief among them—as the chief symbol of all that kept China feudal, poor, and backward. Jiang Zemin now fondly recalls Confucian influences in his upbringing and Gu Mu, the old cultural czar, calls Confucianism and Chinese traditional culture the "mainstay" of society.[2] Even the director Chen Kaige, whose film *Farewell, My Concubine* achieved great success abroad but was banned in China, is among the believers: "I hope one day Chinese will be both wealthy and in love with *li*"—a key Confucian concept that promotes obedience to a strict code of rituals and hierarchy.[3]

"What is the essence of modern Chinese philosophy?" asks the urbane, sophisticated Wang Xuebing, president of the Bank of China during his lunch with us. Wang has run the bank's operations in London and New York and is intimately familiar with Western economic and financial concepts. In his early forties, he is something of a wunderkind and was named an alternate member of the Central Committee in September 1997. Yet for all his worldly knowledge and his youthful outlook, his answer to the question he himself has raised to us is the traditional one: "Confucianism."

Confucian thinking, properly interpreted, could lay the basis for an economy that seeks growth and profit, but also makes a large accommodation to social, moral, and philosophical values. It further creates the possibility for despotic politics to be leavened with benevolent economics and for strong leaders and informal hierarchies to set accepted standards for public morality and behavior without much democratic oversight. The reason Confucianism is back not just at the official level but also among millions of ordinary people is that it provides a means of coping with moral confusion and rapid social change. Its canon—part religion, part ethical code, part social ritual, and part political philosophy—is malleable and can be cited by thinkers of many different outlooks and motivations.

The Party can promote Confucianism's ideals of "harmony" (i.e., stability). The upwardly mobile middle class can take inspiration from its commitment to education and sanctity of the family. Moreover, as the scholar Wm. Theodore de Bary suggests, now that Marxism is no longer available to do the job, Confucianism can guard the gates against Western decadence.[4] Liberal thinkers, on the other hand, can point out that most of Confucius's precepts concerned how princes should govern in a moral, just, and upright fashion.[5]

China undoubtedly will not return to classical Confucianism, however. A more rounded and updated synthesis is needed if the philosophy is to move beyond simply being a prop of support for whatever dynastic establishment holds power. At the intersection of Confucian tradition and the asceticism and egalitarianism of the Communist past, for example, lie what might be called new-paradigm values, an ethos emphasizing self-sacrifice for the sake of the greater good, building a strong new China. It also incorporates a real sense of "get-off-your-butt, dirt-under-the-fingernails, Jeffersonian everyman-ism," to use China analyst James Stepanek's phrase. These new values are particularly strong among Chinese baby boomers who survived the romantic and rebellious years of the Cultural Revolution.

Equality and fairness are important elements in new-paradigm thinking. Even among those who are very well off there exists an unmistakable desire to achieve fairness in the long term, or at least avoid the severity they associate with Western laissez-faire capitalism. "The whole Chinese philosophical tradition is that you do something for people—you don't just exchange value without also some fairness being there," says Zhang Wei, chairman of East China Holdings in Shanghai.

"The job of economics is not to make a bigger cake but to divide it fairly," says Qin Xiao, a veteran of years of manual labor in the countryside during the Cultural Revolution who

One of China's famous young computer hackers on his life and times: "We're not living in a moral society or a moral age. As the old saying goes, 'Only when you have enough to eat and wear do you think of frugality and shame.' We're at the stage of accumulating capital. We're going through a baptism of blood and fire. It's far too early to get onto a moral high horse. Anyway, I'm sick of being poor."

—SANG YE
WIRED

is now the president of Citic, China's most prestigious and diversified investment company. "We are the pioneers for the world for those people who want to create a new thing. We will encourage collectivism more than individualism. We will pay attention to equality and fairness, and encourage people to live in a simple way."

All forms of Chinese and foreign religions and beliefs are also gaining popularity in the search for values that can counter mass cynicism, corruption, and the chase after money. Temples and churches of all descriptions have re-opened in recent years, and those who attend are not just the elderly (as was the case in the 1970s and 80s) but the young, the fashionable, the intellectual elite, and the business class. Islam, Buddhism, Taoism, and a host of folk religions are flourishing. No faith, however, is growing as quickly as Christianity. Despite the concerns of Americans who argue that China is brutally repressing its Christian population, three new officially tolerated Christian churches open every two days.

Religion will continue growing in the coming decade. Not only does it fill a moral void but the government, which once derided it as the opiate of the masses, now considers that normal religious practices, by improving social and personal morality, can enhance rather than impede socialist nation building—as long as the teachings include a healthy dose of patriotism. Aware, no doubt, of the temporal conditions placed upon his house of the spirit, a pastor of the Beijing Christian (United) Church told a visitor, "A Christian church that is not patriotic is not true to its religion."[6]

Economic change and the vibrant mix of new thinking have helped create a fundamental shift in the values of individual Chinese from fatalism to choice, submission to assertion, and, very tentatively, from obligations toward rights. This shift will gather momentum in the decades to come. Just because it is going in a direction with which Americans can identify, however, there is no evidence to suggest that Western values are the goal. "Capitalism" and "democracy" remain words associated more with lifestyles than a realistic understanding of how these Western concepts work in practice. There is simply no underlying habit of individualism, personal rights, or devotion to the principle of liberty, although the Western practice of these ideas is widely admired by many Chinese intellectuals.

"People want to believe in more than just money. Religion will come back, as will an adapted, modern version of Confucianism. You have to have a moral foundation, something to build on, something to dedicate yourself to. We are looking for a system where we can ride the train together as ordinary citizens rather than rely on the government for all our inspiration."

—ALLAN H. LIU
PRESIDENT, CHINA RETAIL FUND

316

Interestingly, there are some surprising parallels between the evolution of Chinese values and what is happening in America and the West. Americans are unconsciously drawing closer to some Asian or Chinese values, even as the Chinese try to incorporate ours on a selective basis. The "market" has never been held in higher esteem in America. But a small counterrevolution is now under way, raising very Asian questions about the limits and failures of unfettered capitalism and global free markets. "A Helping Hand, Not Just an Invisible Hand" was the headline over a *Business Week* article that outlined the case, increasingly being made, that self-interest and laissez-faire policies may destroy capitalism from within.[7] Investor George Soros has been making the same point, as have many figures in the Clinton administration.

Asian societies can keep wages low by preventing workers from organizing, limiting government welfare benefits, and placing the primary responsibility for individuals' behavior on the family. American social problems are seen by some as weakening the country's competitiveness. Thus, in the name of "international competition," the sociologist and China specialist Richard Madsen points out, American companies are breaking the power of the unions, Congress is dismantling the welfare state, and individual liberties are being curtailed to better fight crime.[8] Madsen makes the case that a global shift is taking place from Western liberalism to Asian communitarianism, "a shift as profound as that of the seventeenth century, when the hegemony of Catholic Spain and Austria gave way to that of a Protestant, and eventually increasingly secularized, Northern Europe." This is so because East Asian countries seem better equipped to handle the moral balance between rights and responsibilities and the individual and society than we have been in postwar, early Info Age America. To use but a few small examples, Americans widely approved of Singapore's caning of an American youth convicted of hooliganism. And how many American parents wouldn't agree with the Chinese newspaper that characterized video games as "electronic opium threatening to enslave our country's youth"—and in their hearts slightly envy that society's ability to do something about it?[9]

In this context, it perhaps becomes easier to understand the thinking (if not to agree with the conclusion) expressed in an article that appeared not long ago in *People's Daily*. "The

Simple idealism won't work: "Five years ago, people were very idealistic. They said, 'I can change China! I can change the political system!' But recent polls show people now feel they were not being realistic enough; they have the big picture but don't know how to get there. So now we have to help them find the vocabulary for change. So they can do something on their own, to think independently, and to face everything by themselves."

—LI ZHIPING
EDITOR, *THE YOUTH LIFE WEEKLY*

basic cause of the crisis of contemporary Western culture," the article argued, "lies in the incompatibility between science and religion. If Westerners' morals and their value of life were based on another humanism rather than on Christianity, the above contradiction would not arise. The right solution is Confucianism, because it is a non-religious humanism that can provide a basis for morals and the value of life." Pointing out how East Asia has been able to modernize quickly while avoiding the defects of the West, the article concludes that "As this culture better suits the future era, it will thrive particularly well in the next century and will replace modern and contemporary Western culture." [10]

The Chinese have faced their contradictions for centuries and have continually found ways of adapting to them. They will again. This time, however, there may not be the single set of official values that has both graced and haunted so much of Chinese history. As Walt Whitman, that most American of poets, once wrote: "Do I contradict myself? Very well, then I contradict myself. (I am large. I contain multitudes.)" [11] The same might be said by a poet writing about today's China.

Postcommunist Politics

Slow progress toward political change continues to bubble up from the grass roots. In a country where the Communist Party once appointed every official from the very top to the very bottom of the hierarchy, some 10,000 village and local officials have now been elected by direct popular vote, increasingly in contested elections. Bo Xilai, the mayor of Dalian, a major industrial port city in China's northeast, was appointed to his current post by the Party, like all other big-city mayors and governors. But the forward-looking Bo has gone on the record as calling for mayors and other high-ranking officials to be elected by direct popular vote of local constituents. Bo is handsome and charismatic, not to mention well-connected. (He is the son of one of China's veteran revolutionary leaders, former Politburo member and vice premier Bo Yibo.) He has amassed a solid track record in delivering foreign investment–fueled growth and prosperity to Dalian. He is the sort of younger leader capable of introducing direct popular voting for offices like mayor. But he

Not yet perfected: Tian Jiyun, a vice chairman of the National People's Congress, electrified political circles by publicly proposing multicandidate elections to the posts of vice premier and premier. "Some people do not support this idea," Tian said, "but it is precisely the requirement of a democracy. The way candidates are now elected is not yet fully perfected."

will bide his time until such a reform becomes possible. It is not today.

Under Qiao Shi, the National People's Congress had taken some steps to break away from its rubber-stamp origins— proposing innovative regulations to curb abuse by corrupt officials, voting *against* officials nominated by Jiang Zemin, and criticizing government economic reports as too optimistic and insufficiently substantiated. Those Americans who talk offhandedly of China as one of the world's most repressive dictatorships should consider this recent news account of an NPC session:

> Normally considered the party's lapdogs, deputies openly questioned the government's line that although the microeconomy had plenty of problems (crumbling state industries, banks at risk), the macroeconomy was now healthy. How, inquired some, could the macroeconomy be healthy if the microeconomy was sick? Was something being withheld? Were there echoes of the falsified optimism at the time of the disastrous Great Leap Forward?[12]

Even today, Chinese leaders are increasingly concerned with cultivating public support and popularity in ways that are traditional in the West but new in a country where the leaders' constituency has been confined to Party loyalists. An extra allocation of bank loans to industry in the run-up to the 1997 Party Congress was viewed by one Hong Kong economist as the "Leninist equivalent of willing a pre-election boom."[13] Throughout Chinese society, tolerance of differing opinions is growing, as are the social and legal mechanisms for protecting some individual rights. Yet these steps toward the development of some quasi-democratic institutions are offset to some degree by the chilling effect of rising traditionalism, conservatism, and neonationalism.

Leading Communist Party officials convened a forum in late 1996 to support Jiang Zemin's drive for a "spiritual civilization." Item one on the agenda was to denounce foreign influences such as the "Western concept of human rights." Yet aside from its clarity in foreigner-bashing, Jiang's concept of "spiritual civilization" remains a vague appeal to the traditions of the Party and the socialist state— hardly what China needs to move forward.

On paper, the political system remains committed to Communist goals and beliefs no longer supported either by the

"For 4,000 years we had family structures and a little bit of law. Creating law is a tradition we just don't have. But old customs and traditions are now returning to China—family values, Confucius, invisible rules of conduct. This is more important than laws written by the State Council."

—JIMMY LAI
HONG KONG
ENTREPRENEUR

society as a whole or even by the 56 million members of the Communist Party. The old theories are highly explicit; most Chinese over forty know them intimately. But no new ideology, or even any new theoretical premises, have been made explicit. Such discussion is deliberately avoided in order to keep the society focused on economic growth and unity and prevent new rounds of political conflict.

It is our forecast that political reform will remain a largely unaddressed imperative over the next several years. It will take some type of crisis around 2002–2005 to begin to break down the walls of denial. "Explosion" is a metaphor; what actually happens may not even be visible to the outside world. It could be an elite conflict—a vote in the NPC, a provincial governor defying the central authorities, a dissenting report at a Party meeting. More likely than a mass uprising bringing mass democracy to China, is a step resembling the breakdown of the divine right of kings in medieval Europe. Nearly eight centuries after the Magna Carta, China's new elite may succeed in requiring the senior Communist leaders to agree to a formal system of power sharing, oversight, and resource allocation. It would be the Chinese equivalent of English noblemen forcing King John to spell out some explicit rights and powers for those who were noble but not the king.

On the relationship between the individual and government: "The experience of the Cultural Revolution has already proved that chaos only leads to retrogression, not to progress, and that there must be good order if we are to move forward. Under China's present circumstances it is clear that without stability and unity we have nothing. In their absence, democracy and the policy of letting 'a hundred flowers bloom and a hundred schools of thought contend'— among other things— are out of the question. Since our people have just been through a decade of suffering, they cannot afford further chaos and will not permit it to occur."

—DENG XIAOPING

The Communist Party: A New LDP?

Japanese political analysts may wonder what Chinese theorists would see in Japan's long-ruling Liberal Democratic Party (LDP) as a model. Today the LDP's hegemony has broken up, its leaders are too weak to implement meaningful change, the party is riddled with scandal, and its once-tight bonds with key Japanese voting blocs have frayed. But the 1960s, 1970s, and 1980s were a different story. And it is that history Chinese intellectuals and think-tankers are thinking of when they suggest the Japanese LDP is at least a kind of model for the Chinese Communist Party.

"I cannot see China ever embracing a two-party system like American Democrats and Republicans, or a multiparty parliamentary system as in Europe," says one Chinese intellectual who has written unpublished papers on how to reform the Communist Party. "But something like Japan's LDP could fit the Chinese situation."

The LDP was essentially a one-party government that stayed in power for more than three decades. Japan, of course, had other parties. But the LDP dominated Japanese politics and managed the partnerships and interactions of business and labor with government. Debates, disagreements, and political reshufflings were all looked after behind the LDP's closed doors. Organized factions operated inside, vying with each other for control of the party apparatus. But all this took place within the context of a single party, which put on a face of unity before the Japanese public. Corruption was endemic, but well concealed. And the LDP got the job done, building a modern Japan with an efficiency rarely seen in modern world governments.

One-party systems abound in Asia, even in countries that are economically advanced and politically democratized in some respects. Singapore's ruling party goes to enormous lengths to keep even a single opposition member out of the parliament, even though the opposition is incredibly weak. Lee Teng-hui's KMT in Taiwan, while facing challenges now from multiple parties, is the inheritor of the single party that has ruled Taiwan since Chiang Kai-shek fled there in 1949.

In China, we foresee political reform after 2002 leading to several critical changes in the Communist Party structure:

• Large parts of the traditional Communist program will be formally jettisoned and a new, specific program adopted that addresses China's needs for development, modernization, and economic democracy. In essence, the new Party program will spell out what it means to be both Chinese and modern and will promulgate the goals and methodology of a Confucian social market system, although obviously not in those words.

• "Communist" will be dropped from the Party's name in favor of something more nationalistic and more oriented toward economic development.

• Party organizational methods and rules will be altered to abandon the traditional principle of "democratic centralism" and effect some working form of sustainable inner-Party democracy that allows for open debate. From this will flow the creation of organized factions that will stay together in one party, run by elites, no doubt, but yet more responsive to the needs of China's different constituencies than they are today.

Give them a break: "If China is expected to undergo, in the space of one or two generations, the modernization process that evolved over a century and a half in Britain and America, should we be really surprised that their social fabric is under stress?"

—PAUL KENNEDY
PREPARING FOR THE TWENTY-FIRST CENTURY

New Institutions and Organizations

Alongside reform of the ruling party will come the development of some of the new political institutions for which a society as big and complex as China is now starved:

• Some new, real political parties may be allowed to play a small role in governance at the national level. Formally, there is already a Chinese People's Consultative Congress, an "advisory" body comprising parties left over from China's united-front days fifty years ago. Jiang Zemin has already reached out to some of these groups and the parties may get a stronger (if still minor) voice.

• Direct elections will continue to be introduced at more levels of local politics. For the past several years, contested elections have been held for leadership posts at the village level. More recently, they have been instituted at the next rung up the Chinese political ladder—the township. In the first decade of the next century, direct popular elections for more important posts—at the city and provincial level, for example—may begin to replace the current practice by which appointed officials dispatched by Beijing fill these posts. NPC Vice Chairman Tian Jiyun, considered among the most liberal of Chinese leaders on the Politburo, has given several speeches in the last two years calling for wider use of direct, multicandidate elections not only for the NPC itself, but for other deliberative bodies and even for China's most senior state government positions. "Some people do not support this idea," he notes with understatement. "But it is precisely the requirement of a democracy."[14] It is possible that some kind of direct-election system may *eventually* develop, even for national offices including the presidency or premiership. But the candidate-selection system at the national level will remain highly controlled, as will the campaign process—just as they do in Japan's electoral system.

• State government institutions such as the National People's Congress will continue to become more independent of party leadership as the present generation of power-holders retires. In particular, the verbal genuflection by today's leaders toward the rule of law will be actualized. This will be made manifest not only in more written laws—China has developed plenty of laws in the last twenty years—but

322

through a more independent judiciary capable of more impartiality than is the case today. The "executive branch" — the president, the State Council, and the Politburo — will still be far more powerful than any other branch, but the NPC and the judiciary will provide more inclusionary and diverse politics, as well as the rudiments of checks and balances.

• Mayors and governors will appoint more active advisory councils. This will afford elites other than party members a political voice and a way to participate in politics and governance. As in Europe's early bourgeois revolutions and as in Hong Kong today, councils will be convened at various governmental levels and will include representatives of different functional occupations and interest groups.

• Interest groups, trade groups, and other voluntary associations (to use de Tocqueville's term) are emerging. These loosely defined nongovernmental organizations (NGOs) now number some 180,000; they include associations, foundations, societies, and chambers of commerce. Although they are nowhere near as independent as similar organizations in the United States, they are increasingly autonomous. Some are seen by the government as social organizations that can help devise solutions to emerging problems and amass the resources to implement those remedies, especially since many are supported by financing from abroad.[15] To consider one narrow band: the growth of the middle class is creating, among other phenomena, consumer-protection groups. The China Consumers Association received about 200,000 formal complaints in 1996, and individuals are suing companies and local governments for everything from malfunctioning products to municipal services withheld. Foreigners are not immune — indeed, their deep pockets have made them targets. "Foreign companies must be clear that their business in China can now be impacted by interest groups the same way as the rest of the world," warned Xavier Delacroix, head of crisis management for Edelman Public Relations in Beijing.

• Business has its own interests and concerns, and is making growing claims for attention. Although they are not independently organized, numerous management associations, commercial federations, entrepreneurs' clubs, and so on could evolve into significant forces in the future. One of the most important developments in recent years was the launch in

Preserving stability by pushing for high-speed economic growth is "a very dangerous trap," said Wang Shan in *Looking at China Through a Third Eye*, a highly controversial, widely circulated neoconservative critique of Deng Xiaoping's reforms. "High-speed economic growth will intensify society's inherent contradictions and give rise to new problems with which the Chinese Communist Party is completely unfamiliar."

1995 of a new bank committed to making loans to private entrepreneurs.

• At another organizational level, large-scale enterprises such as SOEs and even the much smaller Township and Village Enterprises (TVEs) will become recognized as new kinds of de facto governments, responsive to the interests and needs of their stakeholders. This will be especially true of the TVEs, which are basically rural enterprise collectives whose profits not only generate the income of the local citizenry but also provide for infrastructure improvement, telecommunications installation, education, health care, and other local needs.

• Finally, individual businesspeople will be heard through a variety of channels; they will be delegates to the NPC and to provincial and local legislatures and councils, for example, or advisors to government bodies at various levels.

These new institutions, organizations, and reforms have a common theme: giving greater voice to more people slowly, gradually, and with constant emphasis on responsibility, order, and stability. It is a political course that will lead to more openness and transparency but does not seem likely to lead to direct democracy, at least not in the next two decades. A Politburo-type group will still monopolize national political power in the future. Yet the members of that Politburo will have many more people to hear from in setting policy, and many more to account to in implementing it.

Toward Chinese Federalism

One of the most important aspects of China's version of political reform and democratization will be the devolution of more power from the center to the regions and localities. This will also be how the system appeases any separatist impulses.

"In the next century, China could move toward a federal system," says He Di, a "fourth generation" intellectual and scholar of Chinese party history. Strong regional leadership and local initiatives, characteristic of federalism, can certainly exist within a framework of national obligations, responsibilities, and standards. Federalization, He Di believes, is in line with the worldwide trend toward smaller, leaner organizations connected through loose networks, rather than through heavy-handed formal ones. Like a good modern corporation, He thinks, China should flatten its hierarchies.

If Beijing could be sold on the virtues of a federal system to address the problems of uneven regional development and the special characteristics of particular regions, then the framework would be in place to solve several other crucial questions, including how to allow greater autonomy for Buddhists in Tibet, Muslims in Xinjiang, the rich metropolitan areas of Guangdong and the coast, and other areas that are chafing under central control. We foresee a situation in which some elements of federalism will be put in place during the first wave of political reform. But it will take at least a quarter of a century for a truly federal system to emerge. When that has happened, China will be ready to reunite peacefully with Taiwan—and Taiwan will be ready for that remarriage as well.

The New Chinese Corporation and the Future of the State-Owned Enterprises

Business and economic development will change China more directly than politics will. If you want to get a sense of the scale of emerging Chinese corporations, consider the plan of Shanghai's city fathers to establish several giant enterprises that will be listed among the world's 500 top firms by the year 2000. In addition, they plan two or three "superlarge" enterprises, each with annual sales of RMB 100 billion ($12 billion). And then there are the plans to set up ten large enterprises, with sales of RMB 10 billion ($1.2 billion) and fifteen enterprises with sales of RMB 5 billion ($600 million).

The management issues for such firms will be extraordinary. But while these companies will be striving for profit, the direction of their management will also be an inherently political question. Consider the views of the urbane and thoughtful president of one of China's most experienced and innovative state-owned companies. China will never adopt Western-style market capitalism wholesale, he says. Even so, he fears that there is too much infatuation with the powers of the market and that not enough thought is being given to the "special characteristics" and institutions that must be blended with the market economy to make it work in China:

Hand in hand toward the (long-term) future: "Economic prosperity and political democracy do tend to go hand in hand sooner or later. But in China's case, the correlation could be much lower than in other countries—and it could take much longer."

—MA GUONAN
SENIOR ECONOMIST,
PEREGRINE BROKERAGE

325

If we just rely on the market we will never catch up to the West in technology and modern economics. In China we need to "organize" the market to make it work in the most innovative and rapid way. We will also have to tolerate some inefficiencies in the market, in order to maintain a sense of fairness and equality in China.

This fourth-generation thinker also questions the Western correlation of democracy and economic development:

Democracy is not needed to promote economic growth. Americans may think there is only one model, but there are many. China is an agriculturally based society, not a trading society like Europe. Agricultural people don't like risks. They stick to routines and leave responsibility for major developments to the emperor. The emperor should build the dams, for example. And if he does, he will be judged as a good emperor. The Chinese need a very good emperor—this is how they treated Mao and Deng.

Companies should serve the interests of the nation, not just those of a small number of owners. "*More* collectivism and *less* individualism" is this executive's prescription.

The "Question of Ownership"

One of the oddities of contemporary China is the oft-discussed "question of ownership." As the state-dominated economy moves more toward the market and allows room for an increasingly vibrant nonstate sector, who actually owns the assets? If a new enterprise was started by a town, or a collective, or a state bureau, and it becomes phenomenally successful, who benefits? How should management in restructured SOEs participate?

China is trying every way possible to avoid straightforward privatization and the handing over of assets to individual, private entrepreneurs. But some "market measures" will be used to force SOEs to compete more directly with each other. Compensation may be tied more closely to performance, and minority stockholders (both domestic and foreign) may be introduced in many cases to reduce financial dependence on the state.

One way to bring greater market forces to bear may be to allow mergers, acquisitions, and bankruptcies among SOEs.

Is this "socialism with Chinese characteristics"? As a new wave of mergers and acquisitions hit China's State-Owned Enterprises in late 1997, one company director explained the process in a way that might be more familiar to J. P. Morgan than to Mao Zedong. "We look at it like this: The big fish eats the small fish and the small fish eats the shrimp. You either buy or you are bought. It's a law of economics."

This is already happening. In Shanghai alone there have been over 600 mergers, although most of them have involved small companies. We anticipate the government will also continue and intensify what has already been done on an experimental basis: trimming the fat off SOEs by restructurings in which healthy units are spun off to draw foreign investment and joint-venturing, while the troubled rump of the business is merged or allowed to go bankrupt. This is also being done with successful results. The first decade of the next century may be China's golden era of mergers and acquisitions and initial public offerings, as the old SOEs are restructured and recapitalized.

In many other cases the major state-owned banks holding nonperforming loans to SOEs will be permitted, and possibly even encouraged, to convert this debt into equity. This could allow the banks to take an aggressive role in operations, just as lenders do with their nonperforming loans in the United States. To the degree that tough choices and harsh measures are needed to keep SOEs functioning, it might be politically preferable for the bank, rather than the government itself, to be seen as the prime mover—even if the major banks are all ultimately owned by the government anyway.

In some cases—where SOE workforces are small, or where economic losses are particularly hopeless, or where the managers are out of political favor—Beijing may bite the bullet and shutter the enterprise. In the first year of a recently passed bankruptcy law, more than 2,000 companies went out of business. Most generally conformed to guidelines that allow for bankruptcy protection after a company has suffered losses for three years and been unable to make debt payments for two years.

Ten to fifteen years from now, economist Fan Gang suggests, Beijing may have scaled down its SOE ownership to a hard core of 1,000 or so of the largest, most strategic firms. (Even a government that desires to get down to 1,000, however, may still end up making exceptions for hundreds more—just ask anyone who went through the U.S. military's base-closing process.) Although the number of industrial SOEs will be whittled down to a fraction of today's 118,000, they could still represent as much as 20 percent of total industrial output. Whatever course is taken, it will still leave the Chinese state in control of a very wide berth along the country's economic waterfront.

Public companies going public: Of the 630 companies listed on China's two stock markets, 85 percent are state controlled. "In the future the State will likewise retain majority interest in key companies, unless, of course, they go bankrupt," says an official with the Commission on Restructuring the Economy.

Meanwhile, other important changes will take place. One of the most important is the rise of workers' retirement and social security programs, which are just now being funded for the first time and will become major sources of investment capital in the future. They will create institutional savings and investment vehicles not unlike what we have started to see in the United States—a kind of pension-fund capitalism.

Although central planning and micromanagement are being phased out, Beijing, as well as provincial and regional authorities, will still *lead* the development process. From moral persuasion to tax breaks, from regulations to political campaigns, the Chinese state will actively macromanage the economic infrastructure.

Arguing about money—lots of money: Moody's Investors Services to China: Your banks' credit ratings must be lowered because of their exposure to bad loans from State-Owned Enterprises. China to Moody's: This reflects either your "ignorance" about the current situation in China or an "intentional distortion of the facts."

One can imagine Chinese equivalents of Japan's MITI or Singapore's Economic Development Board actively targeting industries and regions for investment and development, orchestrating joint R&D, coordinating technology transfer programs from foreign companies, and training the right cadre of skilled workers. Much of such a body's work will also be social and ideological, however, as China tries to ensure some evening-out of the development curves in cities and countryside, coastal areas and hinterlands, and otherwise tries to use economic-development tools to address social problems. At the moment, for example, a drive is on to encourage enterprises, both domestic and foreign, to locate in the hinterlands of China and begin to make up for years of economic neglect during which the high growth has been in coastal cities.

Even several decades from now, ownership of most Chinese assets will still be by collective units. Individual entrepreneurs will be able to build sizable companies; China will have plenty of personal millionaires and a collection of billionaires as well. But the bulk of total assets will be owned by the state, or by the workers of an enterprise, or by the community surrounding the enterprise, or by a university, an army unit, or another collective institution. By the time China's fourth generation is retiring and the fifth generation is taking the reins, the vast pension and savings assets of the Chinese nation will have evolved into a huge institutional-investor community with many of its portfolio allocations made by state agencies and state-run companies.

Big Versus Fast

One of the complexities of the U.S.-China relationship over the next generation grows out of the different strengths and weaknesses the two countries bring to the table of global competition and cooperation. The strengths and weaknesses are little debated in and of themselves. Everyone generally agrees that the United States is the world's leading society in generating new software technology, for example, and that China's disciplined, educated, low-cost labor force is a major advantage in developing manufacturing industries. The real questions lie in what values to assign to these different strengths and weaknesses and how rapidly those values will change, given differing assumptions about the development of the "new economy," the globalization of business, and the ascendancy of the Information Age.

China is already strong, and is gaining strength day by day, in a variety of traditional industrial categories where the United States once led the world. But while mass manufacturing may constitute a good economic development strategy for China, the kinds of power assets from which it derives— a huge population, abundant cheap labor, extensive natural resources, and so on—are deemed by some noted experts (particularly in the West, but also in Asia) to be of declining relevance to future prosperity, wealth, and global leadership.

By contrast, although the United States has lost much of its formerly world-leading manufacturing muscle in recent years, a large contingent of economic futurists modeling the twenty-first century assure us that America has in place the most critical assets for generating future wealth and power: a thriving advanced technology sector; excellent universities and research centers; sophisticated service businesses; vibrant financial markets; and a socioeconomic infrastructure that disseminates information widely, eliminates regulatory barriers, encourages free trade and open markets, and values and promotes innovation, knowledge, creative freedom, flexible systems, customized goods and services, and quick decision making.

As an "emerging" market, China is, not surprisingly, undeveloped and weak in these areas. But even a much-changed China is unlikely to define itself around these values. The Chinese, like many others in Asia, believe they can obtain a sufficiency of what they need technologically

An economy with Chinese characteristics: "The lesson I have learned from studying Western economics and applying it to China is this: In China, our resources are limited, even as our demand is unlimited. The job of economics in China, therefore, is not to make a bigger cake—since its size has been predetermined—but to divide it fairly. The Western way does not make that possible for China."

—QIN XIAO
PRESIDENT, CHINA INTERNATIONAL TRUST & INVESTMENT CORP.

and economically to compete successfully in the twenty-first century without significantly enlarging the scope of personal or business freedom—certainly not enlarging it to the degree seen in the United States. The Chinese are not unlike the Singaporeans, the Japanese, and many others in Asia, all of whom want for their own countries the levels of technological advances, creativity, and innovation for which they admire America. But few are likely to rewrite their social contracts to end up with what are seen as the dreadful results of too much democracy in America: violent crime, erosion of the work ethic, welfare dependency, sexual promiscuity and public indecency, collapsing institutions, government and social leaders who get no respect, and a people who are becoming almost ungovernable.

Ever since the beginning of the reform process in the late 1970s, the Chinese have routinely told all who would listen that their ultimate goal is a society that incorporates the positive features of Western societies *without* the negative features. In official pronouncements (as well as in about 99 percent of unofficial commentary), the Chinese have been crystal clear about the fact that they do not desire to remake their society in the West's image entirely. Rather, the future they wish to see will be a blend of West and East, capitalism and socialism, traditional and new, a market-driven economy and a centrally planned one. This is the meaning of the oft-heard phrase "a market economy with Chinese characteristics."

Some Chinese economists and think-tank specialists say that in the late 1980s, there was some support at very high levels for an ultimate solution to the problems of Chinese socialism by means of radical privatization and unleashing the full power of market forces quickly. But if that was ever the goal—and it is doubtful a Western-style market was ever anything more than an academic theory briefly debated in the inner sancta of Chinese power—it is not now. Most knowledgeable Chinese believe Russia's flirtation with shock therapy and radical privatization to be an unmitigated disaster; they have no appetite to repeat the experience at home.[16]

In the 1980s, *The Third Wave,* by American futurist Alvin Toffler, swept through China in translation; many intellectuals were captivated by the idea that China might skip the "second wave" stage of industrial development and move

The point is, China really is different: "Let us assume that the students had carried the day at Tiananmen and they had formed a government. The same students who were at Tiananmen went to France and America. They've been quarreling with each other ever since. What kind of China would they have today? Something worse than the Soviet Union. China is a vast, disparate country; there is no alternative to strong central power."

—Lee Kuan Yew
   Senior Minister of
   Singapore

right into the new, advanced industries of the Information Age. Then-Premier Zhao Ziyang read the book and spoke on several occasions of the need to prepare China for the third wave.

Today, of course, Zhao is out of favor and so is the third wave, at least in official circles. Jiang Zemin is the ultimate second-wave Communist industrial man, trying to hold big China together as the world's largest unit of second-wave organization. Chinese leaders talk about building a new automotive industry in China and recreating all the other global manufacturing industries as well. Says a senior Chinese economist:

> We discovered we cannot skip stages. Here and there we can move more quickly to incorporate advanced technology. But in a country of more than a billion people, and especially with our huge peasant population, we cannot suddenly emerge overnight as an advanced technology-based economy. To put it simply, we need to industrialize.

Toffler fears that the retrograde forces of the second wave are destroying China's third-wave potential. "To try to build a new, huge, mass second-wave industrial economy today is a prescription for disaster—socially, politically, economically, environmentally, and in every other way," he says. But in Beijing, the national leadership is betting heavily on building just that second-wave economy. If successful, it will be a key part of China's competitive advantage in the world. It could also turn out to be China's Achilles' heel.

In any event, some third-wave pockets persist and grow. Drawing on great cultural strengths in mathematics and physics, plus plenty of help from ethnic Chinese innovators and investors from all over the world, China is developing islands of world-class third-wave technology in numerous fields. Andy Grove, CEO of Intel, is probably not just being paranoid when he predicts his toughest competition in the future will come from China. From these third-wave embryos, Toffler believes, the ideas and leadership for an appropriate Chinese development model will come.

Impact of the third wave: "Although I think the bond between people here is stronger than most imagine, technology will nevertheless destroy some of our traditional values—which I personally would like to see destroyed. For example, feudalistic ideas such as that, as the son or daughter of a bigshot, you are entitled to certain privileges. Or ideas like the boss having to take care of his workers. Bondage cannot be the goal. The boss and the employee must be equal."

—SENIOR CHINESE GOVERNMENT POLICY ADVISOR

"Connectivity": A Vision of China's Future Shape

One argument often cited by Bears and Hawks is that China simply cannot tolerate the growing polarization between the wealthy coastal provinces and the rust belt of the northeast or the backward hinterlands in the west. As evidence that this disparity (and the potential for fragmentation it brings) will only get worse, they point to such places as Guangzhou and Shanghai and note that while their economic ties to Beijing are shrinking rapidly, a third of their economy is supported by world trade and foreign direct investment (and the share is growing). The Hong Kong dollar circulates widely in Guangdong, as does the Taiwan dollar in Fujian.

We would argue that this particular contradiction is not, in fact, likely to pull China apart. Almost no secessionist movement in the world is based primarily on economic differences. Whenever countries have broken apart, the active ingredients have been racial, religious, ethnic, or linguistic differences. These are, of course, exacerbated by economic disparities. But when one looks at the passions that have been aroused in Bosnia, Chechnya, Northern Ireland, Quebec, the West Bank, and on and on, one sees that the role of economics in these conflicts is secondary at best.

Huang Yantian, featured on the cover of an American business magazine as the "Red Capitalist of Guangdong," is the chief executive of the Guangdong International Trust & Investment Corporation (GITIC), the leading provincial-owned diversified investment company in China's richest province. Huang tells of a period a few years ago when he and his crackerjack team of young, ambitious Chinese deal-makers signed a "deal a week" with foreign partners from McDonald's to General Electric. We ask him if there is much desire among the Cantonese of Guangdong to split off and form their own nation-state. After all, Guangdong would rank fourteenth among world nations by population and, with a GDP about the size of New Zealand's, step into the top third of the world's countries if judged by total economic output.

"Such an idea may be very logical to Americans," says Huang. "But we don't really think about it or hear about it in Guangdong province. We are importing labor from poorer areas of China. We are using our capital to invest in other areas of China. We are selling our products all over China. We obtain power and resources from across our provincial borders. It is to our benefit to be part of a big China."

Bo Xilai, the energetic young mayor of Dalian in China's less developed northeast, has a similar message. A tour of the new industrial area of Dalian had reminded us of Kenichi Ohmae's observation that its success is "driven not by clever management from Beijing but an infusion of foreign capital and the presence of foreign corporations." Ohmae, a leading proponent of the theory that nation-states will be superseded by independent economic regions, used his visit to Dalian to buttress his assertion that "There is no country called China. There's really only a dozen independent islands without much interaction."[17]

Mayor Bo, however, paints a different picture. As someone who has personally helped lure some 2,500 foreign companies to the region, he told us, "My vision is to provide the environment of a developed country with the prices of a developing country. Dalian can move in that direction only because it is a product of a national economy and national policies." China as a *national* entity is, for Bo Xilai, not a barrier but a major source of competitive advantage. It is Beijing that builds the infrastructure, secures the common defense, represents the collective interest in international commercial and political negotiations, and provides the symbolic cultural glue that holds the country together.

Despite reports of border conflicts and tariff barriers and other protectionist measures at the provincial and local levels, the bigger news confirms the points made by Huang Yantian and Bo Xilai. Chinese provinces in the Maoist past were encouraged to be self-sufficient units, ready to be cut off from one another if a foreign invasion came. But today, provinces and regions are becoming increasingly interdependent.

One way to understand this process of economic development is to think of China's economic geography as a kind of building using post-and-beam construction methods. Nine "posts"—call them regional economic zones—are being put in place that support three economic "kingdoms." Each kingdom is at its own level of development, so that national policies must be driven as much by development needs as by geography.

Level One includes Greater Beijing (including Tianjin and

The culture gap: Chinese history has produced no single written character to mean "rights," as in the kind of political or human rights that have slowly evolved in the West since the days of the Magna Carta. Of the two characters that make up the phrase *quan li,* one means "power," the other means "benefit"; in other words, rights are benefits to be conferred by those in authority, rather than innate as the U.S. Declaration of Independence states.

the provinces of Hebei, Henan, and Shandong); the Yangzi Delta (including Shanghai and such important regional cities as Wuxi, Suzhou, Hangzhou, and Nanjing as well as the provinces of Jiangsu and Zhejiang); the Midcoast (Fujian, with the cities of Fujian and Xiamen, the area around Wenzhou in Zhejiang, and the "Greater China" economy of Taiwan); and the Gold Coast (including, for example, Guangdong, Hainan, Shenzhen, and Hong Kong). These four "posts" are the most advanced, and are generally pursuing export-led growth strategies reminiscent of Asia's "little dragons" of the 1960s and 1970s.[18]

Level Two includes the Mid-Yangzi (the area that will benefit most from the Three Gorges project, it includes the major cities of Wuhan and Changsha and the provinces of Hubei, Hunan, Jiangxi, and Anhui); the Sichuan Plain (anchored by Chongqing and Chengdu), and Dongbei (the northeast industrial cities of Dalian, Shenyang, Changchun, and Harbin). Especially in the northeast, these three "posts" have substantial, already pre-existing industrial bases rooted in the state enterprise system and attracting them to import-substitution growth strategies.

Level Three includes the Southeast Border (Kunming and the provinces of Yunnan, Guizhou, and Guangxi) and the Great West (the huge east-west stretch between Xian and Urumqi). These macroregions of the interior face severe transportation and geographic constraints that limit their access to markets, although the Southeast Border provinces have built an independent trade network with the countries of Southeast Asia, and the Great West is building similar ties with Kazahkstan and other republics along China's western border.

While each of these levels to some degree stands alone, and will grow at different rates, none is isolated. This is what the devolution-equals-fragmentation equation misses: the overwhelming number of beams that bind these "posts" and regions together, such as government and cross-national investment, commerce, rivers, railroads, highways, and airports. And, most of all, mutual need and a common vision of what it means to have a strong, unified China.

A third of Guangzhou's economy may be transnational, but another full third is tied directly to the interior (in Shanghai's case, the proportion is 50 percent). Just as inland provinces have opened offices and factories in places like

Vanity, vanity, all is vanity: Off to a fast start in trying to catch its long-established rivals, Mary Kay Cosmetics announced it had sales of $2.4 million in 1995, and had reached its 1996 target of $10 million by the end of August. "We're way over capacity right now; our existing cities are growing like crazy," said Cecilia Yang, vice president of sales and marketing.

Shenzhen, Pudong, Qingdao, Tianjin, and Dalian, companies in these cities and zones have in turn invested hundreds of millions of yuan in developing sources of raw material in inland areas. Guangdong, woefully short of energy, is investing in electric power generation and transmission facilities under the banner of the South China Joint Hydropower Company, a joint effort that includes the provinces of Guizhou and Yunnan. The truth, which they realize, is that they all need each other to survive individually.

Any government wishing to remain in power must continue to raise the Chinese people's standard of living. To accomplish that, different policies will have to be devised for different areas, involving different levels of state direction. In the "hinterlands" that economic policy is probably going to have to be more state directed, with massive investment in infrastructure projects, industrial development, and means for dealing with the inevitable dislocation of the peasantry and rural population. Making a virtue of necessity, the coastal regions will be left more to their own devices on the assumption that even as investment declines, these areas are basically on course.

Pessimists will continue to look at the devolution of power and say conflicting interests are driving China apart. We disagree. The pronounced movement toward internal economic integration does not preclude regional separatism. But, with flexibility being shown by the center, it makes such separatism much less likely. When we look at China's sense of itself, at its ability to adapt to the changes so far, at its culture, at the psyche of the people, we see a good case that it can absorb many shocks and pull together. We believe there will be a new meeting of the minds, a confluence (over time) of grassroots demands and top-down imperatives that forces the old pyramidal command-and-control structure to yield more fully to a flexible process. China's leaders will realize that a one-dimensional, overcentralized, hierarchical, and rigidly bureaucratic state cannot get the job done and that it must be replaced by a less centralized, more networked, more heterogeneous environment.

This economically diverse, evolved network will create the space for different political forums, different kinds of experiments with different levels of autonomy and political democracy, and different degrees of market influences. In

China's coming impact on capital markets: "I can imagine a day when China will have a huge current account surplus and will recycle its capital throughout the Asian region. Perhaps China's savers will bail out the Japanese pension system."

—ENZIO VON PFIEHL
SBC WARBURG

short, a new interdependence will set the stage for the new federalist political institutions of the future.

Perhaps the best metaphor for understanding the evolving political economy of China is one adopted from technology: connectivity. It may seem as though China's provinces and regions are like separate computers with separate operating systems. But like everything else in China, they are now being actively networked. By 2024 China's structure will be more flexible, federal, and adaptive, amply able to stand up to the challenges of twenty-first-century global competition. It will be a looser kingdom.

Of course, it will also still be the Middle Kingdom.

Opportunity knocks: Over the next decade, says the World Bank, East Asia will need to invest up to $1.5 trillion in infrastructure. Half will be spent in China.

The Three Gorges Dam: A Study in Environmental Politics

The Yangzi River gorges have always been a source of great imaginings. Chinese legends tell of witches, demons, gods, and giants who inhabit the enormous limestone cliffs that plunge straight as daggers into the swirling torrent. Every rock and cliff has a name, every bend and eddy its epic story. Poets, artists, and writers have celebrated its views and tried to explain its hold on the consciousness. The famous eighth-century poet Tu Fu found "cloven gorges" and a "misty void." John Hersey was spellbound by the "supernatural and malevolent atmosphere."[19]

The gorges have also inspired engineers and planners who dreamed of taming their destructive floods, and rulers bent upon the vanity of grand monuments in the tradition of the Great Wall and the Grand Canal. Sun Yat-sen is credited with being the first to propose a dam, in 1919. Formal planning began under Chiang Kai-shek as early as 1932. Mao Zedong was its modern champion, even writing a poem to launch the revised version of the project in 1956.

Official groundbreaking occurred in 1994, and the largest hydroelectric power project ever attempted in the world—generating fifteen times as much as the standard nuclear power station—is now well under way, with completion scheduled for 2009. Benefits in generating electric power and providing efficient inland water transportation are potentially enormous, as is the dam's potential to end the extremes of the flood cycle.

But will it ever be completed? As far as engineering and construction go, we do not doubt China's ability to see the project through. But if the dam is viewed as a metaphor for the overall economic and political transition China is trying to achieve, significant doubts arise.

The Three Gorges Project (TGP) is a particularly good vehicle for understanding the evolution of political discourse in China. It belies the image most outsiders have of a country where the will of the Party translates into the unquestioning action of the government and people. Hundreds of government agencies, bureaucracies, and academic bodies have time and again participated in detailed studies on all aspects of the megaproject since the mid-1950s, but planning has consistently been interrupted, not only by ideological struggles and the chaos of the Cultural Revolution but also by prolonged debate over its feasibility and political and environmental impact. After all, if fully implemented, the TGP would create a reservoir approximately 400 miles long, permanently submerging about 150,000 acres (including 160 towns and sixteen archeological sites) and requiring the resettlement of 1.3 million people.

At first the debate went on mostly behind closed doors in the upper levels of government. Former premier Zhao Ziyang is said to have opposed it when he was still governor of Sichuan in the early 1970s. By the mid- to late-1980s, however, the project was openly questioned by scientists, engineers, economists, and journalists all over China. A top-level Political Consultative Committee submitted a negative report in 1985. Ten experts withheld their signatures from a 1987 feasibility study in which 400 other experts signaled their approval of the TGP. Most visible of all was Dai Qing, a journalist who gained fame in the early 1980s with her exposure of some of the Communist Party's dirty linen. In early 1989 she published a collection of anti-TGP essays, which gained a wide audience.[20]

In April 1989, the government responded to this wave of criticism by announcing that a decision on building the dam would be delayed five years. But two months later, soldiers opened fire on demonstrators in Tiananmen Square and all dissent, including opposition to the dam, was stifled. Dai Qing was thrown in jail for ten months (ostensibly for her

Power shortage:
China's Ministry of Power says the country needs to install power plants generating 15,000 to 17,000 megawatts each year for at least the next decade. That is the equivalent of each year duplicating all of Southern California Edison's plants, which supply all of southern and central California. Or of producing as much new power over the next decade as the United States generates annually today.

support of the students but also for her outspoken opposition to the dam). Then, in 1990, Premier Li Peng, who had been in charge of the project since 1984, held a meeting to revive the planning.

The debate soon reemerged, however, and it was louder than ever. Opposition reached a climax in 1992, when the project was submitted by the government for presumed rubber-stamp approval by the National People's Congress. Instead, many delegates voiced frustration about being denied access to reports critical of the project and demanded a floor debate. When hushed, one delegate stormed out, shouting, "The NPC has violated its own law!" After order was restored and a vote taken, an unprecedented one-third of all delegates voted no or abstained.

International environmental and human rights groups have been particularly loud in their condemnation of the project. The United Auto Workers tagged it a "Chinese Love Canal, Chernobyl and Three Mile Island rolled into one."[21] The Sierra Club calls it an "environmental, economic and political nightmare" and a worldwide symbol of "unsustainable development."[22] Human Rights Watch/Asia has raised concerns about reports of "forced labor" and described the relocation effort as "blatantly coercive."[23] This moralistic chorus, plus a host of solid financial, technical, and environmental questions raised by experts in China and around the world, led the World Bank and Ex-Im Bank to withhold financing from the project.

At least for now, the government pushes ahead. Madame Qian Zhenying, a longtime leader in China's energy sector, is as passionate about the project as the critics are in trying to stop it. She told us in an interview, "The governor of Sichuan told me, 'I give my regions to you,' because he knows these people will be lifted from poverty to middle-class status in their new houses." But the cost? The annual investment needed from now until completion is "only a small fraction of our GNP." And the environmental impact? "There is strict environmental monitoring and the project will end up reducing pollution [because it will decrease reliance on coal power]," says Qian.

While it may seem out of touch to Western environmentalists and even cavalier to those involved with human rights causes, Qian's position has validity in the context of a government trying to implement Deng's aphorism that "Devel-

Two-track China:
"China today is characterized by a mismatch of economic hardware and political software. The constituency for real change can't do much in politics—so they go into business."

—RICHARD MARGOLIS
MANAGING DIRECTOR,
SMITH NEW COURT
(CHINA)

opment is the only theory." When a country has been as poor as China, and Yangzi River floods have regularly killed thousands and devastated millions of acres of critical farmland, there is an unassailable logic and even an urgency behind projects that will help hundreds of millions, even if a million or so are inconvenienced in the process. China's past experience with huge public works projects—the Grand Canal, the Yangzi River bridge, the endless terracing of hillsides—came at a cost, but all provided big, demonstrable benefits. Like the building of the transcontinental railroad in the United States, the turning of pristine American rivers and canyons into grand hydroelectric, irrigation, and recreation projects, China's vast development projects contribute to the greater good. Is China to be denied development now that the West already has it?

The project and the conflict of views about it demonstrate that China is, by fits and starts, becoming a "normal" country, where pressure groups form and use the media for maximum exposure, and the political system must accommodate them if it is to survive. What is particularly striking to those of us familiar with the China of the 1960s and 1970s is the degree to which individuals—even those in "responsible" positions—are speaking up. A group of fifty-six prominent personages, including the former ambassador to the United States, have formally petitioned Jiang Zemin to hold off so the cultural relics can be saved.[24] The project's leading sedimentation analyst, who lets himself be quoted by name, reveals to *The New York Times* that in his opinion measures to control silt will fall short. An environmental official in Chongqing also openly tells the press, "There are a lot of problems that have to be solved, and the leaders aren't thinking that far ahead."[25] And Dai Qing regularly travels the globe, winning a fellowship at Harvard, accepting awards from environmental groups, and giving interviews in which she continues to speak out vigorously against the dam.[26]

We believe the government will not formally back down. Indeed, the main riverbed has now been successfully blocked; Li Peng, the dam's "godfather," remains at the center of power, and the government is hailing the project as their monument to a new and powerful China. At a ceremony at the dam site in November 1997, Jiang Zemin even claimed that success achieved in the first stage of the project was

China's strategic view? "Be so subtle that you are invisible. Be so mysterious that you are intangible. Then you will control your rival's fate."

—SUN TZU
THE ART OF WAR

proof of the superiority of the socialist system. But the debate about the dam's safety and environmental impact continues to escalate, just as the cost will over time. (For example, while the government now budgets $5,000 per person to be relocated, that figure could easily double as the dam approaches completion.)

Here is a positive resolution we think has a chance: In 2003, when initial powerhouse operation becomes feasible but the water will have risen only to its first (of three) stages, there is already a scheduled hiatus. A period of thorough observation and evaluation is to follow. By then, "only" several hundred thousand people will have had to be resettled instead of the full 1.2 million. Leaders less personally identified with the project will have come to power and prominence. An economic slowdown will have made the cost of bringing the project to full utilization even more problematic. But some of the smaller hydroelectric projects already under construction for key tributaries to the upper Yangzi will be ready to operate. These dams will cost less and yet produce more electricity and provide more precise flood-control benefits. The government will still have accomplished its goal of taming the Yangzi, but the full scope of the TGP as it is now on the drawing boards can be quietly be scaled back. A second-wave dinosaur will have been transformed into something approximating a third-wave dragon. In the process of averting the worst environmental and investment mistakes, the political process will also have opened up somewhat—and it will have "worked," Chinese style.

CHAPTER 17

Fast-Forward to the Future: The Superdragon in 2024

To summarize what we believe lies ahead, we invite you to fast-forward with us into the future and imagine the world in 2024, a Year of the Dragon on the Chinese calendar. China is no longer an "emerging market" but has fully emerged as the first newly minted all-around comprehensive superpower of the new millennium. Consider just a small sampling of new realities that have appeared and evolved between tomorrow and the end of the first quarter of the twenty-first century.

• China has stayed the course of economic reform—although not without sharp veering and pendulum swings—and built an economy approaching America's in total size. After some dips in growth rates in the early years of the century, and a serious recession in 2004 that caused American Bears to question all assumptions about China's continued growth, China by 2024 has arrived at near parity with the United States in total economic output. In the 2030s, it will emerge as the biggest single national economy in the world.

• The rise of China, like the rise of most great powers in previous eras, has provoked intense contradictions and challenges to the existing arrangements of global wealth and power. The United States and China are now the two leading superpowers of the twenty-first century—the two countries with the greatest concentrations of political, economic, military, technological, and cultural power. They, and the world, have gained when their interactions have been positive.

• Unfortunately, there was more confrontation than cooperation during the 1998–2005 period, and many opportunities for these two uniquely complementary societies to draw closer were squandered. A pernicious on-and-off economic and political cold war dominated the early years of the new century.

• After 2005, the cold-war atmosphere began to die down in the United States, thanks to a combination of greater liberalization in China, increased Western confidence that China would not emerge as a strategic threat, and more evident economic benefits to American business.

• China by 2024 is the world's largest producer of most manufactured goods, and the world's largest market for many types of goods as well. The Chinese market has been central to the strategies of many American and global corporations. It has acted as a kind of competitive proving ground, with enormous stakes in terms of market share for the winners and an endless stream of headaches and failures for the losers. The ability to manufacture successfully in China and to capture significant chunks of its domestic market has radically altered the map of global corporate competition in businesses from telecommunications to automobiles to aircraft. The China trade has created millions of jobs abroad and has had a dramatic impact on the fates of hundreds of global corporations.

• However, China's continuous growth as a manufacturing-led economy has put constant downward pressure on the wages of workers and the profits of corporations trying to manufacture for the global market in Europe, North America, and Japan. Consequently, China policy has been the subject of intense debate about "globalization" all over the world. A fierce protectionist current centered on limiting trade with China has risen up throughout the developed world.

• Although Chinese per capita income and output are still only a fraction of Western norms, China's aggregate size gives it enormous bargaining power in the world economy. China is the heart of an increasingly wealthy and powerful

Asia. It is the leading expression of the global shift in the concentration of wealth and power from West to East and from the developed world to the developing world. The world's leading economic powers now include not only China but India, Brazil, Mexico, Indonesia, and Russia. Meanwhile, the traditional "advanced," developed democracies (America, Japan, Germany, etc.) are still strong and rich but have become minority forces in the total structure of global output, trade, and wealth creation.

• The Chinese have evolved their own new political-economic paradigm. It draws on elements of modern, Western-style marketplace capitalism, but it incorporates the impulses of China's 5,000 years of cultural history and, reflecting the legacy of fifty years of Communism as well, still reserves great power for a highly interventionist, activist, agenda-setting state. Despite outward trappings of Westernization, the Chinese have not become all that much "like us" politically or culturally.

• For the sake of developing this new Chinese political economy, however, significant reform and democratization of the Communist Party and Chinese institutions have taken place. In the early years of the twenty-first century, pressure from new stakeholders in China's increasingly prosperous economy and emerging fifth-generation leaders at last forced a showdown over the long-delayed matter of political reform, with positive results.

• China is a more open society than it used to be, but it is still not democratic in the Western sense. Multiple elite factions and trends vie for power; these often represent legitimate broad-based interest groups but still generally carry out their debates behind closed doors. Big government continues to regulate and plan—excessively by Western standards—and to operate in an authoritarian and still largely opaque manner.

• Ideology is still a powerful force, although the content of that ideology is nationalism and economic development first, socialist principles second. "Economic democracy"—by which the Chinese mean growth and development of the national economy—is valued much more highly than personal freedom.

"Remember that famous Tiananmen intersection where that lone Chinese dissident stopped a tank in June 1989? It is now overseen by Ronald McDonald, who sits on a bench there outside the world's biggest McDonald's bearing silent testimony to this new age of mercantile diplomacy. Like it or not, the nightmare of Tiananmen has given way to the daydream of an Asian gold rush."

—Thomas Friedman
The New York Times

343

• Practically every dire scenario once predicted by Western pundits has actually befallen China, but less apocalyptically than was imagined. Social contradictions between the new rich and the new poor have exploded from time to time; armies of migrant laborers have rioted; bankrupt SOEs have collapsed; regions have grabbed powers formerly reserved for the center. Waves of xenophobia have arisen, threatening to drive foreign investors out of China. Overplanned infrastructure projects and top-down efforts to create new cities, industries, and financial markets have sometimes proven embarrassing failures. Ecological disasters have occurred on a substantial scale. Nevertheless, the basic drive for economic progress has been so strong that the center has been able to hold China together, muddle through on most issues, and experience the highest overall average economic growth rates in the world.

• Despite its rich energy resources and traditionally massive agricultural economy, China has become heavily dependent on imported oil and food. This need to be a working part of the global trading system has restrained some of the most nationalist and xenophobic politicians in Beijing, but it has also encouraged the Chinese leaders in their efforts to play global trade partners against each other. China has re-established its leadership of the old "nonaligned" movement, cultivating close ties to other Asian countries and Middle Eastern oil suppliers as a bulwark against overdependence on the West.

• The Chinese may still not be very rich "per capita," but coastal cities like Shanghai, Guangzhou, and Beijing are thriving metropolises, as modern and advanced as any in Asia. Inland cities such as Wuhan, Chengdu, and Chongqing are now also nodes on the network of China's advanced economy, the result of policies launched in the 1990s to begin steering investment, which previously had been confined largely to the coast, into the interior and even the remote hinterlands. China is now dotted with islands of prosperity—cities and regions that are themselves the size of whole Asian economies like Korea or Thailand.

• The market capitalization of the Shanghai Stock Exchange trails the New York Stock Exchange but has surpassed London, Hong Kong, and Tokyo. On the *Fortune* list of the 500 largest global corporations, nearly a hundred are China-based or closely connected to China. The *Forbes* list of the world's richest individuals includes not only the great Overseas Chinese family fortunes of the past decades, but many new ones made inside China and on its periphery.

• Following the difficult but ultimately successful 1997 absorption of Hong Kong, Taiwan has now also been reunited into a federalized China, adding an additional slice of GDP as well as valuable human resources for the management cadre necessary to develop advanced industries and services.

• An advanced, high-tech, third-wave component has developed both within China's economic system—newer, more entrepreneurial businesses—as well as within its geography, such as in the high-growth area of the south. But most economic growth has been accomplished through massive traditional industries. Chinese authorities have only minimally moved away from their past attempts to restrict the flow of knowledge and information. They have continued to think in the second-wave industrial vocabulary of the twentieth century, focusing on building large industries and huge infrastructure projects while organizing the country as a bordered nation-state. Indeed, even as China partakes of and benefits from the new "networked" global economy, it is a force pulling the world back toward the traditional politics of nation-states.

• The contradiction between China's growing global clout and its relatively low average living standard has helped sustain a "poor, backward, and exploited-by-foreigners" self-image. Beijing's leadership utilizes the politics of domestic populism to pursue protectionist, neomercantilist, and neonationalist strategies. China has consistently used its aggregate economic might—and the ability to open or close its market to others—as leverage in making demands on foreigners and in bootstrapping its domestic living standards. This economic nationalism has been contagious in Asia and throughout the world.

• After thirty years of intensive capital formation, based on very high savings rates, China is beginning to emerge as a significant exporter of capital. The 1990s' rush of foreign investors into China is now mirrored by an expansion of China-based companies throughout Asia and the world.

Asian values:
"Spreading wealth evenly in a market economy is far more difficult than spreading poverty evenly in a command economy."

—MALAYSIAN PRIME MINISTER MAHATHIR BIN MOHAMAD

• Sino-Russian relations became a dramatic new issue for American Hawks in the first years of the new century. We heard much scare-mongering about the specter of a new Sino-Russian alliance, with the Russians bartering advanced weapons for consumer goods and raw materials. No real Beijing-Moscow alliance was consummated, however, despite healthy trade relations and China's emergence as the major economic force in the Russian Far East.

• The new "Chinese dream" has come true for hundreds of millions: owning their own homes and apartments. Infrastructure was a huge business in China during this entire period, drawing in massive foreign investment as well as technology and expertise. But beyond the airports, highways, and power generation systems that needed to be built, much of the continuing economic boom was driven by the construction of improved housing for the chronically underserved Chinese masses. This was paid for thanks to China's world-leading household savings rates. As in America after World War II, modern housing fueled the Chinese consumer economy. As during the recent history of Singapore, home ownership was utilized as a social tool to make more people stakeholders in the society and to foster stability and social harmony.

• China, although it still doesn't wish to acknowledge the fact, has become Asia's dominant hegemonic power. Japan, after trying for years to tilt toward the West, has become increasingly enmeshed in the Chinese economy and the Asian sphere. Nearly every pan-Asian corporation thrives or fails based on its connection to China. In almost every Asian political capital, ruling elites seek to accommodate, appease, or assuage China as necessary, having witnessed more than one occasion in the early twenty-first century when China demonstrated its willingness to use force against its neighbors.

• With aligned Japanese-Chinese interests as its fulcrum, with more than a dozen "little dragon" Asian economies connected to China by a thousand threads, and with Overseas Chinese communities and corporations an integral part of the story, the twenty-first century is, in fact, turning out to be the "Asian century" that many have long forecast.

Will we need to learn Chinese? "In the next century . . . Chinese will become very important. The Internet will flourish in China in Chinese. Chinese will be used for communication between Chinese provinces, which are as populous as European nations like France and Germany, and between cities like Shanghai and Hong Kong. There is no need for the Chinese to use an intermediate language like English. Of course, if you want to communicate between Shanghai and Los Angeles, you may need to use English. But there the advantage will be with whoever is bilingual, not with those who only know English."

—GEORGE YEO
SINGAPORE MINISTER OF INFORMATION

Looking Back from 2024

Looking back from the vantage point of 2024, Western historians may conclude that the ascendancy of China and a China-centered Asia has not proven to be quite the us-versus-them, all-or-nothing, good-versus-evil, war-or-peace matter it might have been in an earlier era. Yes, the process has been studded with polarization and confrontation, a cold economic war, and even some significant military conflict. Yes, the world's adjustment to the entrance of a billion and a half Chinese into its economy has been complex and at times traumatic for outsiders, just as it has been for the Chinese themselves.

It would be fair to say that China's growth has severely tested the limits of flexibility and resilience in the world order of the new millennium. It has brought forth a torrent of Joseph Schumpeter's "creative destruction." It has exacerbated many of the difficult challenges American and other policymakers in the developed world already faced—and has generated many new ones.

On the one hand, the process has scarcely resembled the idyll imagined in the 1990s by Pollyanna pundits who saw China chiefly as a giant market for Western goods and as a place to derive Western corporate profits. Indeed, their vision of China as a society that, having quaffed the once-forbidden taste of Coca-Cola, would make a beeline for Western-style liberal democracy has been stood on its head. Instead, China has set a new standard for other parts of the developing world in showing how a high degree of consumerism can coexist with a high degree of authoritarianism.

Yet on the other hand, China has proven the Hawks of the late twentieth century wrong: it has not developed as an overly aggressive force in the world and, on balance, has contributed more to the global order than it challenged.

The global economy and political structure of the twenty-first century have proven sufficiently big, dynamic, flexible, and self-adjusting—even if just barely—to absorb an empowered China and a greatly enriched Asia alongside the other major global centers of power. Napoleon's two-hundred-year-old warning that when the Chinese dragon awoke from its slumber it would shake the world has at last been proven true. China has revolutionized itself and shaken the world, but managed to do so without triggering either a

The father of containment got it wrong: "China doesn't matter very much. It's not very important. It's never going to be powerful."

—GEORGE F. KENNAN, 1949

347

domestic or an international apocalypse. Perhaps the most apocalyptic scenario—of China and the West becoming real adversaries, fighting economic and even military wars—has been averted at least partly because political leaders in the United States and China have actually listened to business leaders and others involved in building the relationship on the ground.

It is said that the world as a whole is shifting its emphasis from politics to economics and that businesspeople in many parts of the world today are often more powerful and can do more good—or at least do it faster—than politicians can. If so, then China traders and the heads of foreign companies doing business in China, along with their counterparts in the emerging class of Chinese entrepreneurs, managers, and businesspeople, will prove to be new kinds of economic heroes. They will have used the powerful leverage of common economic benefit to defuse the highly explosive power of contradictory politics, ideology, and belief systems.

We can also hope that leaders and decision makers in many countries will read and think about the many important books, articles, papers, and other discussions that dramatize the stakes involved in U.S.-China relations and can help convince both sides to think more carefully about the many preferable alternatives to the current collision course. It is a central feature of our forecast, in fact, that when historians of our children's generation look back from the vantage point of 2024, they will conclude that the worst dangers of an institutionalized U.S.-China cold war were skirted because concerned citizens in both countries became aware of them, and acted before it was too late.

Although the apocalypse will have been avoided, those same historians will certainly note that the global political economy of the twenty-first century has been radically altered as a result of China's ascendancy. The very contours of global life in the postmodern era will have been deeply affected by China's course—and by how the international business, financial, and political communities respond to it. The competitive fortunes of companies, the living standards of countries, the political and philosophical systems of societies—and the lives of millions of people—will all be profoundly different because of how China has developed and how Americans have interacted with that process.

Modern China's founding father saw it coming. Sun Yat-sen, founder of the first Chinese republic in 1911, once said: "The world has greatly benefited by the development of America as an industrial and a commercial nation. So a developed China with her four hundred million of population will be another New World in the economic sense. The nations which will take part in the development will reap immense advantages."

PART V

BEYOND THE COLD WAR

One who knows the enemy and knows himself will live to fight a hundred engagements. One who does not know the enemy but knows himself will sometimes be victorious, sometimes meet with defeat. One who knows neither the enemy nor himself will invariably be defeated in every engagement.

—Sun Tzu

We often hear that the U.S. wants engagement with China. But I'm not sure whether engagement means to fight or to marry. If you want to fight with us then you had better let us know. But if you want to engage with us, we'll also welcome that, because American girls are beautiful, and we won't refuse.

—Vice Premier Li Lanqing

The Past, the Future, and a Talk with Deng Xiaoping

China, 1978: The warm sun of new ideas and economic reform is just beginning to melt the ice of Maoism's long bitter winter. Mao is dead. Deng Xiaoping has just returned to the Chinese leadership team. Although he is not yet in full control, he exudes confidence. Dan Burstein sits down with him for an interview.

"You are twenty-five years old; I am seventy-five," Deng observed. "I have had three times more chance to make mistakes as you." He had a reputation for speaking blunt truths, peppered with wit and insight as spicy as his native Sichuan cuisine. Summing up the Maoist era just ended, however, he was still quite cautious. Everyone knew he and his family had been among the Cultural Revolution's persecuted victims. Everyone knew he was already beginning to engineer reforms that were the very antithesis of Cultural Revolution policies. Everyone know that he was poised to become the first emperor who would allow the Great Wall of Chinese insularity to crumble and throw open the imperial gates to the world economy.

Yet Deng was still eager to preserve the precarious political peace that allowed him to outflank and outmaneuver the remaining Maoist hard-liners in power. He used one of Mao's classic Chinese formulations for finding the silver lining in a horrendous experience, describing the Cultural Revolution as "seventy percent positive, thirty percent negative."

But how could something so profoundly destructive be "seventy percent positive"? In reply, Deng acknowledged the agony brought to China by the Cultural Revolution. He claimed only one tangible "benefit" for the Chinese people: having accepted something that turned out to be so terrible, they had learned to be critical in their thinking and would be unwilling to be led astray again.

Time will tell whether he was right in this ironic, circuitous, and quintessentially Chinese bit of logic. So far, it appears his forecast was on the money. But China's greatest time of testing still lies ahead. Moreover, the question has changed in a way Deng probably not have imagined then. It is no longer so much a matter of whether China will be dragged back into the downward spiral of Maoist dogma,

Socialism with Chinese characteristics: "Being poor is not socialism," Deng Xiaoping said when he launched China's economic reform movement. He also said, "That which works we call socialism; that which doesn't we call capitalism." A senior economic planner, echoing Deng's statements, says: "Socialism used to mean government planning. Now it means common prosperity."

which is an unlikely scenario. Rather, can China avoid the pitfalls of excessive nationalism, xenophobia, a gridlocked reform process, and a closing of the door that Deng opened?

This 1978 interview with Deng took place as the United States was moving closer to normalizing relations with China. An issue of the moment was emigration, with voices from within the Carter administration as well as the Congress calling on Beijing to allow disaffected Chinese to leave the country freely.

Deng said he thought American policymakers were being unduly interventionist in China's affairs, as well as short-sighted with respect their own strategic interests. If Beijing opened the door and let all Chinese who wanted to leave the country do so freely, America would find 100 million or 200 million Chinese immigrants seeking admission. Japan and Southeast Asia would be overrun and overwhelmed. Did the United States want that?

The Chinese leadership, Deng opined, was actually protecting America's interests by ignoring the pressure from American political leaders and keeping the Chinese inside China. Regional and world stability was being preserved.

Deng's point was much larger than the emigration issue: Americans, he seemed to be saying, congenitally wish to insist that China adopt their values, without regard for whether American-style democracy or capitalism is appropriate for others—or even for whether American-style democracy in China would be in America's own interests.

Living in a country as peaceful and stable as the United States, Americans have very little ability to understand the fears that exist elsewhere about loss of stability and order. But the Chinese feel very differently about this question. Their history includes deeply painful periods of "warring states," warlordism, and breakdown of central authority. They have been invaded when their national structures were weak. They have had multiple civil wars and decades of Communist politics dominated by apocalyptic political struggles and constant faction fights even among the hard core of true believers.

Thus, they seek to define a unique Chinese road not simply because they wish to control the march along it (which the Communist Party, as China's ruling class, of course wishes to do). Rather, they believe they must develop their own proprietary mix of authoritarianism, nationalism, and

Capturing the vast historical irony: "The present leaders of the Chinese Communist Party spent their youth vowing to bring about a forcible leveling of society through the liquidation of class interests other than those of the proletariat. Instead, they are blessing extremes of exploitation not seen in the West since the mid-19th century. Whereas once they were shooting landlords, now they are dining with them. Some leaders must see this process as a catastrophic error. Some must see it as an inevitable interplay of historical forces which has all been for the best. Others must decline to think about it at all, for fear they will go mad."

—ROBERT COTTRELL
THE ECONOMIST

market solutions because that is the only way China will succeed.

In our view, the United States must be prepared to understand and work with China on that basis. For political strategies as well as for business strategies, the time has come to put aside American dreams, hopes, and fears concerning the China that is not and come to terms with the China that is.

CHAPTER 18

The New Shanghai Compact: Maximizing Opportunity, Minimizing Conflict

For a Policy of "Dynamic Engagement"

The sooner we bring an end to the cold war with China, the better . . .

. . . *for American business,* which will enjoy far better access to the China market in an overall atmosphere of cooperation than in one of hostility and threat. The American corporate community has a chance to be the partner of choice in the development of the world's fastest-growing— and someday largest—economy. We can harness the enormous complementarity and synergies of our two economies. But this opportunity is currently being restricted as its most significant potential is sacrificed on the altar of a cold war that does not need to be fought.

. . . *for the larger interests of the U.S. economy.* Aside from corporate profitability, there are numerous other benefits of an enhanced relationship with China, ranging from domestic job growth to how Chinese imports benefit American consumers and their living standards.

. . . for American strategic and political interests. Washington will have a much greater chance of influencing China positively on questions of concern to Asian and global security in the context of an engaged, involved dialogue between two great powers than it will as a belligerent pursuing a cold war to contain an ascendant China. We have the opportunity to play the leading role in encouraging China's development as a responsible, reasonable superpower that fits—even if not smoothly or easily—into the very positive emerging world order of recent years. Let us not make the mistake of forcing Beijing to conclude it is not welcome in this system and must go its own way.

. . . for the Chinese people themselves. If we, as Americans, want to contribute anything toward hastening the development of a more market-oriented and a more democratic China, in which a more Western-style system of political liberties and human rights may someday prevail, we can do so meaningfully only if we are actively engaged with the Chinese. The Hawks' strategy of isolation and containment will leave Americans preaching a message that cannot be heard in China, or that will be rejected because of its source. And it will undermine the position of the most enlightened and pro-Western forces.

. . . for what the American and Chinese people can do together. In spite of our different cultural backgrounds and histories, our peoples have a strong affinity. Despite political rhetoric of recent years, the Chinese people admire the freedom and creativity of American culture and lifestyles, our pioneering spirit, our open society, and many of our ideals. Americans admire the Chinese for their rich culture, their diligence and work ethic, their ability to shoulder so many burdens and make so many sacrifices, and their eagerness to put the past behind them and come into the modern era. But this powerful potential for our two peoples to work together on many projects of mutual interest and concern is constantly undermined by the politics of confrontation.

. . . for the global interests of peace and prosperity. An increasing number of countries stand at the edge of a vast potential global economic boom that could make the twenty-first century a time of a quantum leap in living standards and provide massive new resources for solving long-

"Of all the bilateral relations between the world's major powers, U.S.-China ties are the most strained and unstable. Further deterioration of this relationship could lead to head-on confrontation and threaten the existing world order."

—WANG JISI
DIRECTOR, AMERICAN DIVISION
CHINESE ACADEMY OF SOCIAL SCIENCES

intractable social and environmental problems. "We're facing twenty-five years of prosperity, freedom, and a better environment for the whole world," says Peter Schwartz, one of the international corporate community's most recognized experts at modeling future scenarios. But he notes that the number one danger to the scenario of extended global boom is posed by "tensions between China and the United States escalating into a new cold war—bordering on a hot one." [1] So how can we resolve this cold war and move on to capture the opportunities and synergies latent in the U.S.-China relationship?

Step one is simple conceptually, although quite difficult politically: *If you want to end the cold war, stop fighting it!* Americans should reject the growing influence of the China Threat school. Instead, we should begin to reconceptualize the relationship as it has been thought of at better times in the recent past, emphasizing its benefits while being open and realistic about its challenges, building upon our shared interests rather than focusing on our differences.

The United States should again seek a long-term strategic partnership with the Chinese as we did in the 1970s and 1980s, rather than pursuing today's range of adversarial tactics. In the twenty-first century, that partnership should be built around economic and other shared interests rather than the geopolitical interests of the past.

Labels are the stock-in-trade of the China policy debate—"engagement," "containment," and so on. We know labels don't do justice to the ideas behind these schools of thought. Nevertheless, for shorthand purposes, we have our own label for our favored approach to China: "*Dynamic Engagement.*" We strongly disagree with the contain-and-confront approach of the Hawks. But while we have said we prefer Engagement to containment, the kind of Engagement recently practiced in Washington is too extreme in its conditionality to serve as a policy that can meaningfully narrow the chasm that separates China and the United States.

Engagement Washington-style means a long list of if-then propositions: "*If* the Chinese change this behavior, *then* we will give them this carrot; *if* they don't, *then* we will hit them with this stick." This suggests a sweeping system of behavior modification therapy. But there is one major problem: the "patient" (China) has not yet been convinced to take part in the process, and is moving further and further away from it. Indeed, while Hawks criticize Engagers for capitulating to

Understatement:
"When President Clinton said the United States would support China's membership in the World Trade Organization as soon as possible and look after it personally, and then at the same time [then–U.S. Trade Representative] Mickey Kantor said that it is still a long way off, and [Special Trade Representative] Charlene Barshefsky says that the United States will adopt a tough stand against China unless we take strong action on some issues, it's confusing."

—VICE PREMIER LI LANQING

China, the Chinese disdain Washington's version of Engagement. As one of China's leading "America watchers," Wang Jisi, points out, engagement "is not a friendly gesture, but, rather, an attempt to pervade China with U.S. economic, political, cultural, and ideological influences."[2]

By "Dynamic Engagement" we do not mean a one-way flooding of China with American views and values, but a commitment to a genuinely mutual dialogue. And we don't mean a calculated system of behavior control, but a willingness on the part of the United States to take the first steps to rebuild trust and cooperation proactively, *without* waiting for all the negative Chinese behaviors to change. Dynamic Engagement means understanding that one of the great, epochal *positive* events of world history is taking place in China and that we, in the United States, wish to be part of it, support it, contribute to it, and benefit from it.

Dynamic Engagement means getting deeply involved in every opportunity offered by China to participate in its economic construction and modernization. Americans need to be on the ground floor of as many of the new things in China as possible. We have to do this through government, business, academic and expert exchanges, and "people-to-people" relationships. A great deal of activity is already taking place, but it must be multiplied, deepened, and *celebrated* publicly, rather than pushed into the shadows or defunded for fear that some Hawk might attack a worthwhile project as dictator coddling.

An American "Marshall Plan" for China is perhaps too much—and is not what the Chinese need or want. Nevertheless, Washington, in conjunction with the private sector, should be providing extensive financial, technical, and other assistance to the Chinese. These public-sector and private-sector partnerships with the Chinese must be vibrant enough to provide a real chance to learn from each other and teach our values by example. Indeed, unless and until we are willing to be engaged closely enough on the ground in China, we cannot hope that any of the great ideas of capitalism and democracy will grow deeper roots.

We favor delinking politics and trade as far as possible. In the modern world of global economics, holding trade hostage to political concerns makes sense only in the most extreme cases. China, despite the efforts of the Hawks to portray it as an extreme dictatorship and moral outlier, is

We'll take the short road, you take the long road, and let's see who has the more successful trip: "In Washington, long-term thinking about China amounts to putting membership in the World Trade Organization ahead of the latest human-rights incident. In Beijing, by contrast, long-term thinking about the United States amounts to assessing when during the next century China will overtake America as the pre-eminent global power and how adversarial the relationship will become in the interim."

—KAREN ELLIOTT HOUSE
    VICE PRESIDENT, DOW
    JONES

simply not such a case at present. We believe that the best hope American-style ideals and values have of winning a role in China is through full, deep, extensive Engagement there by American companies and institutions. Trade and investment should not be restrained by political differences—just the opposite. They should be seen as the antidotes to the potential toxicity of those differences.

Trade and investment involving American corporations, as well as institutional participation by American universities, think tanks, public policy organizations, journalists, and governmental agencies, can minimize our differences by addressing the practicalities of the relationship. They can also expose the Chinese to a fundamentally different working model of political economy that may be influential in China's *long-term* evolution. We don't, however, tout economic interdependence as a cure-all or panacea. But it certainly beats idle threats and evangelism delivered from the sidelines to a people with whom we have decided not to trade because we object to their politics or values.

Starting Points

In its most recent efforts to restore normalcy to the Washington-Beijing relationship and to argue in support of MFN for China, the Clinton administration has come halfway down the road to the line of thinking just described. These efforts are supported by American business and by many voices of reason across the political spectrum. But the administration's impulse to go further in this direction is hemmed in by its prominent critics on both the Left and the Right, both in the Congress and in American society at large, who are trying to manipulate American policy in the direction of a more confrontational stance.

We are keenly aware of the difficulties in changing this political mix, especially since the policy we propose opposes the direction in which the American pendulum has recently been swinging. Our realism about this situation lies behind our forecast that an on-again, off-again cold war with China will continue for the next several years. We do not wish to see that unfortunate reality unfold. Sadly, however, it is made all the more probable by the fact that the Chinese continue to refuse to make the changes in their behavior that

Have it your way: McDonald's developed a potato that could grow in China. Then it taught the Chinese how to grow potatoes. Next, McDonald's showed the Chinese how to produce french fries. Ninety-five percent of its food and paper needs are now supplied domestically.

could best win friends and influence thinking abroad. Some of the greatest excesses have been reined in, but the Chinese pendulum, too, is still in danger of swinging further in the neonationalist direction. Moreover, China has so far shown little evidence of deeply understanding our political process. What it does understand it too often ridicules or resents. Although Ziang Zemin may be able to recite the Gettysburg Address in English, his insistence that China's role in liberating Tibetan serfs is similar to Lincoln's role in freeing African-American slaves is hard for anyone in the United States to swallow.

Nevertheless, we believe that there are policy prescriptions for and proactive involvements with China that could help heal the wounds of recent years, resolve this cold war, and set the two countries on a dynamic and healthy course again. But first allow us to reiterate a few key overarching principles that should guide U.S.-China relations:

- The context in which we choose to see China should be one of challenge, not threat, and the challenge should be to our own creativity, our spirit of innovation, and our immense American resources. How do we maximize the obvious opportunities in the China relationship and minimize the conflicts?

- The United States cannot make China in its own image. To develop a China that is reasonable and responsible in its global behavior, market oriented in its economic practices, and moving toward greater democracy and rule of law in its internal politics, we must rely primarily on the indigenous process of reform, modernization, and transformation that is already working in China. *American policy should aim to support and contribute to these positive directions, not attempt to set the agenda for China.* The best way to contribute to positive developments in China is for the United States, its businesses, and its institutions to become constituents and stakeholders in the Chinese economy and development process.

- To avoid frustration, U.S. expectations of how much influence we can have in China—even if we follow the "right" strategic course—must be modest. The same applies to our expectations of how much total political change can take place in the short and medium term.

- In dealing with the Chinese, we should never lose our commitment to American values and beliefs. Nevertheless,

The information age: According to at least some credible studies, the U.S. Information Agency's international broadcasting arm, the Voice of America, has become the primary news source for 60 percent of educated Chinese.

we must avoid the impulse to be missionaries. Our zeal should be tempered with an understanding of the essentially non-Western nature of Chinese culture. We need to listen to, respect, and learn from the Chinese view. We can evangelize for our values and beliefs if we wish; we can seek opportunities for them to be heard in the budding Chinese marketplace of ideas; we can try to find a constituency in China that supports them. We should respond warmly to all who want our help, and especially to those who want to come to America to study or learn from our experience. But we should never try to force our beliefs down the throats of a people who don't accept them or are not yet ready for them.

• Although we propose a highly engaged and supportive political policy toward China, *no initiative to improve relations should ever be blind to or uncritical of the dark side of what is happening there.* The abuses of human rights are real, as are the huge social and political problems. The potential for China to destabilize Asia or emerge as a long-term strategic threat to American interests is also real. Our critics will allege that we seek to ignore these crucial matters. *We emphatically do not.* Instead, we argue that constructive American criticism and frank dialogue will be more effective when we are seen as partners and builders within the Chinese process, not as outside antagonists. We believe the United States has little leverage today to influence China to change its ways. We want to see the United States develop more leverage through economic interdependency and through the accumulation of goodwill and political capital.

• While we believe the troubling issues must be seen in context (for the negative aspects of China are counterbalanced by much that is positive), we also believe they must be monitored constantly. We should always be prepared to change American policy if the underlying reality in China turns out to be the kind of domestic dictatorship and external aggression and hegemonism that the Hawks forecast.

What Is Strength? What Is Weakness? What Is Leverage?

But won't America appear weak if we take the first step? Don't the Chinese respect strength above all? Isn't Dynamic Engagement a prescription for losing our leverage over Bei-

For want of a policy: "We are in a destructive routine. We accuse the Chinese, they balk, we threaten sanctions, they threaten retaliation. And no one really has a plan for arresting this."

—JEFFREY GARTEN
YALE SCHOOL OF
MANAGEMENT
FORMER UNDERSECRETARY
OF COMMERCE

jing? The truth is we have precious little leverage to lose. China has shown scarcely a sign in the most recent years of listening to American demands, let alone responding to them. Washington policymakers are sometimes even confused when it comes to figuring out the difference between "strength" and "weakness" toward China.

The British, too, are of two minds on China (1): "States are not going to change because you don't happen to like their system. And they expect you to talk to them directly, confidentially, if you want to get anything out of them."

—SIR PERCY CRADOCK
BRITISH DIPLOMAT AND
GOVERNMENT ADVISOR

• Does it send a message of strength when top officials of the United States become consumed by the issue of pirated videotapes and CD-ROMs—and appear ready to fight a trade war over this matter—while another set of officials backs down from charges (almost certainly true) that Chinese entities were selling high-tech equipment for nuclear weapons to Pakistan?

• Is dispatching naval vessels to the Strait of Taiwan an act of strength? What if it is well known that America's defense and intelligence communities doubt that the administration would ever actually intervene against China militarily?

• Is it strong to threaten economic sanctions and then not impose them? What if the United States actually imposed sanctions—and they ended up hurting American interests more than Chinese interests? Would that be strength?

• Is it strong to threaten to use the MFN club, when denial of MFN will mean hurting the very people we should be helping: entrepreneurs in Hong Kong, coastal China, and Taiwan; American consumers benefiting from low-cost consumer products; and those seeking jobs in an expanding export sector?

America is incredibly strong economically and militarily, while China is going to remain relatively weak in these areas for many more years. As former U.S. Secretary of Defense Harold Brown has written, "China does not now have the weight . . . that is ascribed to it by journalists. It is not in a class with the United States economically, militarily or technologically, or in international affairs."[3] Brown thinks China might "begin to approach" American strengths in two decades' time; we think even that is quite optimistic. But assume two decades is the right timetable. The United States, as the sole superpower of the current era, known for its flexibility, dynamism, and adaptability, can certainly afford to get deeply involved with China and see if that involvement yields the expected salutary results over the next few years. If it does not—if we are wrong and China instead emerges as the Hawks envision it a decade from now—we will still have plenty of time to change course.

We like the principle implied in Ronald Reagan's old aphorism about dealing with Mikhail Gorbachev's Soviet Union on nuclear weapons: "Trust but verify." Something similar might be said about our vision of Dynamic Engagement. We can extend an attractive olive branch to China economically. We can hold in abeyance our constant use of trade threats to back up American political criticisms of Beijing. We can become a much better partner and friend to China as it copes with its great internal contradictions and challenges. But we should not consider minimizing the U.S. defense presence in the Asia-Pacific region. In the future, the United States will face public pressure (from China and other Asian countries, as well as on the domestic front) to withdraw from its peace-keeping, power-balancing, stability-enhancing role in Asia. We hope Washington will resist this pressure and keep this most potent of all cards in play.

We are firm believers that American military preparedness is one of the great stabilizing forces in an increasingly complex and at times hostile world. We have argued that the Chinese military spending increases and weapons programs that so exercise the Hawks pose no great threat to Asia or the United States. But our view presupposes that America remains strong militarily, stays in Asia, and leads the world in military R&D. If we lose that edge, the equation could change very swiftly.

Specific Initiatives, Strategies, and Tactics

To be more specific and put some flesh on the bones of our vision of Dynamic Engagement, here are eighteen initiatives, strategies, and tactics we would like to see the United States use in its relations with China in the coming years:

1. Bill Clinton should go to China. Clinton should stop worrying about the effects of a positive China policy on the

The British, too, are of two minds on China (2): "You know, I dare say there are some who, if China was saying, 'Well, our price is slaughter of the firstborn,' would say, 'Well, maybe it is not unreasonable in the circumstances. You know, you have to allow for different cultural traditions.' I mean, do we ever have a bottom line?"

—CHRIS PATTEN
LAST BRITISH COLONIAL
GOVERNOR OF HONG
KONG

* Clinton did indeed go to China in June, 1998, three months after the first publication of this book. The visit had generally positive results, and we would urge that he continue to pursue personal summitry with his Chinese counterparts, including supplementary visits by high-level administration officials.

perpetual Democratic campaign, take the political risk (and the heat, if necessary), and continue the diplomacy to restart a true normalization of the U.S.-China relationship. He knows the stakes for American business and the economy, and he knows what good can come of it. He, of all people, knows that you can talk to those with whom you don't agree and that dialogue does not have to be taken as an endorsement. He can end this cold war if he wants to, by his own actions.

Moreover, he should use the bully pulpit of the presidency to educate the Congress and policymakers about the benefits of an improved relationship and the dangers of carrying on in the cold war vein.

As of this writing, Clinton is tentatively scheduled to visit China in the spring of 1998, following his reasonably successful summit with Jiang Zemin in Washington in late 1997. It is important that he make it to Beijing and not be deterred by the inside-the-Beltway stratagems designed to bring a halt to this next phase of rapprochement with China. In other words, Clinton needs to go to China and make a substantive success of the visit, despite the domestic American forces that will doubtless be arrayed against him.

2. Reestablish an active leadership-level dialogue. Our call is not just for an occasional cosmetic exchange of visits between state leaders—although that would be a start—but for a regular, active dialogue of the type American presidents usually have with leaders of other major countries. It should be followed up by regular exchanges between governmental officials at all levels, including the military.

3. Explicitly delink politics and trade. Build some trust and confidence in the U.S.-China relationship by extending MFN on an ongoing basis. MFN means only a willingness on the part of the United States to have a normal trade relationship with a country. Most countries of the world, even those with despicable governments, enjoy permanent MFN status. China should have it as well.

4. Support China's membership in the WTO. Leading trading nations, including the United States, are eager to get China into the WTO so that the world trade body's multilateral rules and systems of adjudication can be used to try to solve trade disputes, rather than relying on Washington's penchant for unilateral sanctions. But China doesn't wish to be forced

Really important strategic advice: Philippine president Fidel Ramos, after hearing China's president Jiang Zemin sing a rendition of Elvis Presley's "Love Me Tender" on a cruise on Manila Bay during the 1996 APEC summit, told Jiang: "That's the favorite song of Bill Clinton, so you have to prepare. When he visits you, you will surprise him."

into rules it is unprepared to live up to. The appropriate compromise will involve a set of terms that China can live with, perhaps with a comfortable schedule by which Beijing is phased in to "developed country" status.

Some of the contentious issues involve China's continuing preference for issuing internal ministerial guidance and directives on business issues, rather than adhering to the WTO's standard of full transparency and publication of all relevant laws and regulations. Or, while WTO rules allow some countries to protect some early-stage industries from foreign competition, China wants major sectors like automobiles protected, even though the rest of the world very much wants to enter. We believe that in these matters, the critical point would be to get China to agree *in principle* with the WTO rules and to a specific timetable for meeting them.

5. Utilize Washington's global clout to expand China's participation role in the making and setting of international rules. Washington should take the lead in including some Chinese representation in the G-7 summit process and similar global leadership initiatives. Russia is already included in what is now being the called the Group of Eight. Why not China?—especially since these summits are supposed to focus on economics, and in that realm China is a far bigger player than Russia. In fact, in the recent period, Russia has been a cause of global economic insecurity, while China has been a rock of stability, another indicator that the G-8 should become a G-9.

6. Build up and preserve Washington's political capital to use with Beijing on the most pressing matters of national interest. The American side ought to pick its fights with Beijing carefully. If threats of sanctions or other tools are to be used, they should be husbanded for maximum effect when they are worth using—and then implemented to demonstrate our side's credibility, which is now doubted in China. CD-ROM piracy is a commercial issue of medium importance. It should not become the center of a high-stakes Washington-Beijing trade conflict. Bilateral and multilateral organizations devoted to arbitrating trade disputes, such as the WTO, ought to handle such issues. In any event, American governmental bodies must be very careful about how frequently economic sanctions are threatened and in what circumstances. Jeffrey Garten, former undersecretary of commerce for international trade, points out the danger that "sanctions fever will get out

Rational? Or just rationalizing?
"Whenever the Chinese declare that the 'relationship is in trouble,' they can always count on some American voices being raised in self-criticism—indeed, providing more sophisticated rationalizations for the behavior of the Chinese than they themselves could produce."

—LUCIAN PYE
 PROFESSOR EMERITUS,
 MIT

365

of control" if Congress keeps trying to intervene in other countries' political systems by this means. Garten believes that sanctions make the most sense if they are multilateral. He cites the case of U.S. efforts to block commercial satellite sales to China for political reasons: All that happened was that non-American companies made the sales.[4]

7. Press China hard on issues of genuine national and global security. China's sales of nuclear material to Pakistan and chemical warfare elements to Iran; the misuse of dual-use American technology sold to China—these are crucial issues, on which Washington should be in a position to press Beijing hard. By rebuilding some political capital and trust with the Chinese, and by moving dozens of other acrimonious but far less important disagreements to other bodies, Washington will be able to use summit-level discussions with the Chinese to push seriously on the agenda items that matter most.

8. Invest in China's frontiers of development. The many relevant bodies and agencies in Washington should work with the Chinese to designate areas where the United States can create public-private partnerships to invest and provide expertise in solving particular problems in China. Infrastructure, power generation, telecommunications, hinterland development, venture capital for truly private small businesses and entrepreneurship are among the fields to consider. Washington has done some of this kind of investing through funds for Russia and Eastern European countries. There should be a similarly significant public-sector investment program for China. The point is to demonstrate that the United States is part of China's solutions, not part of its problems.

9. Establish or expand programs to sponsor more Chinese students in the United States and train more Chinese on key aspects of our systems. Many good initiatives are already under way in these areas, some sponsored by groups like the National Committee on U.S.-China Relations and the U.S.-China Business Council, as well as by many private companies, professional associations, universities, and foundations. They should be widely expanded. Also, the U.S. government should go well beyond its present limited support of Fulbright programs to establish a permanent, fully funded umbrella agency that expansively offers China's best and brightest the opportunity to learn at first hand how

"It is healthy to have a debate on China and its future," says Winston Lord, former U.S. secretary of state for East Asian and Pacific affairs, "but there is a tendency to demonize it, almost out of nostalgia for the Soviet Union. We shouldn't assume China's hostility in the next century, which could be self-fulfilling and wrong, any more than we should assume China will be benign."

America works in areas from law to securities markets, from pension planning to environmental regulation. There are tens of thousands of Chinese students in the United States, but most of them are in this country more or less on their own, not as part of any specialized program. We should make it *easy* for Chinese professionals and technocrats who wish to avail themselves of American expertise to come to the United States and learn. It is *not* easy to do so now. Even high-ranking delegates from Chinese government ministries have trouble getting visas, sponsorships, and the right American private-sector partners to educate them about their areas of interest. We should be actively increasing exchanges in science, technology, agriculture, teaching, publishing, the fine arts, sports, journalism, military affairs, and every other field. This is the kind of grassroots effort that can contribute far more to China's eventual democratization than can endless public criticism of China for not being democratic enough.

10. Deepen intergovernmental exchanges with China. Some very important American institutions are actively involved with China. The Federal Reserve and the Securities and Exchange Commission, for example, have both been working closely with their counterparts to help develop China's financial system and regulatory controls. But many of these ultra-important bilateral exchange programs have been terminated or restricted in recent years. We must, instead, expand and deepen U.S. government agency involvement at this crucial moment when fledgling Chinese institutions like stock markets, courts, and environmental controls are first being established.

11. Get TDA and OPIC involved in China. Currently, two key U.S. government business-support agencies are barred by Congress from operating in China: the Overseas Private Investment Corporation (OPIC), which offers political risk insurance to U.S. companies, and the Trade Development Agency (TDA), which finances feasibility studies. Both agencies should be working with American companies in China and also must be proactive on a wide scale just to compete with what the Europeans and Japanese are doing in these areas.

12. Establish regular and in-depth exchanges between members of the U.S. Congress and legislators of the National People's Congress in China. Efforts should be made to get more of China's U.S. critics to visit there, see the realities for

China issues? What China issues? In a poll conducted on behalf of the Committee of 100 (a group of well-known Chinese-Americans), less than half of all members of Congress rated themselves "highly familiar" with China issues. Yet this is the same Congress that is seeking to wrest a greater role in China policymaking away from the president.

themselves—and have the chance to make their views known directly to Chinese leaders. Newt Gingrich's 1997 visit to Beijing was useful: the Chinese heard directly his concerns about the future of Taiwan, Hong Kong, and the limitations on the religious freedom of Chinese Christians. And Gingrich came back willing to support the Clinton administration on extending MFN.

13. Convene a Permanent Joint Council, with bilateral panels of "Wise Men" (and Women). The process of narrowing U.S.-China differences can be greatly enriched if leading thinkers from both countries try to work together on elaborating joint solutions to common problems. To that end, we would propose the establishment of a formal Sino-American Joint Council, made up of distinguished persons from both countries. The council would have standing groups of committees—on trade, politics, and security, for example—comprising "wise men and women." While open communication would be one goal, the council could also be charged with taking up specific problems and making concrete recommendations for their resolution. Where meaningful consensus can be reached, joint reports should be published and publicized.*

The Permanent Joint Council should build on a process already pioneered successfully by some key laborers in this important vineyard: The National Committee on United States–China Relations and its counterparts in China, which have fostered a mutual dialogue on governance issues with local and national leaders; the U.S.-China Business Council, which has had positive experiences with joint discussions of business issues; and the Council on Foreign Relations, which has worked with the Chinese People's Association for Foreign Affairs in a similar vein. There are also official joint commissions on economics, commerce and trade, and science and technology, but their work was suspended for nine years in the wake of Tiananmen. Such efforts should be supported and upgraded and the range of opinion and expertise broadened.

Both societies are fortunate in having an able and experienced group of "watchers" of the other in government, academic institutes, foundations, think tanks, and the world

* Something of a precedent already exists. As part of the reassurance mechanisms associated with the eastward expansion of NATO, a Permanent Joint Council was established between NATO and Russia to aid "mutual transparency." While that body is focused on defense policy, we would expand on the idea put forward by Charles Wolf at the RAND Corporation that a similar organization be established with China.

We say we don't want to be involved, but . . . : "Again and again we Americans have said that we should never interfere in the internal affairs of the Chinese. But we know that this is only diplomatically, technically, or legally true. It cannot be historically true. For a half century at least, the United States has been a major and busy maker of Chinese history. Among other things, Americans have fought three major wars in which China was involved."

—RAY HUANG
CHINA: A MACROHISTORY

368

of business, law, and finance. Using them as an active resource will maximize the opportunities to move forward in the relationship and minimize conflict. In short, it ensures the process of "Dynamic Engagement."

14. Get Washington out of the business of appearing to set human rights and other domestic political priorities for China. Since China does not seem to respond to this type of pressure, it is counterproductive anyway. At the governmental level, the United States should only involve itself in the most significant human rights cases. We believe that quiet diplomacy works better with the Chinese than high-profile public pressure. But quiet diplomacy works only in the context of a positive atmosphere in the relationship.

15. Encourage U.S. private citizens and organizations to speak out. The American government should adopt a less interventionist stance toward China's domestic political process, but private citizens would obviously be under no compulsion to follow suit. Just the opposite. In our vibrant American democracy there is every reason for universities to welcome Chinese dissidents, for the media to make the views of Chinese opposition figures known, and for human rights organizations to monitor the situation in China. If a private American university wishes to invite the leader of Taiwan to make a private visit to speak on its campus, that shoud be its prerogative in a democracy. Chinese officialdom in Beijing continuously needs to be educated about how a democracy works and about the difference between official government policy and private free expression of ideas. Private American political, ideological, moral, and artistic views cannot and will not be muzzled to please Beijing— even on sensitive matters such as Taiwan or Tibet. The Chinese must come to understand this fact of life.

16. Develop a depth of China expertise in the U.S. government, academia, and business. In the first few months of the second Clinton administration in 1997, there was an embarrassing void in Washington: no senior advisor to Clinton had anything more than superficial knowledge of China. No one on the senior White House staff could read or speak Chinese. No secretary of state for East Asian affairs was in place. No one close to the secretary of state was well versed in China. And the Commerce Department's two most experienced

Well-intentioned, but ineffective: Using sanctions as a trade weapon "may be well intentioned, but they don't work as intended and often backfire," notes Stan Crock, a *Business Week* reporter. "Take the plan to bar American companies from selling nuclear power technology to Beijing after the 1989 Tiananmen Square massacre." Because American companies couldn't or wouldn't sell China what it needed, the Chinese went elsewhere, spending $8 billion in France, $4 billion in Russia, and $3 billion in Canada. "The end result was that China got the nukes it wanted. Meanwhile, Westinghouse Electric Corp. cut 3,500 workers at a Monroeville (Pa.) plant."

trade negotiators responsible for China suddenly departed for the private sector. Washington cannot make good China policy without at least some experts involved. One reason it has been so easy recently for extreme and irresponsible forces to dominate the debate is that the rational middle does not seem to know what it wants to say or how to argue the case for a better relationship. China is the new global business and political frontier. Our future businesspeople and government policymakers must get ready for its challenges linguistically and culturally. At the moment, there are roughly a hundred times more Chinese studying English than there are Americans studying Chinese. It is highly advantageous for Americans that English is being so widely adopted as the international language of business and technology. But if we are to communicate effectively, there is no substitute for knowing the Chinese language and culture.

Twenty-first century realpolitik, Chinese style: To U.S. objections over China's missile-rattling campaign against Taiwan in 1995, Lieutenant General Xiong Guangkai told a U.S. assistant secretary of defense, "In the end, you care a lot more about Los Angeles than you do about Taipei."

17. Try to avoid confrontation over Taiwan. In the current mini-cycle of events, the tensions of two to three years ago over Taiwan are easing. Washington can contribute to this deescalation by following a few broad guidelines:

• Recognize that this is a case in which realpolitik works. In return for assuring Beijing of what it wants most—a consistent "one China" policy when it comes to all issues of *formal* diplomacy—Taiwan can thrive economically and enjoy de facto self-rule. Injecting sudden bursts of American moralism or using the Taiwan issue to express American displeasure with Beijing is counterproductive. Such actions disrupt a status quo that has served the interest of China, most forces in Taiwan, and the United States quite well for two decades.

• Encourage Beijing-Taipei dialogue. The Taiwan issue *is* a matter for the Chinese and Taiwanese to settle. It is not up to the United States to design a solution.

• Promote restraint on the part of Taiwan's leaders, discouraging them from taking provocative actions that will make renewed confrontation likelier.

• Make clear to China that the United States insists on a peaceful settlement of the Taiwan issue and *will* oppose Chinese threats or military actions against Taiwan. The United States can and should continue to support Taiwan's defense, but it should endeavor to do so with China's tacit understanding—and with Washington fully affirming a one-China policy and preserving good relations with Beijing.

• Oppose both any move toward a unilateral declaration of independence by Taiwan and any unilateral setting of an arbitrary date for reunification by Beijing.

• Work to push a permanent solution off into a more temperate political time. As diplomat and Asia hand Morton Abramowitz has suggested, we should "keep exporting the Taiwan issue to the future," when there may be harmonious economic levels and political systems and a generally improved atmosphere in which to develop a solution for the long term.

18. Study Sun Tzu. American decision makers must learn to think more strategically about Asia. We must also work with our allies to develop multilateral approaches to China. It is foolish to assume that America's European and Asian allies will automatically support our policy goals with respect to China. It is even more of a stretch to imagine that they will carry the water for us in pursuing our agenda, with which many of them disagree. However, if we develop China policy mutually with our allies, we have a greater chance of receiving their support. That is an important part of the process, even if it risks moderating the sharp edges of United States policy. Our allies may help us set more realistic goals, and then be more prepared to help implement them.

Toward a Partnership That Recognizes Differences: The Shanghai Compact of 2002

Twenty-six years ago, China and the United States were able to set aside two decades of mutual invective, fear, and a pair of proxy wars in Korea and Vietnam to reach a new understanding. The means used to accomplish this historic shift included a set of highly dramatic, personal gestures (the Nixon-Mao meetings) as well as a carefully crafted document notable for its informality, its ambiguity, and most of all its willingness to acknowledge that fundamental differences need not obscure mutually shared goals. That document—the Shanghai communiqué—laid the groundwork for a surprisingly smooth and quick normalization of

Evolving a realistic policy toward China:
"The U.S. strategy should be based on the assumption that although China will remain an authoritarian regime in the foreseeable future, it is still plausible to integrate China into the world system as a responsible player. Without such a conceptual breakthrough, any strategy is doomed to failure."

—JIANWEI WANG
EAST-WEST CENTER

relations between two powers that had deliberately walled themselves off from each other for so long.

But, at the dawn of the new century, we are sliding backward, reaching into our mental attic for that "bamboo curtain" of old. The American attitude toward China inclines to hectoring and "getting tough." Even old shibboleths such as "Red China" have made their way back into the congressional vocabulary. As for the Chinese mood, it is prickly, surly, and often given to melodramatic pouting and overstatement.

This new U.S.-China cold war will run its course eventually. Changes in both countries will hasten the end of an extremely negative period. We believe that in time, there will be renewed energy for more substantial economic reform, as well as some appetite for political democratization. That will certainly change both China's reality and our perception of it.

We also believe that Americans will ultimately realize that China is not the fearsome threat Hawks have billed it as. The politics of confrontation and noncooperation with its earth-shaking process of change will come to be recognized as counterproductive for our own interests. The business community will prevail upon Washington to shift its sights once again to a constructive partnership. But reestablishing the idea of a U.S.-China partnership will take some work, including the elaboration of some principles to guide that partnership and prevent us from falling victim again to our persistent differences, which will not disappear any time soon.

To that end, we propose a new document to be signed on February 27, 2002, the occasion of the thirtieth anniversary of the Shanghai communiqué. The most appropriate format would simultaneously serve the sense of continuity and re-invigorate our mutual commitment to a more mature relationship. A treaty seems too formal; another communiqué, too informal. Perhaps we need a new compact—the Shanghai Compact.

The work leading up to this compact would be highly beneficial. It would give whatever administration was then in power a chance to articulate a clear, coherent, bipartisan, and purposeful policy. It could reinforce the importance we attach to the relationship while at the same time signaling that America neither intends to force its values on China nor abandon them. It could give voice to the serious concerns

Americans have about human rights, the environment, nuclear proliferation, and other hot-button issues, while making the point that in general we will not measure the success or failure of the relationship, nor set the economic terms for its operation, on the basis of political disagreements.

The greatest gain for *both* nations would be the rebuilding of a relationship of mutual interest and a new sense of commitment to maintaining that mutuality. In America, too many policymakers and opinion leaders have gone on too long looking at China as the successor "Evil Empire," when, unlike the old Soviet Union, China is not bent on world conquest, has no bases, missiles, or political beachheads abroad, and has been more of an asset than a liability to international stability. In China, too many policymakers and opinion leaders have gone on too long ignoring the validity of foreign criticisms on human rights and other matters, while perpetuating the myths of cultural purity, trampled national dignity, and American hegemonism.

This new Shanghai Compact should indicate that the relationship is special enough to require continual top-level engagement, yet everyday enough so that most issues can be solved through relevant bilateral and multilateral mechanisms rather than being treated as threats to fundamental sovereignty or ideals. It should also make clear that the United States and China will have sharp disagreements and differing interests for a long time to come. But it should commit both sides to respecting those differences and putting them in context. Washington and Beijing should adopt a course of responsibility to each other and to the global community to emphasize and build up the positive elements of the relationship and to negotiate the problems in good faith.

More than the exact words in the Shanghai Compact, the diplomatic developments and the statecraft necessary to arrive at such an agreement would signal that both sides had stepped away from the abyss they faced at the end of the twentieth century. It would tell the world that the two superpowers of the new century were entering the new age with hope and confidence that they could contribute to fulfilling its immense promise of peace, prosperity, and a global economic boom.

The stakes are high:
"The direction China takes in the years to come will help to decide whether the next century is one of conflict or cooperation. The emergence of a stable, an open, a prosperous China, a strong China confident of its place and willing to assume its responsibilities as a great nation is in our deepest interest."

—PRESIDENT BILL CLINTON
SPEECH, NOV. 21, 1996

NOTES

CHAPTER 1

1. Steven Erlanger, "Searching for an Enemy and Finding China," *The New York Times,* April 6, 1997.
2. George Will, "China's Turn," *The Washington Post,* April 17, 1997.
3. Arthur Waldron, "How Not to Deal with China," American Enterprise Institute paper, March 1997.
4. Steven Erlanger, "Chinese Cold War Forecast: Costly, Dangerous," *The New York Times,* February 25, 1996.
5. Chas. W. Freeman, Jr., "Sino-American Relations: Back to Basics," *Foreign Policy,* fall 1996.

CHAPTER 2

1. Jonathan D. Spence, *The Search for Modern China* (New York: W. W. Norton & Company, 1990), p. 129.
2. Ibid.
3. Fred Warner Neal, "American Attitudes, Past and Present," in *Asian Dilemma: United States, Japan and China* (Santa Barbara, Calif.: Center for the Study of Democratic Institutions, 1969).
4. Richard Madsen, *China and the American Dream* (Ann Arbor: University of Michigan Press, 1995), p. 31.
5. Henry Kissinger, *Years of Upheaval* (Boston: Little, Brown and Company, 1982), p. 46.
6. Thomas L. Friedman, "Fruit of the Loom," *The New York Times,* August 20, 1995.
7. Ibid.
8. Patrick E. Tyler, "Why China Has No Ears for American Demands," *The New York Times,* November 3, 1996.
9. "Conference Call," *The Economist,* November 18, 1995, p. 75.
10. Motorola news release, *Business Wire,* September 18, 1996.

CHAPTER 3

1. William H. Overholt, "Asia and America in Clinton's Second Term: A New Cold War?" Banker's Trust Hong Kong, research paper, April 21, 1997.

2. Kathy Chen, "Emboldened by Strong Economy, China Speaks Out and Commands Respect," *The Wall Street Journal,* December 20, 1993.
3. Helene Cooper, "U.S., China Deadlocked in Copyright Talks," *The Wall Street Journal,* May 15, 1996.
4. Charles Krauthammer, *Time,* July 31, 1995.
5. Robert S. Greenberger, et al., "U.S. and China: A Trail of Misperceptions," *The Wall Street Journal,* July 14, 1995.
6. Zhang Xiaobo and Song Qiang, "China Can Say No to America," *New Perspectives Quarterly,* fall 1996.
7. A. M. Rosenthal, "Wake Up, America!" *The New York Times,* October 26, 1996.
8. Zhang and Song, op. cit.
9. *Newsweek,* April 1, 1996.
10. "China: The Issue," *The Weekly Standard,* February 24, 1997.
11. Michael A Ledeen, "No Tyrants Allowed," *The Weekly Standard,* February 24, 1997.
12. "Destructive Engagement," *The New Republic,* March 10, 1997.
13. Albert R. Hunt, "The Get-Tough-on-China Crowd: Appealing but Ineffectual," *The Wall Street Journal,* April 24, 1997.
14. David E. Sanger, "Boeing and Other Concerns Lobby Congress for China," *The New York Times,* April 29, 1997.
15. David Mastio, "Uncle Sam Plays John Huang," *Slate,* March 15, 1997.
16. Alvin Toffler and Heidi Toffler, "Hat-Passing in the Global Economy," *The Los Angeles Times,* March 7, 1997.
17. The firm is Cassidy and Associates, whose three-year contract (1994–97) for $45 million was renewed for another three-year term in June 1997, according to the *Hong Kong Standard* (June 3, 1997).
18. Phil Kuntz, "Thompson Backs Off Assertion of Chinese Plot to Buy 1996 Elections," *The Wall Street Journal,* August 1, 1997.
19. John E. Yang, "Gingrich Unlinks Trade Status, China's Treatment of Hong Kong," *The Washington Post,* May 12, 1997.
20. Patrick E. Tyler, "Why China Has No Ears for American Demands," *The New York Times,* November 3, 1996.
21. "Sell Out," *The New Republic,* December 16, 1996.
22. Interview with CNN, as quoted by Pamela Pun in the *Hong Kong Standard,* May 9, 1997.
23. Zhang and Song, op. cit.
24. *Der Spiegel,* January 16, 1995. Quoted in *Army Times,* November 21, 1995.
25. Kathy Chen, "Anti-U.S. Sentiment Surges in China, Putting a Further Strain on Relations," *The Wall Street Journal,* May 16, 1996.

CHAPTER 4
1. Frances Williams and Michiyo Nakamoto, "China Takes Top Spot in World Steel Production," *The Financial Times,* January 17, 1997.
2. Steven Mufson, "A New World Market," *The Washington Post National Weekly,* March 28–April 3, 1994.

3. Paul Blustein, "China's Trade Challenge: Playing the China Card Correctly," *The Washington Post,* November 7, 1996.

4. Karl Schoenberger, "Motorola Bets Big on China," *Fortune,* May 27, 1996.

5. Monica Showalter, "Getting into the Game," *Far Eastern Economic Review,* November 7, 1996.

6. Ibid.

7. "Commerce Promotes China," *Business Week,* April 17, 1995.

8. Company announcement, quoted in Dean Takahashi and G. Christian Hill, "Motorola Sees Profit Missing Forecasts; Stock Price Drops 11% in Late Trading," *The Wall Street Journal,* September 12, 1997.

9. "How Microsoft Is Penetrating China's Software Market," *Business Week,* June 24, 1996.

10. "Now Departing for China: Boeing Jobs," *Business Week,* November 27, 1995.

11. Quoted in John Maggs, "The Myth of the China Market," *The New Republic,* March 10, 1997.

12. Quoted in Joseph Kahn, "Foreigners Help Build China's Trade Surplus," *The Wall Street Journal,* April 7, 1997.

13. Stephen Baker, "A Slow Boat to China," *Business Week,* September 8, 1997.

14. Neil Weinberg, "Power-hungry Asia," *Forbes,* February 24, 1997.

15. Reuters wire service report, October 17, 1996.

16. "Survey: Business in Asia," *The Economist,* March 9, 1996.

17. Stewart Toy, "Peugeot Picks Up Speed Far from Home," *Business Week,* May 27, 1996 (international edition).

18. The computer market grew 60 percent from 1993 through 1995; the total market in 1996 was over 2 million units—about the size of the U.S. market in the late 1980s.

19. Sang Ye, "Insect," *Wired,* July 1996.

20. Allen Cheng, "Prying into China," *Asia, Inc.,* October 1995.

21. "China: How Much Change?" *Business Week,* June 6, 1994.

22. Joyce Barnathan, et al., "Rethinking China," *Business Week,* March 4, 1996.

23. *The New York Times,* February 20, 1997.

24. Quoted in an interview with Qiao Shi, reported in *South China Morning Post,* May 29, 1997.

25. Some believe the absence of a modern welfare system is one of the keys to the rapid development of the little Asian dragons. See, for example, Jim Rohwer, *Asia Rising* (New York: Simon & Schuster, 1995), and John Naisbitt, *Megatrends Asia: Eight Asian Megatrends That Are Reshaping Our World* (New York: Simon & Schuster, 1996).

26. For this effort to reclaim the liberal side of the Confucian tradition, see, for example, William Theodore de Bary, "The New Confucianism in Beijing," *The American Scholar,* spring 1995; and Jonathan Spence's review of Simon Ley's new translation of the Confucian *Analects* in *The New York Review of Books,* April 10, 1997.

27. "Time for a Reality Check in Asia," quoted in *Business Week,* December 2, 1996.
28. Naisbitt, op. cit., p. 11.

CHAPTER 5

1. China was undoubtedly the world's largest and most advanced economy until the 1500s. In those earlier dynastic years it probably was also a leader in per capita wealth and living standards. Chinese peasants of the Tang Dynasty, for example, were poor, but probably lived better than European peasants of the Dark Ages.
2. Robert J. Samuelson, "Not a New Cold War," *Newsweek,* February 24, 1997.
3. "Price of Power," *The Economist,* March 8, 1997.
4. Michael Oksenberg and Elizabeth Economy, *Shaping U.S.-China Relations: A Long-Term Strategy* (New York: Council on Foreign Relations, 1997), p. 35.
5. Robert Ross, "Beijing as a Conservative Power," *Foreign Affairs,* March–April 1997.
6. Ibid.
7. Kathy Chen, "China's Inability to Keep Subs Running Shows Broader Woes Plaguing Military," *The Wall Street Journal,* August 1, 1997.
8. Owen Harries, "How Not to Handle China," *National Interest,* May 5, 1997.
9. Richard Bernstein and H. Ross Munro, *The Coming Conflict with China* (New York: Alfred A. Knopf, 1997), p. 3.
10. Alastair Iain Johnston, "Cultural Realism," letter to the editor, *The Atlantic Monthly,* June 1997.
11. Quoted in Barry Wain, "Tension Mounts as Vietnam Vies with Beijing over Oil Exploration," *The Wall Street Journal,* July 25, 1994.
12. Andrew J. Nathan and Robert S. Ross, *The Great Wall and the Empty Fortress* (New York: W. W. Norton and Company, 1997).
13. Ruben Alabastro, quoted in Reuters wire service report, May 17, 1995.
14. Andrew Nathan, "Bull in the China Shop," *The New Republic,* August 12, 1996.
15. "Chinese Exercise Strait 961: 8–25 March 1996," paper published by the U.S. Office of Naval Intelligence.
16. Leslie Chang, "Taiwanese Firms Expand in China as Commerce Outweighs Politics," *The Wall Street Journal,* November 23, 1996.
17. William H. Overholt, "Asia and America in Clinton's Second Term: A New Cold War?" Bankers Trust Hong Kong, research paper, April 21, 1997.
18. Nathan and Ross, op. cit., p. 153.
19. Overholt, op. cit.
20. Jan Wong, *Red China Blues* (Toronto: Doubleday/Anchor, 1996), p. 261.
21. Donald MacInnis, "From Suppression to Repression: Religion in China Today," *Current History,* September 1996.
22. Wendell Willkie II, "The U.S. and China: Gary Bauer vs. Wendell Willkie II," *Slate,* Message #4, May 14, 1997.
23. Merle Goldman, "The Importance of Human Rights in U.S. Policy Toward

China," in Thomas A. Metzger and Ramon H. Myers, eds., *Greater China and U.S. Foreign Policy* (Stanford, Calif.: Hoover Institution Press, 1997), pp. 77–78.

24. Harries, op. cit.
25. Thomas A. Metzger, "The U.S. Quest for Morality in Foreign Policy and the Issue of Chinese Democratization," in Metzger and Myers, op. cit., p. 85.
26. Reported by Ted Koppel, *Nightline,* April 28, 1997.
27. Harry S. Rowen, "The Short March: China's Road to Democracy," *The National Interest,* fall 1996.
28. Ibid.
29. Metzger, op. cit., p. 87.
30. Patrick E. Tyler, "Beijing Says It Could Live Well Even if U.S. Trade Was Cut Off," *The New York Times,* March 21, 1994.
31. Richard Bernstein, "China-Basher Bashes Bashing," *The New York Times,* June 29, 1997.
32. Paul Blustein, "Engaging China May Be the Only Choice," *The Washington Post,* April 13, 1997.
33. "China's Wedge," *The Economist,* May 11, 1996, p. 18.
34. Leslie Chang, "Taiwanese Firms Expand in China as Commerce Outweighs Politics," *The Wall Street Journal,* November 23, 1996.
35. Fred Hiatt, "Counterweight to China," *The Washington Post,* May 5, 1997.

CHAPTER 6

1. William H. Overholt, *The Rise of China* (New York: W. W. Norton & Company, 1993).
2. William H. Overholt, "China After Deng," *Foreign Affairs,* May–June 1996.
3. Jim Rohwer, *Asia Rising* (New York: Simon & Schuster, 1995).
4. John Naisbitt, *Megatrends Asia: Eight Asian Megatrends That Are Reshaping Our World* (New York: Simon & Schuster, 1996).
5. "Survey: Business in Asia," *The Economist,* March 9, 1996.
6. Manfred Kronen, chairman and CEO, Igedo. Quoted in Seth Faison, "Chinese Fair Showcases an Old Taboo: Lingerie," *The New York Times,* April 30, 1996.
7. Andrew Tanzer, "Consumer Frenzy in China," *Forbes,* August 2, 1993.
8. Reuters wire service report, July 19, 1995.
9. Dominic Ziegler, "Ready to Face the World?" *The Economist* (special supplement), March 8, 1997.
10. Rohwer, op. cit., p. 348.
11. Jack Goldstone, "The Coming Chinese Collapse," *Foreign Policy,* summer 1995.
12. U.S. Department of Defense, Under Secretary of Defense (Policy), "China in the Near Term" (photocopy, August 1994).
13. Lester R. Brown, et al., *State of the World, 1997* (New York: W. W. Norton & Company, 1997).
14. Arthur Waldron, "After Deng the Deluge," *Foreign Affairs,* September–October 1995.

15. "Asia Needs to Rewrite Its Strategy," *Business Week,* December 2, 1996.
16. David P. Goldman, "A Report Card on Asia," *Forbes,* February 24, 1997.
17. Richard Hornik, "Bursting China's Bubble," *Foreign Affairs,* May–June 1994.

CHAPTER 7

1. China's official population figure for the end of 1995 is 1.2112 billion.
2. Officially, China's population rose by 220 million between 1978 and 1993, while its arable land shrank by 10.6 million acres, equivalent to all arable acreage in Sichuan, the country's most populous province. In 1994, the population climbed by 14 million, and China lost another 265,000 acres. Helpfully, new satellite imagery indicates China may possess more arable land than the official 270 million acres calculated in 1994.
3. Douglas P. Murray, *America's Interest in China's Environment* (New York: The National Committee on United States–China Relations, 1994).
4. There is a well-known classical Chinese saying: "Intellectuals will die for someone who appreciates them."
5. Steven Mufson, "China's Shaky Grip," *The Washington Post,* November 17, 1996.
6. Who qualifies as a peasant? Officially, the number of farm-based residents is 431 million, of whom 250 million are actively engaged in pure agricultural work. Of the remaining, about 100 million are engaged in rural industry. The 900 million figure, which is the one regularly used by elites and the media, refers more accurately to the entire rural population—i.e., those not living in the major cities. This miscalculation may reflect a certain residual "revolutionary" romanticism—or, more likely in the roaring nineties, a prejudice against anyone not as prosperous and "sophisticated" as the urban dweller. Not frequently mentioned is the increased class differentiation among the peasants. As in the pre-Communist era, three distinct categories are now evident: rich, middle-class, and poor.
7. For a further discussion of China's "high equilibrium trap," which prevented an industrial revolution, see, for example, John K. Fairbank, *The Great Chinese Revolution, 1800–1985* (New York: Perennial Library, 1986), and the seminal study by Etienne Balasz, *Chinese Civilization and Bureaucracy* (New Haven: Yale University Press, 1964).
8. "China Plays Down Role of a Model Village in Guangdong," *Far Eastern Economic Review,* November 14, 1996, and, on Nanjie, Lincoln Kaye, "Against the Grain," *Far Eastern Economic Review,* November 17, 1994.
9. Quoted in Reuters wire service report, "Private Sector to Stay 'Supplementary,'" January 22, 1997.
10. Stone's turbulent quest for entrepreneurial success has been documented most recently in Scott Kennedy, "Reaching into All Corners," *The China Business Review,* January–February 1995, and Pamela Yatsko, "Spreading It Thin," *Far Eastern Economic Review,* April 17, 1997.

1. China's own official figure is 58 million poor, and 20 million more "just above the line," using the threshold of 60 cents per day. A cautionary note: statistics about China and its economy often conflict, depending upon the source. We have tried to use generally accepted figures, although we recognize there are other sources with other figures.

2. Wang Dongjin, vice minister, State Commission for Restructuring the Economic System. Quoted in "Finding Jobs for 175m 'Arduous,' " *Hong Kong Standard,* May 7, 1997. Also, Tom Korski, "20m Jobs to Go by 2000 in China's State Sector," *South China Morning Post,* May 7, 1997.

3. Quoted in "U.S., China Deadlock in Copyright Talks," *The Economist,* October 14, 1995.

4. Ivan Tang, "Inner Regions Outraged Over Empty Words," *South China Morning Post,* April 10, 1997.

5. Andrew Nathan, "Beijing Blues," *The New Republic,* January 23, 1995.

6. Matt Forney, "We Want to Eat," *Far Eastern Economic Review,* June 26, 1997.

7. Quoted in *Far Eastern Economic Review,* September 8, 1994.

8. Kenneth Lieberthal, *Governing China* (New York: W. W. Norton & Company, 1995) p. 316.

9. Joseph Kahn, "Foreigners Help Build China's Trade Surplus," *The Wall Street Journal,* April 7, 1997.

10. William Overholt, "China After Deng," *Foreign Affairs,* May–June 1996.

11. Dominic Ziegler, "Ready to Face the World?" *The Economist* (special supplement), March 8, 1997. Also, authors' interview with Fan Gang and various press reports.

12. Matt Forney, "Jiang's Big Bet," *Far Eastern Economic Review,* September 25, 1997.

13. Quoted in Seth Faison, "A Great Tiptoe Forward: Free Enterprise in China," *The New York Times,* September 17, 1997.

14. Jack Goldstone, "The Coming Chinese Collapse," *Foreign Policy,* summer 1995.

15. "China's Bankrupt State Enterprises," *The Economist,* December 14, 1996.

16. Marcus W. Brauchli, "China's Big Problems Are Greenspan's, Too," *The Wall Street Journal,* October 24, 1994.

17. See Reuters wire service report, "Greater Role for Private Sector," June 17, 1997, and "Reform in the Air," *The Economist,* July 19, 1997.

18. Craig R. Smith, "China Is Revitalizing State Sector, Starting at the Factory Level," *The Wall Street Journal,* March 26, 1996.

19. "Illegally Stored Dynamite Kills at Least 95 in China," *The New York Times,* February 2, 1996.

20. Kathy Chen, "As Millions of Chinese Try to Get Rich, Values Get Trampled," *The Wall Street Journal,* May 2, 1995.

21. Quoted in Zha Jianying, *China Pop: How Soap Operas, Tabloids and Bestsellers Are Transforming a Culture* (New York: The New Press, 1995).

CHAPTER 9

1. Jared Diamond, "The Great Chinese Puzzle," *Discover,* March 1996.
2. Ray Huang, *China: A Macro History* (Armonk, N.Y.: M. E. Sharpe, 1990).
3. Jonathan Spence, *God's Chinese Son* (New York: W. W. Norton & Company, 1996).
4. Ray Huang, op. cit., p. 105.
5. Gerald Segal, "China's Changing Shape," *Foreign Affairs,* May–June 1994.
6. Sandra Sugawara, "With Billions at Stake, Boeing Goes to Bat for China," *The Washington Post,* July 7, 1996.
7. Ibid.
8. Seth Faison, "Dalai Lama Movie Imperils Disney's Future in China," *The New York Times,* November 26, 1996.
9. Ibid.
10. "Sell Out," *The New Republic,* December 16, 1996.
11. Samuel P. Huntington, *The Clash of Civilizations and the Remaking of the World Order* (New York: Simon & Schuster, 1996), p. 223.
12. Matt Forney, "Patriot Games," *Far Eastern Economic Review,* October 3, 1996.
13. Ibid.
14. Reuters wire service report, March 14, 1995.

CHAPTER 10

1. Willy Wo-lap Lam, *China After Deng Xiaoping: The Power Struggle in Beijing Since Tiananmen* (Hong Kong: PA Professional Consultants Ltd., 1995), p. 383.
2. Well underreported at the time were the "democratic" manifestos issued demanding "no obstruction" and "total compliance" to the edicts of student leaders. They set up a makeshift society that "resembled the communist state in structure and operation," wrote the *Washington Post*'s Sarah Lubman, who, unlike more "visible" reporters present during the last few days of demonstrations, had spent many weeks on the square among the students ("The Myth of Tiananmen Square," *The Washington Post,* June 30, 1989). For similar sympathetic but myth-debunking reportage see Jan Wong, *Red China Blues* (Toronto: Doubleday/Anchor Books, 1996).
3. Patrick E. Tyler, "Riches Tasted, China Hungers for Freedom," *The New York Times,* May 30, 1997.

PART III: A THOUSAND RIVERS

1. Robert Cottrell, "A Vacancy Awaits," *The Economist,* March 18, 1995.
2. "Fast-Growing Private Enterprises," *China News Analysis,* February 15, 1995.

CHAPTER 13

1. Wm. Theodore de Bary, "The New Confucianism in Beijing," *The American Scholar,* spring 1995.

CHAPTER 14

1. Willy Wo-lap Lam, "Jiang Gives Blessing to Rising Star," *South China Morning Post,* October 1, 1997 and "The 24 Most Powerful Figures in China," *South China Morning Post,* September 20, 1997.
2. Matt Forney and Bruce Gilley, "In Defence of Dad," *Far Eastern Economic Review,* July 25, 1996.
3. Even more ironic, perhaps, is that, according to his daughter, Deng worked for a time in a handicrafts factory, making memorial rosettes with labels proclaiming them the product of French World War I veterans.
4. As quoted in Kenneth Lieberthal, *Governing China: From Revolution Through Reform* (New York: W. W. Norton & Company, 1995), pp. 238–39.
5. Ibid., p. 239.
6. Lucian W. Pye, "What China Wants," *The New York Times,* November 26, 1996.
7. Li Zhisui, *The Private Life of Chairman Mao* (New York: Random House, 1994).
8. Jasper Becker, *Hungry Ghosts: Mao's Secret Famine* (New York: The Free Press, 1996).

CHAPTER 15

1. Steven Erlanger, "Uncle Sam's New Role: Hong Kong's Advocate," *The New York Times,* July 2, 1997.
2. Paul Theroux, "Letter from Hong Kong: Ghost Stories," *The New Yorker,* May 12, 1997.
3. Interview broadcast on *All Things Considered,* January 1, 1997.
4. George Melloan, "Yam's Rule: Don't Just Do Something, Sit There," *The Wall Street Journal,* October 7, 1996.
5. "Global Wrap-up," *Business Week,* September 8, 1997.
6. Kathy Chen, et al., "China's Foreign Minister Issues Warnings," *The Wall Street Journal,* October 16, 1996.
7. Editorial, "Guanxi Maximizing," *The Wall Street Journal,* January 31, 1997.
8. Frank Ching, "Misreading Hong Kong," *Foreign Affairs,* May–June 1997.
9. A "red chip" is a mainland Chinese company listed in Hong Kong.
10. Frank Ching, "Hong Kong Isn't Dead Yet," *Far Eastern Economic Review,* February 20, 1997.
11. This colorful saying, also heard in connection with how China deals with dissidents, is meant to convey a sense of warning, a lesson to be learned. The monkey, which is clever as well as impish, must be scared off. Chickens are not worth much and, besides, can be eaten when slaughtered, so hence to kill one is an easy way to make a blunt point.
12. Joseph Kahn & Marcus W. Brauchli, "Chinese City Is Reborn in Splendor as Leaders Order It to Be Great," *The Wall Street Journal,* May 15, 1997.
13. Nicholas D. Kristof, "Tension with Japan Rises Alongside China's Star," *The New York Times,* June 16, 1996.
14. Kent E. Calder, *Pacific Defense: Arms, Energy, and America's Future in Asia* (New York: William Morrow & Company, 1996), p.8.

15. Lee Kuan Yew, "News from a Time-Capsule," *150 Economist Years* (special supplement), *The Economist,* September 11, 1993.
16. Samuel P. Huntington, *The Clash of Civilizations and the Remaking of the World Order* (New York: Simon & Schuster, 1996).

CHAPTER 16

1. Robert Scalapino, "National Political Institutions and Leadership in Asia," *Washington Quarterly,* autumn 1992.
2. Cited in Wm. Theodore de Bary, "The New Confucianism in Beijing," *The American Scholar,* spring 1995, p. 181.
3. Zha Jianying, *China Pop: How Soap Operas, Tabloids, and Bestsellers Are Transforming a Culture* (New York: The New Press, 1995), p. 102.
4. De Bary, op. cit., p. 183.
5. There is, for example, the oft-cited passage "One may rob an army of its commander-in-chief; one cannot deprive the humblest man of his free will." *The Analects of Confucius,* translated by Simon Leys (New York: W. W. Norton & Company, 1997).
6. Donald McInnes, "From Suppression to Repression: Religion in China Today," *Current History,* September 1996.
7. Karen Pennar, "A Helping Hand, Not Just an Invisible Hand," *Business Week,* March 24, 1997.
8. Richard Madsen, "After Liberalism: What If Confucianism Becomes the Hegemonic Ethic of the Twenty-first Century?" Japan Policy Research Institute Working Paper No. 14, November 1995.
9. "Video Games Attacked," Agence France Press, wire service report. Cited in the *South China Morning Post,* April 10, 1997.
10. Frank Ching, "Confucius, the New Savior," *Far Eastern Economic Review,* November 10, 1994.
11. Quoted in Nicholas D. Kristof and Sheryl WuDunn, *China Wakes* (New York: Times Books, 1994), p. 449.
12. "Second Thoughts," *The Economist,* September 28, 1996.
13. Ibid.
14. "Senior Leader Calls Again for Electoral Reform," *Far Eastern Economic Review,* November 7, 1996.
15. "The Rise of Nongovernmental Organizations in China: Implications for Americans," The National Committee on U.S.-China Relations, China Policy Series, No. 8, May 1994.
16. One of the most potentially significant but little-discussed influences on China's future direction would be Beijing's response if Russia starts to show real signs of success with its post-shock-therapy economy building.
17. Kenichi Ohmae, "China's 600,000 Avon Ladies," *NPQ,* winter 1995.
18. For a good summary of the variations in development strategies used by the three major regions, see Yoichi Funabashi, Michel Oksenberg, and Heinrich Weiss, *An Emerging China in a World of Interdependence* (New York: Trilateral Commission, 1994), p. 25.
19. Tu fu quoted in Erling Ho, "The Long River's Journey Ends," *Natural*

History, July 1996. John Hersey's famous literary account of a young American engineer's coming face to face with the Yangzi (and China) is *A Single Pebble* (New York: Alfred A. Knopf, 1956). An engaging modern portrait of the Yangzi, including its people, culture, and landscape from its upper regions to its mouth, can be found in Simon Winchester, *The River at the Center of the World* (New York: Henry Holt, 1997).

20. Dai Qing has received a great deal of press attention in the West and has been profiled in several recent books: Kristof and WuDunn, op. cit.; Perry Link, *Evening Chats in Beijing* (New York: W. W. Norton & Company, 1992); and Orville Schell, *Mandate of Heaven* (New York: Simon & Schuster, 1994).

21. "UAW Commends U.S. Export-Import Bank for Rejection of Caterpillar Financing of China's Three Gorges Dam Project," UAW press release, May 30, 1996.

22. Sid Tan, "China's Three Gorges Dam Project," Sierra Club position paper, 1996.

23. Meng Xiaoshu, "Dam Investors Warned Off by Human Rights Groups," *Hong Kong Standard,* February 22, 1995.

24. *Straits Times* (Singapore), April 6, 1997.

25. Joseph Kahn, "Despite Vast Obstacles, Chinese Move to Tap Power of Historic River," *The Wall Street Journal,* April 18, 1994. Patrick E. Tyler, "Cracks Show Early in China's Big Dam Project," *The New York Times,* January 15, 1996.

26. Interview with Audrey Topping, *The New York Times Magazine,* January 5, 1997.

CHAPTER 18

1. Peter Schwartz and Peter Leyden, "The Long Boom," *Wired,* July 1997.

2. Quoted in Matt Forney, "Out of Synch," *Far Eastern Economic Review,* December 5, 1996, p. 16.

3. Harold Brown, foreword, in James Shinn, ed., *Weaving the Net: Conditional Engagement with China* (New York: Council on Foreign Relations Press, 1996).

4. Jeffrey E. Garten, "Business and Foreign Policy," *Foreign Affairs,* May–June 1997.

ACKNOWLEDGMENTS

IN A CERTAIN SENSE, *Big Dragon* is the book about China we have been researching much of our adult lives. Our travels to Asia and our thinking about China began more than thirty years ago. Over the course of the last three decades, our understanding has deepened and matured with the benefit of the wisdom and insight of a great many people. Our first debt of gratitude is to our teachers—the Sinologists with whom we studied in college, Chinese friends and colleagues from many aspects of Chinese society who shared their thinking with us even when it was dangerous to do so, the senior figures of the modern Chinese political scene we met over the last decades from the late Vice Premier Deng Xiaoping to today's Vice Premier Li Lanqing, the executives of companies we have advised, and the authors, journalists, and experts who have helped us see the many layers of China's realities and provided us with original insights into the drama of China's rise as well as new thinking about its future.

Over the last three years, as *Big Dragon* has taken specific shape, we have benefited from first-hand interviews with some two hundred political figures, business leaders, academics, economists, futurists, think-tank and public policy experts, financial analysts, journalists, and others in China, Southeast Asia, Japan, Europe, and, of course, North America. A great many American and other global corporations opened their doors to us, made their senior executives available for interviews, and allowed us candid looks inside their operations in China. We also benefited enormously from the behind-the-scenes help given us by those making introductions, setting up meetings, supplying us with research materials, translating documents, and otherwise supporting our efforts to find jewels of enlightenment behind the Great Wall.

In particular, we would like to acknowledge the following individuals:

An Chengxin, Brian Arveson, Bo Xilai, Phil Bowring, Cao Yuanzheng, Richard Chamblin, Annie Chang, Chen Jiahai, Chen Jiang, Chen Luzhi, Chen Ping, Chen Xiaolu, Chen Yuan, Mei Wei Cheng, Aaron Cheung, Frank Ching, Chinh Chu, Ed Cowles, Michael B. DeNoma, Charles de Trenck, Dong Qiu,

Duan Cunhua, Daniel Esty, Fan Gang, Fang Xin, Feng Liwen, Feng Lun, Victor Feng, Feng Yun, Fu Yimin, Gao Xiqing, Goh Toh Sim, Guo Dongpo, Guo Shuqing, David Hale, He Di, Henry Ho, Morton Holbrook, Arthur Holcombe, Sven Hsia, Gavin M. Hu, Hu Deping, Huang Lixin, Huang Yantian, Kenichi Ito, Jia Qingguo, Jin Ligang, Charles K. Kao, Jimmy Lai, Willy Wo-lap Lam, David M. Lampton, Richard Latham, Kimen Leung, Handel C. H. Lee, J. P. Lee, Martin Lee, Li Chuwen.

David K. P. Li, Haiyan Li, Li Lanqing, Li Sanyou, Li Zhaoxing, Li Zhiping, Liang Qiaorong, Lin Hua, Wayne W. Ling, Allan H. Liu, Liu Chuanzhi, Liu Minjun, Liu Shuqing, Liu Yongtao, Lu Haoxing, Luo Yuping, Guonan Ma, Ma Ying, Ma Xiaoli, Clement B. Malin, Mao Bingqiang, Richard Margolis, Rei Masunaga, Mei Shan, Mei Shaowu, Timothy Moe, Robert Ng, Ni Shixiong, William Overholt, Qian Zhengying, Qiao Shi, Qiao Xiaodong, Qin Chaoying, Qin Xiao, Robert Scalapino, Rudolph Schlais, Scott Seligman, Diana Shen, Shen Guojun, Yong G. Shen, Simon Shi, Ryuichi Shoji, James Stepanek, Ronald Suleski, Richard L. Y. Sun, Sun Jian, Yasunobo Suzuki, Seiichiro Takagi, Ross Terrill, Alvin Toffler, Lois Tretiak, Tu Jian, Enzio Von Pfeil, Wang Feixin, Wang Gungwu, Hui Wang, Wang Jinzhen, Wang Jisi, Wang Qishan, Wayne W. Wang, Wang Xiaodong, Wang Xiaoqiang, Wang Xuebing, William J. Warwick, Gordon Wu, Wu Keliang, Wu Xiaoling, Wu Xubing, Xiao Yu, Xu Yimin, Xue Ya, Yan Mingfu, Peter Yan, Yang Guangqi, Yang Ping, Yao Zhenyan, Ye Xiaowei, Yu Chen, Jerry Yu, Yu Peining, Yuan Ming, Zhai Zhihai, Zhang Haoruo, Zhang Wei, Zhang Wenpu, Zhang Zhuoyuan, Zhao Qizheng, Zhao Zhenger, and Zhou Weimin.

With respect to all those acknowledged in these pages, we stress the usual authorial caveat: we thank them for their invaluable advice and support, but, as the views expressed here are entirely ours, ask our readers to hold them blameless for any sins in fact, analysis, or judgment we may have committed.

This book would not exist without the constant support of our editor at Simon & Schuster, Frederic W. Hills. In a time when many bemoan the state of book publishing, Fred stands out as one of the last lions of the business—an editor deeply concerned about his authors, their ideas, and making their books successful. We deeply appreciate all he has done for *Big Dragon*.

Special thanks are also in order for many others at Simon & Schuster who were involved in helping *Big Dragon* move from idea to printed page and into bookstores, especially: Carolyn Reidy, Wendy Nicholson, Victoria Meyer, Pam Dueval, Leslie Ellen, Hilary Black, and Karen Weitzman. Our text benefited greatly from the line and copy editing of Burton Beals and Jolanta Benal. And we were greatly aided throughout the process by another one of the vanishing breed of publishing lions, our agent, Perry Knowlton.

John Scardino helped us get attention for the ideas in the book inside the Beltway. Three U.S. Congressmen—Robert Matsui, Jim Kolbe, and David Drier—were kind enough to circulate *Big Dragon* to their Congressional colleagues and recommend it to their attention during the 1998 MFN debate and President Clinton's visit to China.

We are also extremely pleased there has been so much interest in *Big Dragon* in China. We wish to thank Xue Dezhen, editor in chief of the People's PublishingHouse/Oriental Press, as well as Wang Naizhuang, Dai Lianbin, Sun Yingchun, and the many others who worked so hard to get the Chinese-language edition out in record time. Also very important to this effort have been Madame Hu Muying, Li Haiyan, and Li Lingyan, who helped introduce us to the increasingly vibrant Chinese publishing scene and advised us wisely.

Our travels in Asia were made much more pleasant by the help and support of the Peninsula Hotel in Hong Kong, the Palace Hotel in Beijing, Kate Kelly of the Peninsula Group, and Mary Bakht in New York and her always-efficient, always-helpful, and pleasant colleagues of the Hong Kong Tourist Association in Hong Kong.

Personal Acknowledgments/Daniel Burstein:

Every idea in this book—and virtually every sentence, for that matter—is the product of a profoundly creative and dynamic partnership with my cowriter, colleague, and friend, Arne de Keijzer. Researching and writing *Big Dragon* proved to be a complex and arduous journey into an incredibly vast subject. With his deep understanding of China's soul, Arne was the compass that continually helped us find our course amid a constantly changing landscape (not to mention through Beijing traffic and Devil's Den).

Several other individuals are pillars of emotional and intellectual support in my life—people who make it possible for me to take on extreme challenges and succeed. In particular, my deep thanks to Peter G. Peterson, Chairman of The Blackstone Group, as well as to my colleagues there. Pete's unique insights into politics, government, and public policy on one hand and finance, business, and economics on the other have provided me with a continuous education on a stunning array of subjects over the last decade, many of which relate directly to the themes of this book.

Martin Edelston, President of Boardroom Inc., has been a supporter through all of my books, and an unsung hero of American entrepreneurship, a marketing genius, and a great friend. *Big Dragon* is a better book—and will undoubtedly be a more widely read book—as a result of his help. Bob Dilenschneider lent his prodigious communication skills to the effort. Susan Maday, Joan O'Connor, and Kathy Hartnett provided invaluable logistical assistance.

Les Gelb, Steve Friedman, and Elizabeth Economy invited me to participate in an extended Council on Foreign Relations study group, which included a veritable Who's Who of American experts on China and afforded me a unique opportunity to see U.S. policy toward China debated by the leading authorities at the very moment when the issues grew most acute.

A number of Chinese officials in New York were helpful to me, including Chen Wenqing, Jiang Zhenxi, and Wang Renliang. I can still hear the voices and am always informed by the perspective of those who first helped me to see China in the 1970s and '80s, especially Li Ruisun, Chen Chuanpi, Shen Minghe, Mao Guohua, Liu Zongren, and Chen Yicun. Wherever they are today, and however the views expressed in this book may differ from theirs, they should know how much I appreciate what they showed and taught me.

Working on this book I often thought about my parents, Leon and Dorothy Burstein. I recall my mother, ever the globalist, questioning my elementary school's administrators in the 1960s about why they had no Chinese language program—since China was obviously going to be such an important country in the world's future. And my father, ever the practical accountant, predicting to the day when U.S.-China relations would be normalized based on the increasing trade flows of the late 1970s.

The most important person in my life is my wife, Julie O'Connor. From the very start of our romance, sharing everything meant sharing ideas and experiences about China—like the stories we reported together (Julie in photographs and myself in words) on the birth of China's computer industry, the opening of the first hamburger joint in Beijing, the conflict on the Sino-Vietnamese border, and the last descendants of the once thriving Jewish community of Kaifeng. Julie nurtured this book as she has nurtured my soul and leavened the all too many dark days that I faced on this project with her special magic and beauty.

What's more, Julie has imbued our son David with her love for books. Now nine, he has zestfully taken up the spirit of *Big Dragon* by coming up with designs for the cover and even producing a promotional bookmark with his expectations of the wonderful things the reviewers should say. During many of the hours I spent writing, David was working silently on jigsaw puzzles on the floor of my office. His relentless dedication to completing his puzzles gave me inspiration and encouragement for completing the puzzle I was working on—this book.

Personal Acknowledgments/Arne de Keijzer

There is an old Chinese saying about how a long journey begins with a single step. So it does, but the direction taken and ultimate success of a trip such as this one depends heavily upon experienced guides, local advice, convivial company, and an unflagging support system. Throughout this journey I have been extraordinarily lucky in all these. Most fortunate of all, I have had as my co-adventurer Dan Burstein, whose insights and immense abilities as conceptualizer, writer, and editor made it all possible. It is impossible to express adequately what his dedication to this project—and our friendship—has meant to me.

From my first steps into the Maoist China of the early 1970s through the research and business trips of the roaring '90s, I have had the tremendous good fortune to learn from remarkable people from all walks of life and from all parts of the country. My primary debt is to Allan H. Liu and Henry Ho. They have guided my journey for much of the past twenty-five years and I thank them both for unflagging friendship, unerring advice, constant encouragement, and true cross-cultural understanding. And double thanks are due Allan for his willing help and wise suggestions throughout the writing of this book. Other friends and colleagues who have also added important dimensions to my knowledge of China include Jim Stepanek, David Lampton, Arlene Posner, Mimi Conway, Ming Yim, Ivy Chiang, Xue Ya, Feng Liwen, Lu Fengchun, and Liu Fugui.

The debt of gratitude owed my parents, John and Nel de Keijzer, is enormous. In many ways this book is an homage to their love and support.

The ups and downs of writing a book over several years especially test the patience of those who are closest and dearest. Their heartfelt, consistent caring is a small miracle. I am particularly grateful for the love and affection of my brother, Steven, and my wonderful family, both immediate and extended: Dick and Shirley, Joan, Elkan and Gail, Bob and Carolyn, Dan and Julie, Lynn, and the remarkable, ever-ready Brian. I also acknowledge with deep appreciation and affection the many other personal friends who have enriched my life over many years. I am blessed and truly thankful.

And deep within, my soul resonates with the joy of Helen and Hannah. Helen's warmth, integrity, and deep respect for and profound optimism about people, issues, and community reflect the best in the human spirit. That she is also my best friend, loving partner, and affectionate critic is a gift beyond measure. There would be no book, no life without her. Let alone our daughter Hannah! For a project that took nearly a quarter of her young life, Hannah never complained about the strange hours, interrupted plans of daily life, or storms of frustration. Instead, she gave me boundless encouragement and endless affection, all the while growing into a person of astonishing grace, talent, and vitality.

INDEX

in U.S. foreign business, 246–47, 252, 255, 257, 259
Erlanger, Steven, 21
European Union, 102, 143, 219

Fairbank, John K., 168, 178
Family Research Council, 70
Fan Gang, 197, 209, 311, 327
Far Eastern Economic Review, 197, 269, 294, 295
Farewell, My Concubine (film), 314
"Farewell to Freedom" editorial, 295
Federal Bureau of Investigation (FBI), 131
Federal Express, 87
Federal Reserve, 367
Federation of Industry and Commerce, Shanghai, 185
Feng Lun, 227, 232, 248–54, 257
    background of, 249–50
    business career of, 250–53
    on Chinese-style company, 258–59
    Chinese-style socialism as seen by, 253–54
    described, 249
feng shui (geomancy), 263–64
Feng Xiliang, 291
"fifth modernization," 281
Film Bureau, Chinese, 214
First National Bank of Chicago, 40
Forbes, 166–67, 345
Forbes, Steve, 77, 193
Ford Motor Company, 50
Foreign Affairs, 110, 141, 306, 313
Foreign Affairs Ministry, Chinese, 64
Foreign Ministry, Japanese, 304, 305
Foreign Trade and Economic Cooperation Ministry, Chinese, 287
Formosa Plastics, 127
Fortune, 344–45
France, 98, 102, 129, 161, 171–72, 201, 312, 369
Frankenstein, John, 156
Freeman, Chas. W., Jr., 27
Friedman, Milton, 240
Friedman, Thomas, 40, 41, 176, 343
Fujian province, 194, 332, 334
Fukuyama, Francis, 14
Fulbright programs, 366
Fun Dazzle, 235
Fung, Victor, 108, 196, 294
Fun World, 235, 236

Gang of Four, 41, 137, 152
Garten, Jeffrey, 361, 365
Gates, Bill, 15, 88, 234
General Electric, 15, 50, 86, 332
General Motors, 50, 88
Generation X, 279
George III, King of England, 30
Gephardt, Richard, 69–70, 140, 141
Gere, Richard, 134, 298
Germany, Imperial, 110

Germany, Nazi, 67, 110
Germany, reunified, 98, 111, 201, 225, 312, 343
    social market of, 102
Gettysburg Address, 222, 360
Gingrich, Newt, 62–63, 69, 76, 119, 139, 367–368
Goldman, Merle, 135–36
Goldstone, Jack, 163, 200
Good Morning, Fujian (TV show), 75
Gorbachev, Mikhail, 17, 120, 363
    attempted coup against, 243
Gordon, Charles "Chinese," 212
Gore, Al, 56, 298, 300
    China visited by, 78
Governing China (Lieberthal), 54
Graham, Billy, 135
Grant, James, 166
Great Britain, 84, 98, 103, 108, 115, 171–72, 179, 362, 363
    China trade and, 29–32
    GDP of, 160
    Hong Kong transition and, 285–86, 292–293
    Jardine mission of, 31–32
    Macartney mission of, 30–31
    opium trade and, 31–32
    Treaty of Nanking and, 32
Great Leap Forward, 136, 173, 319
Greider, William, 97, 342
Group of Eight, 365
Grove, Andy, 85–86, 331
G-7, 365
Guangdong International Trust Investment Corporation (GITIC), 332
Guangdong province, 173, 175–76, 191, 194, 211, 304, 325, 332, 334, 335
Guangming Ribao, 276
Guangxi Autonomous Region, 251, 334
guanxi (personal connections), 204, 208
Guizhou province, 334, 335
Gu Mu, 314
Guo Shuqing, 202

Hale, David, 278
Hamilton, Lee, 24
Han Feitse, 154, 180
Harper's, 255
Harper's Index, 71
Harries, Owen, 120, 136–37
Hart, Robert, 29
Havel, Václav, 243, 300
Hebei province, 334
He Di, 324–25
Hegel, G.W.F., 222
Helms, Jesse, 69, 71
Henan province, 334
Hersey, John, 336
Herzog, Roman, 215
Hewlett-Packard, 50
He Xin, 309

Long March, 163, 275
Looking at China Through a Third Eye (Wang), 46, 189, 192, 323
Lord, Winston, 143, 366
Luce, Henry, 33, 34
Lu Hsün, 193, 214, 244
Lu Ping, 290

Macau, 47, 127
Macartney, George, 30, 40, 149, 159, 214, 216
McCarthy, Joseph, 34
McDonald's, 16, 174, 251, 332, 343, 359
McDougall, Walter A., 55
McGrory, Mary, 71
Macke, Richard C., 140
MacLaine, Shirley, 44
Madsen, Richard, 317
Magna Carta, 320, 333
Ma Guonan, 325
Mahan, A. T., 324
Mahathir Bin Mohamad, 112, 345
Major, John, 295
Malaysia, 2, 122, 123, 199, 288–89, 303
Manchurian Candidate, The (film), 35
Mandela, Nelson, 215, 267, 300
Manning, Robert, 142
Maoism, 4, 164, 187, 313
    revival of, 279–81
Mao Zedong, 4, 5, 39, 65, 78, 79, 82, 151, 153, 178, 185, 224, 233, 240, 248, 253, 290, 314, 326, 336, 371
    Cultural Revolution and, 38–39
    death of, 41, 152, 168
    Deng as successor to, 275–76
    national unity and, 212
    place of, in Chinese history, 279–80
    political system of, 182, 192–93
    succession and, 266, 271
Margolis, Richard, 161, 174, 176, 304, 338
Marx, Karl, 222, 280
Marxism, 313, 315
Mary Kay Cosmetics, 334
Mastio, David, 73
Matsushita, 144
media, Chinese, 184, 205–6
    Communist Party and, 134
media, U.S., 55, 314
    China in, 99, 312
    China-Taiwan relations in, 128
    Chinese entrepreneurs in, 183
    Deng era in, 68–69
    Hong Kong transition and, 295
    Tibet issue in, 300
Medicare, 87, 223
Megatrends China, 66
Mercedes-Benz, 58, 93
Metzger, Thomas, 137, 139
Mexico, 98, 343
Meyerand, Michael G., 93
MGM, 214
Microsoft, 88, 95

Middle Kingdom, defined, 213–14
Milholin, Gary, 21
Military Affairs Commission, 267, 268
Mischief Reef, 60, 122
MITI, 328
Mitsui, 185
Mitterrand, François, 312
Mi Zhenyu, 120
Moe, Timothy, 291
Mongolia, 213
Monsanto, 40
Moody's Investors Services, 328
Moses, Robert, 172
Most Favored Nation (MFN) debate, 58, 72, 77, 106, 125, 135, 138
    Clinton administration and, 14–15, 53, 54, 55–56, 70–71, 285, 359, 368
    Clinton and, 22, 70–71, 139–40
    consequences of denial in, 139–41, 362
    Dynamic Engagement policy and, 359, 362, 364, 368
    human rights linkage to, 55–56
    U.S. Congress and, 22, 55, 62, 76, 139–40
Motorola, 15, 50, 51, 66, 92
    China sales of, 86, 87
Mou Qizhong, 172
Moynihan, Daniel Patrick, 59
Mundell, Robert, 201
Munro, Ross H., 69, 116, 120, 142
Murdoch, Rupert, 291
Murray, Douglas P., 176
Myanmar, 213

Naisbitt, John, 106, 159
Nanking, Treaty of (1842), 32
Nansha (Spratly) Islands, 66, 122–23, 308
Nath, Rajendra, 159
Nathan, Andrew J., 26, 74, 130, 222
National Committee on U.S.-China Relations, 366, 368
National Endowment for Democracy, 73
National Interest, 120, 136–37
nationalism, 212–13, 216–19
National People's Congress, Chinese, 82, 151, 219, 268, 318, 319, 320, 324, 338, 367
    in 21st century, 322–23
National Security Council, U.S., 44
Naughton, Barry, 252
Naval Intelligence, U.S., 126
Neighborhood Party Committees, 135
Nelson, Bryan, 88
Nelson, Chris, 159
Netherlands, 102, 108, 115
New Republic, 53, 68, 69, 77, 125, 307
Newsweek, 68, 81, 219
New Yorker, 68
New York Stock Exchange, 50, 344
New York Times, 21, 65, 67, 72, 77, 89, 111, 142, 176, 198, 294, 312, 339, 343, 372
    "Farewell to Freedom" editorial of, 295
New Zealand, 332

400

DATE DUE

BRODART, CO. Cat. No. 23-221